Friedrich Trautwein · Birgit Zürn ·
Heide Lukosch · Sebastiaan Meijer · Tobias Alf
Editors

Shaping the Future through Simulation and Gaming

56th International Simulation and
Gaming Association Conference, ISAGA 2025
Stuttgart, Germany, July 15–18, 2025
Revised Selected Papers

 Springer

Editors
Friedrich Trautwein
Baden-Wuerttemberg Cooperative State
University
Stuttgart, Germany

Birgit Zürn
Baden-Wuerttemberg Cooperative State
University
Stuttgart, Germany

Heide Lukosch
University of Canterbury
Christchurch, New Zealand

Sebastiaan Meijer
KTH Royal Institute of Technology
Stockholm, Sweden

Tobias Alf
Baden-Wuerttemberg Cooperative State
University
Stuttgart, Germany

ISSN 0302-9743   ISSN 1611-3349 (electronic)
Lecture Notes in Computer Science
ISBN 978-3-032-20128-7   ISBN 978-3-032-20129-4 (eBook)
https://doi.org/10.1007/978-3-032-20129-4

Preface

The International Simulation And Gaming Association (ISAGA) Conference 2025 was held from July 15–18, 2025, at Baden-Württemberg Cooperative State University (DHBW Stuttgart) and its Centre for Management Simulation, in cooperation with the Swiss Austrian German Simulation And Gaming Association (SAGSAGA). Focusing on **"Shaping the Future through Simulation & Gaming,"** the conference convened an international and interdisciplinary community of researchers, practitioners, educators, and designers. Continuing ISAGA's long-standing tradition, the event provided a forum for examining how simulation and gaming approaches can advance the understanding of complex systems, foster learning processes, and support collaborative explorations of possible futures.

In the light of contemporary societal and technological uncertainties, simulation and gaming offer structured means to explore dynamics, test assumptions and theories, and engage stakeholders in evidence-informed reflection. Whether applied to analyzing the implications of climate change, anticipating economic developments, or supporting the design of resilient urban systems, these methods provide analytical and experiential frameworks that help illuminate emerging challenges and potential trajectories. The 2025 conference thus underscored the increasing relevance of simulation and gaming as tools for inquiry, communication, and the co-creation of forward-looking insights.

This proceedings volume contains a selection of contributions presented at the 2025 conference. All submissions underwent a double-blind peer-review process, conducted by members of the Scientific Committee. Each paper received at least two reviews, and ambiguous cases were examined in a meta-review discussion by the conference chairs. Out of 51 submissions, 24 contributions were selected for the LNCS proceedings. The editors of these proceedings provided additional feedback after the conference, resulting in the final versions presented here. Contributions accepted for this volume include papers capturing conceptual, empirical, and practice-oriented work across a broad range of domains.

The contributions to this volume are assigned to four topical sections, reflecting the thematic clusters around which the scientific program of the conference was structured. The first section, *Designing Futures: Innovation in Game Design and Development*, presents work on conceptual, methodological, and creative foundations in game design and development. These papers examine the realities created through game-based methods, new modelling approaches and frameworks, and design processes that support creativity, structure, and reflection.

The second section, *Learning and Evaluation in Simulation-Based Environments*, focuses on the use and evaluation of simulation games to support learning, knowledge transfer, and decision-making in educational, organizational, health, and policy contexts. The papers in this cluster highlight how simulation activities promote teamwork, facilitate dialogue among stakeholders, and enable critical reflection on complex social, technological, or organizational challenges.

The third section, *Sustainability, Climate, and Urban Resilience*, brings together contributions addressing environmental and spatial futures. These papers demonstrate how games and simulations can help individuals and communities understand ecological interdependencies, engage in participatory planning, explore climate-related risks, and collaboratively consider interventions for sustainable development and resilience.

The fourth section, *Immersion and Intercultural Perspectives*, explores experiential, immersive, and culturally sensitive dimensions of simulation and gaming. The contributions investigate virtual and augmented reality environments, avatar-based collaboration, embodied debriefing practices, and intercultural learning processes. Collectively, they emphasize the role of inclusive, reflective, and human-centered design in shaping impactful game-based experiences.

Taken together, the contributions in this volume demonstrate the vitality and diversity of contemporary research in simulation and gaming. They show how the field continues to develop innovative design methodologies, foster meaningful learning experiences, address urgent societal and environmental challenges, and cultivate inclusive and immersive environments for exploration and dialogue. The four sections of this volume further underscore the thematic breadth and methodological richness of the 2025 ISAGA community, highlighting the growing relevance of simulation and gaming in supporting collaborative inquiry and in shaping futures through systematic, experiential, and imaginative approaches. The 2025 conference emphasized that advancing the field requires not only technical innovation but also critical reflection, ethical awareness, and interdisciplinary collaboration.

We extend our sincere appreciation to all authors, reviewers, organizers, and participants who contributed to the success of the ISAGA Conference 2025. We hope that this volume will serve as a valuable resource and as an inspiration for future work in simulation and gaming research, design, and practice.

December 2025

Friedrich Trautwein
Birgit Zürn
Heide Lukosch
Sebastiaan Meijer
Tobias Alf

Organization

General Chairs

Friedrich Trautwein   Baden-Württemberg Cooperative State University (DHBW) Stuttgart, Germany

Birgit Zürn   Baden-Württemberg Cooperative State University (DHBW) Stuttgart, Germany

Local Chairs

Tobias Alf   Baden-Württemberg Cooperative State University (DHBW) Stuttgart, Germany

Christof Döhren   SAGSAGA e.V., Germany

Maren Schaal   Baden-Württemberg Cooperative State University (DHBW) Stuttgart, Germany

Annemarie Zimmer   Baden-Württemberg Cooperative State University (DHBW) Stuttgart, Germany

Gabriel Gaa   Baden-Württemberg Cooperative State University (DHBW) Stuttgart, Germany

Advisory Board

Daniel Bartschat   Playful Insights GmbH, Germany

Nicolas Becu   Centre National de la Recherche Scientifique, France

Maria Freese   Otto von Guericke University Magdeburg, Germany

Willy Christian Kriz   FHV Vorarlberg University, Austria

Heide Lukosch   University of Canterbury, New Zealand

Sebastiaan Meijer   KTH Royal Institute of Technology, Sweden

Sebastian Schwägele   Playful Insights GmbH, Germany

Marcin Wardaszko   Kozminski University, Poland

Marieke de Wijse van Heeswijk   Radboud University, Netherlands

Helmut Wittenzellner   Hochschule der Medien, Germany

Scientific Committee

Tobias Alf
Gildas Geraud Assogba
Bryann Avendano-Uribe
Nicolas Becu
Joshua Birenheide
Swen Bos
Marta Brkovic Dodig
Sagnik Chakraborty
Isabelle Charpentier
Chatchai Chatpinyakoop
Juliette Cortes-Arevalo
David Crookall
Robert-Jan den Haan
Sylvain Dernat
Walter Dettling
Anne Dray
Vinod Dumblekar
Martin Esters
Michaela Fenakel Fiedelman
Simon Ford
Holly Franklin
Maria Freese
Kaede Fujita
Gabriel Gaa
Martin Gerner
Shesh Narayan Gupta
Ryoju Hamada
Ciska Harte-Hoogervorst
Casper Harteveld
J. Tuomas Harviainen
Ulrich Holzbaur
Barbara Holzner
Anna Hurova
Carla Jaboyedoff
Michal Jakubowski
Xianbiao Jiang
Mckale Jones
Rouven Kaiser
Christian Karl
Toshiko Kikkawa
Valerie Sophie Krieger
Willy Christian Kriz
Jérémy Le Du
Meike Lehmann

Elyssebeth Ellen Leigh
Nick Ludwig
Heide Lukosch
Ulrike Mascher
Sebastiaan Meijer
Korryn Danette Mozisek
Mieko Nakamura
Robin Neef
Vien-Thong Nguyen
Angelika Pohnitzer
Anastasia Ponomareva
Alexandre Poyé
Patrick Querl
Nantenaina Maminirina Ravoahangilalao
Sundararaman Rengarajan
Stephan Rometsch
Juliette Rouchier
Sayan Saha
Nicolas Salliou
Sourjya Sarkar
Maren Schaal
Malte Schweizerhof
Marvin Soetanto
Micael Sousa
Julika Stenzel
Hiroaki Sugino
Weronika Zuzanna Szatkowska
Longeon Thomas
Marta Toscano
Yusuke Toyoda
Friedrich Trautwein
Eric Treske
Pieter van der Hijden
Miranda Verswijvelen
Marcin Wardaszko
Ivo Wenzler
Britta Werksnis
Marieke de Wijse van Heeswijk
Helmut Wittenzellner
David Wortley
Annemarie Zimmer
Birgit Zürn
Siegfried Georg Zürn

Contents

Learning and Evaluation in Simulation-Based Environments

Sustainability, Climate, and Urban Resilience

Designing Futures: Innovation in Game Design and Development

What Reality Do We Pursue as Designers and Facilitators?

Toshiko Kikkawa[1]([⊠]) [iD], Mieko Nakamura[2] [iD], and Willy Christian Kriz[3] [iD]

[1] Keio University, 2-15-45, Mita, Minato-ku, Tokyo 108-8345, Japan
toshiko.sg@gmail.com
[2] Ryutsu Keizai University, Hirahata, Ryugasaki 301-8555, Ibaraki, Japan
mnakamura@rku.ac.jp
[3] FHV University Vorarlberg, Hochschulstrasse 1, 6850 Dornbirn, Austria
Willy.kriz@fhv.at

Abstract. The study aims to highlight the issue of "reality" within the Simulation and Gaming (S&G) domain, which has been largely overlooked. The research community has struggled to connect game experiences to realities, especially from the perspectives of game designers and facilitators. Awareness of differing perceptions of reality has grown significantly, driven in part by the rapid spread of misinformation and conspiracy theories on social media. Consequently, the realities perceived by players may differ from those intended to be shared by game designers and facilitators. However, this awareness within the S&G community is insufficient. To address this, the authors explore the issue theoretically. First, the importance of increasing awareness is explained using various concrete examples. Second, the role of facilitators, who play an essential role in the S&G process, is explored. Third, insights are derived from foundational research in this field, offering various perspectives to address the issue. Lastly, the authors emphasize the need for actively discussing the issue of realities in the S&G community and reiterate the associated risks.

Keywords: Game Designers · Facilitators · Misinformation · Players · Social Media

1 Introduction

The study aims to highlight the issue of "reality" within the Simulation and Gaming (S&G) domain, which the authors argue has been overlooked in the post-truth era. In this era, with prevalent misinformation, the importance of this issue has been underestimated, and awareness regarding it must be enhanced. Through a theoretical examination, the authors seek to improve awareness regarding the perception of reality within the S&G community, especially given the widespread dissemination of false information. The authors believe that raising the notion of realities in the context of S&G will contribute to shaping the future of this domain.

The authors intentionally use the plural form "realities" to highlight that "reality" is inevitably subjective and varies depending on the perceptions of individuals and groups, among other factors. Throughout history, no single truth has existed.

© The Author(s) 2026
F. Trautwein et al. (Eds.): ISAGA 2025, LNCS 16439, pp. 3–18, 2026.
https://doi.org/10.1007/978-3-032-20129-4_1

S&G fundamentally involves reality issues, as many games require players to assume roles. For example, in the game SIMSOC by Gamson [1], players adopt the roles of inhabitants in different regions with different economic backgrounds. Observations by facilitators suggest that players often become deeply immersed in their roles, with the distinction between the game and their perceptions blurred. For example, players assigned to wealthier regions may exhibit arrogance, whereas those in economically weaker regions may display aggression owing to the inequity in the distribution of wealth. Although the players are comprehensively briefed on the fictitious nature of their roles, this phenomenon frequently occurs, even with careful facilitation and management by facilitators, as an essential aspect of the gaming experience. The key issue here is the degree of immersion: Can we, as facilitators, effectively debrief players and separate their in-game experiences from real-world reality?

Drawing an analogy from theater, audiences clearly understand that actors portray fictional roles on stage, even when the narrative implies or reflects various aspects of reality. For example, in Shakespeare's "Twelfth Night, or What You Will," the character Viola, one of the twins, disguises herself as a man (Cesario). The other characters are confused by this disguised identity, while the audience remains aware of the reality. In other words, the audience fully recognizes the two different realities occurring on the stage. In this context, Shakespeare's works illustrate the concept of multiple realities and S&G, as famously expressed by Jaques in "As You Like It": *All the world's a stage, and all the men and women merely players.*

In S&G frameworks, players are assigned roles in simulated worlds to varying extents. In role-playing games, it is typically evident to the players that the world in the game is different from the real world. In contrast, in business-related games, where players assume roles such as production or marketing personnel, the distinction between the game and reality may be less clear.

2 Realities for Game Designers

The traditional S&G design process begins with an analysis of the systems associated with a given phenomenon. Subsequently, game designers set the learning objectives for the game.

Although system analysis has always been a complex and crucial process for effective S&G design, an additional challenge has arisen in the present environment. For example, the spread of misinformation has been exacerbated by the COVID-19 pandemic and political shifts, and this trend has intensified in recent times.

Historically, people's beliefs have evolved in response to changing circumstances. For example, after WWII, Japanese people transitioned to a democratic society from militarism, despite widespread support for war during wartime. During that period, dissent was discouraged and could even result in imprisonment. Similar instances can be observed in other locations throughout history.

In the modern era, misinformation is being rapidly spread, largely driven by social media. A notable example is the COVID-19 vaccination campaign [2]. Although some individuals chose to be vaccinated, others did not, often because of their belief in conspiracy theories. In such cases, designing games to promote vaccination, even if vaccination is crucial to promote herd immunity, may be counterproductive. For those who believe in conspiracies, games encouraging vaccination may be perceived as offering a "false" reality. Conversely, skeptics could design games discouraging vaccination. If long-term risks or side effects of the vaccination were to be substantiated, those previously labeled as conspiracy theorists may be regarded as having issued early warnings. In this scenario, what type of game can game designers develop? One possible solution is to present both sides to the players and encourage discussions between the opposing viewpoints. However, this carries the risk of indicating that all perspectives hold equal validity, which may inadvertently reinforce conspiracy theories.

Political issues introduce even greater complexity. What objectives should S&G designers set when developing a politically inclined game? As an example of games being used for manipulation, certain games have been designed to instill patriotism in children. As children typically enjoy playing games, games represent an effective tool to shape their beliefs from their childhood. Figure 1 shows a variant of "The Game of the Goose", designed to educate children about daily life during wartime. One of its frames warns of the dangers posed by spies, implying their ubiquitous presence and teaching children to be careful about them, i.e., teaching children to be distrustful of others. Figure 2 illustrates a game where players must work together to extinguish fires, teaching the importance of cooperation with neighbors (*Tonarigumi* in Japanese). Ironically, this emphasis on cooperation was noted to lead to mutual surveillance within communities, fostering division among individuals.

Fig. 1. Game for children, educating them about life during wartime

Propaganda games have been developed for various purposes. Figure 3 illustrates the energy procurement game developed by the Japanese Agency for Natural Resources and Energy and distributed to junior high school students before the 2011 Fukushima Nuclear Disaster. In this game, players try to secure energy resources. However, the "event cards" drawn during the game frequently introduce scenarios such as "A war has broken out in the Middle East," which render crude oil procurement challenging and lead to an energy crisis. Thus, relying on nuclear energy emerges as the best solution to win the game. The message conveyed to students is that nuclear energy is the most

Fig. 2. *Tonarigumi* game for children, educating them about life during wartime

Fig. 3. Energy procurement game

reliable solution for a stable energy supply. This reflects the perspective promoted by the Ministry at the time.

Unintentional biases or improper perceptions of reality can cause game designers to create problematic games. A notable example is a board game recently developed about a former Japanese soldier who remained in hiding for nearly 30 years after WWII, believing that the war had not ended. This game, which successfully secured crowd-funding, depicts his survival in the forest for numerous years as extraordinary, painting him as a "survivor". However, records indicate that the soldier was aware that the war had ended and sustained himself by killing villagers and stealing their food. Ignorance of this fact can mislead the players, as they may believe that the game is based on fact and is thus accurate.

3   Realities for Players and Facilitators

S&G is a collaborative process involving designers, facilitators, and players. As stated by Kikkawa [3], "The whole intake-to-transfer process of S&G is a complex interplay of design requirements, facilitation approaches, context-sensitive implementation, and meaning-making processes to foster transfer from S&G to reality." When considering this transfer, we need to ask, for what purpose and for whom?

Arai [4] discussed the relationship between the real world and S&G from the perspectives of both designers and players. From a designer's perspective, an S&G world is a representation of the real world. The designer structures the S&G based on a certain model that represents an area of interest in the real world. However, from a player's perspective, the S&G world is not merely a representation of the real world but rather an alternative real world structured by the designer. After playing the game, guided by facilitators, the player compares their in-game experiences with real-world experiences. Thus, designers, facilitators, and players together deepen their knowledge and understanding of the real world through S&G.

Figure 4, adapted from Arai's framework [4], shows perspectives of designers, facilitators, and players. First, a designer conceptualizes the area of interest in the real world, develops the corresponding system model, and designs a playable game. Second, a facilitator selects a game for an S&G session and prepares debriefing strategies to foster transfer from S&G to reality. These steps are completed before the S&G session. During the session, the facilitator implements the S&G, while players engage with and experience the S&G world. Later, the facilitator leads the debriefing process, guiding the players to compare their S&G experience with their real-world experiences, analyze the system model, and/or discuss the game structure.

Although Fig. 4 is based on Arai's framework [4], it is different from the original figure. In Fig. 4, the dual roles of facilitators are depicted by two types of arrows. Before the S&G session, a facilitator selects a game and connects it to the area of interest in the real world, as indicated by the hatched arrows. During the debriefing session, the facilitator supports players to reflect upon the area of interest, model, and game itself, as shown by the shaded arrows. In addition to these two roles, the facilitator also executes the S&G session (this function is not indicated by arrows).

In some cases, facilitators also contribute to game design. Figure 5 shows the case where facilitators use existing games as a foundation and integrate them with models or theories associated with a certain real-world situation. In this instance, facilitators assume the role of a designer. The hatched arrows in Fig. 5 represent the responsibilities of facilitators before the S&G session. The shaded arrows represent their role in guiding players during debriefing.

When a designer facilitates their self-developed game, the interpretation of Figs. 4 and 5 becomes somewhat complex. The viewpoints of the designer (in Fig. 4) and facilitator (in Fig. 5) are contrasting. When one person assumes both roles, they must shift between these two viewpoints. The authors believe that in such scenarios, both Figs. 4 and 5 must be retained in their current form, allowing individuals to intentionally adopt either viewpoint depending on the context (designer or facilitator). This metacognitive approach would benefit not only the designer and facilitator, but also players, especially during debriefing.

Although not explicitly shown in Figs. 4 and 5, facilitators are responsible for ensuring organization and safety in an S&G session. Especially in group-based S&G settings, players must be provided with clear instructions to ensure that they adhere to the rules and are respectful. Notably, in the S&G world, players perform actions in condensed

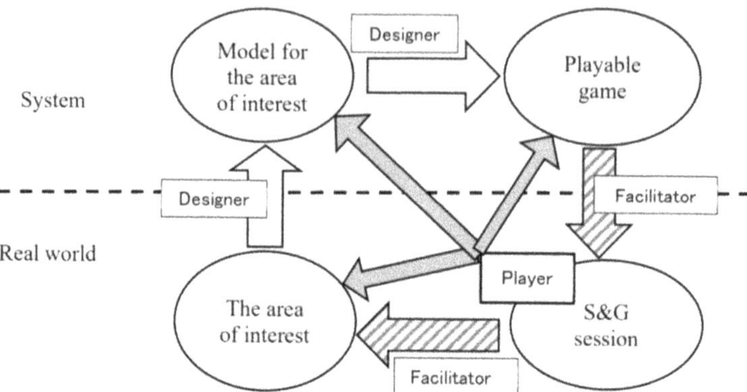

Fig. 4. Role of facilitators in S&G (adapted from Arai's framework [4], p. 34)

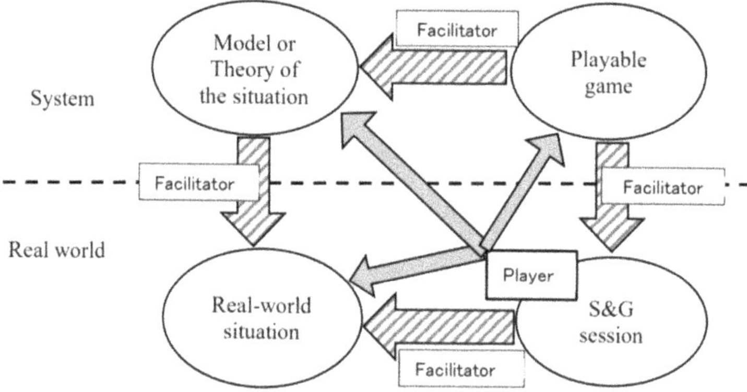

Fig. 5. Alternative function of facilitators in S&G

periods [5]. For example, a single 10-min round may represent one year. Inexperienced players may struggle to adjust to these dynamics in the S&G world. It may be dangerous to give players full authority without any briefing, similar to driving a car without a license. Similar to how all drivers must follow the traffic regulations to ensure safety on the road, e.g., driving on the left side in Japan, the rules must be clear and respected in S&G sessions to establish a sense of security among the players. Facilitators must ensure such safe environments in S&G sessions, and players must cooperate to maintain a safe session for themselves and for others.

In the scenario shown in Fig. 4, a designer is responsible for defining the mechanics of the game. However, the facilitator determines the suitability of a game for a given session. Therefore, facilitators must review the game manual and materials and ensure no flagrant contradiction among them. If inconsistencies emerge, the facilitators bear the responsibility for resolving them before the session, while respecting the designer's intent. Otherwise, players may distrust the validity of the S&G session. To this end, facilitators must fully understand the reality that the designer intends to reflect in the game as well as in the model. Without this understanding, rectification would become extremely challenging. However, facilitators are typically more familiar with the players, which positions them to more effectively deliver the message compared with a designer. During debriefing, the facilitator must help players grasp the designer's perspective of the real world. However, the designer's perspective is one of many possible perspectives. If a player proposes another meaningful perspective during debriefing, it should be explored. The facilitator must be open to a diverse range of perspectives, and in some cases, players and facilitators together may uncover deeper or broader insights extending beyond the designer's intent. Although such discoveries may not always occur, they represent one of the most valuable aspects of debriefing.

In the scenario shown in Fig. 5, the facilitator is responsible for both the mechanics and management of the game. One example of this role in practice can be seen in HACONORI [6], a simple cooperative learning game, in which players are required to describe how a picture looks on the card in their hand and combine fragments of information to form a complete picture. The game mechanics are as follows [7]:

Players work in groups of five, with each group receiving ten cube-shaped boxes and a set of five cards. Each box measures 20 cm per side. Nine boxes are white, and one is red. Group members sit around the ten boxes. Each member receives one card at a time, and the players are not allowed to show their cards to others. Each card contains a two-dimensional diagram, representing a specific view of a three-dimensional object, either from above or from one of four horizontal directions. Each group must arrange the boxes such that the shape of the resulting three-dimensional object fits all five two-dimensional pictures. Each task takes approximately two to five minutes to complete, with difficulty levels ranging from easy to difficult. Once all members of a group concur that the picture on their cards fits one of the five different views of the central object, they proceed to the next task. The total number of tasks is 15. Figure 6 shows a scene from HACONORI.

Fig. 6. HACONORI, a simple cooperative learning game

Through HACONORI, players develop fundamental teamwork skills, including information sharing and active listening. Consider a classroom setting with 60 students divided into 12 groups, each working at different speeds. A facilitator may implement a short break after every five tasks or every 10 min to maintain a balanced pace for the class. During these breaks, groups that have completed their tasks must wait, while those that have not must stop and move on. During the break, the facilitator can encourage knowledge sharing by publicly posing questions or interviewing successful groups about their problem-solving strategies, allowing this discussion to assist groups who faced challenges. This approach allows successful groups to reflect on their methods, while helping the struggling groups better address the tasks. Overall, breaks represent a valuable opportunity for objectively assessing the progress of each group and maintaining motivation. However, the facilitator may unintentionally deprive players of the opportunity to struggle and identify solutions independently.

In the context of debriefing, the problem-solving process in HACONORI can be linked to the concept of "learning from failure" or the Plan-Do-Check-Act (PDCA) cycle. As part of session preparation, a brief introduction to the PDCA cycle may be prepared, if necessary. During the debriefing session, players often present various insights, such as sharing leadership roles among members, introducing trial-and-error strategies, physically moving around the object, and imagining others' viewpoints. Facilitators may be inclined to focus on the topics they had previously planned, steering discussions toward these themes. While this is appropriate when conforming to the learning objective, the facilitators may miss opportunities to discover new perspectives, limit players from developing their own theories and discouraging players from engaging in discussion.

HACONORI provides an excellent example of the concept of multiple realities. A three-dimensional object can appear considerably different when viewed from five different directions as two-dimensional pictures. This serves as a visual analogy for the existence of multiple realities for a single true reality. Facilitators can highlight this by showing how different positions lead to different perspectives and how a lack of imagination can lead to misunderstanding. Although facilitators can provide guidance to help players connect their S&G experiences to real-world experiences, this does not guarantee that players will perceive the connections as expected by the facilitators. Players interpret their experiences from their own viewpoints. Therefore, facilitators should respect the perspectives of the players, while also considering their own intentions as well as those of the designers.

Kolb's learning style [8] provides an additional perspective. People with an accommodative learning style excel in performing tasks and engaging in new experiences. In contrast, people with an assimilative learning style excel at inductive reasoning and theoretical development. The former group is typically highly active in S&G, whereas the latter appears to be somewhat withdrawn. The composition of a group with different learning styles can be either beneficial or challenging. For example, when HACONORI tasks are simple, a trial-and-error approach can be effective. However, as the level of difficulty increases, more sophisticated tactics are required. Members with different learning styles can complement each other, or conversely, experience a sense of alienation and distrust.

Jones [9] offers practical tips regarding facilitation and describes how easily poor facilitation can mar the S&G experience. When facilitators reflect on their experiences, they may recall moments of tension. Obtaining feedback from players who have had negative experiences is challenging, as they are unlikely to return. There may be numerous players who dislike S&G because of poor facilitation. This presents a dilemma: Facilitators can improve their facilitation style learning from their mistakes and failures. However, they must also strive to minimize errors. Moreover, facilitators must learn promptly from their failures, as poor facilitation may lead to emotional distress for the players. Jones [9] repeatedly emphasizes that emotions in S&G are real, and players will vividly remember other players' facial expressions or tone of voice. Facilitators must ensure that players are not physically or emotionally harmed during the S&G process.

4 Fostering Multiple Realities and Participatory Multilogue Processes in S&G

According to Klabbers [10], a *game* is a form of *play*. However, as Sutton-Smith [11] pointed out, there exists significant ambiguity in the definitions of these terms. In the context of *gaming simulation,* games serve as models of reality and focus on well-defined subjects, in terms of both context and content. A *model* is a description and representation of a (real) system or its processes, allowing us to understand how the system works or might work. A *simulation* recreates a set of conditions to explore a real-world system. As previously discussed, "reality" itself, as well as the game as a model of "reality" and "reality of play" may be perceived differently by designers, facilitators, and players. Sutton-Smith [11] introduced the concept of *rhetoric* of play to highlight that we find implicit narratives in games, which represent the active component of a gaming experience. He distinguished seven rhetorics or narratives of play: as progress, as fate, as power, as identity, as imaginary, as the self, and as frivolous. De Caluwé et al. [12] discussed the different meanings that can emerge in playing (simulation) games, which may *"Express the way play is placed in a context within broader value systems ... Rhetorics refer to popular ways of thinking and beliefs that create the cultures and subcultures we live in"* (p. 14). Consequently, the different rhetorics of designers, facilitators, and players lead to different understandings of reality within games, influencing player behaviors.

The ways in which a game is played and interpreted are also shaped by fundamental differences in personalities, value systems, motivation drivers, and interests of players, facilitators, and designers. Marczewski [13] defined six *player types* that may lead to conflicting behaviors in design, facilitation, debriefing, and play. For the typical "players," the objective is to win as efficiently as possible and seek maximum extrinsic rewards. "Disruptors" often want to be the center of attention and may often attempt to change the situation or even break the rules to gain influence over others. "Free spirits" are motivated by opportunities for exploration and creativity. "Achievers" focus on overcoming challenges, performing well, and demonstrating their competencies. They enjoy learning new skills through play. "Socializers" seek inclusion and belonging and view the game as an opportunity to be recognized by peers. "Philanthropists" prioritize helping others by selflessly supporting their needs and improving the overall game experience.

Greenblat [14] introduced the concept of *multiple realities* in the 1970s and 1980s, arguing that game design and game use represent social constructions of reality. She disputed the existence of a common reality underlying game design, facilitation, and play. Different actors negotiate reality throughout the S&G process. Individual mental models provide the basis for multiple realities, which often emerge owing to conflicting objectives among different stakeholders. Although increasing diversity in game design and facilitation may heighten the risk of conflicts, it may also enhance awareness of conceptual borders and help overcome unconscious limitations caused by implicit assumptions, biases, and stereotypes [15].

Debriefing is a critical means to explore the narratives perceived during the game. As simulation games are not intended to replicate reality exactly, it is essential to understand the common points between play and reality. In fact, differences between games and reality benefit players by challenging their existing knowledge and assumptions. Disagreements among players encourage critical discussions, prompting them to articulate their mental models, assumptions, and subjective theories regarding the world. Through the S&G process, players gain a deeper understanding of themselves and others, promoting learning. Occasionally, players may fail to interpret certain aspects of a game, leading to disagreements or even complaints like "This is a bad simulation; reality is not like this". However, these instances may promote curiosity that can be leveraged during debriefing. For example, facilitators may ask "How do you perceive reality?". Even if players do not accept the game as an "accurate" model of (their) reality, its value is not diminished if effective debriefing is conducted. The purpose of S&G is to stimulate thinking about multiple perceptions of reality, different interpretative perspectives, and various interactions and behaviors. Designers, facilitators, and players should strive to adopt a meta-perspective, understanding that a specific view of reality may be "true" under certain conditions, while another viewpoint may offer equally valid insights in different contexts. From an epistemological standpoint of constructivism, knowledge is socially constructed, and games provide a means to examine how we construct reality. Through the process of reconstructing reality within design, play, and debriefing, we may even change our perceptions of reality beyond the game [16]. In addition, debriefing should encourage reflection on multiple realities based on alternative rhetorics of play and the diverse intentions of different player types (see above).

As Greenblat [14] noted, games involve various stakeholders with differing interests and goals. From the design science perspective, games can be used to foster learning at the individual, collective, and organizational levels and support decision-making, policy development, and transformation processes of large socio-technical systems. Simulation games can serve as communication tools to reinforce certain behaviors or promote awareness and mindset shifts. Such games can lead to meaningful learning and contribute to changes in dysfunctional systems toward the betterment of individuals, groups, organizations, and societies [17]. However, all forms of media can be used for manipulation and miscommunication [18]. According to Kriz et al. [15], adverse effects may include the reinforcement of stereotypes and attitudes that reflect the values or interests of the game designers or their sponsors. Games may spread miscommunication, driven by unintentional individual, group, and societal biases.

One example of this issue is evident in many modern business simulation games [19]. Designers, facilitators, and players may believe in neoliberalism and a pure free-market economy. As a result, they may prefer a reductive and normative model of reality, assuming such a model to be ontologically true and fully representative of reality. In addition, they may believe that winning a business game (typically measured by achieving the highest market share or stock price) demonstrates competencies and learning. At present, many business schools evaluate students based solely on their game results. Students with better financial outcomes in simulation games are awarded better grades, even without any meaningful debriefing or reflection on the assumptions and models embedded within the game. These schools do not reveal or challenge the simulated variables and interconnections, and the game model thus remains a black box. This interplay between game and reality reflects a more positivistic and normative way of using games, which we consider inappropriate, and in some cases, even unethical. Thus, even traditional simulation games may intentionally or unintentionally serve as one-dimensional and biased media [18]. In our understanding of S&G, players should be encouraged to question and analyze their assumptions and learn from the debriefing process. Assuming the game to be an accurate representation of reality and grading students solely based on their game performance is inappropriate. Such a strategy deprives students of the opportunity to reflect and experiment in a safe learning environment, openly dispute perceptions, or discuss their perspectives. Without these opportunities, players fail to examine the model or the boundaries within which this model is applicable.

Duke [20], the founder of the International Simulation and Gaming Association Conference (ISAGA), is well-known for introducing the concept of *multilogue*, a holistic form of multi-dialogue. He argued that traditional communication modes do not effectively address complex problems. Duke proposed S&G as a future language for better understanding and adapting complex malfunctioning systems. He viewed S&G as a form of gestalt communication, which is well-suited for managing systems and communicating complex interrelationships of reality. At present, we are facing increasingly complex and wicked problems, which necessitate the adoption of a more participatory and multidisciplinary approach. According to Duke, the design phase should integrate a wide range of meaningful and diverse perspectives. When the simulation model is co-designed, stakeholders often understand their reference system for the first time or develop a shared language to articulate their perceptions of reality. Once the system model is collaboratively built, gaming elements are added to it. The outcome of the game-building process is a game artifact that can be used by players who did not participate in its design. The concept of multilogue is interconnected to a transdisciplinary approach, as it engages different stakeholders and subject-matter experts. The idea is to incorporate not only diverse disciplines, but also other dimensions of diversity, such as genders, cultures, and experience levels. The design process, as a self-organizing and participatory learning environment, helps make the group's communication modes, individual mental models, and system representations of the designers more visible. This interaction fosters the development of shared values, goals, rules, social representations of reality, and strategies for the management of complex systems.

To facilitate such rich communication within S&G frameworks, *meta-debriefing* and *formative evaluation* strategies must be implemented throughout the process [21, 22]. In continuous meta-debriefing frameworks, game designers, facilitators, players, and other stakeholders reflect on shared feedback and game outcomes and examine the game process. This approach helps understand how and why a game functions within specific contexts and identify techniques to enhance its quality for specific target groups. Thus, a multilogue feedback and feedforward loop for multiple realities is necessary to minimize intended or unintended manipulation and raise awareness regarding cultural rhetorics of play, boundaries, and constraints. Debriefing and meta-debriefing enable participants to recognize different views of reality through elaboration and multilogue. The entire process within the *magic circle* of gaming can support the development of competencies and their transfer into the real world [17].

Unfortunately, debriefing can also be misused, and in the worst-case scenario, it may reinforce unethical messages mediated by the game [18]. Allen Feldt, a co-founder of ISAGA, expressed similar concerns in an interview: *"Games are powerful because they teach by experience. But the danger is: it teaches by experience. People are not capable of disbelieving things that happened to them. They believe implicitly it must be true, because it happened to me. Games can be designed to lie, and they give false experience. We must be vigilant in protecting this from happening… Debriefing is important, by an honest debriefer… but you can misrepresent"*. (personal communication; [23]).

To mitigate these risks, additional reflection loops must be incorporated. To ensure that gaming leads to meaningful learning rather than reinforced manipulation, a multi-perspective approach must be adopted. In principle, greater diversity can reduce the danger of manipulation. This can be achieved by assembling diverse player groups (characterized by different cultures, disciplinary backgrounds, genders, and ages) and multiple facilitators. Furthermore, diversifying debriefing methods and game formats within a program can minimize the potential for manipulation. Games come in many forms, including role-playing games, haptic games with tangible game pieces, and digital computer simulation games. Whenever possible, educational programs in schools or corporate training programs should use diverse gaming approaches, as there exist multiple ways to simulate reality. This diversity is also beneficial because different learners (e.g., Kolb's classification [8]) and player types (e.g., Marczewski's classification [13]) are sensitive to different forms of games and debriefing methods.

Feedback loops and meta-debriefing among communities of practitioners should be implemented along with constant and transparent formative evaluation processes and research studies. In particular, a multi-disciplinary multilogue with all relevant stakeholders, including facilitators, designers, educational program managers, and players, should be established throughout the design, learning, and transfer processes. Through debriefing and meta-debriefing, a game can be (partly) accepted as a sufficient and useful model of reality, or the next iteration of design necessary to build a "better" game model can be identified. Regardless of whether the perceived reality of the reference system aligns with or differs from that of the game, this participatory multilogue can provide deeper insights into the reference system. Thus, the iterative nature of gaming provides an opportunity to understand and reconstruct complex systems, processes, situations, problems, and interrelations, while generating ideas for their transformation. Players, as actors, can assume and interpret multiple roles, represent the social organization of the reference system, explore alternative meanings for a set of rules, and envision alternative futures for the use of a set of resources. By leveraging a participatory approach that emphasizes diversity and multiple realities and by moderating this process in a multilogue communication mode, we can overcome unethical and restrictive conditions in games and contribute to meaningful experiences and constructive development for all stakeholders.

The true potential of S&G lies in its ability to create future worlds, hypothetical scenarios, and alternatives for discussion and analysis. The objective is not to depict a specific truth or normative reality, but rather to explore multiple realities when addressing complex problems without a definitive optimal solution and where people do not agree on a common model of reality owing to diverse perspectives. S&G allows these diverse perspectives to be converged through shared model building, participatory game building, and bringing together different stakeholders as players in debriefing and gameplay. Through proper debriefing, multiple realities can be explored, and participants can enhance their awareness of the underlying assumptions and limitations of the game model and gameplay. The risks of stereotyping, miscommunication, and manipulation in game design, play, and debriefing can be mitigated by leveraging meta-debriefing and involving various designers, facilitators, and players, as well as different types of games and debriefing methods. Ultimately, this process fosters critical thinking, creativity, and the development of alternative futures.

Klabbers [24] argues that the current body of knowledge in the S&G community lacks a cohesive structure or a well-defined game science paradigm. The author encourages debate on the three perspectives of philosophy of science, scientific theory, and practical application, and their interconnections in the context of S&G. This debate is also connected with the need to deal with positions on how "reality" is shaped in the process of gaming simulation. This discussion should also promote the construction of shared knowledge through gaming simulations, while recognizing the risks and challenges of the potential misuse of gaming simulations, e.g., through intended or unintended manipulation of "reality" in this era with prevalent "fake news" and "alternative facts". Our paper contributes to this debate from a meta-perspective and advocates for an epistemological understanding of the term "reality" in S&G rooted in social constructivism. Simulation games can be understood as commonly created artifacts and models of socially constructed reality, with the main actors in this construction including players, facilitators and designers of simulation games [16, 25].

5 Implicit and Explicit Manipulation

In line with the conference theme of ISAGA 2025, "Shaping the Future through Simulation & Gaming," this paper highlights that well-designed gaming simulations can act as catalysts for behavioral change and societal transformation. Simulation games are powerful tools for learning and decision-making, allowing individuals and organizations to safely explore complex scenarios and develop future-oriented strategies. Such games can foster learning at multiple levels, from personal skill-building to organizational development, and even support transformation processes in large socio-technical systems by reinforcing constructive behaviors and encouraging mindset shifts. The transformative potential of simulation gaming hinges on aligning the game's "reality" with the perceptions of the players, facilitators, and designers. If misaligned (for instance, owing to conscious manipulation or unconscious bias), games might inadvertently entrench stereotypes or spread misperceptions. In our understanding of social constructivism, players, facilitators, and designers need to constantly meta-debrief and ensure that multiple realities are being discussed in the design and debriefing processes [15, 17]. This meta-debriefing focuses on the common construction and reconstruction of games as models of reality. By addressing this challenge and emphasizing responsible design and facilitation, the work underlines how S&G can be deliberately harnessed to shape better futures through enhanced learning and meaningful change.

Ignorance, especially concerning historical knowledge, is inevitable, as in the game discussed in Sect. 2. Academic disputes regarding historical events can compound ambiguity, which can be exploited by historical revisionists to develop games based on fabricated history, presenting them as authentic descriptions. Even when the truth remains a subject of debate among historians, fake history games may imprint false perceptions on plays, representing implicit manipulation. Revisionists may insist on a distorted version of history, as observed in wartime, and which continues to be a concern today.

Online games pose a notable risk in this context. At present, the development of digital online games is facile, and they can be conveniently popularized through social media such as social networking sites or YouTube, spreading conspiracy theories and misinformation.

Believers of alternative truth recognize gamification as an effective tool for influencing perceptions. For example, the success of "America's Army," [26] a game developed by the U.S. Army for recruiting soldiers, hints at the effectiveness of gamification. Although the realities of military service and wartime may be far more complex than the game suggests, these aspects may not be explicitly shown. While it remains unclear whether such omissions are intentional, S&G researchers have a responsibility to caution players about "what remains untold" in games. Behind every game, there exists another layer of reality, and games may be used as implicit manipulation tactics.

The potential for manipulation exists even if we design games with traditional S&G methods. Game design relies on system diagrams that illustrate the factors affecting systems and their interrelationships (typically indicated by arrows). In some cases, certain factors may be omitted to simplify and improve the game system. However, a designer with malicious intent or alternative beliefs may manipulate the system diagram or intentionally omit critical factors. This represents an explicit form of manipulation.

S&G is widely recognized as a user-friendly tool for learning, and games are often recommended for learning the "truth." Even within the S&G research community, scholars believe in different truths. The authors do not insist that we agree on a single, absolute truth. However, researchers must acknowledge the issues that persist in this era of misinformation. In this post-truth era, as in a Shakespearean play, we are not the audience that knows the truth, but the actual characters on the stage of life who are confused by the realities.

Acknowledgments. This study was funded by the Fusion of Science and Technology. The authors appreciate "The Archives of Daily Living in the Wartime, Shushu area, Japan" for providing photos of wartime in Japan.

Disclosure of Interests. The authors have no competing interests to declare relevant to this article's content.

References

1. Gamson, W.A.: SIMSOC: simulated society. The Free Press, New York (1969)
2. Welch, W. (ed.): Masks, misinformation, and masking do: appalachian health-care workers and the COVID-19 pandemic. Ohio University Press, Athens, OH (2023)
3. Kikkawa, T.: Preface. In: Kikkawa, T., Kriz, W., Sugiura, J., de Wijse-van Heeswijk, M. (eds.) Transferring Gaming and Simulation Experience to the Real World, pp. v–vii. Springer, Singapore (2025). https://doi.org/10.1007/978-981-96-2755-4
4. Arai, K.: Chap.1 What is gaming simulation? In: Arai, K., Deguchi, H., Kaneda, T., Kato, F., Nakamura, M.: Gaming Simulation. JUSE Press Ltd., Tokyo (1998). (In Japanese)
5. Nakamura, M.: Facilitating diversity: Enhancing gaming and simulation activities for varied participants. In: Kikkawa, T., Kriz, W., Sugiura, J., de Wijse-van Heeswijk, M. (eds.): Transferring Gaming and Simulation Experience to the Real World, pp. 23–38. Springer, Singapore (2025). https://doi.org/10.1007/978-981-96-2755-4_3
6. HACONORI. https://joypod.net/haconori/. Accessed 27 Jan 2025
7. Nakamura, M.: Influence of room condition on participants in simulation and gaming activities: analyses of debriefing forms. Simul. Gaming **50**(5), 645–661 (2019)
8. Kolb, K.: Experiential learning: experience as the source of learning and development. Prentice-Hall, Englewood Cliffs, NJ (1984)
9. Jones, K.: Games & simulations made easy: practical tips to improve learning through gaming. Kogan Page Limited, London (1997)
10. Klabbers, J.: The magic circle: principles of gaming & simulation (Third and Revised Edition ed.). Sense Publishers, Rotterdam (2009)
11. Sutton-Smith, B.: The ambiguity of play. Harward University Press, Boston (1997)
12. De Caluwé, L., Hofstede, G.J., Peters, V.: Why do games work? in search of the active substance. Kluwer, Deventer, Netherlands (2008)
13. Marczewski, A.: Even ninja monkeys like to play. Unicorn Edition. Gamified UK, London (2018)
14. Greenblat, C.S.: Designing games and simulations: an illustrated handbook. Sage, Beverly Hills (1988)
15. Kriz, W.C., Nakamura, M., Kikkawa, T.: Crossing borders by revisiting ethical issues of simulation and gaming. In: Lukosch, H., Freese, M., Meijer, S. (eds.) Simulation Gaming Across Borders: 55th International Simulation and Gaming Association Conference, ISAGA 2024, Christchurch, New Zealand, July 8–12, 2024, Revised Selected Papers, pp. 1–18. Springer, Cham (2025). https://doi.org/10.1007/978-3-031-86555-8_1
16. Kriz, W.C.: A systems-oriented constructivism approach to the facilitation and debriefing of simulations and games. Simul. Gaming **41**(5), 663–680 (2010)
17. Kriz, W.C.: Transfer of gaming: designing simulation games as models of reality and gaming simulation to design and model reality. In: Kikkawa, T., Kriz, W.C., Sugiura, J., de Wijse-van Heeswijk, M. (eds.) Transferring Gaming and Simulation Experience to the Real World, pp. 1–12. Springer, Singapore (2025). https://doi.org/10.1007/978-981-96-2755-4_1
18. Kriz, W.C., Kikkawa, T., Sugiura, J.: Manipulation through gamification and gaming. In: Kikkawa, T., Kriz, W.C., Sugiura, J. (eds.) Gaming as a Cultural Commons. Risks, Challenges, and Opportunities, pp. 185–199. Springer, Singapore (2022). https://doi.org/10.1007/978-981-19-0348-9_11
19. Kriz, W.C.: The thorny issue of time. In: Angelini, M.L., Muñiz, R. (eds.): Simulation for Participatory Education: Virtual Exchange and Worldwide Collaboration, pp. 253–267. Springer, Cham (2023). https://doi.org/10.1007/978-3-031-21011-2
20. Duke, R.D.: Gaming: the future's language. Wiley, New York (1974)

21. De Wijse-van Heeswijk, M., Kriz, W.C.: Design science perspective on formative evaluation in simulation games. In: Angelini, M.L., Muñiz, R. (eds.): Simulation for Participatory Education: Virtual Exchange and Worldwide Collaboration, pp. 215–251. Springer, Cham (2023). https://doi.org/10.1007/978-3-031-21011-2_7
22. Kriz, W.C., Harviainen, J.T., Clapper, T.C.: Game science: foundations and perspectives. Simul. Gaming **49**(3), 199–206 (2018)
23. Personal communication (Kriz-Feldt)
24. Klabbers, J.H.: On the architecture of game science. Simul. Gaming **49**(3), 207–245 (2018)
25. Palincsar, A.S.: Social constructivist perspectives on teaching and learning. Annu. Rev. Psychol. **49**, 345–375 (1998)
26. "America's Army" published in 2002. Not accessible after 02/07/2022

Development of Gaming Simulation for Policy Discussion on the Community-Based Integrated Care System

Kaede Fujita^(✉) and Manabu Ichikawa

Shibaura Institute of Technology, Saitama 337-8570, Japan
`i047011@sic.shibaura-it.ac.jp`

Abstract. The Community-Based Integrated Care System (CICS) in Japan integrates five key domains—housing, healthcare, long-term care, livelihood support, and prevention—to support elderly' independent living. However, rising demand for social welfare services and financial constraints challenge its sustainability. Policymaking within CICS requires cross-sectoral coordination, yet traditional approaches often fail to capture interdependencies and long-term impacts.

This study develops a gaming simulation to facilitate policy discussions within CICS, enabling stakeholders to experience decision-making processes and assess the effects of policy choices on service sustainability. Players act as municipal policymakers, allocating budgets across CICS domains and evaluating long-term policy outcomes through a CICS simulator using an agent-based modeling framework. The game is structured on Lasswell's context-oriented approach, organizing stakeholder perspectives, regulatory mechanisms, and decision-making processes.

The simulation evaluates policy sustainability based on short-term indicators, such as service utilization rates and demographic shifts, and long-term indicators, including healthy life expectancy and financial sustainability. By visualizing trade-offs and sectoral interactions, the game serves as a scenario-based learning tool, enhancing stakeholder understanding of policy interdependencies. This research contributes to policymaking by providing an inter-active framework for optimizing care service delivery and fostering co-creation in municipal governance.

Keywords: Policy Simulation · Municipal Governance · Cross-Sectoral Policy Discussion

1 First Section

1.1 Background

The Ministry of Health, Labour and Welfare (MHLW) of Japan has been promoting the development of the Community-Based Integrated Care System (CICS) with the goal of full implementation by 2025 [1]. This system integrates five key domains—housing, healthcare, long-term care, livelihood support, and prevention—to enable elderly to maintain independent living in their familiar communities. With the continued trends of

F. Trautwein et al. (Eds.): ISAGA 2025, LNCS 16439, pp. 19–32, 2026.
https://doi.org/10.1007/978-3-032-20129-4_2

low birth rates, population aging, and nuclear family structures, the demand for social welfare services for elderly has been increasing, necessitating policies that ensure the long-term sustainability of the social security system.

Figure1 illustrates the interrelationship among the five domains within CICS. At the center, housing serves as the foundation, around which healthcare, long-term care, and livelihood support & prevention operate in coordination to support elderly' lives. Municipal governments play a critical role in orchestrating service provision, managing the operation of healthcare and long-term

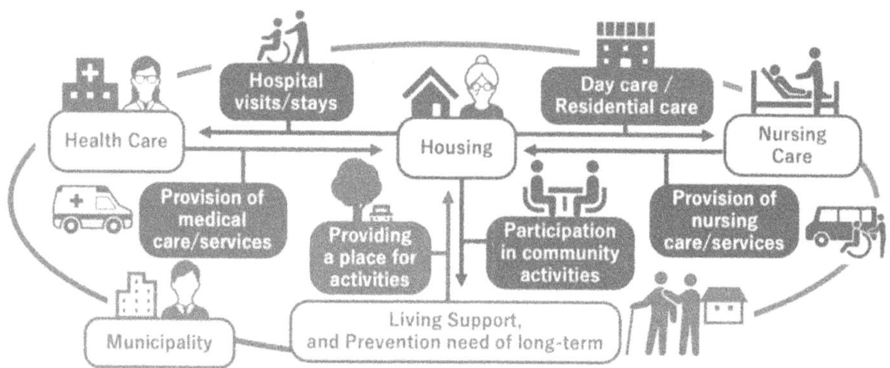

Fig. 1. The Community-Based Integrated Care System in Japan (CICS)

care facilities, and ensuring access to necessary services. Additionally, municipalities are responsible for fostering community participation among elderly, facilitating social activities and opportunities for engagement. Through the integration and coordination of these domains, CICS aims to establish a system where elderly can continue living in their communities for as long as possible while maintaining their quality of life.

Traditionally, Japanese policies have focused on securing local resources to reduce disparities in service availability and quality across regions. However, in recent years, the rapid increase in social security expenditures and financial constraints at both national and municipal levels have become critical issues, particularly due to the rising utilization of hospital beds and long-term care facilities, which places significant pressure on public finances. As a result, optimizing the allocation and operation of services within a limited budget has emerged as a new policy challenge.

Under financial constraints, strengthening livelihood support and preventive measures within CICS has become essential to delay the progression of care needs. The increasing utilization of specialized medical and long-term care services directly contributes to higher social security costs, making early intervention to reduce the risk of care dependency and disease onset a critical priority. For instance, the development of community hubs for elderly and the implementation of health promotion initiatives led by local volunteers can help prevent social isolation and frailty, serving as proactive measures before the need for long-term care arises. Additionally, functional differentiation and coordination among service providers can create a mutually supportive system, allowing elderly to maintain independence while mitigating financial burdens.

To establish an integrated care framework across different service domains, it is essential to visualize supply and demand conditions within municipalities and determine optimal service allocation. This involves analyzing trends in the older adult population, the number of certified care recipients, the distribution and utilization rates of service providers, and municipal financial conditions to objectively assess local resource gaps. These insights not only inform municipal planning, regulatory measures, and policy guidance but also serve as key decision-making indicators for service providers regarding business continuity, withdrawal, or new market entry.

The successful implementation of CICS requires collaboration among healthcare institutions, long-term care providers, municipal governments, non-profit organizations (NPOs), and community residents to foster a co-creation approach to policymaking. Conventional policy discussions have primarily emphasized expert and administrative perspectives, often failing to fully reflect on-the-ground realities and community needs. Therefore, to enhance policy effectiveness and local adaptability, a framework that facilitates stakeholder participation and mutual understanding is necessary.

Existing studies on CICS have predominantly focused on healthcare and long-term care services, with limited research on cross-sectoral integration [3]. This is partly due to the unique characteristics of Japan's CICS compared to other countries, particularly its strong emphasis on livelihood support for elderly as a core system component. According to Tsutsui (2014) [2], Japan's system is characterized by the integration of long-term care, healthcare, and welfare services, with private sector involvement playing a major role in service provision.

In the context of multi-sector policy planning, gaming simulation has proven to be an effective method. Gaming enables multiple stakeholders to simulate future scenarios, enhance mutual understanding, and evaluate the feasibility of policy measures. This study aims to develop a gaming simulation for policy discussions within CICS, focusing on system modeling, methods for translating real-world systems into game mechanics, and the design of collaborative stakeholder processes.

1.2 Purpose of the Research

This study proposes a gaming simulation as a communication tool to facilitate future-oriented policy discussions within CICS. The gaming simulation is designed to engage diverse stakeholders in discussions on demand-supply mismatches and service optimization.

Accordingly, the objective of this study is to present a new approach to policy discussions and provide insights to enhance the sustainability of CICS.

2 Game Design

2.1 Purpose of the Gaming

CICS is composed of five interdependent domains—housing, healthcare, long-term care, livelihood support, and prevention—where policies in each domain influence and interact with one another. The municipal government plays a central role in regulating and guiding policy decisions to ensure coordination across these domains.

In the healthcare sector, regional medical care plans facilitate the attraction of clinics and regulation of hospital beds. In long-term care, livelihood support, and prevention, local long-term care plans are used to allocate subsidies for service expansion and provider recruitment. Additionally, in housing and livelihood support, national grants are utilized to support community-based service development initiatives.

The objective of this gaming simulation is to allow players to experience the policy formation process within CICS, where interactions across the five domains shape decision-making. The simulation enables players to learn about building a sustainable care system by considering how different levels of care needs require varying types of support, incorporating both specialized and non-specialized services.

Table 1 categorizes services based on care needs and distinguishes specialized support from non-specialized support. For individuals with low care needs, services primarily consist of non-specialized support, such as daily living assistance, monitoring programs, preventive care classes, and community salon activities. In contrast, individuals with high care needs require specialized support, including home-visit care, short-term residential care, special nursing homes, and specialized medical treatment. Municipal governments must evaluate the characteristics of each domain to determine how to structure and regulate the overall care system at the community level.

Table 1. Types of Support Based on Care Needs

Care Needs Level	Non-Specialized Support	Specialized Support
Low Care Needs	Livelihood support services (shopping assistance, cleaning, etc.) Monitoring activities Preventive care workshops Community salon activities Meal delivery services Outing support Housekeeping support	Home visit rehabilitation Day rehabilitation Home-visit nursing Day care services Preventive care programs Health education Counseling by specialists
High Care Needs	Monitoring and support by family and local residents Livelihood support by volunteers Community salon activities	Home-visit care (home help services) Short-term residential care (short stay) Special nursing homes Geriatric health facilities Specialized treatment in medical institutions Rehabilitation by specialists

In this game, each player represents one of the five domains within CICS (housing, healthcare, long-term care, livelihood support, and prevention), with a total of five players. Players take on the perspective of municipal governments, engaging in policy discussions and budget allocation negotiations. Through this process, they experience how their decisions impact the overall community care system.

The game is designed to help players understand the diverse perspectives of different stakeholders and learn the decision-making process for building a sustainable care system. By simulating real-world complexities, the game provides a shared framework that enables policymakers to coordinate policies more effectively and adapt their strategies for optimal service integration within CICS.

2.2 Target

In this game, players assume the role of municipal governments responsible for guiding and regulating policies within each domain of CICS. Players engage in policy decision-making while considering the expertise and operational realities of their respective domains to enhance the long-term sustainability of CICS. The game is designed to facilitate collaboration among players, allowing them to negotiate trade-offs and assess interdependencies to explore how overall system optimization can be achieved.

Table2 organizes the key stakeholders involved in policy formation within CICS, based on Lass-well's context-oriented approach [4] Lasswell's framework categorizes the decision-making process into five levels: (1) Actors, (2) Perspectives, (3) Situations, (4) Values, and (5) Actions, demonstrating how different stakeholders make decisions from varied viewpoints.

This game is designed based on Lasswell's context-oriented approach, enabling players to understand the perspectives, values, and decision-making conditions of key stakeholders when making policy decisions in each CICS domain. The objective is to explore optimal policy formation by considering the interdependencies between sectors.

For example, in the healthcare sector, prefectural medical policy divisions coordinate the distribution of hospitals and clinics, while in the long-term care sector, municipal elderly welfare divisions are responsible for securing care resources. Additionally, in livelihood support and prevention, NPOs and volunteer organizations play a crucial role in promoting social engagement and health initiatives for elderly.

Each stakeholder operates from a different perspective and faces unique challenges, yet all con-tribute to the operation of CICS. Through this game, players engage in decision-making from the standpoint of policy guidance and regulation, fostering discussions that highlight the importance of strategic coordination in building a sustainable community-based care system.

2.3 Theoretical Framework

This game simulation is designed to theoretically structure the policy formation process within CICS and integrate its key design elements into the game mechanics. Through this approach, players learn the importance of coordination in building a sustainable CICS. While policy decisions in each domain are made independently, their long-term interactions accumulate, ultimately influencing the overall system. Even if immediate effects are not visible in the short term, understanding their significant long-term impact is crucial.

This game incorporates Lasswell's context-oriented approach, organizing stakeholders' roles, perspectives, and actions within a structured policy decision-making framework. Based on this theoretical foundation, the game progression is structured as outlined in Sect. 3.2.

Table 2. Stakeholders in the Community-Based Integrated Care System

Category	Housing	Healthcare	Long-term Care	Livelihood Support	Prevention
Actors	Prefectural/ municipal governments (Housing Policy Division, Architecture andHousing Division)	Prefectural governments (MedicalPolicy Division,Regional Healthcare Division)	Municipal governments (Elderly Welfare Division, Long-term Care Insurance Division), Prefectural governments (Health and Welfare Di-vision, Elderly Care Support Division)	Municipal governments (Elderly Welfare Division, Com-munity Welfare Division), NPOs, Volunteer organizations	Municipal governments (Elderly Welfare Division, Care Prevention Division, Community-based Support Centers)
Perspective	Improving housing environments, promoting senior housing	Ensuring regional healthcare services, securing medical staff	Providing care services, balancing home and facility care	Supporting elderly daily living, improving convenience	Preventing care dependency, ex-tending healthy life expectancy
Situation	Increaseinelderlysingle households, housing deterioration, urban-rural disparities	Rising healthcare demand, uneven physician distribution, increasing medical costs	Growth in care recipients, care-giver shortages, burden on family caregivers	Elderly social isolation, lack of mobility means, shortage of sup-port personnel	Lack of aware-ness in preventive care, health dis-parities, regional variations in policies
Actions	Promoting senior housing, home modifications, home care services	Developing regional healthcare plans, hospital/clinic net-work, emergency and advanced care	Planninglong-termcare insurance projects,certifying/providing careservices, caregiver training	Implementing livelihoodsup-portprograms (monitoring, shoppingaid, community mutual support)	Implementing preventivepro-grams (exercise, nutritionguidance,dementia prevention)
Values	Enabling elderly to live safely in familiar areas, integrating housing and welfare	Ensuring fair access to health-care, maintaining health and treatment continuity	Supporting elderly independence,sustain-able care services, reducingfamily burden	Promotingelderly community participation, social connections, independent living	Extending healthylife expectancy, reducingmedical/carecosts, community health promotion

2.4 Evaluation

The evaluation of this game is conducted along two axes: short-term and long-term indicators.

For the short-term evaluation, indicators include migration and inflow rates, which measure the impact of municipal policies on resident retention and population dynamics, including elderly. Additionally, to assess the sustainability of the healthcare and long-term care sectors, the availability of medical and care professionals is used as a key indicator.

For the long-term evaluation, changes in healthy life expectancy serve as an indicator to measure the impact of CICS policies on residents' health outcomes. Furthermore, to evaluate the financial sustainability of policies, fluctuations in regional healthcare and long-term care expenditures are considered.

Players must take these indicators into account when formulating policies to address regional challenges, aiming to establish a sustainable community-based care system.

3 Methods of the Gaming

3.1 Component

This game is designed with three key components: player role assignment, policy evaluation through the CICS simulator, and the policy decision feedback process (Fig. 2).

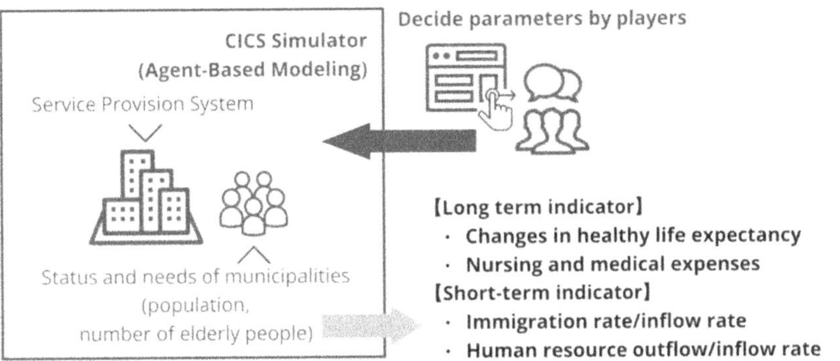

Fig. 2. Key Components of the Gaming Simulation: Role Assignment, Policy Evaluation, and Feedback Process

Player Roles. In this game, players act as municipal policymakers, responsible for guiding and regulating policies in the healthcare, long-term care, livelihood support, and prevention domains. Each player is provided with Role Cards and Profiling Cards, which define their policy responsibilities and perspectives for decision-making.

As illustrated in Fig. 3, the Role Cards are structured based on Lasswell's context-oriented approach[4], organizing information into five key elements: Actors, Perspectives, Situations, Values, and Actions. For example, the healthcare player receives a card

Medical

Entity : Prefectural government (Medical Policy Division, Regional Medical Affairs Division)
Perspective : Overall regional medical service system, hospital and clinic distribution, securing doctors and nurses
Situation : Increasing medical demand due to aging population, uneven distribution of doctors, rising medical costs
Actions : Formulating regional medical plans, developing hospitals and clinics, providing emergency and advanced medical care, securing and allocating medical professionals
Values : Ensuring fair access to appropriate medical care for residents, equitable medical services, disease treatment, and health maintenance

Fig. 3. Role Card

detailing current issues, policy challenges, and priority objectives in healthcare, which serve as the basis for their policy decisions.

Additionally, as illustrated in Fig. 3, the Profiling Cards summarize regional conditions, including the number of elderly, the number of certified care recipients, the availability of healthcare, long-term care, and livelihood support services, as well as the financial status of the municipality. Players use this information to formulate policies.

Furthermore, by referencing the Profiling Cards, players evaluate policy options and determine budget allocations for each domain. Ultimately, the allocated budgets for each sector serve as input parameters for the CICS simulator, influencing the simulation outcomes.

CICS Simulator. The CICS simulator is a policy evaluation tool utilizing Agent-Based Modeling (ABM) to assess the sustainability of policies within the Community-Based Integrated Care System

Medical Profiling Card	
Category	**Data**
Total Population	226,940
Aging Rate	28.10%
Elderly Population	63,953
Medical Institutions	5 Hospitals, 120 Clinics
Medical Personnel	1,421 Doctors, 1,077 Nurses
Nursing and Medical Expenses	Medical: 15.9 Billion Yen, Care: 6.5 Billion Yen

Fig. 4. Profiling Card

(CICS). Players make policy decisions based on municipal demographic data, the number of elderly, and the availability of services, and then visualize their impact using the simulator. Specifically, it analyzes key post-policy implementation factors such as healthcare and long-term care service utilization, financial fluctuations, and resident mobility, allowing players to incorporate these in-sights into subsequent decision-making. This enables policy evaluation not only from a short-term perspective but also in terms of long-term sustainability (Fig. 4).

The CICS simulator is developed using SOARS (Spot Oriented Agent Role Simulator), an ABM framework. SOARS is designed to model agent behaviors based on social and organizational roles, enabling micro-level simulations of individual decision-making and interactions, while capturing macro-level system dynamics. According to Ono et al. [5], SOARS simulates complex social and organizational behaviors by modeling agents with predefined roles and behavioral rules, allowing for the replication of interdependent decision-making processes.

Furthermore, the design of this simulation expands on Fujita (2024) [6], Optimizing Care Service Delivery, by incorporating the five key domains of CICS. In addition to simulating healthcare and long-term care utilization trends, the system evaluates the effects of livelihood support, preventive measures, and community-based elderly independence strategies.

The CICS simulator interface is implemented using Streamlit, a Python-based web application framework, providing an intuitive and interactive environment for users.

Policy Decision Feedback Process. Policy decisions made by players are evaluated based on the short-term and long-term indicators defined in Sect. 2.4 (Evaluation). The results influence subsequent policy decisions, as players review municipal conditions after policy implementation in CICS simulator and adjust their strategies for the following year.

Through repeated iterations of this process, players must consider both immediate effects and long-term impacts in their decision-making, striving to build a sustainable CICS. By integrating these elements, the game provides players with an experiential learning environment where they balance short-term policy effectiveness with long-term sustainability as municipal decision-makers.

3.2 Processes of the Gaming

This game is designed to simulate how municipal governments guide and regulate policies within CICS, allowing players to experience the decision-making process for constructing a sustainable care system. Players are responsible for policymaking within one of the five CICS domains, using the CICS simulator to evaluate policy impacts and collaboratively build an optimized care system. The budget allocation and policy decision-making process in the game follows a one-year cycle, where players assess regional conditions, select policy options, adjust budget allocations, and implement measures. This process is repeated over a five-year simulation period.

Figure 5 presents the interface of the CICS simulator, which is set in Ageo City, Saitama Prefecture, as the target region. The left side of the interface displays a municipal map along with basic demographic information, such as population and aging rate. On the right side, sliders allow players to adjust budget allocations across five domains—healthcare, long-term care, housing, livelihood support, and prevention. By modifying these allocations, players reflect municipal policy decisions in the simulation. Pressing the "Run Simulation" button inputs the allocated budget into the CICS simulator, which then executes the simulation. After progressing through five years, CICS simulator visualizes changes in healthcare and long-term care expenditures as a graph. Through

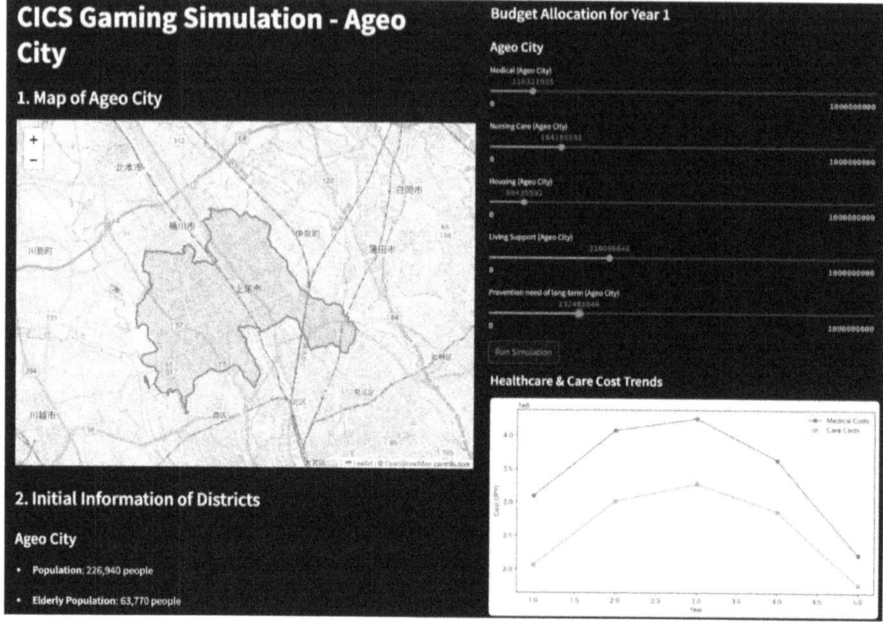

Fig. 5. The CICS simulator

this simulation, players can evaluate how policy choices impact service provision and financial sustainability at the municipal level.

3.3   0. Role Assignment (Pre-GAME Distribution)

Before the game begins, each player receives a Role Card, which outlines their domain's long-term policy direction, challenges, and responsibilities regarding regulation and guidance. Players must understand their sector's perspectives and responsibilities in advance and use this knowledge when selecting policy options.

3.4   1. Situation Assessment

Players review the current municipal conditions displayed by the CICS simulator, including:

- Number of elderly
- Number of certified care recipients
- Availability of healthcare, long-term care, and livelihood support services
- Municipal financial conditions

This allows players to analyze the existing challenges and organize necessary information for decision-making.

3.5 2. Confirmation of Long-Term Policy Perspectives

Players review their Role Cards, which outline long-term policy objectives, to understand how their sector contributes to CICS as a whole. This phase does not involve discussion but serves as a process where players confirm their sector's role and responsibilities before making decisions.

3.6 3. Selection of Policy Options

Based on the Situation Assessment, players select policy options within their domain. In doing so, they must consider:

- Types of necessary interventions (e.g., introducing new policies, expanding existing services, strengthening regulations)
- Policy prioritization (which measures should be prioritized)
- Interdependencies between policy decisions (how one player's decision may impact others)

3.7 4. Budget Allocation

Each player proposes a budget required to implement their selected policies. The total municipal budget is distributed among all sectors, requiring negotiation and consensus-building. The final allocated budget is then input into the CICS simulator as a key parameter.

To assist players in decision-making, Role Cards and Profiling Cards are provided:

- Role Cards: Outline each sector's regulatory and policy direction as well as its long-term goals.
- Profiling Cards: Present detailed municipal data on demographics, aging rates, the number of healthcare and long-term care facilities, and the availability of medical professionals.

By referring to these cards, players simulate real-world sectoral perspectives and adjust policies accordingly.

3.8 5. Policy Implementation

Once the final budget allocations are set, the selected policies are executed, and the CICS simulator calculates their impact. The results are reflected in key indicators such as:

- Changes in healthcare and long-term care service utilization rates
- Changes in elderly' health conditions
- Regional demographic changes (migration and inflow rates)
- Availability of healthcare and long-term care workers
- Municipal financial conditions (fluctuations in healthcare and long-term care expenditures)

Through this process, players can evaluate the long-term impacts of their policy decisions on municipal sustainability.

4 Results and Discussion

Through the design of this game, the decision-making process in CICS policy formation was visualized, demonstrating the potential to facilitate co-creative discussions among diverse stakeholders. In particular, the Role Cards and Profiling Cards, designed based on Lasswell's context-oriented approach, functioned as key elements that supported players in adopting a policymaker's perspective and making realistic, issue-based decisions.

The primary outcomes of this game can be summarized in three key points: First, it was con-firmed that players could experience how short-term policy choices impact the long-term sustain-ability of the overall system. Specifically, the balance between healthcare and long-term care service provision and budget allocation was shown to significantly influence regional healthy life expectancy and the sustainability of social security expenditures.

Second, the game enhanced players' understanding of sectoral interdependencies in policy formation. Players were observed to consider not only the policy decisions within their own domains but also the broader systemic impact of policy choices in other sectors.

Third, this gaming simulation demonstrated the potential to serve as an effective scenario analysis tool in real-world policy formation. By utilizing this game, municipal officials and policymakers could visualize region-specific policy challenges and compare different policy scenarios, making it a valuable decision-support tool.

In addition, one of the key strengths of this simulation lies in its ability to replicate the operational flow of real-world CICS policy formation in a compressed and expe-riential format. While policy implementation in actual municipalities often takes years to manifest measurable outcomes, this game enables participants to simulate multi-year policy impacts within a few hours. By engaging with realistic decision-making con-straints, players can internalize the dynamics of resource allocation, sectoral trade-offs, and demographic shifts. Regardless of whether the simulated outcome is successful or not, the experience itself supports a deeper understanding of municipal governance and service coordination.

At this stage, the game does not yet incorporate a formalized evaluation framework to measure learning outcomes or behavioral changes among participants. Establishing robust methods to assess how players grasp system-level interdependencies, exercise judgment under uncertainty, and engage in collaborative decision-making will be an essential future direction. In this sense, evaluating the educational and transformative potential of the game remains an important area for continued research.

From a social and academic perspective, this study contributes by presenting a new approach to policy evaluation in CICS. While traditional simulation studies primarily rely on statistical analysis and mathematical modeling, this game is characterized by its ability to replicate the cognitive processes and consensus-building mechanisms of decision-makers. As a result, the game extends beyond policy evaluation, positioning itself as a learning tool for policy formation.

However, this player experience inherently depends on the validity of the underlying simulation model, which represents a key limitation of this study. To ensure the validity and relevance of the simulation model, ongoing dialogue with real-world stakehold-ers—such as municipal officials, healthcare providers, and community organizations—is essential. Their practical insights can help refine the model's assumptions, structure, and parameters, thereby enhancing both the accuracy of the simulation and the authenticity of the player experience. Such collaboration will also strengthen the applicability of the game to actual policy design processes.

From a social and academic perspective, this study contributes by presenting a new approach to policy evaluation in CICS. While traditional simulation studies primarily rely on statistical analysis and mathematical modeling, this game is characterized by its ability to replicate the cognitive processes and consensus-building mechanisms of decision-makers. As a result, the game extends beyond policy evaluation, positioning itself as a learning tool for policy formation.

To expand the applicability of this game, it is necessary to conduct players with actual policymakers and verify its alignment with real-world decision-making processes. Incorporating the perspectives of policymakers, municipal officials, healthcare and long-term care providers, and civic organizations will further enhance its practical utility in real-world policy discussions.

Disclosure of Interests.   The authors have no competing interests to declare that are relevant to the content of this article.

References

1. Ministry of Health, Labour and Welfare: about the community-based integrated care system. https://www.mhlw.go.jp/stf/seisakunitsuite/bunya/hukushi_kaigo/kaigo_kourei sha/chiiki-houkatsu/. Accessed 24 May 2025
2. Tsutsui, T.: Implementation process and challenges for the community-based integrated care system in Japan. Int. J. Integr. Care **14**, e002 (2014)
3. Tsuruta, Y.: Trends and future issues in regional comprehensive care research. J. Jpn. Soc. Health Econ. 33(1), 33–40 (2017)
4. Lasswell, H.D.: A Pre-View of Policy Sciences. American Elsevier, New York (1971)
5. Ono, I., Ichikawa, M., Deguchi, H.: Proposal of SOARS toolkit for large-scale agent-based simulation. In: Proceedings of the SICE System and Information Division Annual Conference (SSI 2020). The Society of Instrument and Control Engineers (2020)
6. Fujita, K., Ichikawa, M.: Optimizing care service delivery in aging Japan: an agent-based simulation approach. Paper presented at the International Conference in Management on Emerging Markets (ICMEM) (2024)

Influence of Game Genre Choice
on Computational Thinking Development
in School-Based Video Game Design Activities

Jérémy Le Du[1]([⊠]), Julian Alvarez[2], and Daniel Schmitt[1]

[1] Université de Lorraine, Metz, France
Jeremy.Le-Du@hrsk.fi, daniel.schmitt@univ-lorraine.fr
[2] Université de Lille, Lille, France
Julian.alvarez@univ-lille.fr

Abstract. This study examines the influence of game genre choice on the development of computational thinking (CT) in school-based video game design activities. While previous research highlights the engagement and motivation benefits of game design, limited quantitative evidence exists regarding its impact on programming skills. In this paper, we investigate the relationship between game mechanics or content and CT concepts development. A quasi-experimental study was conducted with 146 students from Finland and France (2022–2024). Students selected from ten game models spanning diverse genres, and their choices were analyzed based on initial programming proficiency and gender. Platform and jumping games emerged as the most popular, while quizzes and visual novels were preferred by female students. Results indicate that game genre choice correlates with both student interest and programming difficulty. Post-test results show overall CT skill improvement, with variation depending on the game type created. Platform games and visual novels yielded the highest learning gains, whereas quiz games showed the lowest. The presence of gameplay elements involving specific CT concepts, such as loops and conditionals, was directly linked to improved mastery of these concepts. Based on these findings, a progression of game types has been proposed, beginning with simpler games before advancing to more complex designs. These results contribute to educational game design research, supporting the hypothesis that game types and mechanics influence programming knowledge acquisition. Future studies should explore broader contextual factors and their impact on CT development through game design activities.

Keywords: computational thinking · game design · game genre · loop · conditional

1 Introduction

The new generation of learners has grown up with technology and many learned to use it from an early age. However, the assertion that today's students, the so-called "digital natives" [1], inherently understand information and communication technologies simply

F. Trautwein et al. (Eds.): ISAGA 2025, LNCS 16439, pp. 33–48, 2026.
https://doi.org/10.1007/978-3-032-20129-4_3

because they have been exposed to them throughout their lives seems exaggerated, as shown by [2] for simple use of standard equipment. Schools play a crucial role in promoting equity in innovation [3] by fostering creative and academic use of digital technologies and, more broadly, developing computational thinking [4].

Even today, computational thinking lacks a universally agreed-upon definition [5]. Reintroduced by [6] as the ability to "solving problems, designing systems, and understanding human behavior that draw on the concepts fundamental to computer science", definitions of computational thinking have multiplied since then. Some consider it a 21st-century skill [7], a cognitive process [8], a set of skills [9], or a problem-solving process [10]—multidisciplinary and thus essential for all children [11]. Some researchers even recommend a broader definition of computational thinking to focus research efforts on developing its teaching, learning, and assessment [12].

A useful way to operationalize computational thinking was proposed by [13], who distinguish computational concepts, practices, and perspectives. Computational concepts refer to elements common to many programming languages: sequences, loops, events, parallelism, conditionals, operators, and data. To implement these concepts, students engage in computational practices—activities such as being incremental and iterative, testing and debugging, reusing and remixing, abstracting and modularizing. Finally, computational perspectives relate to the worldviews, interpersonal connections, and self-perceptions that designers develop while interacting with digital media, including expressing, connecting, and questioning.

All these authors agree that computational thinking goes beyond simple programming skills. It enables individuals to adapt to the digital world and solve problems across multiple disciplines using computational tools, models, and ideas [14]. This is the case, for instance, in video game design, which is at the core of this study.

Video game design appears to offer a particularly rich context for reinforcing computational concepts [15], more effectively than creating video clips or stories when it comes to mastering computational thinking (CT) concepts such as variables, conditions, or loops [16]. Werner, Denner, and Campe confirmed this in their study of 221 games designed by 325 middle school students [17], noting the use of both simple and more complex CT concepts such as parallelism or abstraction. However, not all CT concepts are equally mastered, as shown in the analysis by [18] of 500 games created with Scratch. The limited use of variables and randomness in programs highlights the need for specific support in these areas.

The meta-analysis by [19] laments the lack of quantitative evidence that game design improves programming skills. Most evidence describes engagement without measuring learning. "Moreover, the generalizability of these findings is limited by a lack of data [...] that can be used to form conclusions about what kinds of game mechanisms or game content result in different kinds of programming knowledge."

This article aims to investigate the link between the game mechanisms or content and the CT concepts reinforced during school-based game design activities.

A practical method for categorizing game mechanics or content is through the concept of genre. While standardized criteria for defining genres remain absent [20], we broadly define genre as a collection of video games with shared gameplay characteristics.

Drawing on the framework of [21] regarding game genre classification, we developed ten models of video games spanning diverse genres for the purposes of this study.

2 Purpose of the Study

Our investigation begins by examining students' choice of game genres, focusing on variations influenced by initial programming levels and gender. For instance, [22] found that embedding programming into narrative activities enhanced engagement for girls, particularly in the complexity of their scripts. This suggests a possible preference among girls for games with strong narrative elements. Our first research question is:

RQ1. What kinds of games do students prefer to design?

Next, we will analyze whether the game mechanisms or game content impact the benefits of video game design activities. The associated research question is:

RQ2. Is there a link between the types of games created and the potential improvement of CT concept skills during video game design activities?

Our hypothesis posits that such a link exists. To investigate this, we employed a quasi-experimental pre-test and post-test design involving 146 students who participated in the Educational Game & Play Design project, a video game design program implemented in schools across Finland and France since the 2022–2023 academic year.

Through an analysis of both test results and the games created by the students, we aimed to uncover the influence of game genre—encompassing its content and mechanics—on the development of learners' CT concepts. To our knowledge, this research offers a novel contribution to the field, providing valuable pedagogical recommendations for researchers and educators on selecting the most suitable game types for effective learning in game design activities.

3 Method

3.1 Research Design

All the students designed their video games following the protocol outlined by the EGPDP program, described below. A pre-test and post-test quasi-experimental design was used to examine the above research questions. The research design is shown in Fig. 1.

The dependent variables assessed in this study were the level of CT concepts proficiency and the video games designed by the students.

Among the various tests evaluating computational thinking concepts [23], we selected the Computational Thinking test (CTt) developed by [24], which has demonstrated both criterion validity [25] and cross-cultural validity [26]. The CTt provides a decontextualized assessment based on 28 multiple-choice questions, lasting approximately 45 min. A paired pre- and post-test design measures how young participants express specific computational thinking skills: Basic directions and sequences; Loops

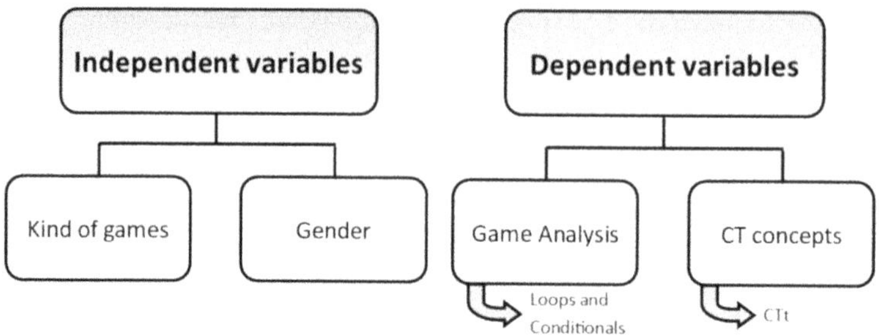

Fig. 1. Schematic diagram of research design.

repeat times; Loops–repeat until; If–simple conditional; If/else–complex conditional; While conditional; Simple functions.

In parallel, we measured the CT concepts used in the video games designed, providing complementary information to the tests. Specifically, we counted the number of blocks associated with different CT concepts, focusing on loops and conditionals, which are analyzed in this study.

The type of video game created, and the student's gender, necessary to answer RQ1 and RQ2, were the two independent variables in this study.

3.2 Context and Participants

This study was conducted as part of the Educational Game & Play Design (EGPDP) project, a video game design program offered to schools in Finland and France since the 2022–2023 academic year. The characteristics of the four primary and secondary schools participating in this study are summarized in Table 1. In total, 146 students from Grades 5 to 6 are included (90 girls and 56 boys).

Table 1. Name of the school, number of students participating, and location.

School	Number of students	Location
Forcalquier	18	Alpes-de-Haute-Provence
Caudry	57	Nord
Deuil-la-Barre	2	Val-d'Oise
Lycée français	69	Helsinki

3.3 Educational Game and Play Design Project

Figure 2 summarizes the main characteristics of the EGPDP program, developed based on a pilot study and a critical analysis of previous video game design experiences [27].

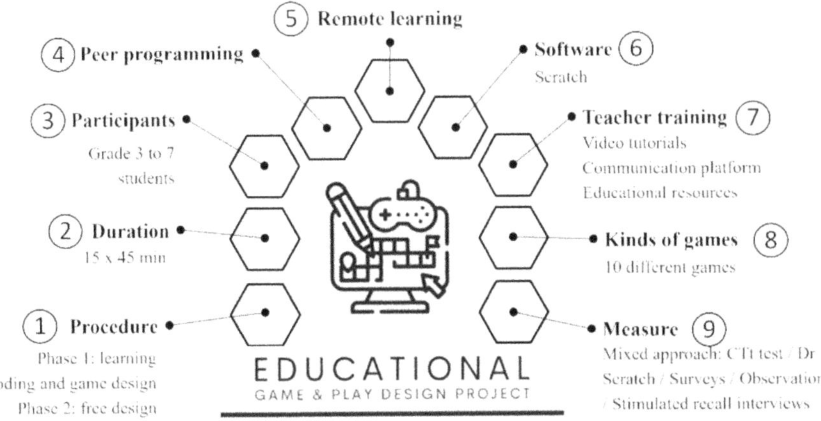

Fig. 2. Experimental protocol followed in EGPDP [26]

In the EGPDP, students design educational video games for their peers using Scratch software (6 in Fig. 1). Peer programming, where two students share a computer with distinct roles, is a promising approach [28] that was implemented in the EGPDP (4).

To maximize participation among students and teachers while ensuring a solid foundation in computational learning, the program is divided into two distinct phases (1): the first focuses on learning programming and game design strategies, while the second emphasizes free game creation. To adapt to the constraints of a school setting where time is limited, the EGPDP includes fifteen 45-min sessions (2), two of which are dedicated to pre-test and post-test evaluations (9).

Sessions 2 to 5 focus on mastering Scratch blocks and developing computational thinking skills. These sessions include 15 min of learning activities built around tutorial videos lasting under three minutes. The videos are designed following [29] instructional design principles: concise content targeting a single objective, using concrete examples, and followed by immediate implementation in the form of a gamified challenge.

Sessions 6 to 8 leverage game templates to help students acquire game design skills. To maximize student engagement, regardless of prior programming experience, 10 game templates are provided (8), visible on Fig. 3. Each template is based on distinct game mechanics and involves computational concepts of varying difficulty. Three indicative difficulty levels were introduced to guide novice designers, based on the CT concepts, game mechanics, and the number of blocks required for their creation.

The difficulty associated with the game mechanics required for designing the model game was assessed through an inventory of the gameplay bricks used [30], shown in Fig. 3. Beyond the number of gameplay bricks, some represent different levels of difficulty, depending on the type of programming involved. A move, for example, is often more complex to program than a choice. Last but not least, the complexity of programming a visual novel is reflected in the number of tree structures required.

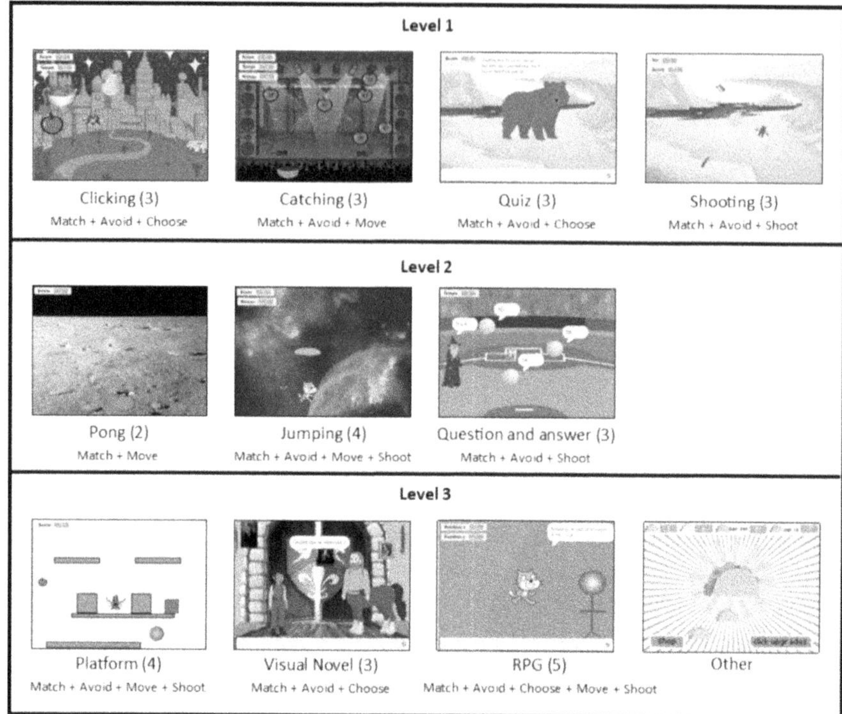

Fig. 3. Model of games offered to students in the EGPDP. The number of gameplay bricks needed to design the game is shown in parentheses.

Sessions 9 to 14 are dedicated to the free design of students' own video games. This period is deemed sufficient to foster creativity by encouraging students to move beyond the templates studied in previous sessions. During this phase, two testing sessions are scheduled, followed by peer feedback exchanges.

Teachers participating in the EGPDP have access to a set of pedagogical resources. Online training sessions are offered (5, 7), along with various educational tools (preparation videos, display materials, game templates). Their primary role is to guide students through the game development process and help them utilize the available resources effectively.

4 Results

4.1 Game Chosen by Students

Figure 4 illustrates the distribution of students according to the type of game designed. The distinction between boys' and girls' declared choices reveals certain preferences based on gender. Some game genres (Shooting, Question and answer, RPG) were not chosen, while other students chose to program a game without being inspired by a given model ("Other").

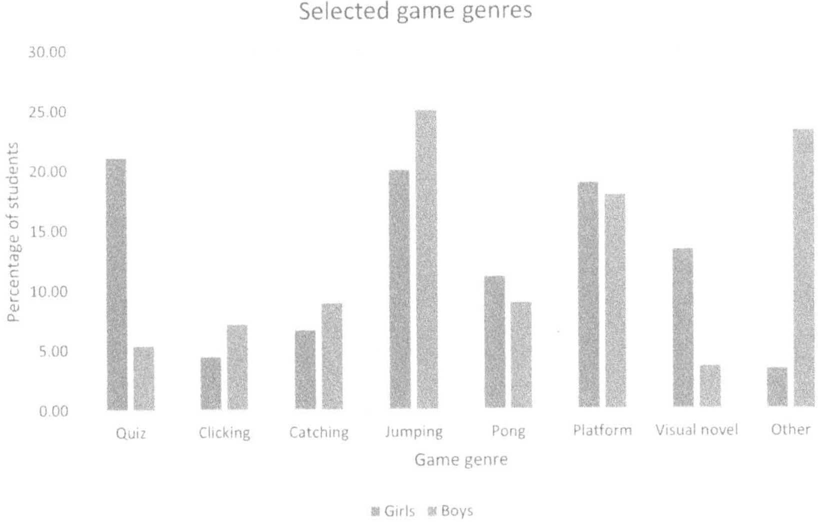

Fig. 4. Distribution of students based on the type of game designed for girls (blue) and boys (orange).

4.2   Results on the CTt Test

Results by Gender

Figure 5 shows box plots of the pre- and post-test scores for boys and girls.

The mean pre-test scores were 14.91(0.60) for boys and 14.44(0.48) for girls. The t-test result shows that there was no significant difference between the two groups (t = 0.60, p > 0.05). Therefore, both groups of students had equivalent prior knowledge before the learning activity.

The mean post-test scores were 16.24(0.44) for boys and 15.83(0.47) for girls. The change in learning was positive for both genders: the normalized learning gain for girls was 14.87%, while for boys it was 15.66%. The t-test result shows that there was no significant difference between the two groups (t = 0.36, p > 0.05). Therefore, both groups of students achieved the same learning gains on CTt through the EGPDP project.

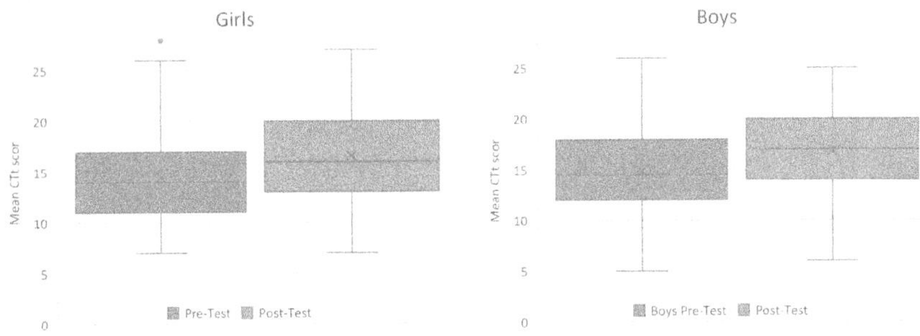

Fig. 5. Box plots of pre- and post-test results for girls (left) and boys (right).

Results by Game Type Created

To analyze variations based on the type of game chosen by students, we examined the mean pre- and post-test CTt scores for each game type group across all program participants. Table 2 provides descriptive statistics, including means, standard errors, standard deviations, differences, and t-test results for CTt scores across the eight groups. Figure 6 shows the average scores obtained in the pre-test (in blue) and post-test (in orange) by type of game created.

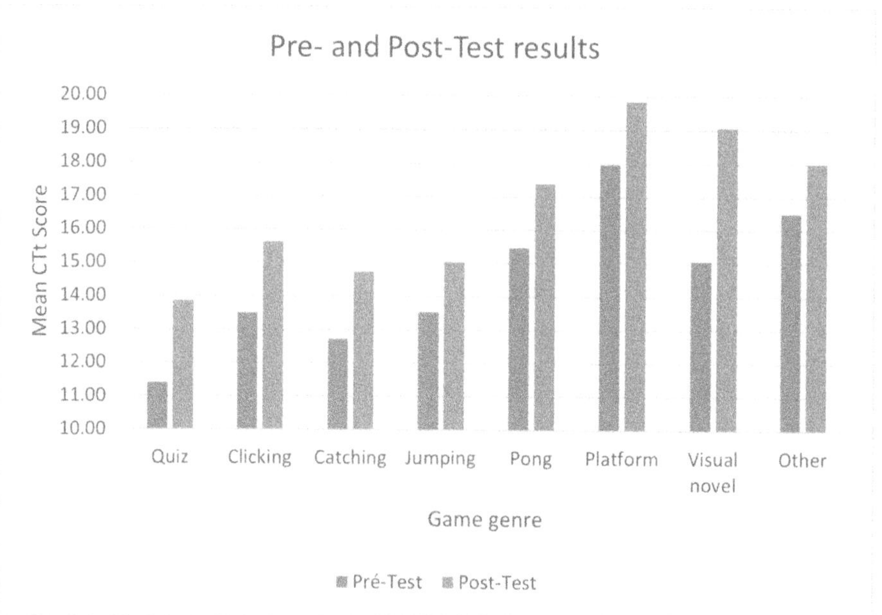

Fig. 6. Distribution of CTt scores by game type. Pre-test scores are represented in blue, post-test scores in orange.

Table 2. Descriptive data and paired samples t-test results from pre- to post-test.

Group	Size	Pre-test Mean	SD	Post-test Mean	SD	Differences Absolute	Normalized Gain	T-test
Quiz	22	11.41(0.76)	3.58	13.86(0.76)	3.55	2.45(0.44)	14.79%	5.64(p < 0.001)
Clicking	8	13.50(1.16)	3.30	15.63(1.19)	3.38	2.13(1.08)	14.66%	1.97(p < 0.05)
Catching	11	12.73(1.58)	5.24	14.73(1.61)	5.35	2.00(0.93)	13.10%	2.14(p < 0.05)
Jumping	32	13.53(0.67)	3.79	15.03(0.82)	4.62	1.50(0.51)	10.37%	2.95(p < 0.01)
Pong	14	14.79(1.19)	4.46	16.71(1.21)	4.53	1.93(0.67)	14.59%	2.89(p < 0.01)
Platform	28	18.21(0.86)	4.54	20.11(0.75)	3.99	1.89(0.50)	19.34%	3.81(p < 0.001)

(continued)

Table 2. (*continued*)

Group	Size	Pre-test Mean	SD	Post-test Mean	SD	Differences Absolute	Normalized Gain	T-test
Visual novel	14	15.07(0.97)	3.65	19.07(0.85)	4.27	4.00(0.79)	30.94%	3.87(p < 0.001)
Others	16	16.50(0.93)	3.71	18.00(1.06)	4.23	1.50(0.84)	13.04%	1.78(p < 0.05)

4.3 Specific Analysis

This section presents results for two CT concepts: loops (Loops repeat times) and conditionals (If–simple conditional). For each concept, we compare the specific results measured using the CTt and the number of associated blocks in the games designed by students.

Loops

Figure 7 depicts the average number of loops created by students for each type of game, based on the average score obtained on loop-related questions in the CTt, for both the pre-test (left) and post-test (right). A strong correlation is observed between the Average number of "loops" and the Pre-test mean CTt "loop" score for both the pre-test (r = 0.64) and the post-test (r = 0.62). For the latter, the correlation becomes very strong (r = 0.98) if we do not take point A into account, which we have good reasons to do as we will explain in the discussion.

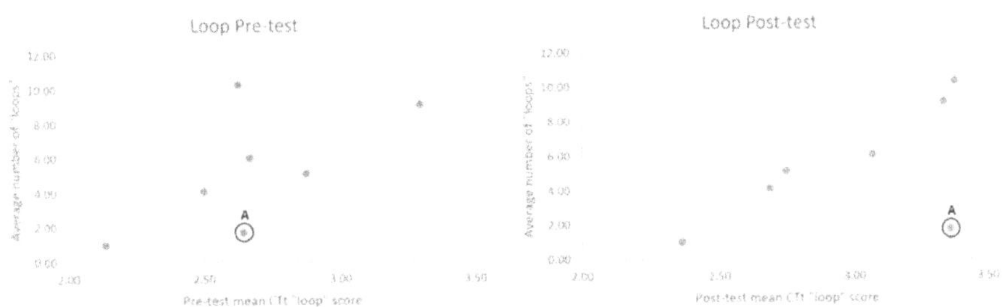

Fig. 7. Average number of loops per game type based on the average CTt score for pre-test (left) and post-test (right). Point A corresponds to the visual novel type game.

Conditionals

Figure 8 illustrates the average number of conditionals created by students for each type of game, based on the average score obtained on conditional-related questions in the CTt, for both the pre-test (left) and post-test (right). A very strong correlation is observed between the Avertage number of "conditionals" and the Pre-test mean CTt "conditional" score for both the pre-test (r = 0.88) and the post-test (r = 0.91).

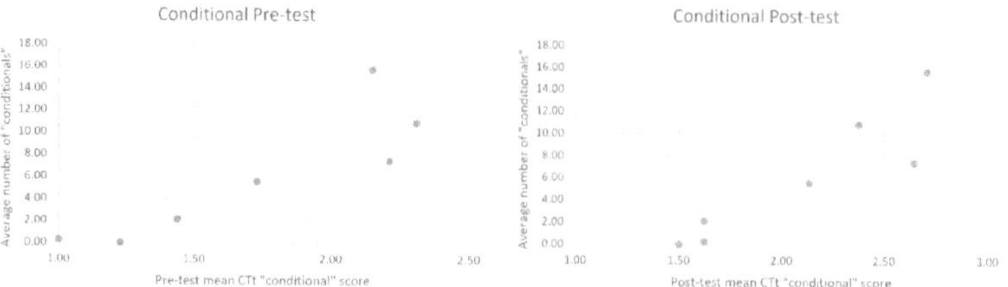

Fig. 8. Average number of conditionals per game type based on the average CTt score for pre-test (left) and post-test (right).

5 Discussion

5.1 Kind of Game Designed by Students

Among the game models offered by the EGPDP program, some genres were preferred over others. Figure 4 shows that platformer and jumping games were the most widely chosen by students overall. However, differences emerged based on gender. Many girls opted to program quizzes and visual novels, while a significant number of boys created games that deviated significantly from the proposed models.

The first explanation for these choices lies in the students' interest in these game genres. For example, platformer games are likely familiar to many students and resemble what they might play outside of school. Thus, it is understandable that they would want to design video games they are accustomed to. The deliberate choice of character designs resembling iconic figures of the genre (e.g., "Mario") supports this notion. Similarly, the choice by girls to program quizzes and visual novels aligns with this reasoning. Quizzes are strongly associated with the school context and may be appreciated for that reason. Visual novels, on the other hand, resonate with findings by [22], who observed that girls are more engaged in game design activities when narrative elements—key gameplay components of visual novels—are involved. Boys' preference for creating games that diverged from the proposed models, often inspired by maze, horror, or sports genres, further illustrates how personal interests shape their choices. [31] previously demonstrated the influence of popular games on students' game design choices. Our findings align with this trend, and we encourage future research to explore these patterns further and examine their potential implications for CT learning.

Another explanation lies in students' programming proficiency. Figure 6 indicates that students largely considered the estimated programming difficulty when selecting their games. Simpler games to program (e.g., quizzes, clicking, catching) were chosen more frequently by students with lower pre-test scores. The widespread selection of the jumping game supports this: it was the primary learning model during the initial phase of the EGPDP program, which focused on acquiring core computational thinking (CT) concepts. Students spent significant time understanding its code and possibly generating additional ideas for their own games through program challenges. Some children may have chosen to build upon these ideas rather than start from scratch. Similarly, students who created entirely original games, uninspired by the proposed models, which required designing the entire code, tended to have higher pre-test scores.

In conclusion, students appear to have selected the type of game they wished to create based on both their interest in the genre and the perceived programming difficulty. This balance is particularly interesting, as it suggests that their choice extends beyond mere game popularity to include a form of self-assessment of their ability to model a game in all its complexity, and we encourage future research to investigate this balance in more detail. Some game genres were not chosen and might be considered for removal from the EGPDP program in the future.

5.2 Variation in the Benefits of Video Game Design Activities Based on the Content of the Games Created

If we now examine the impact of the type of game designed on learning out-comes, Fig. 6 and Table 2 show that the results vary depending on the type of game created. All game types led to improvements observed between the pre-test and post-test, indicating that students generally progressed after participating in the EGPDP program, an initial response to the limitations identified by [19]. Quiz games resulted in the lowest average post-test scores, which confirms the study of [32]. On the contrary, platformer games, visual novels, and "other" games resulted in the highest average post-test scores. However, the interpretation differs for each of these cases.

In the case of platformer games, the absolute learning gains measured fall within the average range for the various game models. The high post-test scores are primarily attributed to the fact that the most skilled programmers chose this type of game, the most challenging to program in terms of the CT concepts mobilized as game mechanisms, requiring four gameplay bricks. Nevertheless, platformer games were the only model proposed that incorporated a true gravity system—a challenging gameplay element that extends beyond basic computational thinking (CT) concepts and concerns also physics. It is plausible to assume that students who chose to program this type of video game experienced additional learning gains beyond the CT concepts measured in this study. This highlights one of the limitations of this study, which focuses solely on the benefits related to CT concepts.

Regarding visual novels, they not only resulted in the highest post-test scores but also had the highest normalized learning gains. These findings contrast with those of [32], who observed that narrative games tend to limit the development of logical skills compared to other game genres. Since Fig. 5 did not reveal significant gender differences, the positive effects of visual novels seem to stem from the game itself, which appears to provide a favorable framework for developing CT concepts without requiring mastery of numerous game mechanics (three gameplay bricks required). This could be due to the extensive use of other CT skills not measured by the CTt, such as reusing, parallelism, and incrementation, which may contribute to improvements in the measured CT concepts. This explanation is supported by the specific case of loops shown in Fig. 7 (point A): although visual novels require few loops in their programming, students who designed such games significantly improved their mean CTt "loop" scores from pre-test to post-test.

For students who created "other" games, not based on one of the proposed models, their progress was among the lowest. Although their high average pre-test scores mitigate this observation, it is possible that the lack of a model to imitate limited their opportunities to discover new gameplay elements involving unfamiliar CT concepts. Having a model can provide valuable guidance in this regard, at least when focusing solely on CT concept development. However, should students be prevented from designing games freely? This is not our recommendation, as the motivational aspect is a significant factor in the educational potential of video game design activities in schools [33]. Furthermore, unless the sole goal is to develop programming skills, a game design module also fosters other 21st-century skills, such as creativity [34], which free game design inherently supports.

Returning to all the game models used, Figs. 6 and 7 reveal correlations between students' progress in certain CT concepts, measured by the CTt (loops and conditionals), and the presence of blocks associated with these concepts in the designed game. In other words, students' CT skills, measured in a decontextualized manner via the CTt, directly correlated with the average number of associated blocks integrated into their games. Using these blocks to design their own games appears to enhance students' mastery of the associated CT concepts, as suggested by the increased correlation observed in the post-test results.

Returning to research question RQ2, we identified a clear link between the type of video game created and the improvement of CT concept skills during game design activities. However, it seems that the key factor is not merely the game type itself but rather the computational thinking concepts and practices involved in designing its elements—namely, the game content and mechanics. Nonetheless, the preferences of novice designers discussed in the previous section should not be overlooked.

Based on this consideration, a proposed progression in game models can be developed to guarantee all students improve their mastery of CT concepts, regardless of their initial programming skills. This progression would account for the gameplay and coding elements involved as well as students' personal preferences. Programming could begin with one of the three Level 1 models: quiz, clicking, or catching games. These accessible models, which are similar in effectiveness, would allow beginners to achieve a basic level of CT concept mastery, sufficient to tackle a more complex game. A visual novel could then be introduced, leveraging its strong potential as previously discussed. Finally, a platformer game or free creation for the most advanced programmers could conclude this progression. This progression could be integrated into an improved version of the EGPDP program and proposed in future years.

These findings are significant and support [19] hypothesis from their meta-synthesis that game mechanisms and content foster distinct types of programming knowledge. The progression outlined here could inform the development of a computational thinking curriculum centered on video game design, providing students with an engaging and motivating learning environment that offers unique learning opportunities compared to more traditional approaches [35].

6 Conclusion

The goal of this article was to examine the impact of the type of game designed by students on the development of CT concepts. To this end, we conducted a design-based study from 2022 to 2024 involving 146 students in grades 5 and 6 from various schools in France and Finland.

We observed that among the ten game models proposed, certain types were preferred over others for two main reasons: students' interests and their programming proficiency. Jumping and platformer games were the most popular choices overall, with quizzes and visual novels also preferred by female students, and non-model-based games by male students.

Students who participated in the EGPDP program generally improved their CTt scores, regardless of the type of game they chose to design in the second part of the program. Some game types were associated with higher post-test scores, but these were predominantly selected by students with higher pre-test scores. Overall, the selected game types proved similarly effective, apart from visual novels. Their relatively accessible programming requirements and game design mechanisms make them an ideal choice as a video game model for maximizing the development of CT concepts.

We also found that the video games created, depending on the gameplay elements involved and the CT concepts enabling them, directly reinforced those same concepts. This was specifically observed in the use of loops and conditionals. Repeatedly using these concepts in game design led to better performance on the decontextualized test assessing mastery of these concepts.

Based on these findings, a progression of game types has been proposed for implementation in future versions of the EGPDP program. For beginner programmers, this progression begins with coding one of the three Level 1 game models used in this study: quiz, clicking, or catching games. After students reach the first threshold in computational thinking, they will design a visual novel, allowing them to assimilate more complex CT concepts alongside a broader range of game design elements. Finally, the most advanced programmers may consider creating a platformer game or a game not based on any of the proposed models.

This study could be further developed. A larger sample size would strengthen these findings and allow us to investigate whether a link exists between the development of specific CT concepts and particular gameplay elements rather than the type of game created. Qualitative methods, such as in-depth or stimulated recall interviews, would also allow for a deeper focus on the affective domain of players, as well as on how students implement the game mechanics they use—thus making it possible to link these mechanics to underlying learning processes. Other contextual factors, which were not considered in this study, could also influence the outcomes and should be explored in future research. These factors include age, socioeconomic status, academic achievement, and student motivation. Additionally, broadening our measurement tools could provide a more comprehensive view of the benefits of video game design activities, focusing more broadly on the development of 21st-century skills.

References

1. Prensky, M.: Digital game-based learning. McGraw-Hill, New York **1** (2001). https://doi.org/10.1145/950566.950567
2. Pittman, C.: Teaching with portals: the intersection of video games and physics education. LEARNing Landscapes **6**, 341–360 (2013). https://doi.org/10.36510/learnland.v6i2.620
3. Barron, B.: Learning ecologies for technological fluency: gender and experience differences. J. Educ. Comput. Res. **31**, 1–36 (2004). https://doi.org/10.2190/1N20-VV12-4RB5-33VA
4. Ito, M., et al.: Connected learning: an agenda for research and design (2013)
5. Durak, H.Y., Saritepeci, M.: Analysis of the relation between computational thinking skills and various variables with the structural equation model. Comput. Educ. **116**, 191–202 (2018). https://doi.org/10.1016/j.compedu.2017.09.004
6. Wing, J.: Computational thinking. Commun. ACM **49**, 33–35 (2006). https://doi.org/10.1145/1118178.1118215
7. Voogt, J., Fisser, P., Good, J., Mishra, P., Yadav, A.: Computational thinking in compulsory education: towards an agenda for research and practice. Educ. Inf. Technol. **20**(4), 715–728 (2015). https://doi.org/10.1007/s10639-015-9412-6
8. Wing, J.: A definition of computational thinking from Jeannette Wing. Computing educational research blog (2011)
9. Fagerlund, J., Häkkinen, P., Vesisenaho, M., Viiri, J.: Computational thinking in programming with Scratch in primary schools: a systematic review. Comput. Appl. Eng. Educ. **29**(1), 12–28 (2021). https://doi.org/10.1002/cae.22255
10. Standl, B.: Solving everyday challenges in a computational way of thinking. In: Dagienė, V., Hellas, A. (Éds.) Informatics in Schools: Focus on Learning Programming, vol. 10696, p. 180–191. Springer International Publishing (2017). https://doi.org/10.1007/978-3-319-71483-7_15
11. Denning, P.: Computational thinking in science. Am. Sci. **105**, 13–17 (2017)
12. Selby, C., & Woollard, J. (2014). Refining an understanding of computational thinking. *Working paper*
13. Brennan, K., Resnick, M.: New frameworks for studying and assessing the development of computational thinking. 2012 Annual Meeting of the American Educational Research Association, vol. 1, p. 25 (2012). http://scratched.gse.harvard.edu/ct/files/AERA2012.pdf
14. Denning, P.J., Tedre, M.: Computational thinking. The MIT Press (2019)
15. Peppler, K., Kafai, Y.: What videogame making can teach us about literacy and learning: alternative pathways into participatory culture. Situated Play: Proceedings of the Third International Conference, pp. 369–376 (2007)
16. Adams, J.C., Webster, A.R.: What do students learn about programming from game, music video, and storytelling projects? In: Proceedings of the 43rd ACM Technical Symposium on Computer Science Education, pp. 643–648 (2012). https://doi.org/10.1145/2157136.2157319
17. Werner, L., Denner, J., Campe, S.: Using computer game programming to teach computational thinking skills. In: Learning, Education and Games, p. 37–53. ETC Press (2014)
18. Kafai, Y.B., Peppler, K.A.: Youth, technology, and DIY: developing participatory competencies in creative media production. Rev. Res. Educ. **35**(1), 89–119 (2011). https://doi.org/10.3102/0091732X10383211
19. Denner, J., Campe, S., Werner, L.: Does computer game design and programming benefit children? a meta-synthesis of research. ACM Trans. Comput. Educ. **19**, 1–35 (2019). https://doi.org/10.1145/3277565
20. Clarke, R., Lee, J., Clark, N.: Why video game genres fail: a classificatory analysis. Games Cult. **12** (2015). https://doi.org/10.1177/1555412015591900

21. Harteveld, C.: Triadic game design—balancing reality, meaning and play (2011)
22. Howland, K., Good, J.: Learning to communicate computationally with Flip: a bi-modal programming language for game creation. Comput. Educ. **80**, 224–240 (2015). https://doi.org/10.1016/j.compedu.2014.08.014
23. Cutumisu, M., Adams, J.C., Lu, C.: A scoping review of empirical research on recent computational thinking assessments. J. Sci. Educ. Technol. **28** (2019). https://doi.org/10.1007/s10956-019-09799-3
24. Román-González, M.: Computational thinking test: design guidelines and content validation. In: 7th International Conference on Education and New Learning Technologies, pp. 2436–2444 (2015). https://doi.org/10.13140/RG.2.1.4203.4329
25. Román-González, M., Pérez-González, J.-C., Jiménez-Fernández, C.: Which cognitive abilities underlie computational thinking? Criterion validity of the Computational Thinking Test. Comput. Hum. Behav. **72**, 678–691 (2017). https://doi.org/10.1016/j.chb.2016.08.047
26. Wiebe, E., London, J., Aksit, O., Mott, B.W., Boyer, K.E., Lester, J.C.: Development of a lean computational thinking abilities assessment for middle grades students. In: SIGCSE '19: The 50th ACM Technical Symposium on Computer Science Education, pp. 456–461 (2019). https://doi.org/10.1145/3287324.3287390
27. Le Du, J., Alvarez, J., Schmitt, D.: Développer la pensée informatique à travers la conception de jeux vidéo éducatifs Educational Game & Play Design Project : Élaboration de la méthode. Distance et Médiation des savoir**48** (2024). https://doi.org/10.4000/12xon
28. Campe, S., Denner, J., Green, E., Torres, D.: Pair programming in middle school: Variations in interactions and behaviors. Comput. Sci. Educ. **30**(1), 22–46 (2020). https://doi.org/10.1080/08993408.2019.1648119
29. Mayer, R.: Thirty years of research on online learning. Appl. Cogn. Psychol. **33** (2018). https://doi.org/10.1002/acp.3482
30. Alvarez, J.: Approche atomique du jeu vidéo : Briques Gameplay 3.0 (2018)
31. Kafai, Y.B.: Minds in play: computer game design as a context for children's learning. Lawrence Erlbaum Associates (1995). http://www.amazon.fr/exec/obidos/ASIN/0805815120/citeulike04-21
32. Troiano, G., et al.: Exploring how game genre in student-designed games influences computational thinking development, pp. 1–17 (2020). https://doi.org/10.1145/3313831.3376755
33. Repenning, A., et al.: Scalable game design: a strategy to bring systemic computer science education to schools through game design and simulation creation. ACM Trans. Comput. Educ. **15**(2) (2015). https://doi.org/10.1145/2700517
34. Bowden, H.: Problem-solving in collaborative game design practices: epistemic stance, affect, and engagement. Learn. Media Technol. **44**, 1–20 (2019). https://doi.org/10.1080/17439884.2018.1563106
35. Kafai, Y.B., Burke, Q.: Constructionist gaming: understanding the benefits of making games for learning. Educ. Psychol. **50**(4), 313–334 (2015). https://doi.org/10.1080/00461520.2015.1124022

LEGO® SERIOUS PLAY® and Simulation Games: A Meaningful Combination or a Distracting Influence?

Maria Freese[1](✉), Hans-Christoph Gründler[2], Petra Hövelborn[3],
Willy Christian Kriz[4], Nadine Meidert[5], Helmut Wittenzellner[6], Susann Zeiner-Fink[7],
Sara Zumhasch[8], and Birgit Zürn[9]

[1] Otto von Guericke University Magdeburg, Universitätsplatz 2, 39106 Magdeburg, Germany
maria.freese@ovgu.de

[2] Turner Consult Unternehmensberatung, Krackhardtstr. 4, 96047 Bamberg, Germany
hcg@turnerconsult.de

[3] Business Coaching | Wirtschaftsmediation Petra Hövelborn, Martin-Schmeißer-Weg 10, 44227 Dortmund, Germany
info@petra-hoevelborn.de

[4] FHV University of Applied Sciences Vorarlberg, Hochschulstrasse 1, 6850 Dornbirn, Austria
willy.kriz@fhv.at

[5] Freelance Trainer and Process Facilitator, Leinerstraße 21, 78462 Konstanz, Germany
info@nadinemeidert.de

[6] Stuttgart Media University, Nobelstraße 10, 70569 Stuttgart, Germany
wittenzellner@hdm-stuttgart.de

[7] Chemnitz University of Technology, Erfenschlagerstr. 73, 09125 Chemnitz, Germany
susann.zeiner-fink@mb.tu-chemnitz.de

[8] Innovation Lab Consultant and Facilitator, Düsseldorf, Germany
info@sara-zumhasch.de

[9] Baden-Wuerttemberg Cooperative State University Stuttgart, Paulinenstr. 50, 70178 Stuttgart, Germany
birgit.zuern@dhbw-stuttgart.de

Abstract. Both LEGO® SERIOUS PLAY® and simulation games have gained attraction as innovative methods for use in education and beyond. Where LEGO® SERIOUS PLAY® makes use of haptic LEGO® bricks, simulation games come in many different forms. Although the two methods exist separately, the question has arisen as to what extent the two methods can create synergies in the different phases of a simulation game: briefing, game play and debriefing. To be able to answer this question, a four-hour workshop with fifteen simulation gaming experts from Germany, Switzerland and Austria was held. Based on the three phases of a simulation game, LEGO® SERIOUS PLAY®-visions were developed within smaller groups to show how synergies between LEGO® SERIOUS PLAY® and simulation games could look like. In three discussion rounds, best practices were discussed and critical reflections derived.

Keywords: Briefing · Debriefing · Education · LEGO® SERIOUS PLAY® · Game Play · Simulation Games

F. Trautwein et al. (Eds.): ISAGA 2025, LNCS 16439, pp. 49–62, 2026.
https://doi.org/10.1007/978-3-032-20129-4_4

1   Introduction

LEGO® SERIOUS PLAY® (LSP[1]) and simulation games have both gained popularity as innovative methods for use in education and beyond. LSP was developed to enhance team performance through encouraging reflection, communication and problem-solving. It is based on the Serious Play theory [1]. Simulation games have also been present in education and research for a long time, with a wide range of applications across diverse disciplines [2]. While LSP uses haptic LEGO® bricks, simulation games come in many different forms. There are many parallels between the playful elements of LSP and those of simulation games. These include aspects, such as narrative and storytelling, visualization and imagination (e.g., [3–5]). This has led to studies on the use of LSP during the game play (e.g., [6]), or in which LSP itself is considered as a form of simulation or serious game (e.g., [7]). However, to the best of the authors' knowledge, LSP and simulation games have tended to coexist and be used separately, at least without being used consciously in the different phases of a simulation game. This raises the question to what extent the two methods can create synergies across the different phases of a simulation game.

The paper is structured as follows: The second section provides an overview of the theoretical background relating to the functioning of LSP and the different phases of simulation games. As part of the presentation of the theoretical background, a literature review was carried out to find out whether the two methods have been combined before. The third section describes a workshop that was held with simulation game experts to discuss and test possible applications of LSP in the different phases of simulation games. Fourthly, the results of the workshop will be presented and discussed (5th section) in relation to the use of LSP in the different phases of a simulation game. Finally, best practices and critical reflections will be derived.

2   Theoretical Background

The following sub-sections provide an overview of LSP and the different phases of a simulation game.

2.1   Lego® Serious Play®

LSP can be understood as a strategy and planning method and was invented out of dissatisfaction with previous strategy development processes. Kristiansen et al. [8] designed LSP as an alternative strategy and planning method by combining theories of learning and developmental psychology with management approaches. The aim was to use LEGO® bricks to reveal unconscious knowledge and experience potential, to communicate and constructively reflect [9].

LSP is based on an iterative learning process consisting of *construction, attribution of meaning, presentation* and *reflection.* By building LEGO® models and using them as a metaphor, implicit experiences can be transformed into explicit, tangible insights

---

[1] For ease of reading, LEGO® SERIOUS PLAY® is abbreviated to LSP.

[10]. During the *construction* process, participants go through a process of reflection and are inspired to 'think with their hands' [11]. The *attribution of meaning* and the *presentation* of the models enable them to reflect on their own construction, to address specific problems and to share ideas. During the *reflection*, feedback and questions are only asked in relation to the model [11].

The LSP method is fundamentally based on the constructivism theory of [12] and [13], who assume that the complex interaction of the finger-hand combination stimulates 'object thinking' in the brain, which releases creative energy during play. The 3D constructions that are built lead to questions and models that are not only visualized but also made tangible, reactivating forgotten thoughts and perceptions [8].

By using LSP, various topics such as strategic developments, the development of specific solutions or conflict resolution can be addressed and a shared understanding can be developed [8, 14]. Through the joint construction, team processes, interactions and improvisational skills of the users are strengthened. The central aim of the method is to combine the advantages of playing and modeling with real-life problems [10].

2.2 Simulation Gaming

According to [15], simulation games offer participants the opportunity to engage in a complex and dynamic environment where strategic tasks have to be dealt with and where conflicting or challenging situations arise. The structure of a simulation gaming session can often be divided into three distinct phases: the briefing, the game play, and the debriefing [4, 16]. These phases can partially overlap, for instance parts of the briefing can be included in the game phase. It is also possible to initiate the debriefing during the game itself [16]. The central key objectives of each phase are:

- The aim of the *briefing* is to open the scenario of the simulation game, explain the rules and give an overview of the setting. If part of the session and/or simulation game, roles are assigned and information is provided in the form of a presentation or manual (e.g., [17]).
- The main objective of the *game play* is to let participants experience the actual simulation game. It refers to the actual play period, during which participants assume roles and act within the established rules of the game taking into account limited resources (e.g., [18]).
- The aim of the *debriefing* is to establish a connection between the in-game experiences and the real world of the participants. This involves reflecting on emotions, events, and experiences in order to apply what has been learnt in a realistic context (e.g., [19–21]).

2.3 Literature Review: LEGO® SERIOUS PLAY® and Simulation Gaming

Different scholars describe the effective use of simulation games in different application contexts (e.g., [22, 23]), emphasized by interaction and innovation. The advantages of LSP over traditional methods have also been highlighted by various authors (e.g., [8, 24]). In order to understand whether both methods have been used together, we conducted a literature review. We used Scopus because it is one of the largest databases for scientific publications worldwide [25]. Relevant publications were identified by using the search strings shown in Table 1. This search resulted in a total of 37 publications. After removing duplicates, proceedings and publications without access to the full paper, 31 papers were selected for full-text screening.

Table 1. Overview of search strings.

Number	Search string	Search result
1	"LEGO® SERIOUS PLAY®" AND "Gam*"	36 publications
2	"LEGO® SERIOUS PLAY®" AND "Brief*"	0 publications
3	"LEGO® SERIOUS PLAY®" AND "Debrief*"	1 publication

The analysis of the publications showed that LSP is used primarily in higher education (see Fig. 1). For instance, [6] developed a simulation game that also makes use of LSP. The goal of the game is to develop and enhance the participants' technical project management knowledge and their soft skills.

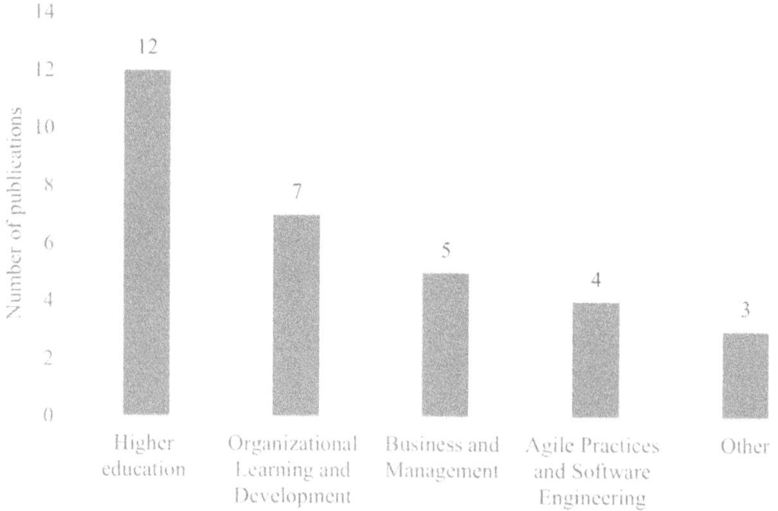

Fig. 1. Overview of LSP areas of application. The category "Other" includes topics around communication optimization, innovation and digitalization.

This is also confirmed by the analysis of the target groups. 58% of the publications target students when using LSP (see Fig. 2). For instance, the work of [26] included research on a serious game based on LSP with software engineering students.

The publications show that LSP itself is often understood as a simulation game, but, to the best of our knowledge, none of the publications have addressed the extent to which simulation games and LSP can create synergies in the different phases of a simulation

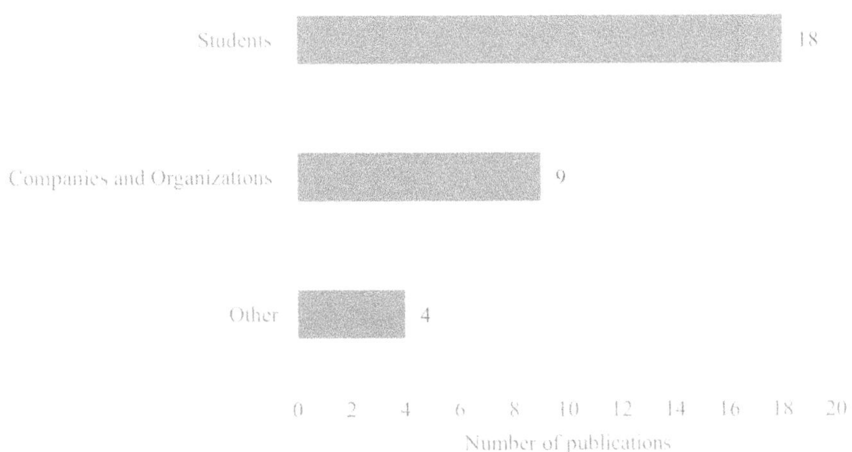

Fig. 2. Overview of LSP target groups. The category "Other" includes educators, administration, and industry.

game. This led to the following research question: *To what extent is LSP a suitable complement within the briefing, game play, and debriefing of simulation games?*

3   Method

In order to answer this question, we conducted an expert workshop as a qualitative approach to explore and evaluate potential applications of LSP in the different phases of simulation games.

3.1   Attendees

Fifteen simulation gaming experts from Germany, Switzerland and Austria took part in a four-hour workshop. Their experience with LSP varied from beginner to expert. All authors of this publication were also participants in the workshop.

3.2   Procedure

According to [10], the traditional LSP workshop consists of two phases: 'skill building' and 'playing' using one or more of the seven 'application techniques'. However, how these phases are designed and which specific steps need to be taken is insufficiently described in the literature [10, 11, 27]. Figure 3 shows one possible approach to describing these phases. During 'skill building' (first phase), participants are introduced to the LSP method (step 1.1). They familiarize themselves with the LEGO® bricks by taking on an initial construction challenge (step 1.2) and try out storytelling (step 1.3). In the second phase ('playing'), participants first briefly summarize what they have learned so far and create their individual models based on a given question (step 2.1). In the next step (2.2), these models are further developed into a joint model. Subsequently, each participant in the workshop develops another individual model, that is linked to the subject (step 2.3). Finally, the participants combine their own model with the shared model and explain their built construction in the form of a story (step 2.4). Finally, solutions and alternative courses of action discussed on the basis of the built 3D constructions are summarized in 'simple guiding principles' and prepared for all participants [10, 11, 28].

The implementation of the method depends on the type and scope of the objective and can be conducted within a defined framework of between two hours and two days. In this case, four to a maximum of twelve people can take part in an event. The method and the materials are publicly accessible, but must be presented in the context of a LSP workshop by a trained facilitator [11].

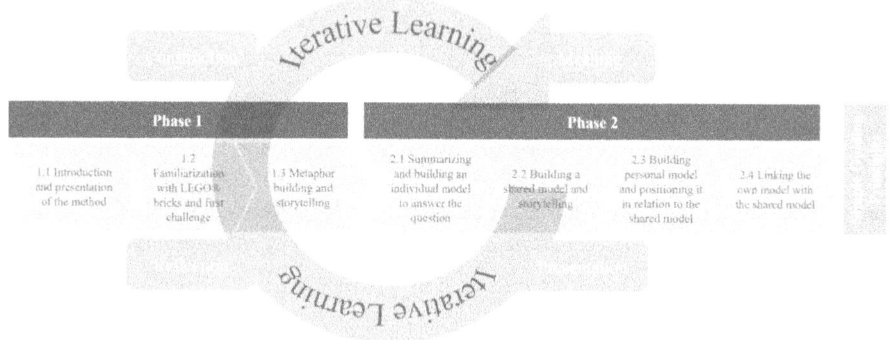

Fig. 3. Traditional LEGO® SERIOUS PLAY® process (own figure based on [11] and [27]).

The workshop described in this paper and conducted for the data collection consisted of the following steps in detail:

- In the first step, we worked with a random assortment of LEGO® bricks in black boxes, independent of LSP. Each participant had ten minutes to build a model and introduce themselves by showing it.
- In three iterations, four groups discussed the extent to which LSP could be integrated in the three different phases of simulation games. This was worked out directly on the basis of LSP models. After each phase, the models were presented to the other groups and discussed, what the main outcomes for the respective phases are.
- At the end of the workshop, the black boxes with limited and given bricks were used again (different from the ones at the beginning). Here the participants had the task of reflecting on what they had learned by building a LSP model.

3.3 Materials

Different sets can be chosen depending on the aim and setting of the workshop. In this workshop the following sets have been provided to allow a choice from a pool of LEGO®

bricks: LSP *Identity and Landscape Set*, the *Starter Set*, *Window Exploration Bags* and *Building Plates*. In addition, moderation cards, pin boards and corresponding markers were also used. The results for the individual phases are presented in the following sections. An impression of a workshop situation can be seen in Fig. 4.

Fig. 4. Workshop impression.

4   Results

The results explained below are based on the discussion between the workshop participants after they had built the models in groups for each phase. An overview of all identified content is shown in Fig. 5.

Fig. 5. Results of the discussion rounds. Graphic displays the English translation of the photographic documentation of the pinboard.

4.1   Use of LEGO® SERIOUS PLAY® in the Briefing Phase

The use of LEGO® in the briefing process of a simulation game requires a stringent and focused facilitation that clearly presents LSP as a methodological part of the briefing and distinguishes it from the simulation game.

4.1.1   Best Practices

LSP enables the visual representation of complex issues and supports thinking in a creative way and can therefore be used at various points in the briefing of simulation games:

- Expectations: Participants' expectations regarding the session and the simulation can be expressed through the building of LSP models.
- Description of objectives: A LSP model developed in the briefing can function as a visualization of the target state to be achieved in the simulation game. These models could therefore also be used by the groups as a haptic reminder of the pre-defined objective during the game.
- Roles: If the simulation game is role-based, participants can create LSP models of their roles or personas individually or as a group. By doing so, the person is playing a predetermined role. This role does not have to and often will not correspond to the person's own typical character traits. Such an approach can be used to reflect on the characteristics of the role and improve the participants' identification with their role.
- Team building: A LSP model developed jointly by the participants can promote communication within the team and thus serve as a good basis for cooperation or collaboration in the actual simulation game.
- Reduction of complexity: The facilitator can build a LSP model of, i.e., the content, rules or goals of the simulation game in advance and use it for visualization in the briefing. In a rather complex simulation game setting, this can serve to reduce complexity and increase the comprehensibility of rules and procedures. This could make the briefing process more efficient.

4.1.2   Reflection Points

The use of LSP as a method itself should be guided and time should be created for individual construction and presentation of the models as well as the categorization of the results in the overall context. Haptic methods in simulation games generally have a positive appeal for the acceptance of the game and support the positive emotionality in connection with the game. However, haptic methods generally require more time for their use, so when using LSP in the briefing of simulation games, care must be taken to ensure that the time planned and ultimately used for the briefing is in a healthy relationship to the simulation game itself. Although we are in the briefing phase of a simulation game, the use of LSP itself requires a briefing, a game phase (= building phase), and a debriefing. This is where the participants explain the models they have built and the facilitator puts the method into the overall context of the briefing of the simulation game. The resulting use of additional time resources represents one of the most important challenges when using LSP in the briefing phase of simulation games. Accordingly, an important prerequisite for the use of this method is the availability of sufficient time and strict time management during implementation. In reality, however, time resources are often limited, which can make it difficult to use LSP as an additional method in the briefing of simulation games.

4.2   Use of LEGO® SERIOUS PLAY® During Game Play

To address the question of how LSP can be effectively used in the game play of simulation games, it seems essential to differentiate between the various formats and purposes of simulation games (e.g., [29]). It is not the aim of this paper to provide a complete overview of all formats of simulation games, rather the following categories seemed useful with regard to the research question:

– Analogue simulation games: These games frequently include tangible physical objects such as game boards, cards, or tokens that represent real-world systems or environments. In some games, LEGO® bricks are used to symbolize resources or processes (e.g., HEX Game [30]).
– Digital simulation games: In this type of simulation, computer systems mimic real-world or fictional scenarios. Participants interact with a digital environment.
– Hybrid simulation games: These formats combine elements of computer-based and board-based simulation games, combining computer simulation with tangible components.

4.2.1   Best Practices

Participants can use LSP to visualize and physically engage with abstract concepts or processes, thereby fostering deeper cognitive and emotional involvement. For instance, in a management simulation game, participants might use LSP bricks to build a physical representation of a company's production process. By building models of workflows, supply chains, or operational structures, participants can better understand the complex systems. Another example could be the use of LSP in a political simulation game, where understanding the perspectives and motivations of different actors is critical. LEGO® bricks can be used as a tool to visualize the 'inner landscapes' of characters. Participants might build models to represent their emotions, priorities, or decision-making processes of their roles.

In addition to these examples of integrating LSP into existing simulation games, we discussed how LSP itself can be used to develop a simulation game (e.g., [31]) or how a (new) simulation game using LSP could be designed. From the simulation games experts' opinion, it might be possible to conceptualize a game concept with LSP for real-world problems, future-oriented scenarios or displaying outlook perspectives on a given topic.

4.2.2   Reflection Points

An exclusion criterion for the use of LSP in the game play is the possible proximity to the materials used in the simulation game itself. If the materials and the task of building models (e.g., 'FutureCity' simulation game by Metalog®) are too similar, we believe there is a risk that the participants will not recognize a clear distinction between the material for the supplement briefing (= LSP) and the material for the simulation game (= e.g., wooden blocks in 'FutureCity'). This could lead to frustration and confusion among the participants and jeopardize the objective of the simulation game. However, when making use of digital simulation games or simulation games with a manageable use of materials, such as card games, the use of LSP for the game play can be of added value. Since the haptic bricks add another perspective to the entire game process, this can positively support the experience of a purely digital simulation game and the insights to be gained. In addition, the important aspect of facilitation comes into play, without which, in our opinion, LSP cannot be used sensibly in the context of simulation games.

4.3 Use of LEGO® SERIOUS PLAY® in the Debriefing

While LEGO® SERIOUS PLAY® provides clear guidelines for facilitation with defined time limits for its phases, a more general debriefing using haptic elements like LEGO® can be flexibly adapted to different contexts, topics, target groups and time frames. This allows for a wide range of applications in combination with simulation games.

4.3.1 Best Practices

Debriefing often begins by capturing the emotions that have arisen during the game play and that need to be processed (emotional processing). For this purpose, it would be conceivable to build LEGO® models that visualize these emotions. By examining the models created by others, learners develop an interest in understanding the reasoning behind them. Furthermore, the act of sharing explanations allows for deeper internalization. Listening to others and observing their reactions can facilitate learning by providing a wider perspective. Four key reflections were related to:

- Visualizing Change: For example, if a change process was involved in the simulation game, this could be visualized with an illustration focusing on the situation before and after the process.
- Perspective-Taking: A change in perspective can also be visualized with LSP. In a simulation game, different stakeholders or roles may be represented, and their perspectives can be built as individual models. The team can then create a large joint model from these individual models to visualize and further reflect the whole system.
- Organizing Learnings: The lessons learnt are often collected on cards in the debriefing of simulation games. LEGO® can be used as an alternative method at the individual or team level to actively engage with what has been learned. On a LEGO® board, for example, categories (different areas, such as soft skills, hard skills, transfer to reality) can also be arranged. Such a playful approach motivates active involvement and participation.
- Transfer to the real world: LSP elements could be helpful as embodiments of mental models. For example, a LSP model can be taken from the debriefing to the workplace to remind oneself later of what has been learned, or LEGO® bricks can be sent in advance of the debriefing session with a preparation task (e.g., about expectations or the role of the player). This could be particularly useful for virtual simulation games to have something 'tangible' and as an online icebreaker (everyone shows their sculpture in front of the camera). The aim here is to support immersion into the magic circle [18].

4.3.2 Reflection Points

Working out the learnings is an important part of the debriefing. LSP can contribute to an immersive and impressive experience. It allows unconventional thinking or thinking outside the box. The planning and use of LSP costs additional time, which is often an already limiting factor in simulation games. Facilitators are required to design an appropriate didactic approach according to the circumstances. This means limiting the number of methods used in the debriefing phase. They should know how to use both divergent and convergent methods, how to strike a balance between brainstorming and internalized learning, and how to facilitate the different stages of the process for orientation and elaboration.

In addition, participants may be overwhelmed at the end of a challenging session, especially one with haptic elements, by the variety of stimuli in a debriefing session using even more different haptic elements. This could lead to a loss of 'thread' and a perception of 'chaos', which could hinder participants' ability to retain learning in a structured way.

As the debriefing is often a group experience, it is very important to handle the individual results of the game play and the debriefing responsibly, as otherwise there is a risk of 'negative group learning' in the sense of model learning according to [32].

5 Discussion

The present publication has addressed the question of whether and, if so, how LSP meaningfully complements the briefing, game play, and debriefing phase of simulation games. To answer the question, a workshop was held with 15 experts from the German-speaking simulation and gaming community, in which answers to this question were discussed by actively using LSP.

The use of LSP as a method in the briefing phase of a simulation game depends on the objectives of both the briefing and the simulation game, while also requiring that the process and objectives are clearly defined and understood by the participants. It is therefore recommended 1) to describe the aim and role of LSP, 2) to tailor the task of building a LSP model precisely to the knowledge to be gained, 3) to allow sufficient time for construction, and 4) to establish a connection between the models and the simulation game when presenting the results.

The integration of LSP in the game play provides a range of options for addressing different learning objectives [33, 34] and it is also a useful tool to develop simulation games. However, combining LSP with existing simulation games is difficult without losing the game flow or learning objective of the game. Using LSP during the game play was considered challenging in board-based and hybrid formats, as these formats already have a tactile component. LSP can become a distracting element, as it can divert attention away from the core objectives of the simulation game. On the other hand, tangible elements, physical interaction and embodiment of learning are conducive to learning processes and emotionality. LSP offers particular added value for simulation games that are otherwise only available in digital, online, or text-based formats.

The use of LSP in the debriefing phase of simulation games should be carefully planned and facilitated. It is helpful to depict emotions, visualize desired outcomes, and illustrate necessary or desired changes to make them more manageable and imaginable. Tactile and visual elements in debriefing can reveal even subtle learning outcomes and latent competencies in simulation games.

6   Conclusions and Future Directions

It is undisputed that many people like LEGO® bricks and associate them with childhood and playing around freely. Therefore, all sorts of attitudes and emotions come from the minds into the hands and then into the mouth and are being made explicit. This openness creates space for discussions.

The most important prerequisite and at the same time the greatest challenge is the meaningful and targeted integration of the LSP methodology into the overall context of the simulation game and the three phases of briefing, game play, and debriefing. This requires a clear and unambiguous description of the objectives of the application of LSP, and great importance is attached to the facilitation, as the use of the methodology must always be focused on the actual objective of the simulation game.

The workshop results show recurring themes regardless of the respective phase. The time available to use LSP in addition to a simulation game and the materials to be used seem to be important. Regarding the latter, it is important to consider the form of the simulation game. For example, the use of LSP can be rather distracting in complex analogue games, but in digital games it can add an analogue component. In doing so, it is important to think about the time component and the use of materials in advance. Otherwise, participants could be irritated by a duplication of playful approaches and haptic methods.

In the workshop, initial ideas for integrating LSP into simulation games were discussed. Future research should aim to implement these ideas and thus actually integrate LSP into the different phases of simulation games. This would allow empirical research into the extent to which LSP has an influence on learning outcomes by testing different groups with and without LSP in the different phases of a game.

As described at the beginning, LSP is currently used primarily in the context of higher education, but we would like to take this opportunity to highlight that LSP itself, and also in combination with simulation games, has great potential in other areas of application, too. A relevant example could be facilitating change in organizations as it helps to think about and understand complex situations.

Acknowledgments. We are grateful to all workshop attendees for their insightful discussions and useful feedback.

Disclosure of Interests. The authors have no competing interests to declare that are relevant to the content of this article.

References

1. Roos, J., Victor, B.: How it all began: the origins of LEGO serious play. Int. J. Manage. Appl. Res. **5**(4), 326–343 (2018)
2. Chernikova, O., Heitzmann, N., Stadler, M., Holzberger, D., Seidel, T., Fischer, F.: Simulation-based learning in higher education: a meta-analysis. Rev. Educ. Res. **90**(4), 499–541 (2020). https://doi.org/10.3102/0034654320933544
3. Dann, S.: Facilitating co-creation experience in the classroom with Lego Serious Play. Austral. Market. J. **26**(2), 121–131 (2018) https://doi.org/10.1016/j.ausmj.2018.05.013

4. Kriz, W.C.: A systems-oriented constructivism approach to the facilitation and debriefing of simulations and games. Simul. Gaming **41**(5), 663–680 (2010)
5. Naul, E., Liu, M.: Why story matters: a review of narrative in serious games. J. Educ. Comput. Res. **58**(3), 687–707 (2020). https://doi.org/10.1177/0735633119859904
6. Geithner, S., Menzel, D.: Effectiveness of learning through experience and reflection in a project management simulation. Simul. Gaming **47**(2), 228–256 (2016)
7. Martin-Cruz, N., Martin-Gutierrez, A., Rojo-Revenga, M.: A LEGO® Serious Play activity to help teamwork skills development amongst business students. Int. J. Res. Meth. Educ. **45**(5), 479–494 (2021). https://doi.org/10.1080/1743727X.2021.1990881
8. Kristiansen, P., Hansen, P.K., Nielsen, L.M.: Articulation of tacit and complex knowledge. In: Schönsleben, P., Vodicka, M., Smeds, R., Riis, J.O. (eds.) Learning and Innovation in Value Added Networks. Proceedings of the 13th IFIP 5.7 Special Interest Group Workshop on Experimental Interactive Learning in Industrial Management, pp. 77–86. ETH Zürich, BWI (2009)
9. LEGO Group: The origins of the Lego® Serious Play® methodology. (2018). https://www.lego.com/en-us/themes/serious-play/about . (24-01-2025)
10. Kristiansen, P., Rasmussen, R.: Building a better business using the lego serious play method. Wiley, New Jersey (2014)
11. LEGO Group: LSP: Open-Source: Basic Principles and Philosophy. (2010). http://davidgauntlett.com/wp-content/uploads/2013/04/LEGO_SERIOUS_PLAY_OpenSource_14mb.pdf (18-01-2025)
12. Piaget, J.: Principal factors determining intellectual evolution from childhood to adult life. In: Rapaport, D. (ed.) Organization and Pathology of Thought: Select-ed Sources, pp. 154–175. Columbia University Press, New York (1951) https://doi.org/10.1037/10584-006
13. Papert, S.: The connected family: bridging the digital generation gap. Long Street Press, Atlanta, GA (1996)
14. Grabmeier, S., Grassler M.: Spiel, Spass und Innovation? Personalmagazin, 09. spezial Start-ups (2017)
15. Schwägele, S.: Planspiel – Lernen – Lerntransfer: Eine subjektorientierte Analyse von Einflussfaktoren. Dissertation, Otto-Friedrich-Universität Bamberg (2015)
16. Schwägele, S., Zürn, B., Lukosch, H.K., Freese, M.: Design of an impulse-debriefing-spiral for simulation game facilitation. Simul. Gaming **52**(3), 364–365 (2021). https://doi.org/10.1177/10468781211006752
17. Vlachopoulos, D., Makri, A.: The effect of games and simulations on higher education: a systematic literature review. Int. J. Educ. Technol. High. Educ. **14**(1), 22 (2017). https://doi.org/10.1186/s41239-017-0062-1
18. Klabbers, J.H.G.: The magic circle: principles of gaming & simulation. Sense Publishers, Rotterdam, The Nethernalds (2006)
19. Crookall, D.: Serious games, debriefing, and simulation/gaming as a discipline. Simul. Gaming **41**(6), 898–920 (2010). https://doi.org/10.1177/1046878110390784
20. Kriz, W.C., Sugiura, J., Kikkawa, T.: Gaming simulation: terminology and fundamentals. In: Kikkawa, T., Kriz, W.C., Sugiura, J. (eds.) Gaming as a Cultural Commons: Risks, Challenges, and Opportunities, pp. 3–23. Springer (2022)
21. Roungas, B., Meijer, S., Verbraeck, A.: The tacit knowledge in games: from validation to debriefing. In: Wardaszko, M., Meijer, S., Lukosch, H., Kanegae, H., Kriz, W.C., Grzybowska-Brzezińska, M. (eds.) Simulation Gaming Through Times and Disciplines. ISAGA 2019. Lecture Notes in Computer Science, vol. 11988. Springer, Cham (2021) https://doi.org/10.1007/978-3-030-72132-9_7
22. Kriz, W.C.: Creating effective interactive learning environments through gaming simulation design. Simul. Gaming **34**(4), 495–511 (2003)

23. Klabbers, J.H.: The gaming landscape: a taxonomy for classifying games and simulations. In: Proceedings of "LEVEL UP: Digital Games Research Conference", pp. 54–68, University of Utrecht, The Netherlands (2003)
24. James, A., Nerantzi, C.: Guest editors: a potpourri of innovative applications Of LEGO® in learning, teaching and development. Int. J. Manage. Appl. Res. 5(4), 153–156 (2018) https://doi.org/10.18646/2056.54.18-011
25. Schotten M., el Aisati M., Meester W.J.N., Steiginga S., Ross C.A.: A brief history of scopus: the world's largest abstract and citation database of scientific literature. In: Schotten, M., el Aisati, M., Meester, W.J.N., Steiginga, S., Ross, C.A. (eds.) Research Analytics, 1st edn. Auerbach Publications (2017). https://doi.org/10.1201/9781315155890-3
26. Gordillo, A., López-Fernández, D., Mayor, J.: Examining and comparing the effectiveness of virtual reality serious games and LEGO serious play for learning scrum. Appl. Sci. 14(2), 830 (2024). https://doi.org/10.3390/app14020830
27. Gauntlett, D.: Creative explorations. New approaches to identities and audiences. Routledge, London. New York (2007)
28. Rasmussen, R.: When you build in the world, you build in your mind. Des. Manage. Rev. 17, 56–63 (2006)
29. Freese, M., Bekebrede, G.: Digital versus analogue simulation games: influence on validity, play(er) experience and learning outcomes. In: Marfisi-Schottman, I., Bellotti, F., Hamon, L., Klemke, R. (eds.) Games and Learning Alliance. GALA 2020. LNCS, vol. 12517. Springer, Cham (2020) https://doi.org/10.1007/978-3-030-63464-3_44
30. Duke, R.D., Geurts, J.L.A.: Policy games for strategic management. Dutch University Press (2004)
31. Karl, C.K.: Designing educational games for project management using the MyPMgame Canvas©. Develop. Bus. Simul. Experien. Learn. 43, 192–206 (2016)
32. Bandura, A.: Social learning theory. General Learning Press, New York (1971)
33. Bedwell, W.L., Pavlas, D., Heyne, K., Lazzara, E.H., Salas, E.: Toward a taxonomy linking game attributes to learning: an empirical study. Simul. Gaming 43, 729–760 (2012)
34. Bloom, B.: Taxonomy of educational objectives. Book I: Cognitive Domain. David Mckay, New Yorks (1956)

Modelling In-Game Events in Game Scenarios: A Comprehensive Framework

Marcin Wardaszko[1]($\boxtimes$) (iD) and Willy Christian Kriz[2] (iD)

[1] Kozminski University, Warsaw, Poland
`wardaszko@kozminski.edu.pl`
[2] Vorarlberg University of Applied Sciences, Dornbirn, Austria
`willy.kriz@fhv.at`

Abstract. This paper presents a comprehensive framework for modeling in-game events in serious games, integrating game design, simulation, and educational theories. Serious games serve as tools for learning and problem-solving by simulating real-world scenarios, requiring structured in-game events to enhance engagement and decision-making. The study explores the classification and role of in-game events, distinguishing between player-triggered and system-generated events and their impact on gameplay dynamics. The paper delves into various event modeling techniques, such as Finite State Machines, Event Sourcing, and Behavior Trees, influencing player interactions, narrative structures, and adaptive game mechanics. Additionally, it examines the balance between randomness and player control, emphasizing how unpredictability can foster engagement while maintaining a sense of agency. Insights from game theory and psychology highlight how random elements can shape player experiences, impacting motivation and learning outcomes. The study addresses the challenge of balancing complexity and engagement in game design. The interplay between randomness and structured events is crucial for maintaining immersion while preventing frustration. The paper also discusses iterative design methodologies for optimizing serious games, ensuring meaningful and effective player experiences.

Keywords: game design · in-game events · game systems modeling · player motivation · theory-crafting

1 Introduction

Modeling in-game events in serious games is a game design feature combining game design, simulation, and educational theory elements. Serious games, designed for a purpose beyond mere entertainment, often simulate real-world processes to address complex societal challenges [1]. The design of these games requires careful consideration of the rules and mechanics that govern player interactions, which serve as constraints that shape the gaming experience [2]. In the context of serious games, modeling in-game events is crucial for creating engaging and educational experiences. The integration of simulations allows for exploring various scenarios and outcomes, which can enhance learning and

© The Author(s) 2026
F. Trautwein et al. (Eds.): ISAGA 2025, LNCS 16439, pp. 63–78, 2026.
https://doi.org/10.1007/978-3-032-20129-4_5

decision-making processes [3]. For instance, serious games can be employed in environmental management, facilitating stakeholder collaboration and social learning [1]. Simulating real-world events enables players to engage with complex systems, fostering a deeper understanding of the subject matter [4]. Event-based modeling techniques can optimize player engagement and enhance the overall gaming experience by stimulating player behavior and simulating meaningful in-game events; designers can create dynamic environments that respond to player actions and decisions [5].

Game-theoretic principles in simulation models can also provide insights into player interactions and decision-making processes, further enriching the gaming experience [6]. This paper addresses the use of in-game events as a mechanism in simulation games, which we would also like to examine from both video and serious game theories, analyzing definition, classification, and the role of in-game events in serious game design. Incorporating in-game events is vital from the perspective of modeling real-world systems and creating meaningful experiences [7]. Furthermore, we aim to analyze the feeling of randomness, unpredictability in games, and control of the players from the research perspective, as the in-game events can potentially significantly impact those factors in simulation game implementation and experimental or educational roles.

2 Theoretical Background

Games are played for various reasons: to pass time, to escape reality, for entertainment, or for educational purposes. Generally, games are engaging because they offer immersive experiences. Gameplay experience, as defined by Ermi and Mäyrä [8], involves the player's emotions, thoughts, actions, and interpretations. Boyle et al. [9] conducted a comprehensive review highlighting the increasing interest in engagement within digital entertainment games. Serious games are imitations of real-world systems designed to solve a problem or to educate, train, and influence decision-making processes [7]. However, research on engagement in serious games is still developing. Some argue that serious games lack motivation [10], but Whitton [11] suggests their value lies in offering meaningful challenges and interactions rather than simply being motivational.

Games are almost unavoidably cyclical. Cycles, in which players make decisions more or less sequentially, permit the game to ask iterative questions that must be resolved in the total context of the game [12]. One way to introduce issues and problems of iterative decisions to the player's decision cycles is by infusing them with events. The events can be pre-programmed or triggered by circumstances that develop or random events that focus the players' attention on some new problem or aspect of the situation [12]. The balance between the iterative cyclicality of the game and in-game events introducing new issues, challenges, or modifying existing cycles was first described by Duke [12, p. 126] with the term "pulses". Pulses are the key to systematically presenting aspects of the total problem represented in the game and may be either issue-oriented or systemic. If systemic, they are self-generated as the players progress through some scheduled sequence of events, leading them deeper into understanding the problem. Issues introduced by in-game events are set off automatically, by predefined conditions or by the facilitator, and used to trigger an exchange of messages between players. Through an intensive communication process, the game and its initial conditions transform into tangible artifacts that embody a conceptual model. This model remains open, allowing players to modify it during gameplay through a deeper understanding of the concept. Introducing new events (topics for discussion) stimulates dialogue between players and leads to adjustments in the original model. This form of multi-actor communication was described by Duke [12] with the term "multilogue" (p. 34). As players progress through the game's cycles, they generate and explore new realities. A reviewing critique after each cycle and a final debriefing help connect the game's models to the participants' real-world perceptions [13]. This process is essential to create the multilogue (Fig. 1).

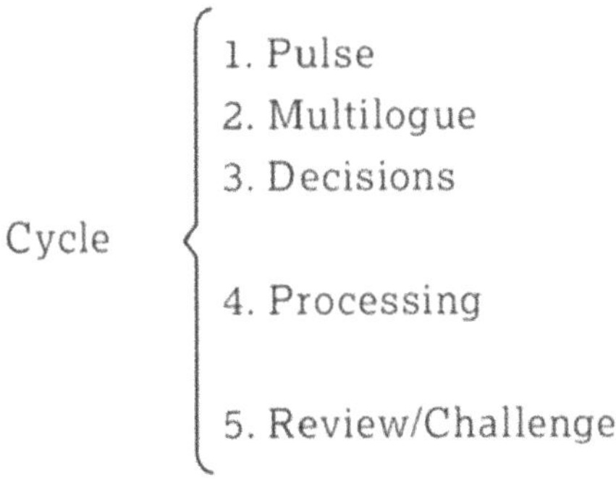

Fig. 1. Game cycle. [12, p. 67].

Using a well-designed mixture of game elements significantly contributes to engagement in entertainment games, yet this dimension is underexplored in serious games [14]. The right choice of game mechanics is important because positive game experiences can enhance learning outcomes. Efforts have been made to merge instructional and game design principles to improve serious games [15], but understanding players' experiences is equally crucial. Emotional engagement influences cognitive decisions, meaning unengaging games may fail to retain players, while positive experiences encourage deeper involvement. Game mechanics are crucial in engaging players across various games, including board games, video games, and serious games. They are foundational elements shaping player experiences, motivations, and interactions. Understanding how these mechanics influence engagement can provide insights into effective game design and player retention strategies. Implementing tutorials and adaptive mechanics can significantly impact player engagement, especially for new or non-expert players. Tutorials that effectively introduce game mechanics can create a "safe zone" for players, enhancing their flow and continuous-use intentions [16]. Adaptive game mechanics that adjust the difficulty based on player performance can also maintain engagement by ensuring that challenges remain appropriate to the player's skill level [17, 18]. This balance between challenge and skill is crucial for sustaining player motivation over time [19]. One of the adaptive game elements can be in-game events that are tailored to enhance players' experience. In-game events are a pivotal game mechanic that enhances player engagement and interaction within the gaming environment. These events can be defined as triggering specific responses or changes in the game state, often impacting gameplay dynamics and player experience. Integrating in-game events into game mechanics can significantly influence player behavior, decision-making, and overall game enjoyment. One of the primary functions of in-game events is to create a structured environment that encourages player interaction and collaboration. Oksanen and Hämäläinen highlight that effective game mechanics can facilitate social interaction and collaborative activities among players [20] and is further supported by Zagal et al., who discuss how collaborative game mechanisms can enhance player engagement and foster a sense of community [21]. The design of these events must be carefully considered to ensure they align with the game's objectives and enhance the overall experience.

Various methodologies, including finite state machines (FSM), can inform the design and implementation of in-game events. Nursobah et al. describe how FSM can control game agents, allowing for dynamic responses to player actions and environmental changes [22]. This approach enhances the game's realism and allows for more complex interactions between players and the game world. Similarly, the work of Smith et al. on prototyping games emphasizes the importance of triggering events that interact with specified game mechanics, thereby allowing designers to create more engaging and responsive gameplay experiences [23]. In addition to enhancing player interaction, in-game events can also serve educational purposes. For instance, serious games often incorporate surprising events that challenge players and stimulate deeper learning [24]. By introducing unexpected elements, designers can create scenarios that require critical thinking and problem-solving, making the learning experience more impactful. This aligns with the findings of Díaz-Ramírez, who notes that game mechanics can be effectively utilized to enhance learning outcomes in educational contexts [25]. The role of in-game events extends to the broader context of game design, where they can be seen as part of a more extensive system of mechanics that govern player interactions. Nelson and Mateas discuss the concept of recompilable game mechanics, which allows for the automated design of games that can adapt to player behavior and preferences [26]. This adaptability is crucial in maintaining player interest and ensuring the game remains engaging.

3   In-Game Event Definition and Classification

The game design literature presents the most common definition of in-game events. In-game events are structured occurrences within a game that can be triggered by player actions, game progress, or external factors (e.g., time-based events). They are a key component of game mechanics, influencing player behavior, engagement, and the overall gameplay experience [27–29]. The in-game events can also be defined as the game's state, which evolves through events resulting from interactions between game entities and influencing the player's actions and decisions. Some events directly impact the player's choices and behaviors, known as player-triggered defining events (PTE). Other events occur independently of the player's decisions, arising from interactions among game elements – these are non-player-triggered defining events (NPTE). In some instances, players may not directly perceive an NPTE but can experience its effects and consequences. As NPTEs unfold, they create a sequence of game state changes that play a vital role in the player's meaning-making process [30, p. 13543]. Both of those definitions are pretty similar but have distinctive differences in underlying logic. The first definition focuses on actions and player agency, which are the game's core from the game design perspective. The second definition is more oriented toward modeling in-game events with internal and external events as a discriminator of both trigger and effect.

In-game events can be classified into several categories using different criteria. Most classifications are defined with game design or game analysis in mind. The simplest and most common classification was already introduced in the second definition mentioned above, and it is player- and non-player-centered events. In the simulation gaming space, Peters and van de Westelaken provide an outlook on classifying in-game events [31], and they consider the events part of the game scenario. Events in the game scenario are a way to provide new elements and unexpected changes to the course of the game. In this way, game designers or facilitators can regulate the gameplay's dynamics, focus the participants' attention on specific elements, or repel unwanted developments [31, p. 27–28]. They also group all events into three categories:

- Planned events – The timing and content of each event are precisely planned in the game design process. However, for participants, these events appear unexpectedly. Such events strategically guide the simulation game in a predetermined direction or introduce new complexity layers.
- Random events – In this category, the timing of an event is predetermined, but its specific nature is not fixed. Participants randomly receive one from predefined incidents at a designated moment and must follow its instructions. These events introduce an element of chance into the scenario, influencing the game's progression based on which events occur.
- Ad hoc events – This type of event can be introduced at the discretion of the game facilitator, who is aware of the structure and dynamics of the simulation game. Events can be introduced into the game on the spot to change the game's difficulty or group dynamics. However, the events must be tailored to the specific situation, and the game structure must be open to such intervention.

The classification presented by Peters and van de Westelaken is primarily oriented toward haptic games, and the typology is quite simple. However, using this classification in serious digital game design might be challenging as they require a much more detailed design structure. Thus, we propose the following classification based on the provided definitions, literature [27–30], and our own experience in game design. We can divide all in-game events into the following categories:

1. Based on Player Involvement
   a. Player-Triggered Events (PTE)
      (1) Action-Based Events – Triggered by direct player actions (e.g. engaging in conflict, opening a door, selling an item, standing on the moving platform).
      (2) Choice-Based Events – The result of player decisions (e.g., selecting a dialogue option or choosing a quest path).
      (3) Exploration-Based Events – Activated by the player discovery (e.g., entering a hidden area, interacting with an object, entering a new market).
   b. Non-Player-Triggered Events (NPTE)

(1) System-Generated Events – Occur based on game mechanics without player input (e.g., day-night cycles, random NPC spawns, seasonality).
(2) AI-Driven Events – Result from autonomous NPC actions (e.g., AI-controlled factions waging conflict, the evolution of the resource markets, innovations).
(3) Scripted Events – Predefined occurrences set by game designers (e.g., cutscenes, boss fight introductions, new entities appearing on the market and for the player, like banks or trade unions).

2. Based on Gameplay Impact
  c. Core Gameplay Events
    (1) Mechanics-Driven Events – Affect core mechanics (e.g., unlocking a new ability, resource depletion).
    (2) Failure and Success Events – Outcomes of player performance (e.g., game over, mission success, draw).
  d. Narrative Events
    (1) Story Progression Events – Move the plot forward (e.g., character deaths, major reveals, plot twists, or the discovery of a clue).
    (2) World-Building Events – Provide lore and context (e.g., finding ancient texts, overhearing NPC conversations, reading a book or smartphone message).

3. Based on Timing and Structure
  e. Real-Time Events
    (1) Dynamic Events – Unfold organically (e.g., enemy reinforcements arriving, currency exchange courses fluctuation).
    (2) Random Events – Occur unpredictably (e.g., procedural weather changes, sudden ambushes, unexpected changes to law or policies, market crashes).
    (3) Quasi-random Events – occur unpredictably, but probability changes based on game state or player actions (e.g., increased probability of flooding based on the weather conditions, decreased likelihood of player action success based on the player character situation like exhaustion)
  f. Predefined Events
    (1) Scripted Sequences – Triggered at specific moments (e.g., cinematic cutscenes, the appearance of the new in-game faction).
    (2) Progression-Gated Events – Occur when a milestone is reached (e.g., leveling up, unlocking a new area).

4. Based on Multiplayer Interaction
  g. Single-Player Events
    (1) Player-Exclusive Events – Affect only the individual player (e.g., personal quest choices, setting individual goals).
  h. Multiplayer Events
    (1) Shared World Events – Impact multiple players (e.g., MMO world bosses, seasonal events, gatherings, voting).
    (2) Player-Created Events – Result from social interactions (e.g., forming alliances, initiating trades, building alliances).

Interestingly, this list is not finite. As a game designer, types of in-game events can combine two or more event categories into a more sophisticated version of a game event, e.g., a combination of system-generated events and random events, and create an event that arrives at the beginning of the new season in the game, however, the event is chosen randomly from the predefined list of events, and the event's size (impact on the game world) is randomized. This way, more compelling and life-like game systems can be created using predefined event categories or custom in-game events.

4 Event Modeling Techniques

Several techniques can be employed to model events in digital games:

- Finite State Machines (FSM) [32]: A computational model mostly used to design the behavior of game entities based on their current state and events. This form of modeling is based on the game script [33]. A game script is a software framework supporting game functions and rules. In a performative way, it collects player data input (decisions and actions). It presents them with the outcome of their decisions and actions based on the execution of the player data input calculated with scripted game functions and rules. This method is best suited for games with rich interaction environments.
- Event Sourcing [34]: A design pattern that involves storing the state of a system as a sequence of events, allowing for easier debugging and state management. This method is less common as it works mainly for the traditional create, read, update, and delete (CRUD) model. It is perfect for sequence modeling as the systems store and remember all the sequences of action, and not just the current state of the models and events like in FSM. In this way, the system can store past, current, and future state of events with selected sequences and generated outcomes. It can be used for narrative-driven systems and a large number of events can be stored at the same time.
- Behavior Trees [35]: A hierarchical model that enables complex decision-making processes for game entities, particularly useful for NPC behavior. Traditionally, they are scripted behavior patterns based on the provided set of tasks and behavior building blocks. In this way, we can structure the response and switching tasks in an autonomous agent, such as a robot or a virtual entity in a computer game [36, p. 3]. This form of modeling is the most common in agent-based modeling for games. We can explore a player's interaction with a computer-simulated agent or the interaction between computer-simulated agents. Until recently, scripting games with behavior trees was a relatively difficult task, requiring many technical skills. However, with the proliferation of widely available Large Language Models (LLM), this task can be outsourced to an LLM system based on simple system training techniques, like feeding the system with texts describing agent behavior or data sets [37].

Deciding on the type of modeling, density, and types of used-in-game events will significantly impact player engagement and the perceived complexity of the game [38]. This, in return, can impact the player and the ability of the game to create a state of meaningful play [39]. The game can produce unpredicted states or outcomes from the player's perspective, contributing to the feeling of randomness and low locus of control. On the other hand, overcoming challenges with unforeseen circumstances can contribute enormously to the players' feeling of control. In the following steps, we would like to examine both effects and find a common ground.

5 Randomness and Unpredictability

Randomness in games is a design concept that plays an important role in shaping player experiences, strategies, and game dynamics. One of the primary aspects of randomness in games is its influence on player strategies and outcomes. Milchtaich's work on random-player games illustrates how randomness can lead to different equilibrium states, such as pure-strategy, mixed-strategy, and correlated equilibria, which are essential for understanding strategic interactions in games with uncertain player behavior [40]. This randomness is not merely a nuisance; it can enhance the complexity and richness of gameplay, as players must adapt their strategies in response to unpredictable elements [41]. For instance, the introduction of mixed strategies allows players to randomize their actions, making it difficult for opponents to predict their moves, thereby increasing the game's strategic depth [42]. Randomness is integral to the design of games that aim to create engaging and immersive experiences. For example, dynamic difficulty adjustment (DDA) leverages randomness to tailor challenges to player skill levels, thereby maintaining engagement and satisfaction [43]. This approach underscores the importance of uncertainty in enhancing player immersion, as players often report that unpredictability contributes significantly to their enjoyment of games [44]. The balance of randomness is crucial; too much unpredictability can lead to frustration, while too little can result in monotony [45].

In game theory, randomness is also pivotal in modeling player behavior and decision-making processes. For instance, the iterated prisoner's dilemma (IPD) demonstrates how strategies involving randomness, such as extortionate tactics, can outperform more generous approaches under certain conditions [46]. This highlights the strategic value of randomness, as players can exploit it to gain advantages over opponents who may not effectively incorporate randomization into their strategies [47]. Furthermore, the study of games with population uncertainty reveals how randomness can affect equilibrium outcomes, suggesting that understanding these dynamics is vital for theoretical and practical game design applications [48]. Integration of randomness into game mechanics can lead to innovative gameplay experiences. For example, augmented reality games that incorporate non-player interactions introduce elements of unpredictability, creating intense and engaging experiences for players [49]. This unpredictability can be a double-edged sword: At the same time, it enhances excitement, while also requiring careful design to ensure that players remain engaged rather than frustrated by excessive randomness [44], which can foster a feeling of losing control over the outcome of the game. One significant study by Westera discusses how randomness can impact performance assessment in serious games. The research indicates that random guess scores can account for a substantial portion of total scores, with findings suggesting that randomness can explain up to 41% of performance outcomes in certain games [50]. This highlights the need for game designers to consider how randomness affects player performance and learning, as it can lead to variability in outcomes that may not accurately reflect a player's skills or knowledge.

Another concept mentioned in the research can be "productive negativity" in game design, as explored by Gauthier and Jenkinson, which suggests that challenges and failures – often perceived as random events – can facilitate deeper learning and conceptual change. This approach encourages players to engage with the material actively, restructuring their understanding in response to unexpected challenges [51]. Such dynamics can create a sense of randomness that enhances the learning experience by pushing players to adapt and rethink their strategies. The systematic review by Abd-Alrazaq et al. on serious games for cognitive impairment emphasizes the role of randomness in maintaining player engagement. The authors argue that the unpredictability of game elements can enhance motivation and participation, particularly among older adults with cognitive challenges [52]. This suggests that incorporating random elements can be beneficial for sustaining interest and promoting cognitive engagement in serious games. Integration of randomness in serious games can be strategically employed to simulate real-world scenarios where unpredictability is a factor. For instance, in medical training games, the random occurrence of patient scenarios can prepare healthcare professionals for the variability they encounter in clinical settings [54]. This application of randomness enhances realism and fosters critical thinking and adaptability among players. The design and implementation of serious games often grapple with the inherent unpredictability of player interactions and game mechanics. This unpredictability can be an asset, enhancing engagement and learning outcomes, but it also poses significant challenges for developers. Understanding the multifaceted nature of unpredictability in serious games is crucial for creating effective and engaging experiences. One of the primary sources of unpredictability in serious games stems from the dynamic interactions between players and the game environment. Multiplayer games, for instance, are characterized by complex human behaviors that can lead to unpredictable outcomes. This complexity necessitates a more intricate design process than single-player games, as developers must account for multiple players' varied strategies and responses [54]. Additionally, the unpredictability inherent in player interactions can foster a more engaging and immersive experience, as players must adapt to the actions of others, thereby enhancing their problem-solving skills and adaptability [55, 56]. Integrating procedural generation techniques in game design can significantly contribute to unpredictability. Procedural generation allows for creation of unique game scenarios and environments, which can lead to unexpected player experiences. This method increases replayability and encourages exploration and discovery within the game [57]. The unpredictability introduced by procedural elements can challenge players to develop new strategies and adapt their gameplay, ultimately leading to a richer gaming experience [58, 59]. In the context of serious games aimed at educational or training purposes, unpredictability can serve as a critical pedagogical tool. Games designed to simulate real-world scenarios, such as military training or emergency response, must incorporate elements of unpredictability to prepare players for the complexities of actual situations [55, 56]. This unpredictability can enhance cognitive skills such as decision-making and situational awareness, essential in high-stakes environments [56, 60]. Furthermore, incorporating unexpected challenges can stimulate curiosity and engagement, prompting players to invest more effort into their learning [61]. However, the unpredictability in serious games also presents challenges that must be carefully managed. Game designers must balance providing enough unpredictability to keep players engaged while ensuring the game remains accessible and comprehensible [62, 63]. Overly complex or chaotic game mechanics can lead to frustration and disengagement, undermining the educational objectives of the game [64]. Therefore, iterative design processes that allow continuous testing and refinement based on player feedback are essential for navigating these challenges [62, 65].

6 Perception of Control and Autonomy

One way of how serious games can foster a feeling of control is through adaptive difficulty settings. Research indicates that games that allow users to choose their level of challenge or adapt to their performance can enhance enjoyment and engagement, leading to better learning outcomes [66]. This user-guided approach empowers players and aligns with self-determination theory [67], which posits that autonomy supports intrinsic motivation [68]. When players feel they can influence their experience, they are more likely to remain engaged and motivated to progress through the game. The design of serious games often incorporates feedback mechanisms that give players a sense of control over their actions and decisions. For instance, games that track performance and offer real-time feedback can help users understand the consequences of their choices, reinforcing their sense of agency [69]. This is particularly important in rehabilitation contexts, where users must learn to navigate new skills or regain lost abilities. The ability to see progress and receive feedback can enhance motivation and encourage continued engagement with the game [70].

Additionally, serious games' narrative and thematic elements can contribute to a player's sense of control. Games that present challenges within a compelling story or context can motivate players to overcome obstacles, reinforcing their agency as they navigate the game [72]. The emotional engagement fostered by a well-crafted narrative can enhance the overall experience, making players feel more invested in their progress and outcomes.

7 Between Challenge and Control

The use of in-game events as game mechanics is connected to a few key concepts. The introduction of in-game events is understood as a game pulse, which can present key concepts and provoke a multilogue between players [13]. Introducing new or unexpected elements to the game through in-game events can deliver challenges to the players within the game's iterative and cyclical decision process. The same iterative, cyclical decision process provides feedback and contributes to understanding and the perception of control and self-determination, which is the key to the player's agency and locus of control [67]. On the other hand, the combination of the game's complexity [38] and the pace of introduction changes and challenges through in-game events can create uncertainty and a feeling of randomness for the players. This might lead to a decrease in perceived control and autonomy or lead to a situation of too much stress and being overwhelmed by workload (Fig. 2).

The role of the in-game events can be connected to the flow theory [72]. The flow state is connected to the feeling of control, which is provided by feedback structures and tangible and achievable goals. Also, the state of flow needs a challenge to be introduced to the player within the zone of optimal development [75 after 76]. The whole gameplay process and, thus, the flow state is dynamic by nature. A lack of new challenges will result

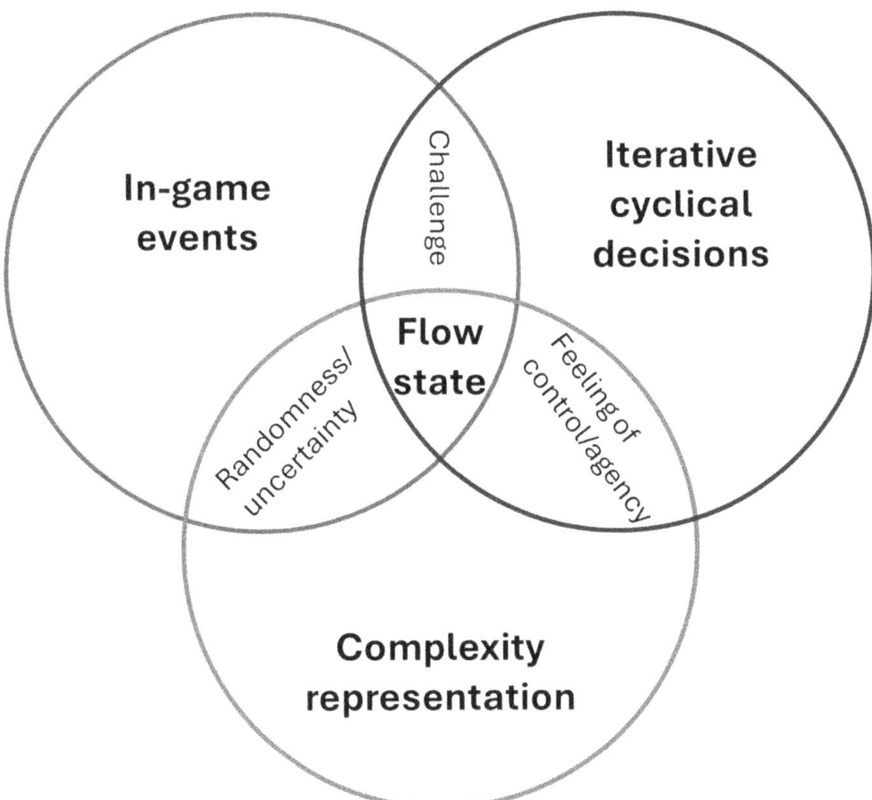

Fig. 2. Dependency between in-game events and players' reception. Own elaboration.

in boredom as the task becomes repetitive and trivial. Too many changes or challenges not within the perceptive skill level of the player can lead to feelings of anxiety. From this perspective, we can say that the right combination of both effects supporting player agency and excitement from uncertainty is crucial for supporting the motivation of the players.

8   Discussion and Conclusions

Modelling events in game scenarios is not trivial and requires a deep understanding of game mechanics, player psychology, and narrative structure. By employing a combination of event classification and modeling techniques, game designers can create immersive and responsive game worlds that enhance player engagement. However, to achieve this state, we have to address several issues.

First, the saturation of events introduced through the gameplay can contribute to player engagement and motivation to play, or it can create the feeling of being overwhelmed. There is no one recipe for the right mixture, but game design frameworks help us guide better game design. Modeling games based on real-world systems requires a design choice of level of abstraction [75] and the process of complexity redux [38]. This will allow us to create a base level of complexity. Choosing the model of in-game events can support the level of complexity selected by the designer, and it should be adjusted to create enough fidelity, abstraction, and resolution of the simulated system [76] to achieve its learning or experimental goals. Of course, this is not an easy task. Thus, it should be supported with an iterative game design process [77] and be evaluated internally and externally [75]. The choice of modeling is secondary in this process, and the chosen method should support the game model and the amount of data available in the game.

Second, the cognitive balance between the feeling of randomness and the perception of control is tricky and entangled. At first glance, those might be mutually exclusive. However, upon closer examination, it appears they can be separated but remain co-dependent, which means they can exist simultaneously in the same space. One example of this phenomenon are the so-called "loot boxes" in video games, virtual boxes containing randomized rewards. Thus, loot boxes introduce randomness to the gaming environment, and their use can diminish the player's sense of agency and control, leading to frustration and potentially addictive behaviors [78]. Of course, serious games rarely introduce gambling-like behavior to the players, but responsible use of randomness and player agency is crucial. Thus, this topic requires more research using new approaches to understanding the interdependence between game design elements and the socio-psychological construct of playing a game.

References

1. Medema, W., Furber, A., Adamowski, J., Mayer, I., Zhou, Q.: Exploring the potential impact of serious games on social learning and stakeholder collaborations for transboundary watershed management of the st. lawrence river basin. Water **8**(5), 175 (2016). https://doi.org/10.3390/w8050175
2. Lameras, P., Arnab, S., Dunwell, I., Stewart, C., Clarke, S., Petridis, P.: Essential features of serious games design in higher education: linking learning attributes to game mechanics. Br. J. Edu. Technol. **48**(4), 972–994 (2016). https://doi.org/10.1111/bjet.12467
3. Stolpe, A., Rummelhoff, I., Hannay, J.: A logic-based event controller for means-end reasoning in simulation environments. SIMULATION **99**(8), 831–858 (2023). https://doi.org/10.1177/00375497231157384
4. Brakovska, V.: Multiplayer game for decision-making in energy communities. Int. J. Sustain. Energy Plan. Manage. (2023). https://doi.org/10.54337/ijsepm.7549
5. Guitart, A., Chen, P., Bertens, P., Periáñez, Á.: Forecasting player behavioral data and simulating in-game events, pp. 274–293 (2018). https://doi.org/10.1007/978-3-030-03402-3_19
6. Poropudas, J., Virtanen, K.: Game-theoretic validation and analysis of air combat simulation models. IEEE Trans. Syst. Man Cybern. - Part a Syst. Hum. **40**(5), 1057–1070 (2010). https://doi.org/10.1109/tsmca.2010.2044997
7. Roungas, B., Bekius, F., Meijer, S.: The game between game theory and gaming simulations: design choices. Simul. Gaming **50**(2), 180–201 (2019). https://doi.org/10.1177/1046878119827625
8. Ermi L., Mäyrä F.: Fundamental components of the gameplay experience: Analysing immersion. In: de Castell, S., Jenson, J. (eds.), Changing views: Worlds in play: Selected Papers

of the 2005 Digital Games Research Association's Second International Conference, pp. 15–27. Digital Interactive Games Research Association, Vancouver, British Columbia, Canada (2005)

9. Boyle, E., Connolly, T., Hainey, T., Boyle, J.: Engagement in digital entertainment games: a systematic review. Comput. Hum. Behav. **28**, 771–780 (2012)

10. Van Eck, R.: Digital game based LEARNING it's not just the digital natives who are restless. EDUCAUSE **41** (2006)

11. Whitton, N.: Learning with digital games. A practical guide to engaging students in higher education. Routledge, New York, NY (2010)

12. Duke, R.D.: Gaming: the future's language. Sage Publications, Great Brytain (1974)

13. Duke, R.D., Geurts, J.: Policy games for strategic management. Dutch University Press, Holland (2004)

14. Oksanen, K.: Subjective experience and sociability in a collaborative serious game. Simul. Gaming **44**(6), 767–793 (2013). https://doi.org/10.1177/1046878113513079

15. Bedwell-Torres, W.L., Pavlas, D., Heyne, K., Lazzara, E., Salas, E.: Toward a taxonomy linking game attributes to learning an empirical study. Simul. Gaming **43**, 729–760 (2012). https://doi.org/10.1177/1046878112439444

16. Passalacqua, M., Morin, R., Sénécal, S., Nacke, L., Léger, P.: Demystifying the first-time experience of mobile games: the presence of a tutorial has a positive impact on non-expert players' flow and continuous-use intentions. Multimodal Technol. Interact. **4**(3), 41 (2020). https://doi.org/10.3390/mti4030041

17. Kazmi, S., Palmer, I.: Action recognition for support of adaptive gameplay: a case study of a first person shooter. Int. J. Comput. Games Technol. **2010**, 1–14 (2010). https://doi.org/10.1155/2010/536480

18. Andrade, K., Fernandes, G., Caurin, G., Siqueira, A., Romero, R., Pereira, R.: Dynamic player modelling in serious games applied to rehabilitation robotics, pp. 211–216 (2014). https://doi.org/10.1109/sbr.lars.robocontrol.2014.41

19. Alserri, S., Zin, N., Wook, T.: Gender-based engagement model for serious games. Int. J. Adv. Sci. Eng. Inform. Technol. **8**(4), 1350 (2018). https://doi.org/10.18517/ijaseit.8.4.6490

20. Oksanen, K., Hämäläinen, R.: Game mechanics in the design of a collaborative 3d serious game. Simul. Gaming **45**(2), 255–278 (2014). https://doi.org/10.1177/1046878114530799

21. Zagal, J., Rick, J., Hsi, I.: Collaborative games: lessons learned from board games. Simul. Gaming **37**(1), 24–40 (2006). https://doi.org/10.1177/1046878105282279

22. Nursobah, N., Andrea, R., Kurniawan, B.: Development finite state machine agent in edugame "hangug word" learning media of korea hangul letters. Jurnal Media Informatika Budidarma **5**(2), 669 (2021). https://doi.org/10.30865/mib.v5i2.2944

23. Smith, A., Nelson, M., Mateas, M.: Prototyping games with biped. Proc. Aaai Conf. Artific. Intell. Interact. Dig. Entertain. **5**(1), 193–194 (2009). https://doi.org/10.1609/aiide.v5i1.12344

24. Spek, E., Oostendorp, H., Meyer, J.: Introducing surprising events can stimulate deep learning in a serious game. Br. J. Edu. Technol. **44**(1), 156–169 (2012). https://doi.org/10.1111/j.1467-8535.2011.01282.x

25. Díaz-Ramírez, J.: Gamification in engineering education – an empirical assessment on learning and game performance. Heliyon **6**(9), e04972 (2020). https://doi.org/10.1016/j.heliyon.2020.e04972

26. Nelson, M., Mateas, M.: Recombinable game mechanics for automated design support. Proc. Aaai Conf. Artific. Intell. Interact. Dig. Entertain. **4**(1), 84–89 (2021). https://doi.org/10.1609/aiide.v4i1.18677

27. Salen, K., Zimmerman, E.: Rules of play. MIT Press, Wielka Brytania (2004)

28. Schell, J.: The art of game design: a book of lenses. CRC Press, Holandia (2008)

29. Adams, E., Dormans, J.: game mechanics: advanced game design. New Riders, Great Britian (2012)
30. Fabricatore, C., Gyaurov, D., López, X.: An exploratory study of the relationship between meaning-making and quality in games. Multimedia Tools Appl. **78**(10), 13539–13564 (2019). https://doi.org/10.1007/s11042-019-7232-1
31. Peters, V., van de Westelaken, M.: Simulation games - a concise introduction to the design process. Samenspraak. Nijmegen, The Netherlands (2014). https://doi.org/10.13140/2.1.4259.1367
32. Wagner, F., Schmuki, R., Wagner, T., Wolstenholme, P.: Modeling software with finite state machines: a practical approach. CRC Press, USA (2006)
33. Unity. Common game development terms and definitions | Game design vocabulary | Unity. Unity (2025). https://learn.unity.com/learn/. Accessed 06 Feb 2025
34. Microsoft. Event Sourcing pattern (2025). https://learn.microsoft.com/en-us/azure/architecture/patterns/event-sourcing. Accessed 06 Feb 2025
35. Unreal. Unreal Engine: Behavior Trees (2025). https://dev.epicgames.com/documentation/en-us/unreal-engine/behavior-trees-in-unreal-engine. Accessed 06 Feb 2025
36. Colledanchise, M., Ögren, P.: Behavior trees in robotics and AI: an introduction. CRC Press. arXiv:1709.00084 (2018). https://doi.org/10.1201/9780429489105. ISBN 978-1-138-59373-2. S2CID 27470659
37. Alto, V.: Building LLM powered applications: create intelligent apps and agents with large language models. Packt Publishing, Germany (2024)
38. Wardaszko, M.: Interdisciplinary approach to complexity in simulation game design and implementation. Simul. Gaming **49**(3), 263–278 (2018). https://doi.org/10.1177/1046878118777809
39. Kriz, W.C.: A systemic-constructivist approach to the facilitation and debriefing of simulations and games. Simul. Gaming **41**(5), 663–680 (2010). https://doi.org/10.1177/1046878108319867
40. Milchtaich, I.: Random-player games. Games Econom. Behav. **47**(2), 353–388 (2004). https://doi.org/10.1016/j.geb.2003.05.002
41. Esquivel, M.: On completely random games. SMCS **3**(2) (2023). https://doi.org/10.61485/smcs.27523829/v3n2p2
42. Chatterjee, K., Doyen, L., Gimbert, H., Henzinger, T.: Randomness for free, pp. 246–257 (2010). https://doi.org/10.1007/978-3-642-15155-2_23
43. Sepúlveda, G., Besoaín, F., Barriga, N.: Exploring dynamic difficulty adjustment in videogames, pp. 1–6 (2019). https://doi.org/10.1109/chilecon47746.2019.8988068
44. Kumari, S., Power, C., Cairns, P.: Investigating uncertainty in digital games and its impact on player immersion (2017). https://doi.org/10.1145/3130859.3131311
45. Power, C., Denisova, A., Papaioannou, T., Cairns, P.: Measuring uncertainty in games, pp. 2839–2845 (2017). https://doi.org/10.1145/3027063.3053215
46. Wang, Z., Zhou, Y., Lien, J., Zheng, J., Xu, B.: Extortion can outperform generosity in the iterated prisoner's dilemma. Nat. Commun. **7**(1) (2016). https://doi.org/10.1038/ncomms11125
47. Press, W., Dyson, F.: Iterated prisoner's dilemma contains strategies that dominate any evolutionary opponent. Proc. Natl. Acad. Sci. **109**(26), 10409–10413 (2012). https://doi.org/10.1073/pnas.1206569109
48. Voorneveld, M.: Maximum likelihood equilibria in games with population uncertainty. Int. Game Theory Rev. **04**(04), 391–403 (2002). https://doi.org/10.1142/s0219198902000768
49. Feltwell, T., Wood, G., Linehan, C., Lawson, S.: An augmented reality game using face recognition technology (2017). https://doi.org/10.1145/3064857.307911

50. Westera, W.: Performance assessment in serious games: compensating for the effects of randomness. Educ. Inf. Technol. **21**(3), 681–697 (2014). https://doi.org/10.1007/s10639-014-9347-3

51. Gauthier, A., Jenkinson, J.: Serious game leverages productive negativity to facilitate conceptual change in undergraduate molecular biology. Int. J. Game-Based Learn. **7**(2), 20–34 (2017). https://doi.org/10.4018/ijgbl.2017040102

52. Abd-Alrazaq, A., et al.: Serious games for learning among older adults with cognitive impairment: systematic review and meta-analysis. J. Med. Internet Res. **25**, e43607 (2023). https://doi.org/10.2196/43607

53. Graafland, M., Bemelman, W., Schijven, M.: Game-based training improves the surgeon's situational awareness in the operation room: a randomized controlled trial. Surg. Endosc. **31**(10), 4093–4101 (2017). https://doi.org/10.1007/s00464-017-5456-6

54. Muñoz, J., Dautenhahn, K.: Robo ludens. ACM Trans. Hum.-Robot Interact. **10**(4), 1–28 (2021). https://doi.org/10.1145/3451343

55. Mun, Y., Oprins, E., Bosch, K., Hulst, A., Schraagen, J.: Serious gaming for adaptive decision making of military personnel. Proc. Hum. Factors Ergon. Soc. Annual Meet. **61**(1), 1168–1172 (2017). https://doi.org/10.1177/1541931213601776

56. Giglioli, I., Ripoll, C., Parra, E., Raya, M.: Expanse: a novel narrative serious game for the behavioral assessment of cognitive abilities. PLoS ONE **13**(11), e0206925 (2018). https://doi.org/10.1371/journal.pone.0206925

57. Cook, M., Colton, S.: A rogue dream: automatically generating meaningful content for games. Proc. Aaai Conf. Artific. Intell. Interact. Digital Entertain. **10**(3), 2–7 (2021). https://doi.org/10.1609/aiide.v10i3.12745

58. Mubin O., Bartneck C.: Do as I say: exploring human response to a predictable and unpredictable robot. In: Proceedings of the 2015 British HCI Conference (British HCI '15), pp. 110–116. Association for Computing Machinery, New York, NY, USA (2015). https://doi.org/10.1145/2783446.2783582

59. Koenitz, H., Eladhari, M.: The paradigm of game system building. Trans. Digital Games Res. Assoc. **5**(3) (2021). https://doi.org/10.26503/todigra.v5i3.123

60. Chenais, N.: Immersive interfaces for clinical applications: current status and future perspective. Front. Neurorobot. **18** (2024). https://doi.org/10.3389/fnbot.2024.1362444

61. Laine, T., Lindberg, R.: Designing engaging games for education: a systematic literature review on game motivators and design principles. IEEE Trans. Learn. Technol. **13**(4), 804–821 (2020). https://doi.org/10.1109/tlt.2020.3018503

62. Eladhari, M., Ollila, E.: Design for research results. Simul. Gaming **43**(3), 391–412 (2012). https://doi.org/10.1177/1046878111434255

63. Bergervoet, E., Sluis, F., Dijk, B., Nijholt, A.: Let the game do the talking: the influence of explicitness and game behavior on comprehension in an educational computer game, pp. 120–127 (2011). https://doi.org/10.1109/cw.2011.30

64. Lischer, S., et al.: Response to the regulation of video games under the youth media protection act: a public health perspective. Int. J. Environ. Res. Public Health **19**(15), 9320 (2022). https://doi.org/10.3390/ijerph19159320

65. Shaw, A., et al.: Analyzing iterative training game design: a multi-method postmortem analysis of cycles training center and cycles carnivale. Multimodal Technol. Interact. **2**(3), 46 (2018). https://doi.org/10.3390/mti2030046

66. Nagle, A., Novak, D., Wolf, P., Riener, R.: The effect of different difficulty adaptation strategies on enjoyment and performance in a serious game for memory training, pp. 1–8 (2014). https://doi.org/10.1109/segah.2014.7067088

67. Deci, E.L., Ryan, R.M.: Intrinsic motivation and self-determination in human behavior. Springer, US, USA (2013)

68. Wouters, P., Nimwegen, C., Oostendorp, H., Spek, E.: A meta-analysis of the cognitive and motivational effects of serious games. J. Educ. Psychol. **105**(2), 249–265 (2013). https://doi.org/10.1037/a0031311
69. Cohard, P.: Evaluation of serious game user experience: the role of emotions. Electron. J. Inform. Syst. Eval. **22**(2) (2019). https://doi.org/10.34190/ejise.19.22.2.005
70. Garske, C., Dyson, M., Dupan, S., Nazarpour, K.: Perception of game-based rehabilitation in upper limb prosthetic training: survey of users and researchers. Jmir Serious Games **9**(1), e23710 (2021). https://doi.org/10.2196/23710
71. Sinclear, D., Flensborg, L., Fogsgaard, A., Löchtefeld, M.: Face-the-waste - learning about food waste through a serious game (2021). https://doi.org/10.1145/3490632.3505171
72. Nakamura, J., Csikszentmihalyi, M.: Flow theory and research. Handbook of Positive Psychology, vol. 195, p. 206 (2009)
73. Daniels, H.: Vygotsky and pedagogy. Routledge/Falmer, Great Britain (2001)
74. Vygotsky, L.S.: Mind in society: the development of higher psychological processes. Harvard University Press, Massachusetts (1978)
75. Kriz, W.C.: Creating effective learning environments and learning organizations through gaming simulation design. Simul. Gaming **34**(4), 495–511 (2003). https://doi.org/10.1177/1046878103258201
76. Raghothama, J., Meijer, S.: Rigor in gaming for design: conditions for transfer between game and reality. Simul. Gaming **49**(3), 246–262 (2018). https://doi.org/10.1177/1046878118770220
77. Macklin, C., Sharp, J.: Games, design and play: a detailed approach to iterative game design. Pearson Education, Great Britan (2016)
78. Yokomitsu, K., Irie, T., Shinkawa, H., Tanaka, M.: Characteristics of gamers who purchase loot box: a systematic literature review. Curr. Addict. Rep. **8**(4), 481–493 (2021). https://doi.org/10.1007/s40429-021-00386-4

Managing the Creative Storm – Game Brainstorm Sessions Based on the Triadic Game Design Philosophy

Heide Lukosch[1](✉) and Daan Groen[2]

[1] HIT Lab NZ, University of Canterbury, Christchurch, New Zealand
`heide.lukosch@canterbury.ac.nz`
[2] Preludens, Delft, The Netherlands

Abstract. Developing a game concept to tackle complex problems is a challenging process. It requires the collaboration of experts from different fields, from game design to technological development, and from content matter experts to pedagogical knowledge holders. Many books and articles have been written about the design of Simulation Games – from Richard Duke's seminal 40-steps game design process to recent approaches from 1981 to Freese and Lukosch's Funnel of Game Design in 2023, and many in between. All these approaches have carefully reviewed related work and analysed game design processes to learn from. As game researchers and developers, we have faced some challenges in applying the existing models when working with content-matter experts without any knowledge of game design. We have therefore developed a new tool, based on the Triadic Game Design Philosophy [1], which we used for participatory game design. We call this tool a GameStorm and describe how we developed it and what we have learned so far.

Keywords: Triadic Game Design · Workshop · Brainstorm · GameStorm

1 Introduction

Simulation Gaming focuses on the analysis and design of complex problems. Simulation games have a long history in helping different actors to better understand and give shape to complex systems and processes. As societies have increased in complexity, the analysis and design of the systems composing them has also become more difficult [2].

Multiple simulation game design approaches, such as Duke and Greenblat's [3], and Duke and Geurts' books [4], exist, yet they are often not explicitly practice-oriented and rather focus on their contribution to the scientific field. Duke and Greenblat [3] for example argue that the design of a simulation game is a systematic translation of understandings of a system into another operational model. Klabbers [5], in his extensive academic work on the science of games, warns that simulation games could provide a misleading feeling of realism. He distinguishes between games as design and as analytical science. He further notes that there is an interesting relationship between reality

© The Author(s) 2026
F. Trautwein et al. (Eds.): ISAGA 2025, LNCS 16439, pp. 79–86, 2026.
https://doi.org/10.1007/978-3-032-20129-4_6

and simulation game, with the elements of reality being translated into rules, roles, and resources of a simulation game [5]. Peters and van Westelaken have also attempted to provide guidelines for science-based simulation game design, following the same tradition [6]. Freese and Lukosch [7] include various phases in their game design process called IDEAS - **I**nterviews, **D**iscussion rounds with **E**xperts, moscow **A**nalysis and game**S**torm, but do not provide details on their distinct steps. However, their IDEAS game design model includes a GameStorm at the end yet only provides a high-level description of this participatory brainstorm session. We add more detail to this phase in this paper and provide a brief overview of the Triadic Game Design framework that serves as design foundation for the GameStorm first.

2 Triadic Game Design

The Triadic Game Design Philosophy (TGD) [1] is a theoretical framework to guide the development of simulation or serious games—games designed for purposes beyond entertainment, such as education, training, or social change. The philosophy of TGD is based on the interplay between three core elements: Reality, Meaning, and Play.

Reality refers to the real-world context in which the game operates. This includes the subject matter, domain knowledge, and constraints from the environment, such as technological limitations, societal needs, or the intended audience.

Meaning represents the purpose of the game, encompassing the intended message, learning objectives, or behavioral outcomes. Meaning ensures that the game aligns with its educational, persuasive, or transformative goals.

Play embodies the interactive and experiential aspects that make the game engaging. This includes mechanics, rules, and player agency, ensuring that the game remains enjoyable while effectively conveying its intended message.

The TGD framework emphasizes balancing these three elements to create a coherent and effective simulation game. If one element dominates at the expense of the others, the game may lose its effectiveness—for instance, a game overly focused on realism may become tedious, while one that prioritizes play may dilute its intended message. By considering the dynamic interplay between Reality, Meaning, and Play, TGD provides a structured approach for designers to create serious games that are both engaging and impactful.

However, while TGD comes with a comprehensive workshop to 'teach' game design, the philosophy itself does not include concrete, practical advice for teams going through the process of simulation game design and development. Especially the communication between game design experts with no or only limited knowledge of a certain domain and the content matter experts with sometimes little prior understanding of the game design process can lead to misunderstandings and challenges. For example, game designers may only be able to grasp the high-level details of a certain field, as they have not been trained in or work in the field for a long time. Likewise, content-matter experts may not understand the complexity of iterative game design processes.

We have encountered such challenges in our own work and have dedicated many hours of observing, communicating, gathering feedback, and testing game concepts with experts. We experienced that the tool we have developed can speed up the process of understanding the first requirements for the further game development.

3 The GameStorm Tool

3.1 GameStorm Elements

Following the TGD framework, the GameStorm session is structured along the three worlds of Reality, Meaning and Play. From a game design perspective, we added the dimensions target group, (learning) goal, and (expected) result to these dimensions. This led to a matrix of nine criteria for the game design, shown in Fig. 1.

GameStorm	REALITY	MEANING	PLAY
TARGET GROUP	What is the current behaviour of the target group?	Which behaviour do we expect from the target group?	Which actors will play a role in the game?
(LEARNING) GOAL	Which processes do you encounter in your work?	What is the desired (learning) goal of the game?	What is the desired play goal of the game?
RESULT	What will we develop within the project?	When do we consider this project to be successful?	How can you win or lose the game?

Fig. 1. GameStorm Elements and Worksheet

For each of the criteria, we developed a question that is addressed by the participants of a workshop. To better understand the current behaviour (interests, attitudes etc.) of the target group, we included the question "What is the current behaviour of the target group?" in the intersection 1of Reality and *Target Group*. The target group is one of the main lenses for the development of simulation games, which often are focused on a specific group of players (the stakeholders in a specific system). This question is aimed to trigger the analysis and discussion of the current state of the system, especially the actions and behaviors of the actors involved. Such analysis, especially when conducted in a team, can lead to fruitful insights in how the system and its actors is perceived at the moment of the analysis. This part of the GameStorm follows processes of analytical science and aims to identify elements, actors and relationships of the reference system for the game. For Meaning and Target Group, we asked "Which behaviour do we expect from the target group?". This question fosters a conversation about the goals of the game to be designed, with a strong focus on how the system and its actors are envisioned to operate in the future. This phase utilizes processes of design science, as participants think about the 'desired' state of the system the game refers to. In highly complex situations, the aim might be less clear, but perceptions of different actors can still be helpful to formulate a design objective. To understand how to design game elements in this area, we asked "Which actors will play a role in the game?". The last question can include roles played by actual players, or roles represented in the game, but not played – such as roles that are mentioned on an action or event card for example.

We also included the perspective of the *(learning) goal* to the matrix to enable discussions on current practices and processes, and related (learning) goals. We understand learning as a broad concept of gathering knowledge, which can support understanding, awareness, or decision-making processes. For this aspect, we again start with an analysis of the current system, then move on to (learning) goals of the system, with the last step in this row to design goals in the game that are connected to the (learning) goals of the game.

The third aspect we have added in the GameStorm matrix is the *result* row. Two questions of this aspect are related to the scope of the specific game design project and define its boundaries as well as the success criteria. These are translated into the winning and losing conditions in the game itself.

We developed these questions as a research team of game researchers and game developers, based on our own experiences. Currently, we are adapting these in the context of developing games for children, and for the use with indigenous communities. We will report on our experiences with these groups in the future.

3.2 GameStorm Applications

As game researchers and developers, we rely on the input of content-matter experts to design meaningful game experiences. This means that these experts must commit a considerable amount of their time to communicate and collaborate with the game developers. In general, we have good experiences with techniques such as focus group interviews, observations, and even role-play (e.g. [8]) to understand the field and requirements for a simulation game. However, we were looking for a structure to make this process more efficient and more effective at the same time.

In a research project focused on the use of simulation games for transport and logistics, we applied the structured GameStorm tool for the first time. As described in [9], the game design process started off with a GameStorm session with ten stakeholders from rail, road, and waterway management, and four researchers with expertise in multimodal transportation. Using the GameStorm method, we were able to extract the core roles in the system, the operating procedures of the system, several possible scenarios, and the game's scoring mechanism, defining its winning and losing conditions. The

GameStorm session for this project was held as an in-person, one-day workshop, and led to the development of a single-player digital game called 'Modal Manager Game'.

The 'Modal Manager Game' is a result of a research project that aimed to exlore the use of simulation games to develop understanding of the concept of multimodal freight transportation, and to showcase related opportunities and challenges. The multimodal transportation of freight includes multiple stakeholders with different interests and can be identified as complex socio-technical system [9]. The GameStorm session served as starting point for the development of the 'Modal Manager Game', and defined the roles of the game, its processes, and scenarios.

The GameStorm defined the game to be developed as a digital, single-player game composed of various missions that simulate a network of road, rail, and barge transport routes, along with associated intermodal terminals, within a hypothetical transport corridor in the Netherlands. In the game, the player takes on the role of an infrastructure manager and interacts with four simulated Logistic Service Providers (LSPs). Each LSP is designed to make routing decisions based on different priorities set for each of them. These priorities are reliability, sustainability, cost-efficiency and one role without consistent preference. Performance of the players is measured along the criteria of network performance and LSP satisfaction.

The engagement in the workshop was high, and feedback of the participants was positive. We were able to identify enough information from the workshop to develop a high-fidelity prototype that could be tested with experts from the domain, who provided further feedback for improvement. The goals of the game were defined as helping players to understand the system of multimodal transportation, and what actions and decisions are needed from the stakeholders involved. While the game that resulted from this initial process is quite complex, we saw that the GameStorm session itself created awareness among the stakeholders that participated, who developed scenarios and discussed first actions to 'make multimodal transport happen' already during the GameStrom session. For us, this is a clear sign that a simulation game design process in itself can be valuable for the analysis and design of a complex system, and not the end result (the game) alone.

4   Discussion and Conclusions

4.1   What We Have Learned

The GameStorm session is a useful tool to engage with different stakeholders in the design process of simulation games. The tool adds structure to the process and helps problem owners to formulate ideas and provide input into the game design process. As game design is a complex process that only experienced and trained researchers and designers can conduct, it can be difficult for stakeholders to formulate their needs and goals. The questions formulated in the GameStorm sheet help to express ideas and discuss different perspectives. There are several learnings that we have collected throughout multiple GameStorm sessions, summarised below. These are the result of rather unstructured observations of ourselves as researchers, designers, and facilitators of the GameStorm sessions, but nonetheless hopefully helpful for others.

1. **The Why and the What -** The GameStorm often is a mirror for the participants of the workshop. Especially the question about the learning goal(s) of the real system shows to be an effective way to make the participants reflect on their actual problem. When Simon Sinek speaks about the "why" in marketing versus the "what", he addresses a similar principle [10]. In GameStorm sessions, we have rephrased the question into: What keeps you awake at night? Often the participants don't have a clear answer to that question, and it requires some digging to identify and express the actual problem. In our experience, serious games involve the risk of failing to achieve their goal when the actual problem is not fully clear – a problem Freese & Lukosch also addressed in [7]. The GameStorm (hosted by a well-trained facilitator) is an effective method to explore that question. The GameStorm also helps to reduce the time of the design phase since it forces all stakeholders to spend significant time together for the design groundwork.

2. **Facilitator** – The success of the GameStorm is highly dependent on the facilitator. Even though the questions are clear, often a sharp ear is needed to hear all remarks in the discussion. The facilitator needs to make sure that the conversation stays on track, but more importantly, the facilitator is responsible for the 'digging' (see above). Often, a question must be asked multiple times before a satisfactory answer is given. The facilitator needs a certain amount of authority to get the participants to answer or debate with each other. Also, experience and knowledge of game design is crucial for a successful facilitation of a GameStorm session. Partnering up with a more experienced facilitator can be a way to develop the necessary skills.

3. **Materials** - In our sessions, we use a large, A0, printed poster to show the matrix with the 9 questions along with big markers to write down important quotes or answers, during the discussion and the workshop. The facilitator is doing the writing and can, together with the participants, formulate the answers and write them on the spot. The posters are also good for capturing additional notes and thoughts. The facilitator has an important role in leading the discussion, making sure that the questions are answered thoroughly and the answers are written down in a structured way. Having the facilitator collecting the feedback of the participants provides a bit of a breathing and thinking moment for the participants and is part of a humble inquiry process [11].

   In one session, sticky notes were used by the participants to answer the questions instead of the facilitator writing down the answers. This session was less successful. In our opinion, the main reason for this was because the biggest value of the GameStorm is the discussion between the participants. We also learned and advise to restrict a GameStorm to just a handful of participants. In our experience, a centralized discussion, with a facilitator to guide the conversation, provides the best outcomes.

4. **Flexibility** – We have noticed that the biggest value of the GameStorm is the way it guides the discussion. With 9 questions we can cover most of the information which is needed for a first design. Sometimes other, valuable questions are introduced. In those cases, there is enough room to write on the poster. If the discussion is heading in the wrong direction or if focus is shifting, the facilitator is needed to steer the discussion back and focus on a different question.

5. **GameStorm as a contract** – Some participants struggle with the concept of investing in serious game development. For many, it is an unknown and uncertain process, and sometimes the problem owner has only limited knowledge of what to expect or how

to appreciate the product. Often, during the process, the problem owner will start to intervene with the design or development process, maybe driven by a wish to gain more control. Especially when the problem owner is outside of their comfort zone, they tend to intervene and bring the design or development back to a process which they understand or control. This can be quite disruptive for the game designer and developer since they are forced into a defensive position and then might struggle to explain their decisions to the problem owner. The GameStorm offers a contract between the problem owners and the game developer, where important decisions are made (together). The result section plays an important role in what to expect and how to set the scope for the project.

When using the GameStorm session, we have seen that users also provided feedback that the tool did not only help them to understand the idea of a game, but that the discussion led by the questions also increased their understanding of the underlying complex problem to address. This way, the GameStorm session is a helpful tool in the analysis of complex systems and problems before a game has even been designed. We propose designers who want to engage with a number of stakeholders early in the design process to use the GameStorm format for their brainstorm sessions.

4.2 Limitations

We have used the GameStorm structure with many stakeholders and problem owners, but have not validated the workshop format in a structured way yet. Our own observations tell us that the participants were engaged with the topic and with each other. Furthermore, the workshop helped us in the design process of simulation games, as a tool next to other instruments such as in-depth interviews and literature reviews. In the future, we would like to apply the workshop to other groups (children, local communities) and carry out a structured reflection on the workshop effectiveness and experience.

Acknowledgments. We would like to thank all our colleagues and participants who helped make the GameStorm sessions and resulting games a success. There are too many to name, but a special thanks goes out to Alexander Verbraeck, Shalini Kurapati, Ioanna Kourounioti and Lorant Tavasszy.

Disclosure of Interests. The authors have no competing interests to declare that are relevant to the content of this article.

References

1. Harteveld, C.: Triadic game design: balancing reality, meaning and play. Springer Science & Business Media (2011)
2. Lukosch, H.K., Bekebrede, G., Kurapati, S., Lukosch, S.G.: A scientific foundation of simulation games for the analysis and design of complex systems. Simul. Gaming **49**(3), 279–314 (2018)
3. Duke, R.D., Greenblat, C.S.: Gaming—simulation, rationale, design and applications: a text with parallel readings for social scientists, educators and community workers. Wiley, New York, NY (1975)

4. Duke, R.D., Geurts, J.: Policy games for strategic management. Rozenberg Publishers, Amsterdam, The Netherlands (2004)
5. Klabbers, J.H.G.: On the architecture of game science. Simul. Gaming **49**, 207–245 (2018)
6. Peters, V., Westelaken, M.: Simulation games—a concise introduction to game design. Samenspraak Advies, Nijmegen, The Nethernalds (2014)
7. Freese, M., Lukosch, H.: The funnel of game design–an adaptive game design approach for complex systems. Simul. Gaming **55**(2), 323–341 (2024)
8. Lukosch, H., van Ruijven, T., Verbraeck, A.: The participatory design of a simulation training game. In: Proceedings of the 2012 Winter Simulation Conference (WSC), vol. 2012, pp. 1–11. Berlin, Germany (2012)
9. Kurapati, S., Kourounioti, I., Lukosch, H., Tavasszy, L., Verbraeck, A.: Fostering sustainable transportation operations through corridor management: a simulation gaming approach. Sustainability **10**(2), 455 (2018)
10. Sinek, S.: Start with why: how great leaders inspire everyone to take action. Penguin Books (2011)
11. Schein, E.H., Schein, P.A.: Humble inquiry: the gentle art of asking instead of telling. Berrett-Koehler Publishers(2025)

Playing for Urban Security: A Co-design Analog Serious Game Process to Support Collaborative Spatial Planning

Micael Sousa^(✉)

CITTA—Research Centre for Territory, Transports and Environment, Department of Civil Engineering, University of Coimbra, Coimbra, Portugal
micaelssousa@gmail.com

Abstract. Serious games can be planning support tools to establish collaborative planning processes for urban issues. We proposed a co-design method to adapt and develop analog games inspired by modern board game design traits, reducing the game development time and cost. The stakeholders, invited by Leiria Municipality (Portugal), played two preparatory sequences of the game to collect priorities and concerns that supported the final serious game (budget allocation). The sequence of game sessions and the final analog serious game for the *UrbSecurity* (Urbact) project delivered support tools for planners and local authorities, allowing them to engage stakeholders and collaborate to plan their city to increase security. There are game design requirements, data collection, and facilitation guidelines and requirements to guarantee future replication. The playability requirements may affect the granularity and accuracy of the simulation. However, achieving the serious game goal of establishing a collaborative planning support tool is still possible.

Keywords: Board Games · Co-design · Urban Security · Urban Planning · Serious Games

1   Introduction

We live in an age of urban complexity, and finding solutions to address all issues and claims related to urban realities is difficult [1]. Even the most evolved technologies associated with Smart City trends struggle to deal with it, especially human factors [2]. These planning problems are "wicked" since there is no optimal or perfect solution to deal with all the claims and constraints [3]. The increasing complexity of urban affairs results from interconnected societal domains, different values, and perspectives of those using the same space [4]. Solving these problems is not easy when there seems to exist a crisis of participation, disengagement, and inefficiency [5]. Traditional rational-systemic panning approaches might not be enough to deal with these problems [6, 7].

Collaborative planning (CP) seems to be a way to deal with complexity, aiming to generate collective decision-making that can reach some consensus. For CP to be

F. Trautwein et al. (Eds.): ISAGA 2025, LNCS 16439, pp. 87–102, 2026.
https://doi.org/10.1007/978-3-032-20129-4_7

effective, planners need to engage the stakeholders actively. CP processes must be representative and have as diverse participants while providing learning, experimentation, and building proposals[7, 8]. Games share many of these characteristics [9, 10], and there are many cases of Serious Games (SG) approaches successfully applied to planning [11, 12]. Despite this, developing planning-based approaches is not easy. It demands resources, knowledge, and openness to try new methods, including co-design practices that can make them more effective [13].

We propose a co-design method to develop a serious game through several stages and play sessions. In the first session, stakeholders identified problems while interacting and fostering empathy and collective awareness. We propose using modified versions of modern board games (creative party games) to identify the urban problems of the zone at stake (played by the participants in workgroups). This is followed by voting stages, where all participants vote on the results from the work groups. This new design framework, described in Sect. 4, supported the development of a new serious game approach, including a new game in the last stage of the process (stage 3).

Our game-based method (Fig. 1) aims to simplify and facilitate the participatory process compared to designing consultation processes that are unable to deliver tangible results. The final game, where participants can help plan the city, is a board game with modern mechanisms focusing on the users and the urban issues at stake. We expect that planners can replicate and adapt this design process to their practices, being aware of the existing limitations (e.g., balancing playability and simulation).

2   From Collaborative Planning and Co-design to Serious Games

Collaborative planning (CP) approaches intend to empower participation in planning [7], considering that stakeholders can be motivated to think, learn, and find solutions to solve collective spatial problems [14]. CP practices aim to deliver consensus when dealing with complex spatial issues [15, 16]. Stakeholders are the human representatives engaged in a CP process to discuss, negotiate, and decide according to their collective goals and claims [17]. In CP, planners act as facilitators, supporting decision-making, providing information, and collecting data for planning processes [18, 19]. Through CP, planners can collect local knowledge that would be difficult to access or predict in any other way [20, 21] and tackle problems during the planning process that appear later [22]. CP is a way to build up trust and commitment from the participants toward the decision-making results [23].

Since the 1960s, Serious Games (SGs) have been explored by several fields of research and practice, including planning [24]. Knowing that a planning process will have a playful dimension, like a game, influences the users to adopt a less confrontational approach, lowering the conflicts [25]. A game can be a way to plan and change the participants' perceptions about the issues at stake, invoking concepts of fairness and making them visual and tangible [26].

Introducing visualization tools and interactive features, like those in games, where users can make decisions and see the effects as spatial representation, helps engage and generate planning information for users [27]. Digital tools can be powerful but generate inequality participation opportunities [28]. Increasing the complexity of the simulation within a game to deliver more realistic experiences can jeopardize the participation objectives because some participants might not understand how to play it within the available time [26, 29], which can be frustrating and inefficient [30]. Analog game solutions have proven easy to use and effective, exploring the advantages of face-to-face interactions [12, 31, 32]. The social interaction is one of the reasons modern board games are growing as a worldwide trend despite the dominance of digital games [33, 34].

Because building an analog game is easier and less expensive than doing a digital one [9, 35], and the face-to-face interactions increase the participants' empathy and foster collaboration [36–38], we propose to explore Modern Board Game (MBG) design for planning, following previous approaches like those defined by Sousa and his colleagues [32, 39, 40]. Although SGs can result from modifying standard entertainment games [10] or created from scratch [41], both are valid approaches. We process a method that combines the two approaches.

3 Methodology

Our co-design process (three steps) resulted in an analog collaborative serious game (S3) where participants (stakeholders, city councilors, planning experts, and civil servants) can play to set the priorities and solutions to increase urban security. We followed a co-design and design-thinking approach where the creations from the previous steps (S1 and S2) generated data for serious game development (S3). The co-design method required two game sessions (S1 and S2) where stakeholders interacted and identified options to explore in the final serious game (S3). Stakeholders were invited by the municipality to represent local institutions. They played all game stages (S1, S2 and S3).

In S1, all the stakeholders ($n_{S1} = 17$) were together, working on three separate tables. Stakeholders were divided into two groups in S2 ($n_{s2.1} = 4$, $n_{s2.2} = 6$) and S3 ($n_{s3.1} = 5$, $n_{s3.2} = 4$. The sessions for City Councilors (CC) ($n_{cc} = 11$) and Department Leadership (DL) ($n_{DL} = 10$) did not have these restrictions. Due to the low number of participants per session (≤ 20), we present median ($\tilde{x}$) values and their variations (before and after) of the participants' perceptions. Sessions had a duration of approximately two hours.

In each session (S1, S2, and S3), post-workshop surveys collected information about the game-based process, the perception of the effectiveness of the process, suggestions, and general comments [26, 42], detailing the play experiences and the serious game goals (generating collaborative planning proposals) [43]. Only during S3 was the serious game ready to be evaluated according to the purposes set for the *Urbsecurity* project because S1 and S2 were necessary to develop S3. For S3, we asked additional questions to participants, such as if the collective proposals improved their individual ideas/claims, if the overall set of proposals was coherent, and if they should be implemented in reality.

During S3, maps were video recorded to track the game's progress (for research purposes). All the other outputs were photographed, including the voting results and the post-game surveys (form) done with post-its, paper, and pens. The surveys and the graphical information generated summary tables and graphics (With less than 20 participants per session, statistical analyses lacked statistical validity).

4   Building a Co-design Process for the Serious Game

We defined a three-step process with three different sessions to deliver a game-based CP for the *Urbsecurity* project (Urbact) in Leiria city (Portugal), fowling multi-step co-design principles combining planning where the knowledge from professionals and stakeholders/citizens helped to design the game [13, 44]. In Session 1 (S1) and Session 2 (S2), we modified a set of MBGs (i.e., *Dixit*, *Telestrations*, *Ikonikus*) to engage participants and foster collaboration and creativity [45]. Before session 3 (S3), we developed a new game by combining MBG mechanisms, PO information/suggestions, and the stakeholders' preferences from S1 and S2. The schematic flowchart to implement our three-step co-design proposal is presented in Fig. 1, detailing the purpose of each session, game usage, and outcomes to be classified as an overall SG approach. After the games, there was a moment of debriefing and discussion with the participants conducted by the Research Team (RT) and Planning Officials (PO) facilitators. The game sessions (S1, S2, and S3) should deliver ways for the participants to express themselves in a collaborative playable environment (yellow box, Fig. 1).

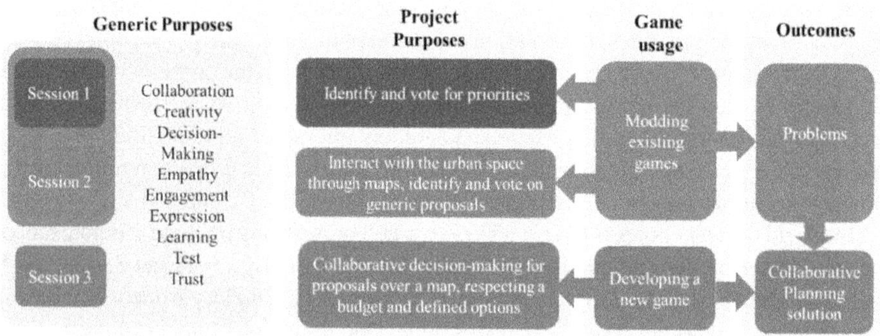

Fig. 1. Development process with co-design sessions (S1 and S2) support the final game (S3).

In S1, participants used storytelling, drawing, and communication games to share information and establish empathy. The S1 process (Fig. 2) was set to introduce the participants to the process, do the ice-breaking, foster teamwork, and divergent and convergent thinking (creative process) to define the collective priorities to increase the urban security of the zone [46, 47]. These collective experiences helped stakeholders to frame the problems collectively. Participants sat at tables with no more than six persons, forming three groups (One PO facilitator per table). Detailed game information can be found at BGG [48].

First, each participant picked a *Dixit* [49] card (illustrated with surrealistic pictures) from a table to do their self-presentation for the group. Then, they played a modified version of *Telestrations* [50], writing a word that represented their priority to increase security in the city in their notepads. After, the participants played a modified version of *Ikonikus* [51] to explore their identified priorities as a group. Each participant would play once as a narrator and expose a security concern. Each other participant played

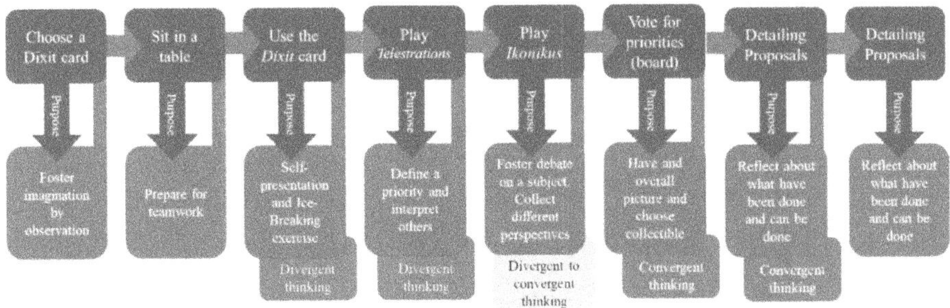

Fig. 2. S1 process detailing game usages, purposes, and divergent/convergent thinking.

cards to deliver feedback. Then, the session general facilitator (RT) asked each table to propose priorities to add to a board. Giving six votes per participant, the participants distributed the votes per priority (Fig. 3). After this, each group of stakeholders filled out Form 1, where they detailed the most voted priorities (e.g., writing how to solve it, who should solve it, when, and with what resources). Participants voted in a second voting round (six votes per person).

Fig. 3. Voting on Form 1 (left) and proposals presentation (right) during S1.

In S2, participants added more details about their priorities as groups. Again, MBGs were used to generate interactions, collaboration, and expression. In S2, the purpose was to complement the results from S1, allowing the participants to deal with maps and graphical representations of the urban area subject to analysis. We adapted *Fake Artist Goes to New York* [52]. In this game, a narrator expressed a problem, passing written information about it to all participants except one. Then, the narrator sketched the same problem on the urban zone map, and all the other participants completed the drawing without ever telling what the problem was. The result was a graphical representation of the problem using the map layout of the urban zone (combining/integrating the game mechanisms with the map). Next, the narrator explained the problem at stake. After this, all the participants defended/pitched their drawings/sketches, discussed, and voted to find which participant ignored the information (the "fake artist" that did not know the word). After all the participants played as narrators, they discussed generic proposals expressed in the collective drawings. They voted on the generated proposals (Fig. 4) as in S1 to define the most important ones (same voting system).

S3 demanded a longer development process and working together with the PO. The available options/choices for participants in the S3 game resulted from the identified

Fig. 4. S2 sessions: Playing *Fake Artist Goes to New York* modified version (1), a drawing result regarding accessibility (2) and the voting system with several post-its per participant (3).

priorities and problems during S1 and S2. S3 was divided into two stages (S3.a/S3.b) (Fig. 5). In S3.a, participants vote on problems by replacing the colored cubes with their white cubes (votes) and placing the colored ones on the map of the urban zone (divided into hexagons). This process resulted in a graphic of priorities (replaced white cubes on a table) and the spatial location of the problems (colored cubes over the map). S3.b occurred on another table near the first one (S3.a) so the participants could track the identified problems. In the second table, participants played four rounds (one round per year, representing a municipal government term) where they could spend part of their budget represented by the game coins (each player got limited coins per cycle) to choose from the available options. The available options were co-designed by the RT and PO, using information from S1, S2, and internal data from the Municipality (ML). Each session was supported by a facilitator from the RT and several from the PO.

Each coin represents an average of 30K€ (according to the ML internal costs). The game was tested with 10K€ per coin, but it increased the game duration by over an hour, and the stacks of coins were prone to falling during handling in the proposals with a higher cost. After spending the four-year budget, participants filled in Form 2, describing and summarizing how the overall solution increased safety in the urban zone. F1 and F2 forms were introduced to help participants summarize, reflect, and justify their collective decisions during the games and provided the PO with data to build the *UrbSecurity* project report (https://urbact.eu/networks/urbsecurity). Information about the forms (F1 and F2) is available in an appendix at: https://estudogeral.uc.pt/handle/10316/114583.

Fig. 5. Participants playing S3.a (left) to identify problems and S3.b (right) to define proposals.

5   Results

The codesign sessions with stakeholders and data from the municipality (maps and costs for actions) supported the development of the S3a/S3b game (Fig. 5). Table 1 shows the budget % allocation to each game option per session (S3.b).

Table 1. Percentage of the budget allocation per proposal type for S3.b sessions

Proposals/Game options	ID	S3.1	S3.2	$S3_{cc}$	$S3_{dl}$	$(\bar{x})$
Cleaning and hygiene	1	4.78	4.98	5.43	2.50	4.42
Public illumination	2	9.57	9.96	10.86	5.83	9.05
General public infrastructures	3	10.43	4.98	16.29	18.75	12.61
Parking	4	17.39	12.45	9.05	8.33	11.81
Sidewalks and bicycle lanes	4	8.70	9.13	2.71	5.83	6.59
Public Transportation	4	4.35	9.13	11.76	12.50	9.44
Pedestrianization	4	3.48	4.15	0.90	2.50	2.76
Roadways	4	6.52	17.43	16.29	16.25	14.12
Policing	5	4.35	4.98	1.81	3.33	3.62
Civilian and social welfare programs	6	3.48	3.32	2.71	2.92	3.11
Marketing, signals, and information	7	3.48	3.32	2.26	2.92	2.99
Urban renewal programs	8	10.43	9.96	10.86	10.00	10.31
Green and leisure parks	9	13.04	6.22	9.05	8.33	9.16

The visual results for each S3 session were different, even among similar participants like the stakeholders' groups (S3.1 and S3.2). Figure 6 presents the final game results (S3) in digital format for spatial analysis.

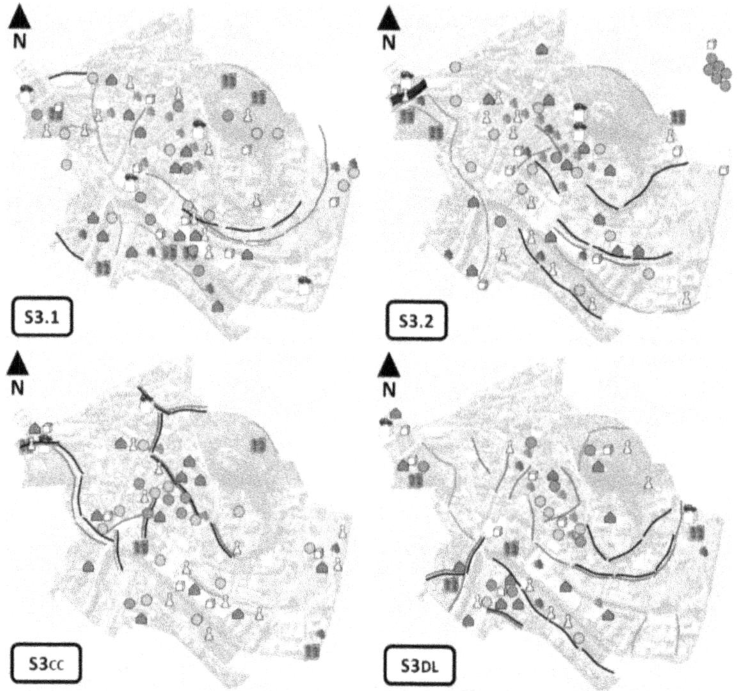

Fig. 6. Spatial game results from S3(.b) sessions.

Table 2 represents the qualitative results from the post-session surveys (Likert scale 1 to 7). The S3 survey included new questions to address the effects of playing the serious game. S3 was the final serious game tool to identify and propose proposals to increase urban safety. Which was the serious game that we wished to evaluate. S1 and S2 were also important as a process to develop S3.

Table 3 shows the overview of comments from the post-test questionnaires, organized per statement type, according to the grounded theory principles [53]. The 46 participants in all sessions produced 24 comments: 55 referred to positive issues, while 4 to negative ones. We considered positive the comments that highlighted the purposes of the serious game (e.g., debating, collaborative decision-making, enjoyment, etc.). As negative, we considered the comments that revealed failures to deliver a collaborative decision-making process, including the game dimensions like duration and the required number of players to play the game.

Table 2. Results regarding participants' perceptions for the sessions (S1, S2 and S3) ($\tilde{x}$ values).

Session	Empathy with facilitators	Feeling of Competence	Difficulty level	Collaboration	Sharing ideas	Generated Learning	Addressed urban security	Collective improved individual	Coherent solution	Different priorities	Should be implemented	Should be Repeated	Participate again
S_1	7.0	6.0	2.0	6.0	7	7.0	6.0	–	–	2.0	–	7.0	7.0
S_2	6.0	6.0	2.0	6.0	6.5	6.0	6.5	–	–	5.5	–	7.0	7.0
S_{31+2}	6.0	5.0	3.0	6.0	6.0	6.0	6.0	7.0	6.0	2.0	6.0	6.0	6.0
S_{3CC}	6.0	6.0	2.0	6.0	6.0	6.0	6.0	6.0	6.0	3.0	6.0	6.0	6.0
S_{3DL}	6.0	6.0	2. 0	6.0	6.0	6.0	5.0	6.0	6.0	3.0	5.5	6.5	7.0
S_1	7.0	6.0	2.0	6.0	7	7.0	6.0	–	–	2.0	–	7.0	7.0

Table 3. Type of statements referred by the participants in the comments.

Session	Type/content of statement	Number of comments
Positive	Collaborative	7
Positive	Meaningful debate	5
Positive	Generic positive	14
Positive	Idea sharing/generation	7
Positive	Interactive/Involving	11
Positive	Useful results	11
Positive	Manageable/enough time	2
Positive	Need more participants	1
Negative	Some options were individualistic	1
Negative	Collaborative	7
Negative	Meaningful debate	5

6 Discussion

Participatory Action Research and co-creation principles helped establish the proposed SG approach. The unpredictable number of attendants demanded that the games be adapted for each session. Despite following a predefined protocol (Fig. 1), we learned and collected new information from each session. Playtesting with the PO defined the SGs, but each session with the users (stakeholders, CC, and DL) revealed improvements for the game. This shows that developing serious is an ongoing iterative improvement that follows the design thinking process and co-design applied to collaborative planning [13]: define ideas, test, and adapt to purpose. To maintain the same game (e.g., game economy), we only improved the quality of the game components. Introducing yellow pawns that looked like public lamps helped the participants to differentiate from other generic game components like colored discs (St3.b). Using white cubes for voting in the S3cc and S3dl helped to visualize the information (e.g., the table to place the votes for S3a generated a bar graph of priority objects (Fig. 7).

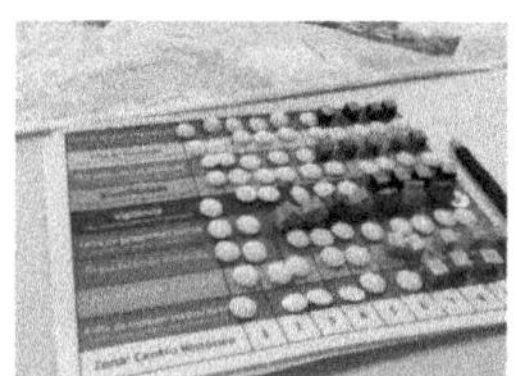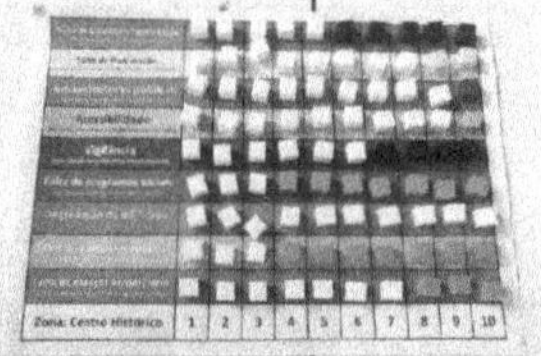

Fig. 7. Table to place the votes for the stage s3.a (discs/meeples and cubes versions)

Each group of participants proposed different solutions (S3.1 and S3.2) (Fig. 6). Stakeholders should be representative of the urban zone at stake, people, claims, activities, and others. [54]. Defining who will participate in the game is crucial because it affects results (in this case, it was set by the ML). Table 1 shows the percentages of budget allocation per session, highlighting the highest values per type of proposal. Stakeholders were the ones more concerned about the need for more parking solutions. CC focused on the renewal of public buildings, whereas the stakeholders focused on the private ones that affected the city's image the most, such as the central bus station. DL was concerned with the infrastructure, the flooding, and the efficiency of the transport system. Nevertheless, all agreed that some spaces needed more public illumination, and some parks should become more agreeable and less frightening due to abandonment and excessive vegetation (Fig. 6). The Pedestrianization of the main historical street was unanimous since it is the primary source of conflict between automobiles and pedestrians due to its narrow section. The S3 proposals reinforce the claims of the residents and shop owners. New parking was something stakeholders and CC agreed on, namely, locating it near the City Hall and the Castle.

Regarding the participants' (stakeholder, CC, and DL) perception, Tables 2 and 3 reveal that the participants found the experience valuable and reached the purposes of collecting their contributions and providing collective proposals (scores above 5.0). Participants (all sessions) considered that the sessions generated empathy (min. of 6.0 after play), were not complex (max. of 3.0), helped to create ideas (min. 6.0), and fostered learning (min 6.0), which are traits of collaborative planning (Table 2). The perception of collaboration was high during all the sessions. In $S3_{CC}$, the facilitator noticed that the freedom to play without a turn order and that all players had the same votes and money helped to level the power relation (there were institutional hierarchical differences between the participants).

Table 2 reveals that all participants wanted to repeat the session (min. 6.0), but S1, S2, and $S3_{CC}$ classified it higher (7.0). These were the sessions where the desire to implement the proposals was higher. Free comments can shed some light on this. Participant 31 (P31) said, *"You should repeat the game with the people that live there,"* while Participant 34 (P34) wrote, *"I hope that these proposals are done for real."* It seems that stakeholders are willing to participate (7.0), and we interpret that they demand more participation and that the results of their participation are consequent (desire to see the proposals implemented.

None of the participants stated that the available choices were incorrect or that other ones were missing, neither during the game nor in the commentaries. We argue that this can be interpreted as an apparent success of the co-design process, at least for problem identification (S3.a) and the proposals to spend the budget (S3.b). The only negative feedback was the downtime in S2, which was related to the time some participants took to make their moves, which made others wait. Also, during the $S3_{DL}$, P51 asked for more time to discuss the choices. In $S3_{CC}$, P39 argued that the game was prone to individual moves. A single participant could place a game piece without other players' contributions (coins) because the coins they received per turn were enough to pay for some proposals (e.g., policing, public illumination) but not for others (e.g., Parking). Considering the players' perspective, the difficulty of directly paying the required coins for some pieces is a design fragility. But it was an intentional design choice. We offered individual and collective choices because the individual actions would reduce the available money for expensive collective plans. These situations lead to discussions in every S3 session. It was a way to enforce negotiation among participants. We were also aware that the unpredictability regarding the number of participants in each session demanded redefining the available coins per player [55]. Reducing the coins per player/cycle would increase the game duration by more than two hours. Increasing the value (number of coins) for choices like "Policing" and "Cleaning and hygiene" would distort the prices when compared to costly options like "Parking." These design choices are clear examples of the balance between playability and simulation of serious games [41].

The overall low perception of complexity (maximum of 3.0) and desire to participate again (minimum 6.0) are indicators of adequate playability. Because half of the participants (stakeholders) played all the games during S1, S2, and S3, the novelty effect of using games and already knowing the other participants might have reduced the empathy with the group for S2 and S3. We interpret that public servants and their leaders considered the SG methods as solutions to improve participation and collaboration. DL comments corroborate this interpretation: *"Very interesting session. I liked the methodology. To repeat."* (P48); *"This methodology should be used for the local participatory budget"* (P53); *"Very dynamic. Allowed us to reflect about the problems and solutions with pairs. Something we cannot do regularly."* (P54).

6.1 Conclusions, Limitations, and Future Research

Designing SGs for CP is challenging when we need to keep the participants engaged during long and continuous sessions. A game can be a tool to explore complex problems, deal with chaotic interactions, foster collaboration, and reinforce collective decision-making. In our case, we adopted a step-by-step co-design method that allowed us to use simple rule sets of game mechanisms, maps, tables, and analog game components (Fig. 1). This serious game development process helped the PO build the *UrbSecurity* project action plan [56]. As expected, the proposals approached security as the result of improving generic urban dimensions.

However, the serious game that resulted from the development process (S3) was prone to some problems. Establishing the game economy forced us to adopt 30K€ per coin, which confused some participants. Another direct effect was that the participants could select some of the proposals without discussing them with other participants (their individual income was sufficient). This economic dimension is a serious game design problem due to the need to balance playability and simulation [41]. The game demanded considerable logistics (two tables 2.0 × 2.0 m) and a permanent facilitator to enforce the rules, provide income (coins), control time, and clarify doubts. How they explain the rules can make suggestions that affect the participants' decisions. The facilitators' experience conducting the game can also affect the participants' experiences of enjoyment and mastering the game. However, the participants' perceptions seem to indicate that the developed game (S3) was perceived with higher potential as a tool for planning purposes (Tables 2 and 3).

Games can be useful tools for planners, although the game design and the facilitators' performance may affect the outcomes. Our experiment revealed that the results might be perceived as less coherent than desired because this dimension did not get the higher classification in any session (always 6.0). Stakeholders seem eager to find new, effective ways to participate and influence decisions, but they demand results. The ability to generate proposals appears to surpass the value of the ludic dimension. Adopting cocreation approaches helps develop tools for expressing the stakeholders' claims and delivering data for planners. However, serious games resulting from co-design can be useful as planning support systems (PSS). We argue that our method (Fig. 1) was a tool to engage participants and provide them with means to discuss, decide, and generate data, not a solution to replace the standard planning process. However, we did not test whether planners could run SGs independently or how much external is required.

Despite the absence of negative comments and criticism regarding the game design process, we have not done extensive interviews with the participants to evaluate this. The novelty of using a game for planning purposes, the face-to-face interactions, and the formality of the survey might have restrained the participants' negative comments or critiques. Doing a focus group and structured interviews with the participants, conducted by a different facilitator, might clear up these doubts. Having sessions where several groups play the games (simultaneously) would deliver new interactions that could enrich the testing of the serious games. The ML invited the stakeholders directly. Some never appeared in the session because it was voluntary participation. Other stakeholders' representatives changed from session to session. This methodological difficulty generates data variability, and we cannot know why people miss the sessions.

Analog game design techniques are compliant with the co-design and participatory approaches for collaborative decision-making, delivering flexible game-based tools that demand low resources. However, they require game design and facilitation expertise (e.g., similar to a game master in narrative games that keeps the game evolving and progressing according to the designed rules), like the ability to treat the collected information and transform it into useful data for planning. The major difficulty was defining a method to analyze and collect the data from the game sessions. We combined quantitative and qualitative methods and faced the same challenges as referred to in the literature [43, 57, 58].

Acknowledging the limitations and potential of analog game-based approaches is utterly important. We recommend future research on these dimensions.

References

1. Portugali, J.: What makes cities complex? In: Complexity, Cognition, Urban Planning and Design, pp. 3–19. Springer (2016)
2. Goodspeed, R.: Smart cities: moving beyond urban cybernetics to tackle wicked problems. Cambridge J. Reg. Econ. Soc. **8**, 79–92 (2015)
3. Innes, J.E., Booher, D.E.: Collaborative rationality as a strategy for working with wicked problems. Landsc. Urban Plan. **154**, 8–10 (2016)
4. Loorbach, D.: Transition management for sustainable development: a prescriptive, complexity-based governance framework. Governance **23**, 161–183 (2010)
5. Legacy, C.: Is there a crisis of participatory planning? Plan. theory. **16**, 425–442 (2017)
6. Albrechts, L.: Reframing strategic spatial planning by using a coproduction perspective. Plan. theory. **12**, 46–63 (2013)

7. Innes, J.E., Booher, D.E.: Planning with complexity: an introduction to collaborative rationality for public policy. Routledge (2018). https://doi.org/10.4324/9781315147949

8. Healey, P.: Planning through debate: the communicative turn in planning theory. In: The Argumentative Turn in Policy Analysis and Planning, pp. 233–253. Duke University Press (2013)

9. Salen, K., Zimmerman, E.: Rules of play: game design fundamentals. MIT Press, Cambridge, Massachusetts, USA (2004)

10. Elias, G.S., Garfield, R., Gutschera, K.R.: Characteristics of games. MIT Press, Cambridge, Massachusetts, USA (2012)

11. Dodig, M.B., Groat, L.N.: The routledge companion to games in architecture and urban planning: tools for design, teaching, and research. Routledge (2019)

12. Tan, E.: Play the city: games informing the urban development. Jap Sam Books (2017)

13. Champlin, C.J., Flacke, J., Dewulf, G.P.M.R.: A game co-design method to elicit knowledge for the contextualization of spatial models. Environ. Plan. B Urban Anal. City Sci. 23998083211041372 (2021)

14. McCann, E.J.: Collaborative visioning or urban planning as therapy? The politics of public-private policy making. Prof. Geogr. **53**, 207–218 (2001)

15. Törnroth, S., Day, J., Fürst, M.F., Mander, S.: Participatory utopian sketching: a methodological framework for collaborative citizen (re) imagination of urban spatial futures. Futures **139**, 102938 (2022)

16. Purbani, K.: Collaborative planning for city development. A perspective from a city planner. Sci. Rev. Eng. Environ. Sci. **26**, 136–147 (2017). https://doi.org/10.22630/PNIKS.2017.26.1.12

17. Fisher, F.: Building bridges between citizens and local governments to work more effectively together: through participatory planning. UN-HABITAT (2001)

18. Healey, P.: Collaborative planning: shaping places in fragmented societies. Macmillan International Higher Education (1997)

19. Innes, J.E., Booher, D.E.: Consensus building and complex adaptive systems: a framework for evaluating collaborative planning. J. Am. Plan. Assoc. **65**, 412–423 (1999)

20. Corburn, J.: Bringing local knowledge into environmental decision making: improving urban planning for communities at risk. J. Plan. Educ. Res. **22**, 420–433 (2003)

21. Caspary, W.R.: Dewey on democracy. Cornell University Press (2000)

22. Moote, M.A., McClaran, M.P., Chickering, D.K.: Theory in practice: applying participatory democracy theory to public land planning. Environ. Manage. **21**, 877–889 (1997)

23. Brody, S.D., Godschalk, D.R., Burby, R.J.: Mandating citizen participation in plan making: six strategic planning choices. J. Am. Plan. Assoc. **69**, 245–264 (2003)

24. Mayer, I.: The gaming of policy and the politics of gaming: a review. Simul. Gaming. **40**, 825–862 (2009)

25. Innes, J.E., Booher, D.E.: Consensus buildings as role playing and bricolage. J. Am. Plan. Assoc. **65**, 9–26 (1999). https://doi.org/10.1080/01944369908976071

26. Goodspeed, R., Babbitt, C., Briones, A.L.G., Pfleiderer, E., Lizundia, C., Seifert, C.M.: Learning to manage common resources: stakeholders playing a serious game see increased interdependence in groundwater basin management. Water **12**, 1966 (2020)

27. Fox, N., Campbell-Arvai, V., Lindquist, M., Van Berkel, D., Serrano-Vergel, R.: Gamifying decision support systems to promote inclusive and engaged urban resilience planning. Urban Plan. **7** (2022)

28. Van Dijk, J.A.G.M.: The deepening divide: inequality in the information society. Sage publications (2005)

29. Billger, M., Kain, J.-H., Niwagaba, C.B., McConville, J.R.: Lessons from co-designing a resource-recovery game for collaborative urban sanitation planning. In: IOP Conference Series: Earth and Environmental Science, p. 42041 (2020)

30. Nakamura, J., Csikszentmihalyi, M.: Flow theory and research. Handb. Posit. Psychol. **195**, 206 (2009)

31. Ferri, G., Hansen, N.B., van Heerden, A., Schouten, B.A.M.: Design concepts for empowerment through urban play. DiGRA **2018**(1), 1–20 (2018)

32. Sousa, M., Antunes, A.P., Pinto, N.: Fast serious analogue games in planning : the role of non-player participants. Simul. Gaming 1–19 (2022). https://doi.org/10.1177/104687812110 73645

33. Booth, P.: Board games as media. Bloomsbury Publishing, USA (2021)

34. Calleja, G.: Unboxed: board game experience and design. MIT Press (2022)

35. Fullerton, T.: Game design workshop: a playcentric approach to creating innovative games. AK Peters/CRC Press (2014). https://doi.org/10.1201/b16671

36. Zagal, J.P., Rick, J., Hsi, I.: Collaborative games: lessons learned from board games. Simul. Gaming **37**, 24–40 (2006). https://doi.org/10.1177/1046878105282279

37. Rogerson, M.J., Gibbs, M.R., Smith, W.: Cooperating to compete: the mutuality of cooperation and competition in boardgame play. In: Proceedings of the 2018 CHI Conference on Human Factors in Computing Systems, pp. 1–13 (2018). https://doi.org/10.1145/3173574.3173767

38. Duarte, L.C.S., Battaiola, A.L., Silva, A.H.P.: Cooperation in Board Games. An. do XIV Simpósio Bras. Jogos e Entretenimento Digit. Soc. Bras. Comput. (2015)

39. Sousa, M.: Moving pieces and allocating budget together: a framework for using analog serious games in sustainable collaborative planning. Sustain. **16** (2024). https://doi.org/10. 3390/su16198348

40. Sousa, M.: Modeling urban spaces with cubes: building analogue serious games for collaborative planning. Int. J. Film Media Arts. **8**, 8–35 (2023)

41. Dörner, R., Göbel, S., Effelsberg, W., Wiemeyer, J.: Serious games. Springer (2016). https:// doi.org/10.1007/978-3-319-40612-1

42. Rouwette, E.A.J.A., Fokkema, E., van Kuppevelt, H.H.J.J., Peters, V.A.M.: Measuring MARCO POLIS management game's influence on market orientations. Simul. Gaming **29**, 420–431 (1998)

43. Mayer, I., et al.: The research and evaluation of serious games: toward a comprehensive methodology. Br. J. Educ. Technol. **45**, 502–527 (2014). https://doi.org/10.1111/bjet.12067

44. Van Empel, C.: The effectiveness of community participation in planning and urban development. WIT Trans. Ecol. Environ. **117**, 549–556 (2008)

45. Sousa, M.: Serious board games: modding existing games for collaborative ideation processes Modding board games to be serious games, vol. 8, pp. 129–147 (2021). https://doi.org/10. 17083/ijsg.v8i2.405

46. Kaner, S.: Facilitator's guide to participatory decision-making. Wiley (2014)

47. Wates, N.: The community planning handbook: how people can shape their cities, towns and villages in any part of the world. Routledge (2014)

48. BGG: Board Game Geek. https://boardgamegeek.com/

49. Roubira, L.: Dixit (2008)

50. Användbart Litet Företag: Telestrations (2009)

51. Palau, M.: Ikonikus (2013)

52. Sasaki, J.: A fake artist goes to New York, (2012)

53. Charmaz, K.: Constructing grounded theory. Sage (2014)

54. Calderon, C., Westin, M.: Understanding context and its influence on collaborative planning processes: a contribution to communicative planning theory. Int. Plan. Stud. **26**, 14–27 (2021)

55. Sousa, M., Antunes, A.P., Pinto, N., Zagalo, N.: Fast serious analogue games in planning: the role of non-player participants. Simul. Gaming **53**, 104687812110736 (2022). https://doi. org/10.1177/10468781211073645

56. Urbact: UrbSecurity: Planning Safer Cities. https://urbact.eu/networks/urbsecurity

57. Rumore, D., Schenk, T., Susskind, L.: Role-play simulations for climate change adaptation education and engagement. Nat. Clim. Chang. **6**, 745–750 (2016)
58. Wouters, P., van Nimwegen, C., van Oostendorp, H., van Der Spek, E.D.: A meta-analysis of the cognitive and motivational effects of serious games. J. Educ. Psychol. **105**, 249–265 (2013). https://doi.org/10.1037/a0031311

Games for Harm and Remedy: Using Video Games to Promote Sex Worker Rights

Miranda Verswijvelen$^{(\boxtimes)}$ and Holly Franklin

Geo AR Games, Auckland, New Zealand
`{Miranda,Holly}@geoar.com`

Abstract. Sex workers are often misrepresented in mainstream video games, reinforcing harmful stereotypes, marginalizing lived experiences, and creating associations with violence. This paper presents the design of two game prototypes that demonstrate how game design affordances can foster empathy and promote social change. The prototypes advocate for sex worker rights while challenging conventional portrayals. Though different in approach, both leverage the persuasive power of games: one engages players with the political history of sex work decriminalization in New Zealand, while the other cultivates human connections with non-player characters to encourage destigmatization. Both designs are grounded in Ruberg's [19] feminist media analysis theory and employ distinct methodological approaches. The first game design applies Aristotelian rhetoric, and the second game uses empathy-focused design strategies. The design process also involved close collaboration with the Aotearoa New Zealand Sex Workers' Collective (NZPC) to ensure accurate representation. The designers aim not only to challenge players' conscious and unconscious biases but also to promote guidelines on how to create authentic representations of sex workers and their communities in future designs of video games.

Keywords: Video Games · Sex Worker Rights · Decriminalisation · Persuasive games · Destigmatisation · Sex Work · Prostitute · Hooker

1   Introduction

Two entrenched stereotypes dominate mainstream media portrayals of sex workers: the "happy hooker" fantasy and the trauma-porn victim narrative. In the former, exemplified by Pretty Woman (1990), Secret Diary of a Call Girl (2007–2011), and The Girlfriend Experience (2009; 2016–2021), sex workers are framed as glamorous, empowered, and emotionally fulfilled, glossing over the material realities of stigma, precarity, and systemic violence. In the latter, typified by Law & Order: SVU, Requiem for a Dream (2000), and Leaving Las Vegas (1995), sex workers are depicted as broken figures defined by addiction, victimisation, and despair. Together, these polarised depictions erase the diversity of lived experiences and reinforce punitive social attitudes toward sex work.

van der Meulen and Durisin's [25] analysis demonstrates that sex workers are consistently portrayed either as victims in need of rescue or as threats to public health and

© The Author(s) 2026
F. Trautwein et al. (Eds.): ISAGA 2025, LNCS 16439, pp. 103–118, 2026.
https://doi.org/10.1007/978-3-032-20129-4_8

moral order. Weitzer [27] similarly critiques these binary portrayals for entrenching marginalisation while denying sex workers' agency. The enduring popularity of Pretty Woman epitomises this dynamic: as McLaughlin [16] argues, the film sanitises prostitution through the rescue fantasy, offering redemption only through romantic escape rather than systemic change.

In one of the fastest growing forms of media, video games, these issues are very prominent. Sex workers rarely have names or a specific role in a game, nor do their characterisations allow players to explore the issues that these individuals face in day-to-day reality. Moreover, sex workers mostly appear in situations that include violence.

In recent decades, the power of games is increasingly employed to promote prosocial behaviour or social and emotional learning. In this paper, we present a project that intends to turn the tables on the representation of sex work in games by using the medium to promote sex worker rights and tackle destigmatisation. We report on the early prototyping phase of two video games, co-designed with subject matter experts connected to the Aotearoa New Zealand Sex Workers' Collective (NZPC).

2 Background

2.1 Theoretical Perspective

Drawing on Ruberg [19], this paper employs a feminist framework to analyse media representations of sex work. Ruberg critiques mainstream feminist scholarship for predominantly using sex work portrayals as examples of women's objectification. This view neglects the insight that the systematic devaluation of sex work as legitimate labour actually inflicts greater harm on women [19]. Following Fullagar's [6] assertion that feminist media analysis must centre the lived experiences of those being represented, the current project recognises that those involved in sex work are uniquely positioned to identify the harms caused by misrepresentation [28]. Accordingly, we develop our game prototypes in active collaboration with subject matter experts from sex worker collectives.

2.2 The Representation of Sex Work in Video Games

Sex worker characters have been fixtures in video games since early titles like Sierra's infamous Leisure Suit Larry (1988). However, as Evans and Tarver [4] point out, the troubling conflation of violence and sex work in game narratives is a relatively recent phenomenon. Much media and scholarly criticism has misdirected its focus, targeting the erotic portrayal of sex worker non-player characters (NPCs) rather than confronting the violence that frequently surrounds their presence in game worlds. This critical oversight reflects broader societal tendencies to moralise sexuality while overlooking systemic violence against marginalised groups. Scholars like Bezio [1] and Ruberg [19] have begun challenging this analytical gap, arguing that the problem lies not in the sexual representation itself, but in how games position sex workers as disposable bodies meant to absorb player violence without narrative consequence.

Grand Theft Auto V [18] allows players to buy sex workers' services and subsequently rob or kill them. A YouTube video with 3.6 million views exemplifies this: after purchasing sex acts, the player jokes, "in regular GTA fashion, you can't let her get away with your money," then runs over, shoots, and incinerates the woman [11]. This action is enabled by the game's open mechanics rather than a specific design choice [8]. However, while such violence in the game is not exclusively related to sex workers, the harm lies in denying sex workers agency, reducing them to disposable props, and reinforcing their cultural devaluation [19].

In contrast, Baldur's Gate 3 [12] offers a rare, respectful depiction of sex work. The brothel in the game is populated with named characters who have distinct identities, agency, and intrinsic value. As an example, the Drow twins, present in the brothel, are depicted as autonomous participants instead of disposable NPCs. In one interaction (Fig. 1), Nym Orlith refuses a player's request for rough sex, underscoring the consensual nature of the exchange.

Fig. 1. Nym Orlith, Drow sex worker in the game Baldur's Gate 3 [12], rejects players' requests for rough sex. Copyright © 2023 Larian Studios. Used under Fair Dealing Provision.

The harmful impact of sex work representation in gaming therefore, stems not from its mere inclusion, but from the systematic devaluation and dehumanization of sex worker characters. As Hoffin and Lee-Treweek [9] demonstrate, these portrayals actively contribute to rape culture by normalising the misconception that violence and exploitation are intrinsic elements of sex work rather than products of criminalisation and stigma. *Baldur's Gate 3* offers a notable counterexample by depicting sex workers as autonomous agents with respected boundaries, positioning players as welcomed clients rather than dominant figures. The contrast highlights that sex work itself isn't inherently problematic in gaming narratives. It is the perpetuation of harmful tropes and exploitative mechanical interactions that cause societal damage by reinforcing dangerous behaviours [7, 9].

3 Designing Video Games to Shift Perception

3.1 Game Design for Empathy and Compassion

While some of the examples demonstrate that games can move beyond simplistic depictions and engage with themes of labour, autonomy, and societal perception, representation is still far from ideal. Moreover, the main purpose of the games discussed earlier is to entertain, with only partial scenes dedicated to sex work. A large body of research discusses the power of games for learning and behaviour change [8, 15]. This includes enhancing compassion, empathy, and associated skills and concepts, often by placing players amidst other's struggles [20].

Some voices warn to nuance this power of games, rightly stating that creators need to accept that a digital game can never confer a full understanding of a lived experience, including marginalisation in society or personal struggle [2]. However, while not resulting in full understanding, games can at least create reminiscences and comparisons with past personal experiences if not a total understanding of another's plight [2, 3].

3.2 Design Principles for Empathy Games

In a recent UNESCO report [5] researchers identified the following three design recommendations to evoke player empathy. A game's narrative needs to encourage player exploration and integrate commonplace interactions in the narrative world, expanding the player's interactive opportunities instead of providing only major decisions. Moreover, it needs to support the player to build relationships with NPCs, building trust and intimacy over time. The report also suggests that reducing the opportunity to make meaningful choices can be a powerful driver for empathy. A poignant example of the last technique is Zoe Quinn's Depression Quest (2013), a text-based game where the strikethrough of options simulates how burdensome some mundane decisions can feel for someone suffering from depression. Quinn uses a perceived loss of agency to evoke empathy in the player, demonstrating the connection between agency and emotions [10, 23].

The US-based iThrive Games Foundation suggests an empathy model (Fig. 2) that identifies six essential design features which promote empathic feelings and/or behaviour in games [14].

First there is "perspective taking", which can be achieved by providing players with opportunities to embody different characters in the narrative, or by allowing them to make decisions about the relative importance of other characters. Experimentation with different personalities also allows players to practice "emotional regulation", the second feature of the model, which can be as straightforward as selecting a kind or less kind dialogue option. A third feature, "empathetic accuracy" can be interpreted as predicting the emotions of other game characters. For example, when an NPC has an emotional back story, the player may need to make a decision that can impact the NPC's feelings.

Game designers can achieve "emotion contagion" by aligning all game elements to express a specific emotion that the designer wants the player to feel. In addition, a game can instil a feeling of melancholy by presenting all NPCs as sad and adding music and visuals to enhance this atmosphere. Another example of emotion contagion is

Fig. 2. Components of Empathy Model by IThrive. From IThrive Games Foundation (2018). iThrive design kit: Empathy. Retrieved from https://ithrivegames.org/resources/game-design-kits/. Used under Fair Dealing Provision.

introducing an NPC who other NPCs have discussed negatively earlier in the game, which may bias the player against them. Finally, "perspective engagement" provides players with opportunities to care deeply, and have "concern for others". The discovery of an NPC's back story is an example of a narrative technique that supports this component of the model.

iThrive's model provides a useful tool to support the multi-faceted approach to detailed design to elicit player emotion, which we needed for the prototype designs described in this paper. It shows the complex interplay of all narrative design elements to achieve desired results: character design for players and NPCs, meaningful choices and dialogue, and non-verbal narrative design elements.

4 Two Game Prototypes Addressing Decriminalisation and Destigmatisation

Leveraging the insights gleaned from empathetic game design, this paper proposes two distinct game concepts, arising out of a need to target two lanes of the conversation, that is, the changing of the law and the challenging of stigma.

These games - developed in close consultation with a sex worker advocacy group - aim to directly challenge the societal perceptions of sex work, by humanising and destigmatising the sex workers themselves. The two games employ specific narrative and interactive techniques to create experiences that foster empathy and advocacy, with a goal of creating meaningful societal change.

4.1 One Vote: The Decriminalisation Game

One Vote is a serious game that places the player amid a historically significant legislative moment: the 2003 decriminalization of sex work in New Zealand, achieved by a single vote, leading to the Prostitution Reform Act 2003. This bill decriminalised sex work (excluding for migrants), and allowed sex workers to unionise, act as independent contractors and operate without fear of police harassment or arrest [17]. The game reframes sex workers not as damsels in distress, nor as objects, but as constituents fighting for civil rights.

Players enter OneVote as the winner of a recent by-election, on the first days of their new political career. Upon arrival at Wellington (the capital city of New Zealand, where the government is located) they meet Lily, a transgender sex worker, at a bus stop. The police arrive, interrogate Lily, and arrest her for having condoms in her purse. The player is powerless and cannot prevent this from happening. This design choice is deliberate. Having the introduction strip the player of agency draws on the principle that removing the opportunity to make a meaningful impact is a powerful driver of empathy [5]. It immediately situates the player inside the systemic violence sex workers face daily under criminalisation, grounding emotional engagement in injustice, rather than spectacle.

The player's journey continues through a series of character stories. Each encounter provides information that must be strategically brought into parliamentary debates to influence the final vote. Advocacy—not action heroics—becomes the true "superpower." Players are rewarded for careful listening, for understanding, and for persuasive argument. Rather than framing success through domination or saviour tropes, One Vote intentionally positions the player as an advocate, a supporting character in a larger civil rights movement. The game's narrative complexity engages with Sicart's concept of the "wicked problem," where clear moral binaries dissolve, and challenges players to form and articulate their own stances [22].

To deepen the persuasive impact of One Vote, the game draws explicitly from classical rhetorical frameworks. Specifically, it utilises a persuasion mechanic based on Aristotelian rhetoric—Ethos, Pathos, and Logos (Fig. 3). This framework is particularly fitting for a political game, aligning with Aristotle's argument that "political speech should bridge the gaps between the public and private spheres, passions and reason, individual interests and the common good, equity and law" [24, p.742]. Each primary NPC represents an element of this triad (see Appendix A). Lily embodies Pathos, designed to evoke emotional resonance and draw on the player's empathy. Fiona, the head of the New Zealand Sex Workers Collective, anchors Ethos, providing a moral and ethical center. Mia, a migrant sex worker, embodies Logos; her story unfolds as a litany of injustices that expose the systemic and structural inequalities faced by marginalized individuals. Through this rhetorical structure, One Vote aims not only to persuade players of the importance of legislative change but also to foster systemic empathy by linking personal narratives to broader political contexts.

The game inverts the hero's tale of traditional games. The player's role as a politician is deliberate as it places them in a position of relative power. However, - the game emphatically does not want the player to play a 'white knight' here. They are the supporting character - advocacy unlocks success, but the victory is collective.

To further ground the emotional weight, and strengthen emotional resonance of the experience, the first working prototype of *One Vote* uses Metahuman technology and VR. By creating a realistic, embodied environment, the game leverages findings that suggest

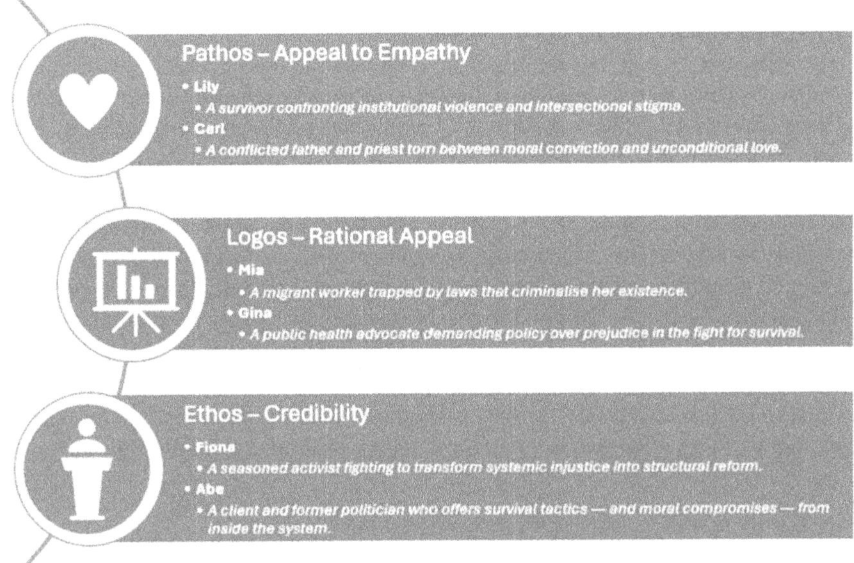

Fig. 3. Application of the Aristotelian Rhetoric within the game design of OneVote.

higher realism strengthens emotional impact and persuasive power [21]. Importantly, players do not "become" sex workers in the game; they advocate for them. This maintains a sex worker-first approach while sidestepping the pitfalls of false embodiment. By equipping players with facts, emotional insight, and rhetorical tools, *One Vote* aims to cultivate not just empathy, but meaningful allyship—a small step towards progressing societal acceptance and pushing towards full decriminalisation.

4.2 Safe Haven: A Cosy Game to Promote Destigmatisation

Cosy games emphasise safe low-risk environments and comforting aesthetics, providing players with a sense of security and well-being [13]. Despite their casual appearance, this genre has increasingly been utilised as a vehicle to explore serious topics within protective emotional frameworks. "Spiritfarer" (2020) exemplifies this approach: a cosy management game that addresses themes of death and grief. It demonstrates how the genre can facilitate engagement with sensitive subjects while maintaining player comfort.

We therefore selected this game genre to carry the gameplay and content for destigmatisation. In "Safe Haven", players assume the role of a newly-appointed interior designer who creates personalised spaces for residents in a town. Through conversations with townspeople about their design preferences, players develop relationships. The player progressively discovers that several town inhabitants are or were sex workers. These revelations are presented with the same narrative weight as discovering other professional roles (e.g. The town mayor or local mechanic) establishing an overall atmosphere of normalisation and acceptance. The gameplay alternates between furniture placement, decoration and conversation, allowing the interactive narrative to reveal the everyday challenges faced by the sex workers.

The game design actively applies design features that encourage empathetic gameplay (Fig. 4). The social interaction with NPCs and gradual involvement in their everyday lives encourages player's perspective taking and perspective engagement. Player empathy is leveraged as they gain insights in previously unknown lives and develop a growing interest in the character's back stories. At the same time, this facilitates non-confrontational examination of the player's personal biases about sex work. Carefully structured narrative discovery encourages alignment with character's feelings. For example, players meet Tyra, the town librarian who supplements her income through erotic webcam performances. As trust and friendship develop, she reveals aspirations to establish a business, providing safe working spaces for other webcam artists. However, she faces institutional discrimination when seeking financial services - banks demonstrate bias against her business model despite its legality. Similarly, other townsfolk encounter stigma-based issues related to family relationships, insurance and housing.

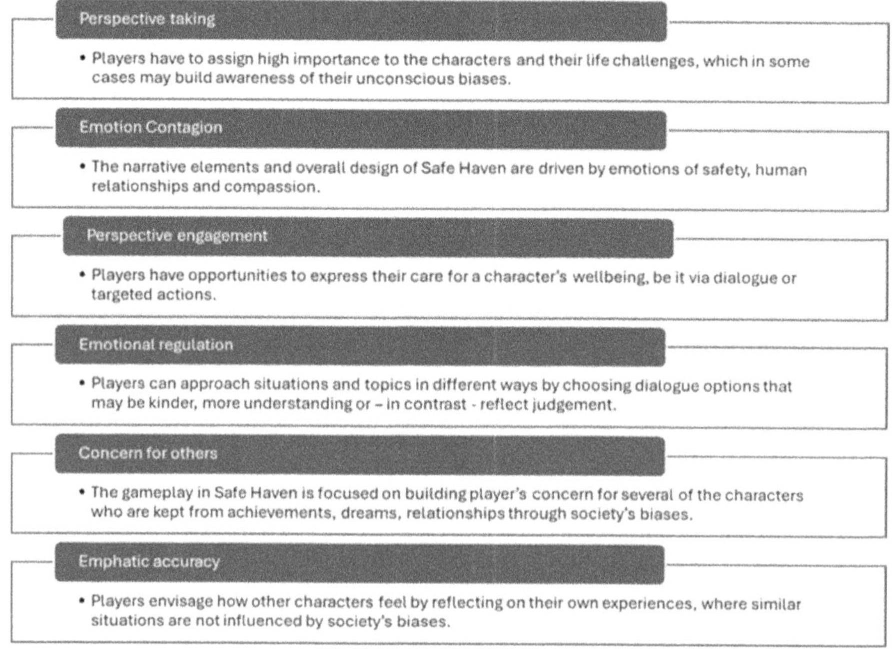

Fig. 4. Application of the iThrive empathy model within the game design for the Safe Haven game prototype.

Safe Haven capitalises on players' desire for connection by building personalised relationships. Linking characters to the emotions portrayed in the game makes characters relatable – regardless of whether they are likable. Universal themes, such as family bonds, loss, loneliness or friendship can significantly deepen players' connections with game characters [26]. Through community-building and empathy, embodied by low-stress, enjoyable and safe gameplay and creating a need to listen, the game aims to show the player that sex workers are professional individuals, not different from people with other jobs. From that viewpoint, showing their struggles with ordinary problems evokes the player's compassion.

5 Iterative Design with Expert Input

The games' development happens at a slow pace, leaving ample space for research, and consultancy with sex work experts.

5.1 Pre-development Workshops

Initially, weekly pre-workshop development sessions were founded on collaboration with subject matter experts, whose generosity in sharing their lived experience, political insight, and deep foundational knowledge fundamentally shaped the project's direction. Early sessions focused on exploring how interactive media could authentically represent sex work advocacy, with the development team offering guidance on the capacities of games for fostering empathy and change. However, it was the subject-matter experts who provided the essential foundation: opening their networks, sharing the complex legal and social realities they navigate daily, and grounding the designs in truths that no external research could replicate. Their contributions were not just advisory but transformational, in some cases confronting team members with their own unconscious biases. This collaborative relationship ensures that as the games evolve, they remain not only authentic and ethically sound but deeply accountable to the communities they aim to represent [28].

5.2 Workshop 1: Prototype Testing

A first workshop focused on prototype testing involved two distinct participant groups of six participants consisting of game developers not involved in the project and subject-matter experts. During this session, both groups of participants engaged with both games.

For Safe Haven, players attended a guided playthrough of a paper prototype emulating a board game experience of the envisaged mechanics. For OneVote, participants evaluated a text-based digital interactive narrative designed in Yarnspinner, an interactive fiction tool.

Results revealed design insights across both prototypes. The complexity of the layered cosy gameplay mechanics in Safe Haven emerged as a barrier to player engagement in the narrative. However, participants valued the contemplative pacing and emotional respite the experience provided.

Feedback on OneVote highlighted that the protagonist's characterisation aligned too closely with problematic tropes. In addition, the dense content delivery using YarnSpinner overwhelmed players. These findings provided direction for subsequent prototype refinements.

5.3 Workshop 2: Revised Prototype Testing and Narrative Expansion

The second workshop featured a plenary session where adapted game concepts were presented to all participants for comprehensive evaluation.

The Safe Haven presentation incorporated finalised artwork for both the cosy gameplay, and the narrative sequences of the game. Additionally, subject matter experts read a web-based exploration of all character storylines in interactive format and were invited to play a sample of the interior design activities.

For OneVote, to prevent content overwhelm, facilitators conducted guided verbal playthroughs focusing on three storylines identified as central to the narrative. Participant feedback revealed areas requiring refinement across both prototypes. For Safe Haven, concerns emerged regarding terminology used in character descriptions, which required greater sensitivity and authenticity. Additionally, participants questioned the aesthetic coherence of transitioning between 2D art assets and pixel art styles, suggesting a need for greater visual consistency. The OneVote prototype garnered more historically-oriented feedback, with participants offering detailed critique regarding the accuracy of depicted discussions surrounding the New Zealand Prostitution Reform Act 2003, emphasising the importance of aligning fictional narrative elements with the historic reality of legislative development and advocacy. These insights provided targeted direction for future development.

6   Limitations and Future Work

The ongoing development and production of these games remains contingent upon securing additional funding resources in the coming years. In the interim period, there exists significant potential to leverage the established characters and conceptual frameworks across diverse creative outputs that support the NZPC initiatives focusing on destigmatisation and awareness.

Cross-media application will extend the impact of the original research while reinforcing consistent messaging across platforms. Furthermore, this project aims to produce comprehensive best practice guidelines for the ethical and authentic portrayal of sex workers in video games—an area currently lacking in standardised industry guidance. These guidelines will address representation gaps while providing developers with concrete frameworks to avoid harmful stereotypes and mischaracterisations that have historically dominated media depictions of sex work and sex workers.

7   Conclusion

Through the two game design prototypes discussed in this paper, we hope to contribute positively to the portrayal of sex workers in video games, by offering counter narratives to the more common representation in entertainment video games.

These games directly answer the challenge posed as they represent sex workers as full and nuanced characters - they have agency, a purpose, and the interactions with them are not to fulfil any base desire of the player. The games will reward the player for being open, empathetic and strategically kind. The games assume that players have some level of acceptance of sex worker rights, and do not claim to be able to change the minds of those convinced otherwise. However, they may encourage a more tasteful representation of sex work in video games, mindful of the context and individuals within the profession.

Disclosure of Interests. Holly Franklin and Miranda Verswijvelen were employed by Geo AR Games and conducted this research as part of their employment. This research was funded by Geo AR Games. While the authors have endeavoured to maintain objectivity, readers should be aware of this potential conflict of interest when evaluating the findings presented in this paper.

Appendix

Table 1. Characters and their game function in the OneVote game

Character	Themes	Rhetorical Mode	Narrative Function
Fiona	Advocacy under criminalisation, grassroots organising, ethical leadership	Ethos	Fiona embodies the tempered, battle-worn optimism of a long-term activist who understands both the hope and the exhaustion of fighting structural injustice. While deeply committed to sex worker rights, she is no idealist: she knows advocacy is often a negotiation with ugly systems and imperfect allies. Fiona is sharp, strategic, and quietly furious—but channels her fire into careful, relentless political work. Her role in the narrative is not to preach purity, but to model resilient, strategic resistance that refuses to sacrifice dignity for expediency. Through Fiona, the player encounters the reality that changing a system requires not only courage, but discipline, coalition, and unglamorous persistence
Lily	Transphobia, racialised policing, colonial legal structures, survival under stigma	Pathos	Functions as the emotional and moral fulcrum of the narrative. Her experiences highlight the legacy of colonial law and the ongoing marginalisation of transgender and Pacific communities. Initiates the player's confrontation with institutional violence and demands recognition of intersectional vulnerability
Mia	Migrant exploitation, legal precarity, labor vulnerability, survival ethics, system-rigged injustice	Logos	Embodies the unsolvable logic of structural oppression. Mia's life is a brutal cascade of cause-and-effect failures engineered by the immigration and labor systems: a puzzle where every answer leads to punishment. Her story resists simple emotional catharsis; instead, it confronts the player with an inescapable rational conclusion: survival is impossible within a system designed to criminalise existence. Through Mia, the player is forced to accept that systemic reform isn't about individual moral failings or bad luck—it's about the rigged design of the rules themselves

(continued)

Table 1. (*continued*)

Character	Themes	Rhetorical Mode	Narrative Function
Gina	healthcare disparities, public health infrastructure, harm reduction	Logos	Embodies the pragmatism of public health activism. Gina channels lived experience into a cold, clear articulation of how criminalisation policies breed disease and death. She rejects moral grandstanding in favor of empirical proof, showing that survival depends not on judgment, but on transparency, resources, and systemic reform. Through her, the player encounters the harsh reality that facts—not moral panic—win public health wars. Gina demands strategic thinking from the player: to argue not for sympathy, but for *results*
Carl	Familial estrangement, moral conflict, religious values vs. lived experience	Pathos	Offers a deeply personal view of the ideological and emotional tensions around sex work. As a priest grappling with his daughter's precarious situation after being kicked out of their home, Carl embodies the collision between institutional morality and personal love. Challenges the player to confront the human cost of abstract moral judgments.
Abe	Loneliness, societal taboo, shifting masculinity norms, blackmail	Ethos	Abe represents the collision of systemic cynicism and human vulnerability. As a former politician and current client, he understands both how the system fails and how individuals survive within it. He offers the player insider knowledge and morally ambiguous strategies, including the possibility of blackmail, framed not as corruption but as protection for a community he has come to care for personally. His loneliness, loyalty, and willingness to get his hands dirty create a complex moral tension, forcing the player to grapple with whether purity or effectiveness best serves justice

Table 2. Character stories in Safe Haven

Character	Life summary	Challenge	Interior design request
Tyra Feathers	Town librarian and erotic webcam artist. She dreams of her own webcam business, a safe place where she and others can perform and earn well	Encounters bias from banks who refuse bank accounts and business investment despite solid financial plans	Decoration of a cosy comfortable waiting space for the webcam performers between performances
Molly Fairchild	Retired dominatrix with a rock band past, having left her family at 16. Lives quietly in Safe Haven	Craves a closer, grandmother-like relationship with her only niece who is nine but is judged by her family because of her past in sex work	Design of a young girl's room for when her niece comes for a sleepover
Sage Holloway	Sex worker and business owner of Safe Haven's small brothel. Mum of three, wife of Bruce, a former client, and balancing work with motherhood	Sage's children sometimes face bullying situations at school because of their mother's work even though her eldest children are fully aware of her work	A cool rumpus room with a TV, game console and ping pong table to create a fun space for kids where they can have their friends for visits

References

1. Bezio, K.M.: Ctrl-Alt-Del: GamerGate as a precursor to the rise of the alt-right. Leadership **14**(5), 556–566 (2018). https://doi.org/10.1177/1742715018793744
2. d'Anastasio, C.: Why video games can't teach you empathy. Vice, 16 May 2015. https://www.vice.com/en/article/mgbwpv/empathy-games-dont-exist
3. Dussault, J.: Empathy games tread a thin line between 'edutainment' and virtual voyeurism. The Christian Science Monitor, 20 September 2017. https://www.csmonitor.com/Technology/2017/0920/Empathy-games-tread-thin-line-between-edutainment-and-virtual-voyeurism
4. Evans, K., Tarver, E.: Sex workers and video games: an exploration of the relationship between sex work, gender, and violence in AAA game titles. First Person Scholar (2017). https://www.firstpersonscholar.com/sex-workers-and-video-games/
5. Farber, M., Schrier, K.: The strengths and limitations of using digital games as "empathy machines," working paper for the UNESCO MGIEP (Mahatma Gandhi Institute of Education for Peace and Sustainable Development (2017)
6. Fullagar, S., Rich, E., Pavlidis, A., van Ingen, C.: Feminist knowledges as interventions in physical cultures. Leis. Sci. **41**(1–2), 1–16 (2019). https://doi.org/10.1080/01490400.2018.1551163
7. Game Assist.: "The Oldest Game": Gender-based violence, exploitation and sex workers' rights in video games. YouTube (2021)
8. Gee, J.P.: What video games have to teach us about learning and literacy, New York (2003)

9. Hoffin, K., Lee-Treweek, G.: The normalisation of sexual deviance and sexual violence in video games. In: Video Games Crime and Next-Gen Deviance: Reorienting the Debate, pp. 151–174. Emerald Publishing Limited (2020)

10. Isbister, K.: How Games Move Us: Emotion by Design. The MIT Press (2016)

11. JoblessGarrett: GTA 5 first person - picking up a prostitute! GTA V hooker pick up [Video]. YouTube (2014). https://www.youtube.com/watch?v=u7__X3B3Vkk

12. Larian Studios: Baldur's Gate 3 [Computer game]. Larian Studios (2023)

13. Lambertsen, C.: What Cozy Games Are (& What Cozy Gaming Really Means). ScreenRant, 7 October 2024. https://screenrant.com/what-cozy-gaming-really-means/

14. McDonald, H.: Making them care: The narrative burden for creating empathy [Video File]. YouTube (2018). https://www.youtube.com/watch?v=-fR27Ad9lPQ

15. McGonigal, J.: Reality Is Broken. Vintage (2012)

16. McLaughlin, L.: Discourses of prostitution/discourses of sexuality. Crit. Stud. Mass Commun. **8**(3), 249–272 (1991)

17. New Zealand Prostitutes Collective: Decriminalisation of sex work in New Zealand. [Brochure] (2013). https://www.nzpc.org.nz/pdfs/Video-Booklet-Decriminalisation_of_Sex_Work_in_New_Zealand.pdf

18. Rockstar North: Grand Theft Auto V [PlayStation 3]. Rockstar Games (2013)

19. Ruberg, B.: Representing sex workers in video games: feminisms, fantasies of exceptionalism, and the value of erotic labor. Fem. Media Stud. **19**(3), 313–330 (2019)

20. Schrier, K., Farber, M.: A systematic literature review of 'empathy' and 'games.' J. Gaming Virtual Worlds **13**(2), 195–214 (2021). https://doi.org/10.1386/jgvw_00036_1

21. Seiffert, J., Nothhaft, H.: The missing media: the procedural rhetoric of computer games. Public Relat. Rev. **41**(2), 254–263 (2015)

22. Sicart, M.: Moral dilemmas in computer games. Des. Issues **29**(3), 28–37 (2013)

23. Salter, A.: Playing at empathy: representing and experiencing emotional growth through Twine games [Paper presentation]. In: IEEE International Conference on Serious Games and Applications for Health (SeGAH), Orlando, Florida, USA, 11–13 May 2016

24. Triadafilopoulos, T.: Politics, speech, and the art of persuasion: toward an Aristotelian conception of the public sphere. J. Polit. **61**(3), 741–757 (1999)

25. van der Meulen, E., Durisin, E.M.: Why decriminalize? How Canada's municipal and federal regulations increase sex workers' vulnerability. Can. J. Women Law **20**(2), 289–311 (2008)

26. Verswijvelen, M.: Reimagining the virtual patient: Crafting Game-inspired Interactive Stories for Compassion Training. Doctoral Thesis, Auckland University of Technology, Auckland (2024)

27. Weitzer, R.: Resistance to sex work stigma. Sexualities **21**(5–6), 717–729 (2017). e10.1177/1363460716684509. (Original work published 2018)

28. Trans Empowerment: Nothing About Us Without Us: Sex Work HIV Policy Organizing. Transgender Empowerment. Research report by Best Practices Policy Project and Desiree Alliance (2015). http://www.bestpracticespolicy.org/wp-content/uploads/2015/10/NOTHINGABOUTUS_REPORT_COLOR_2015.pdf

MyCrystalBall - A Game-Based Learning and Foresight Framework Based on PETIES

Christian K. Karl[(⊠)] [iD]

University of Duisburg-Essen, Universitätsstr. 15, 45141 Essen, Germany
`christian.karl@uni-due.de`

Abstract. Digital transformation creates both opportunities and uncertainties, demanding approaches that anticipate systemic impacts while fostering collaboration and reflection. Traditional foresight methods often remain abstract and lack experiential components that support participatory learning. MyCrystalBall addresses this gap through a game-based learning approach that integrates foresight, systems thinking, and interactive decision-making. The game is structured around the newly developed PETIES framework (Politics, Economy, Technology, Individual, Education, Society), which extends classical strategic management models such as PESTEL by emphasizing the human and educational dimensions of transformation. Within this framework, participants analyze systemic interdependencies and explore cascading effects of innovation across multiple domains. Results from two exploratory sessions on Big Data in construction and VR/AR in HVAC systems illustrate that successful digital transformation depends on the alignment of political, technological, and societal factors. Thus, MyCrystalBall represents a versatile and practical framework for foresight and collaborative learning, enabling participants to navigate uncertainty, enhance systems thinking, and co-create strategies for sustainable innovation in an increasingly VUCA world.

Keywords: Digital Transformation · Foresight · Game-Based Learning · Innovation · PETIES Framework · Scenario Planning · Strategic Foresight · Systems Thinking · VUCA

1 The Need for Experiential Foresight

Digital transformation and the rapid diffusion of emerging technologies create both unprecedented opportunities and significant uncertainty. Navigating these developments requires strategic foresight, systems thinking, and the ability to anticipate and define complex problems within their contextual environments. Developing actionable solutions in such settings demands openness, creativity, and effective communication across disciplines and audiences.

Traditional foresight methods, however, often remain abstract and lack interactive elements that engage participants in collaborative, experiential learning. To address this gap, MyCrystalBall was developed as a turn-based, multi-actor board game that integrates design thinking, foresight, and systems thinking. The game simulates future

© The Author(s) 2026

F. Trautwein et al. (Eds.): ISAGA 2025, LNCS 16439, pp. 119–129, 2026.

https://doi.org/10.1007/978-3-032-20129-4_9

challenges and enables participants to evaluate long-term implications of technological and social innovations through structured scenario-based exercises. By engaging in role-based decision-making, players practice identifying systemic interdependencies, debating strategic choices, and reflecting on possible outcomes.

This paper introduces MyCrystalBall and presents empirical findings from four exploratory sessions. For this contribution, we focus on two scenarios most relevant to digital transformation: the integration of Virtual and Augmented Reality (VR/AR) in HVAC systems and the adoption of Big Data and analytics in construction and real estate. These sessions highlight critical dynamics at the intersection of technology, society and policy, making them highly illustrative of digital transformation processes [1].

Other sessions (automation in construction through robotics, and sustainable housing concepts) are briefly referenced but analyzed in detail elsewhere. The focus here is on demonstrating how MyCrystalBall can serve as a versatile tool for foresight, innovation and collaborative learning in contexts shaped by uncertainty and rapid technological change.

2 Foundations of Game-Based Foresight

Strategic foresight is a key competence for navigating technological and societal transformation. Traditional methods such as scenario planning, Delphi studies or trend analysis provide structured approaches but often face limitations: they are linear, struggle with wicked problems [2], and tend to lack engagement and practical applicability [3, 4]. In our own workshops, some participants even described these methods as "too abstract to be useful", which is a telling sign of their limitations in practice.

Game-based learning (GBL) has emerged as an effective response to these shortcomings. Rooted in experiential and constructivist theories, GBL promotes active learning, collaboration and problem-solving in immersive settings [5–8]. Studies show its effectiveness in diverse contexts, from engineering education [9] to environmental training [10] and medical education [11]. In line with these findings, our own sessions revealed how quickly participants immersed themselves in the gameplay, often forgetting that they were "just" in a foresight exercise. As a result, by combining structured foresight with interactive play, GBL fosters motivation, creativity and long-term retention.

Building on earlier research, MyCrystalBall continues a line of studies in which game-based approaches were applied to construction management and education [12, 13] as well as to disaster management training [14]. These projects demonstrate how simulation and gaming can foster decision-making under uncertainty, collaboration among stakeholders and systems thinking in practice. Related work has also explored decision behavior in auction environments [15], showing how serious games can model complex dynamics and support learning. This background provides the methodological foundation for applying game-based foresight to the challenges of digital transformation.

Beyond engagement, creativity, systems thinking and critical thinking are crucial theoretical foundations. Lateral thinking encourages unconventional approaches [16], while systems thinking highlights interdependencies and unintended consequences [17]. Critical thinking supports evidence-based judgments in uncertain contexts [18]. Foresight methodologies build on these competencies by systematically exploring possible futures and testing adaptive strategies [19, 20].

Figure 1 illustrates the conceptual framework underlying MyCrystalBall, showing how different thinking modes in game-based learning (GBL) interrelate and collectively lead to foresight thinking (FT). The framework integrates creativity, lateral thinking, systems thinking, and critical thinking as complementary competencies that foster future-oriented learning and decision-making. Creativity acts as a meta-competence linking and enhancing the other three modes of thinking. In line with international frameworks such as the OECD Learning Compass, UNESCO's Futures Literacy approach, and the EU 21st-Century Skills framework, the model emphasizes competence in navigating uncertainty, connecting cognitive, social, and reflective dimensions of learning.

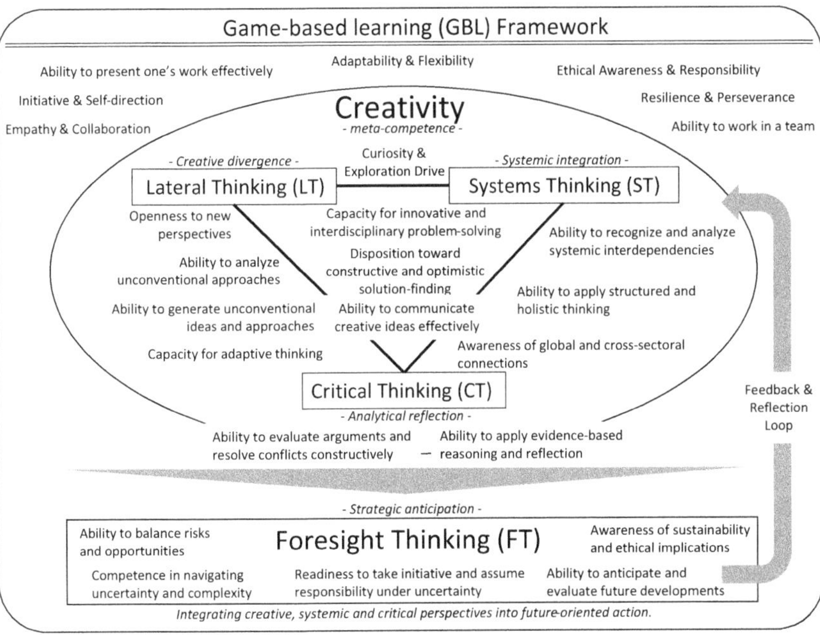

Fig. 1. Interrelation of thinking modes in game-based learning (GBL) leading to foresight thinking (FT) with exemplary competencies. (Own illustration).

Despite advancements, most foresight methods still emphasize passive knowledge transfer and isolated variables [21, 22]. Recent approaches like the Scenario Exploration System [23] show how games can bridge this gap, but few integrate both systemic analysis and interactive decision-making.

Building on these insights, MyCrystalBall provides a hands-on framework where participants actively explore systemic consequences of technological and societal innovations. Unlike computationally intensive simulations, the analog design keeps complexity manageable while maintaining analytical depth. This makes it particularly suitable for exploring sector-specific transformations such as digitalization, data-driven governance and the adoption of emerging technologies.

The initial concept of MyCrystalBall was developed during a research stay at the University of Cambridge (Faculty of Education, Design & Technology Education, Prof. Bill

Nicholl). This collaboration provided a foundation for integrating design-based learning principles into the foresight-oriented game design, emphasizing creativity, systemic reflection, and innovation literacy.

Especially innovation and foresight are closely interlinked. Foresight activities do not only anticipate change but also act as enablers of innovation by broadening perspectives and stimulating creative solutions. Classic models such as Rogers' Diffusion of Innovations [24] outline the systemic conditions under which innovations spread across societies, emphasizing the role of early adopters, social acceptance and contextual drivers. Similarly, foresight studies have shown how anticipatory practices can accelerate innovation by aligning technology development with societal and political needs [20, 21]. In this sense, MyCrystalBall positions itself at the interface of foresight and innovation: it provides a structured environment where participants explore not only possible futures but also the pathways by which innovations such as VR/AR or Big Data may succeed or fail. This dual focus reinforces the game's relevance as both a foresight tool and an innovation-oriented learning platform.

3 Methodology and Game Design

The development of MyCrystalBall followed a structured design process combining game-based learning, design thinking, and foresight methodologies. The aim was to create an accessible but analytically sound tool that fosters systems thinking, strategic foresight and collaborative problem-solving.

3.1 Conceptual Framework

The conceptual model integrates creativity, lateral thinking, systems thinking and foresight. Design thinking methods such as need-finding, ideation and iterative prototyping guided the game's development. For systemic analysis, the design draws on Vester's Paper Computer [25], enabling the classification of factors into active, critical and buffering roles. In the context of gameplay, these concepts are simplified into a scoring mechanism based on activity (Q) and passivity (P) values.

The six domains in MyCrystalBall, Politics, Economy, Technology, Individual, Education, and Society, are not only designed for gameplay purposes but also align with established frameworks in strategic management. A well-known example is the PESTEL analysis (Political, Economic, Social, Technological, Environmental, Legal), which structures environmental scanning and strategy development [26].

Building on this logic, MyCrystalBall introduces the PETIES framework (Politics, Economy, Technology, Individual, Education, Society), which extends the classical PESTEL model by emphasizing the human and educational dimensions of transformation. Education acts as a driver of workforce readiness and knowledge transfer, while Individual represents micro-level factors shaping adoption, perception, and acceptance.

This alignment demonstrates that the game does not reinvent analytical categories but rather operationalizes and enriches them in an interactive and systemic way. Consequently, MyCrystalBall can be understood as a hands-on, game-based extension of strategic management tools like PESTEL, enhanced through the PETIES perspective that combines analytical rigor with experiential learning.

3.2 Research Design and Data Collection

A mixed-methods approach was used to assess the game:

- Observation: Researchers monitored participant interactions, decision-making and engagement.
- Quantitative scoring: Players assessed systemic interrelations with an Excel-based tool, calculating simplified Q and P values.
- Group discussions: Guided reflections captured qualitative insights on foresight skills, teamwork and learning outcomes.

This triangulation ensured reliability while balancing analytical depth with playability. For this conference paper, the mathematical details are condensed; a full methodological treatment will be provided in forthcoming publications.

3.3 Game Design and Implementation

MyCrystalBall is a turn-based, multi-actor board game designed to foster systemic and critical thinking about complex, uncertain situations and to explore their multidimensional long-term impacts. Participants engage with innovation scenarios across six analytical domains, Politics, Economy, Technology, Individual, Education, and Society (PETIES), to examine interrelations and cascading effects of decisions.

The game facilitates knowledge sharing, reflection on values, and collective impact assessment through structured group discussion and effect analysis. The game material is deliberately straightforward, following the "Keep It Short and Simple" (KISS) principle [27]:

- Game board with the six domains (Fig. 2).
- Innovation, Event and Strategy cards to introduce technologies and disruptions.
- Voting chips to assign impact values.
- Excel tool for structured analysis and debriefing.

The game proceeds through six phases:

1. Context framing (Innovation Card introduction)
2. Domain team analysis
3. First impact assessment (voting chips, inner circle)
4. External disruptions & strategies (optional Event/Strategy cards)
5. Second impact assessment (outer circle, systemic influences)
6. Debriefing & reflection

Sessions typically last approx. 120 min, including briefing and structured debrief. Facilitators guide discussions, while participants collaboratively explore decision paths and reflect on systemic outcomes.

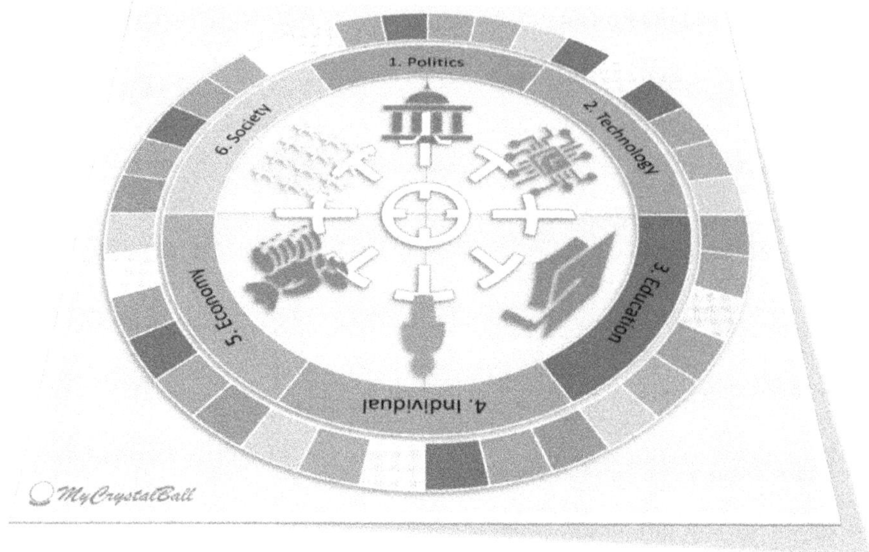

Fig. 2. Game board of MyCrystalBall integrating the PETIES framework (Politics, Economy, Technology, Individual, Education, Society) to structure the foresight analysis within the gameplay (Own illustration).

3.4 Application Contexts

The game has been tested with university students in engineering and construction programs. Its flexible design allows adaptation to other domains such as policy, business strategy or sustainability. The following sections present results from two sessions most relevant to digital transformation: VR/AR in HVAC systems and Big Data in construction and real estate.

4 Results

MyCrystalBall has been applied across multiple scenarios, including automation in construction through robotics, sustainable housing concepts, the adoption of Virtual and Augmented Reality (VR/AR), and the use of Big Data in construction and real estate. The following sections focus on the two scenarios most relevant to digital transformation: VR/AR and Big Data. These cases illustrate distinct systemic dynamics within the PETIES framework and address central challenges in the digital transformation of the construction and real estate sectors. Together, they provide a representative insight into the analytical capacity of the MyCrystalBall approach and demonstrate how the interplay between political, technological, and societal factors shapes the adoption of digital innovations.

4.1 VR/AR in HVAC Systems

This session explored the adoption of Virtual and Augmented Reality in the operation of HVAC systems (Heating, Ventilation, and Air Conditioning systems).

Findings

- Technology emerged as the strongest driver (highest Q-value), shaping regulations, market adoption and workforce training.
- Society was the most critical factor (highest P-value), indicating that trust, usability and workforce readiness largely determine adoption.
- Politics and Education played supportive roles, with regulation following technological developments and training needs increasing over time.
- Economy was less influential than expected, suggesting that financial incentives alone cannot overcome societal skepticism.

Key Insights

- Public trust and workforce adaptation are decisive. Without societal acceptance, technological progress remains limited.
- Regulation must address privacy, safety and ethical concerns, but adoption will depend on social readiness.
- Workforce training should integrate VR/AR competencies into HVAC curricula and provide targeted upskilling.

Takeaway. The session highlights that while VR/AR innovation is primarily technology-driven, its diffusion remains socially constrained. Sustainable adoption will depend on addressing public acceptance and workforce training in parallel with technical advancement. This observation is consistent with recent studies [28–30] and sector analyses on VR/AR readiness in construction [1].

4.2 Big Data in Construction and Real Estate

This session examined the systemic adoption of Big Data and analytics in construction and real estate.

Findings

- Politics emerged as the most active factor, shaping adoption through governance, standards and incentives.
- Technology was the most critical constraint, highlighting the need for digital infrastructure, AI-driven analytics and interoperable platforms.
- Economy and Education played secondary roles: incentives facilitated adoption, while digital skills training remained a growing need.

- Society and Individual factors influenced acceptance indirectly through trust in data governance.

Key insights

- Regulatory clarity and investment incentives are essential to accelerate adoption.
- Technological readiness (cloud, AI, data interoperability) ultimately determines feasibility.
- Financial incentives alone are insufficient without reliable digital infrastructure.
- Workforce upskilling in data analytics will be critical to sustain long-term transformation.

Takeaway. Big Data adoption is politically enabled but technologically limited. A coordinated approach between policymakers, technology providers and industry leaders is required to align governance, infrastructure and workforce training (see [31], on behavioral data and governance challenges).

5 Discussion

The two sessions illustrate how MyCrystalBall can reveal systemic dynamics of digital transformation. Across both scenarios, a clear pattern emerges: technology often acts as a driver, but societal and political factors determine the pace and scope of adoption.

In the VR/AR scenario, society proved decisive. Even though technological progress was strong, trust, usability and workforce readiness constrained implementation. This demonstrates that digital innovations cannot be evaluated purely on technical merits; social acceptance and training are equally essential.

In the Big Data scenario, politics acted as the main enabler. Regulatory clarity, data governance and infrastructure investments were found to be critical. Without political commitment to standards and interoperability, even advanced technology remains under-utilized. Interestingly, some groups initially equated "Big Data" simply with surveillance, while others focused on efficiency gains; a contrast that sparked lively debate (see also [31]).

Together, these cases emphasize that digital transformation requires alignment of three domains:

- Policy frameworks that create stability and trust.
- Technological infrastructure that ensures feasibility.
- Societal readiness through education, acceptance and ethical considerations.

These three domains mirror the core logic of the PETIES framework, where transformation emerges from the interaction of political, technological and social dynamics.

Compared with traditional foresight methods, MyCrystalBall offers a playful but structured environment in which interdependencies become visible. The board game format reduces abstraction, engages participants actively, and stimulates collaborative reflection.

While classical analytical tools such as the PESTEL framework (Political, Economic, Social, Technological, Environmental, Legal) provide a valuable macro-level perspective, the PETIES framework (Politics, Economy, Technology, Individual, Education, Society) used in MyCrystalBall extends this logic by adding the dimensions Individual and Education. These additions make it possible to capture human behavior, perception, acceptance, and learning processes. These factors are essential for understanding the adoption and impact of innovations. As a result, PETIES enables a more nuanced and practice-oriented analysis of socio-technical transformation than PESTEL alone.

6 Conclusion and Outlook

MyCrystalBall demonstrates the potential of combining foresight, systems thinking, and game-based learning into a practical and adaptable tool for exploring digital futures. By focusing on the scenarios of VR/AR in HVAC and Big Data in construction, the study highlights the interplay of politics, technology, and society as decisive levers of digital transformation, an alignment also emphasized in industry perspectives [32]. Additionally, this triangulation is consistent with socio-technical transition theory [33, 34] and with practice-oriented foresight formats that combine scenario work with decision gaming [35].

The game's strength lies in its simplicity: minimal materials, clear phases, and a structured analytical framework make it suitable for various educational and professional contexts. While this paper presented two exemplary sessions, additional applications in robotics and sustainable housing confirm the broader applicability of the approach. Future work will extend the game to include topics based on emerging domains such as Artificial Intelligence, Quantum Technologies, and Circular Economy. Forthcoming publications will provide deeper methodological insights and quantitative analyses, complementing the practice-oriented perspective presented here.

In an increasingly volatile, uncertain, complex, and ambiguous (VUCA) world, MyCrystalBall serves as both a research instrument and a catalyst for dialogue among stakeholders. It enables participants to co-create strategies, reflect on systemic interdependencies, and translate foresight into action. By continuously refining its methodology and exploring future integrations, such as AI-supported evaluation, MyCrystalBall has the potential to evolve into a versatile tool for strategic foresight, learning, and innovation-driven decision-making. Future work will focus on integrating adaptive, data-driven analysis modules to further operationalize the PETIES framework and enhance its analytical depth. In doing so, MyCrystalBall bridges foresight research and educational innovation, offering a tangible format for operationalizing systemic thinking in practice.

Further information and materials are available for free at: https://www.uni-due.de/bautechnik/mycrystalball.php.

Acknowledgments. The author would like to express his sincere gratitude to Prof. Bill Nicholl from the University of Cambridge, Faculty of Education (Design & Technology Education), for his invitation to collaborate on research exploring creativity and technology, and for enabling the research stay during which the initial concept of MyCrystalBall was developed.

Disclosure of Interests. The author has no competing interests to declare that are relevant to the content of this article.

References

1. Karl, C.K.: Auswirkungen der Digitalisierung auf das Baumanagement. BauVolution. ISSN 2942-9145 (2023)
2. Rittel, H.W.J., Webber, M.M.: Dilemmas in a general theory of planning. Policy. Sci. **4**(2), 155–169 (1973)
3. Bootz, J.-P.: Strategic foresight and organizational learning: a survey and critical analysis. Technol. Forecast. Soc. Change **77**(9), 1588–1594 (2010)
4. Miethke, M.: Strategic foresight in high-hazard organizations. Master's thesis, OCAD University (2020)
5. Liang, H.-Y., Hsu, T.-Y., Hwang, G.-J., Chang, S.-C., Chu, H.-C.: A mandatory contribution-based collaborative gaming approach to enhancing students' collaborative learning outcomes in science museums. Interact. Learn. Environ. **31**(5), 2692–2706 (2023)
6. Fusco, N.M., Foltz-Ramos, K., Jacobsen, L.J., Gambacorta, J.: Educational game improves systems thinking, socialization, and teamwork among students of 13 health professions programs. J. Interprof. Care **38**(1), 176–181 (2024)
7. Irabor, T.J., Yameogo, P.S.A., Perrin, L., et al.: Gaming for change – exploring systems thinking and sustainable practices through complexity-inspired game mechanics. Humanit. Soc. Sci. Commun. **12**, 680 (2025)
8. Schmahl, T., Strumann, C., Goetz, K., et al.: Investigation of the psychometric properties of the German System Thinking Scale in an interprofessional learning setting using the game "Friday Night at the Emergency Room®": a cross-sectional study. BMC Med. Educ. **25**, 875 (2025)
9. Karl, C.K.: Construction Giant: a multi-purpose business game for education and training in the construction industry. Proc. Annu. ABSEL Conf. **42**, 241–250 (2015a)
10. Onencan, A., Walle, B., Enserink, B., Chelang'a, J., Kulei, F.: WeShareIt Game: strategic foresight for climate-change induced disaster risk reduction. Procedia Eng. **159**, 307–315 (2016)
11. Xu, M., Luo, Y., Zhang, Y., Xia, R., Qian, H., Zou, X.: Game-based learning in medical education. Front. Public Health **11**, 1113682 (2023)
12. Karl, C.K.: Simulation and gaming in construction business: design of a module-oriented modeling approach based on system dynamics and its prototypical implementation in research and education. Dissertation, University of Duisburg-Essen (2015b)
13. Karl, C.K.: Designing educational games for project management using the MyPMgame Canvas. Proc. Annu. ABSEL Conf. **43**, 192–206 (2016a)
14. Karl, C.K.: Das Planspiel "Einsatz in Grimhausen." Bevölkerungsschutz **3**, 61–64 (2024)
15. Karl, C.K.: Investigating the Winner's Curse based on decision making in an auction environment. Simul. Gaming **47**(3), 324–345 (2016)
16. de Bono, E.: Lateral Thinking: Creativity Step by Step. Harper & Row, New York (1970)
17. Meadows, D.H.: Thinking in Systems: A Primer. Chelsea Green Publishing, White River Junction (2008)
18. Jacob, E., Duffield, C., Jacob, D.: Development of an Australian nursing critical thinking tool using a Delphi process. J. Adv. Nurs. **74**, 2241–2247 (2018)
19. Nowack, P., Endrikat, J., Guenther, E.: Review of Delphi-based scenario studies: quality and design considerations. Technol. Forecast. Soc. Change **78**(9), 1603–1615 (2011)

20. Saritas, O.: Systemic foresight methodology. In: Meissner, D., Gokhberg, L., Sokolov, A. (eds.) Science, Technology and Innovation Policy for the Future. Springer, Heidelberg (2013). https://doi.org/10.1007/978-3-642-31827-6_6

21. Daheim, C., Hirsch, J.: Emerging practices in foresight and their use in STI policy. STI Policy Rev. **6**, 24–53 (2015)

22. Padbury, P.: An overview of the Horizons Foresight Method: using the "inner game" of foresight to build system-based scenarios. World Futures Rev. **12**, 249–258 (2020)

23. Bontoux, L., Sweeney, J., Rosa, A., et al.: A game for all seasons: lessons and learnings from the JRC's Scenario Exploration System. World Futures Rev. **12**, 103–181 (2020)

24. Rogers, E.M.: Diffusion of Innovations, 5th edn. Free Press, New York (2003)

25. Vester, F.: Ballungsgebiete in der Krise - Vom Verstehen und Planen menschlicher Lebensräume. dtv Verlagsgesellschaft, Munich (1983)

26. Andersen, P.D.: The PESTEL framework and its variants for analysing the strategic environment: evolution, limitations and adoption in energy policy research. SSRN (2025)

27. The Minneapolis Star: Keep it short and simple (KISS). The Minneapolis Star, p. 20 (1938)

28. Liu, H., Miao, X., Shi, C., Xu, T.: Exploring the acceptance of virtual reality training systems among construction workers: a combined SEM–ANN approach. Front. Public Health **12**, 1478615 (2024)

29. Dallasega, P., Schulze, F., Revolti, A.: Augmented reality to overcome visual management implementation barriers in construction: a MEP case study. Constr. Manag. Econ. **41**(3), 232–255 (2022)

30. Akindele, N., Taiwo, R., Sarvari, H., Oluleye, B.I., Awodele, I.A., Olaniran, T.O.: A state-of-the-art analysis of virtual reality applications in construction health and safety. Results Eng. **23**, 102382 (2024)

31. Karl, C.K.: Internet of behaviors: Verhaltensdaten in der Bauwirtschaft. BauVolution (2025). ISSN 2942-9145

32. Karl, C.K.: Im Dialog: Dr. Thomas Wilk über digitale Transformation in der Bauwirtschaft. BauVolution (2024). ISSN 2942-9145

33. Geels, F.W.: Technological transitions as evolutionary reconfiguration processes: a multi-level perspective and a case study. Res. Policy **31**(8–9), 1257–1274 (2002)

34. Geels, F.W.: Socio-technical transitions to sustainability: a review of criticisms and elaborations of the multi-level perspective. Curr. Opin. Environ. Sustain. **39**, 187–201 (2019)

35. Schwarz, J.O., Ram, C., Rohrbeck, R.: Combining scenario planning and business wargaming to better anticipate future competitive dynamics. Futures **105**, 133–142 (2019)

Learning and Evaluation
in Simulation-Based Environments

The Health Insurance Game – A Simulation Game and a Simulation of a Health Economic Experiment

Tobias Alf[1(✉)], Jürgen Wasem[2], and Florian Buchner[2,3]

[1] Baden Württemberg Cooperative State University, Stuttgart, Germany
`tobias.alf@dhbw-stuttgart.de`
[2] Universität Duisburg Essen, Duisburg, Germany
`Juergen.Wasem@uni-due.de, F.Buchner@fh-kaernten.at`
[3] CUAS University of Applied Science, Villach, Australia

Abstract. Simulation games are applied in a lot of different areas. We investigate for the Health Insurance Game, an economic simulation, how students evaluate this simulation (1), whether students learn economic concepts when playing this simulation (2), whether different roles show different progress (3) and whether we see the results expected by economic theory (4). Students are quite satisfied with the game. By playing and debriefing the Health Insurance Game students can significantly improve their knowledge on health insurance markets. A significant difference in the learning effect between different roles in the game cannot be observed. We find a significant difference in risk scores between insured and not insured consumers in the expected direction in two of three scenarios, for which health economic theory does expect it. Overall, we come to the conclusion that students learn about health insurance markets when playing the HIG and that the HIG represents in a simplified way real effects of health economics. We found these results although the sample size is relatively small. Results may become even clearer when collecting more data from more courses.

Keywords: Health Insurance Market · Simulation Games · Evaluation

1 Introduction

1.1 Learning with Simulation Games

Simulation games are widely used in higher education in various disciplines. Political and economic education might be the most prominent fields in which simulation games are applied – at least in the German speaking area. The Federal Agency for Civic Education lists more than 250 simulation games on political education (https://www.bpb.de/lernen/angebote/planspiele/datenbank-planspiele/). The Federal Institute for Vocational Education and Training has over 500 simulation games and serious games, mainly on economic topics [1]. However, simulation games are not only used in the fields of politics and economy: simulation games are also used in IT programs [2], healthcare [3],

F. Trautwein et al. (Eds.): ISAGA 2025, LNCS 16439, pp. 133–147, 2026.
https://doi.org/10.1007/978-3-032-20129-4_10

theology [4] and increasingly in teacher education [5]. This raises the question why simulation games are developed and used on such a broad scale. Why do they enjoy such popularity in education? Very (subject) specific answers can be found to this question, such as learning about the topic represented in a particular simulation game. However, overarching answers can also be given beyond specific specialist topics. Without claiming to be exhaustive, we can identify three overarching reasons why simulation games are used in teaching: the multidimensionality of learning, the depth of learning and the experience of systemic contexts.

Simulation games are multidimensional teaching/learning arrangements: they make it possible to acquire specialist knowledge, practice social-communicative skills and learn methodological-strategic competencies [6]. The authors emphasize that simulation games open up several learning opportunities at the same time. Factual topics are always integrated into a specific use case. Key economic figures are learned and at the same time applied to decision-making in business simulations. Formal democratic decision-making processes are learned and at the same time run through in political simulations. The use case is always integrated into a social context. For example, learners explain an economic indicator to each other and discuss how they come to a decision based on it. In political simulation games, participants take part in a simulated election campaign and discuss from the perspective of their respective roles. The learning of a certain content does not take place in isolation; it is integrated into a meaningful network of social and methodological requirements that learners have to deal with simultaneously. Learning with simulation games thus becomes a multidimensional, holistic experience.

Taxonomies are often used to describe learning and learning objectives in a differentiated way. Bloom's advanced taxonomy [7], for example, distinguishes between different dimensions of knowledge (factual knowledge, conceptual knowledge, procedural knowledge, metacognitive knowledge) on the one hand and different dimensions of the cognitive process in which this knowledge is applied on the other (remember, understand, apply, analyze, evaluate, create). As simulation games are a very action-oriented teaching and learning method, it can be assumed that they can be used to reach deeper levels of learning in the sense of this taxonomy: Simulation games require students to learn and use different kinds of knowledge: For example they learn a specific formula (factual knowledge) but also to apply the formula to solve a certain problem (procedural knowledge). Meanwhile various mental processes are performed. To play simulations successfully one must remember and understand things but also to take decisions based on the information processed. The content must therefore be applied, analyzed and evaluated. So, simulation games include processing the learning content at deeper levels.

In simulation games, learners are not confronted with isolated problems, but with entire systems and their multifaceted causal and functional interactions; they are encouraged to think in systems. "A system is an interconnected set of elements that is coherently organized in a way that achieves something. (…) a system must consist of three kinds of things: elements, interconnections, and a function or purpose." [8]. What sounds very straightforward in theory can be difficult to understand in reality: Which elements belong to the system, what are the connections and what purpose does the system fulfill? According to Monat and Gannon [9], systems cannot be adequately grasped using linear patterns of thinking. Holistic thinking is needed that incorporates multiple spatial and temporal influences at the same time. According to Duke and Geurts [10], simulation games should depict systemic relationships: "the intended end product of the design process is an operating model of a real-life system. In the game model, people in different but interrelated roles create, at least partly, the dynamic behavior of the model." In simulation games, learners experience how system elements interact in a temporal and spatial manner and can also explore the options for action with which they can "move" in a (political or economic) system. This also includes realistic trial actions (trying out behavioral patterns, strategies) and changing perspectives by taking on other people's roles [6]. So, the third general reason for the use of simulation games in teaching can be concluded: By simulating systemic contexts, simulation games are suitable for action-oriented (trying things out, taking on roles) learning of how to behave in complex systemic contexts – and health insurance is such a complex systemic context.

1.2 The Health Insurance Game (HIG)

In health insurance markets, several market failures are to be faced which are often counter-balanced by different types of government regulations. There is no first-choice solution to these problems, different kinds of regulatory frameworks for health insurance systems represent different second choice solutions. But this comes with a trade-off between the consequences of market failures in free health insurance markets and the consequences of government regulations resulting in different kinds of selection processes.

The health insurance game HIG gives participants a kind of real-life experience of such effects and confronts them with a situation in which they have to calculate health insurance premiums. It reflects some basic parameters of different health insurance systems in a quite simple way, helping participants to get familiar with basic concepts like actuarially fair premiums, adverse selection, risk selection and risk adversity and serves as a first step into the quite complex framework of health insurance systems.

The basic principle of the game works as follows: participants are divided into health insurers and consumers. Consumers are characterized by different risk scores and may negotiate health insurance premiums with insurers under different regulatory frameworks like free market, community rating or premium regulation combined with risk adjustment. The aim of the game is for both sides, consumers and insurers, to earn as much money as possible or to make as little loss as possible in each individual round (and also over all scenarios).

In more detail, the HIG is played in the common three phases of briefing, experience and debriefing [11].

In the briefing (1), participants are introduced to the simulation, the rules of the game are explained, and they get an introduction to the website used. Therefore, a manual is available in English and in German, so participants have a chance to get some information in advance.

At the beginning of the actual game phase (2), participants take on the role of either an insurer or a consumer. Consumers are randomly assigned risk scores between 1 and 6, which reflect their probability of becoming ill (between $1/6 = 17\%$ and $6/6 = 100\%$). All consumers get the same annual income. The random component of the illness is simulated by throwing a dice: whether a person falls ill or not depends on the ratio of the risk score to the number of eyes on the respective dice roll. If someone falls ill, a fixed amount of medical costs is to be paid regardless of the risk score. This is fully covered by the insurance company when taking out insurance, otherwise it is to be borne by the consumer him-/herself. Insurers and consumers can freely negotiate premiums. In practice facilitators usually ask students to volunteer for the insurance role. The idea is to find students that are more confident with calculating insurance fees. At the same time, it could be expected that students playing insurances might have a benefit in learning, because the game forces them to invest more effort in calculating premiums according to different market scenarios.

Four different market scenarios are played out:

- In the free market with perfect information, there are no regulations on premium calculation and consumers interested in insurance are obliged to disclose their risk score to the insurer.
- In the free market with asymmetric information there is no obligation to disclose the risk score.
- In the community rating/premium regulation scenario, the insurer must charge the same premium to all its insured parties.
- In the risk adjustment scenario, the insurer receives payments from a pool for insured parties with a high-risk score and must pay into this pool for insured parties with a low-risk score.

In all four scenarios, there is no obligation for consumers or insurers to take out an insurance contract. For each scenario, three years are played, i.e., the dice are rolled three times (with the same premium and risk score). By rolling the dice three times per scenario, the influence of chance on the game results is considerably decreased compared to rolling the dice only once. For each new scenario, consumers are assigned new risk scores, and new premiums are negotiated. After each scenario round, the leaderboards of the ranking of the consumers as well as the insurers are shown – what is considerably increasing motivation and fun of participants.

In the debriefing (3), after all four rounds have been completed, the different results of the scenarios are analyzed together with the participants. The calculation of actuarially fair premiums is discussed, and concepts such as risk selection, adverse selection ("insurance death spiral") and risk aversion are explained using the game results. A summary of some calculations delivers an overview so teachers can link the game results with theoretical concepts from health economics. Teachers who have international experience in the field of financing health systems can discuss the different simulation scenarios with corresponding examples from real-world health insurance systems.

Originally the game was a paper and pencil simulation. In the times of Covid19 pandemic and of widespread online teaching, we transferred the concept into a web-based online version, which is available in English and in German. The dice were replaced by a random generator and the insurance contracts were recorded on the online platform instead of on paper. After the Covid19 pandemic we returned to playing on campus but keeping the website as central element. The online version and the translation into English brought the occasion to test the simulation with health economists from all over the world in the context of a webinar of the Special Interest Group Teaching Health Economics of the international Health Economists Association (iHEA).

1.3 The Research Questions

The teaching objective of the HIG is to open students' eyes in a direction, that health insurance may work differently from what they are used to from the conditions in their home country and to make them experience the consequences of different frameworks in this context. In this way they should understand different selection processes at the health insurance market. More specifically the students should understand, how the different scenarios of the simulation influence the behavior of consumers and become able to analyze respective data and evaluate selection processes. At the same time, it is not obvious, that the behavior patterns expected by health economic theory can be observed even for small samples of participants in this simulation game, in the sense of Klabbers [12] inquiry scheme of design science (design-in-the-small) and the question "Does it work in this context for this audience? This leads in detail to the following four research questions (RQ):

1. How do students evaluate courses that are lectured using the HIG?
2. Do students learn basic economic concepts of health insurance markets when playing the HIG?
3. Does learning differ between roles taken over in the game (insurer/consumer)?
4. To what respect do results of the simulated market in the game reflect results expected by health economic theory?

The first of these research questions refers to students' satisfaction with the game, the second and third question refer to the learning effect of the game and the fourth and last question refers to whether the health economics experiment works or not.

2 Data Gathering and Methods

Data used in this study was gathered at the Business Faculty at the DHBW Stuttgart University of Cooperative Education in Germany in April and September 2024. Altogether the game was applied in three courses, always lectured by the same two facilitators. One of the facilitators was mainly in charge of gameplay and the other more as an expert in the field of health insurance markets. All participants study bachelor programs at the business school but with different profiles. The students who played the game in April 2024 studied Business Informatic while the students who played the game in September 2024 had a focus on insurance. One could ask why Business Informatic students should play a health insurance game. The answer is that all students in this course (university of cooperative education) work in insurance companies. Applying the game students can learn basic concepts of their industry.

2.1 Data Gathering RQ 1–3

Over all three classes we administered a pre-test ($N = 63$) at the very beginning of the seminar and a post-test ($N = 57$) at the very end of the seminar. As this is often the case, slightly fewer participants took part in the post-test or could not be matched by a randomized identification code.

Table 1. Overview Participants.

Pretest/Posttest	N63/N57
Program of study	Business Informatics: 22 Insurance: 35
Gender	Male: 23 Female: 30 Divers: 1 No answer: 3
Role in the Simulation Game	Consumer: 38 Insurance: 17 No answer: 2

To evaluate the game and answer the research questions we used two instruments. On the one hand, we used the ZMS-questionnaire that combines questions typical for student evaluation of teaching and questions that are relevant for the evaluation of simulation games [13]. It consists of seven constructs that are formed of 25 items evaluated using six-point Likert scales. To investigate the above outlined research questions only four of the seven constructs were used:

Satisfaction and Learning: Evaluates the overall satisfaction with the simulation game-based teaching and contains a student-self-assessment on learning. It consists of three items related to learning and three items related to overall satisfaction.
Facilitation: Addresses teaching specific aspects of facilitation such as structure of the seminar or communication between instructors and students.
Simulation Game Reality/Relevance: Students evaluate to what respect the game represents corresponding real-world issues.
Simulation Game Comprehension: Students evaluate how well they understand how the game proceeds and the results provided.

The questionnaire is based on students' self-assessment and therefore suitable to answer RQ1. It is designed for post-evaluation and was therefore only administered with the post-test.

On the other hand, we used a self-developed learning test to evaluate the learning achievement. As the HIG pursues very specific learning objectives it was not possible to use an already existing test instrument to answer RQ2 and RQ3. The self-developed learning test includes one question in which students must calculate an actuarially fair premium and three multiple choice questions on community rating, risk adjustment and adverse selection. All topics included in the test are covered by the game. The test was mainly developed by one of the developers of HIG and validated by other experts in the field (content validation). To score the test results we used the following system:

Question 1 (calculation): 3 points for the correct calculation of question one, 0 points for no or wrong calculation of question one.

Questions 2–4 (multiple choice): We scored one point for each correctly marked and each correctly not marked option. We also scored one minus point for each incorrectly marked and each incorrectly not marked option.

This means that the scores could range from -13 points (everything incorrect) to 16 points (everything correct).

2.2 Data Gathering RQ4

In this section we use a different database, because the results come from a Master thesis which comprises the data of 91 consumers from five different international courses [14]. In her master thesis, Flaschberger examined whether and to what extent this simulation can reflect market failures in real health insurance markets and how the simulation can help students understand these phenomena. The thesis included a literature review as well as quantitative and qualitative evaluations. Here we refer to the results of her first research question. The data came from courses at the Carinthia University of Applied Sciences, Austria, the University of Duisburg-Essen, Germany and the Erasmus University in Rotterdam, Netherlands. A t-test was used to test statistical significance of the differences of mean risk scores between those consumers who subscribed an insurance and those who did not at the 5%-level.

3 Results

In this section we present results on the outlined research questions: how satisfied are students playing the game as a learning activity (RQ1), whether they learn some relevant issues of health economics (RQ2 and RQ3) and whether the health economics experiment works out (RQ4).

3.1 RQ1: How Do Students Evaluate Courses that Are Lectured Using the HIG?

To answer RQ1 we present the descriptive data we have collected using the ZMS-questionnaire developed by Trautwein and Alf [13]. We focus on four unobserved variables: Satisfaction and Learning, Facilitation, Simulation Game Reality/Relevance and Simulation Game Comprehension. We can compare the results found for the HIG with evaluation results of a variety of business simulation games (BSG). These results were published in prior research [15] (Table 2).

Comparing means, medians and standard deviations of the four variables (scale from one to six, Table 2), we find that the means represent the variables well. Standard deviations are moderate while means and medians are very close. With a minimum of 3 and a mean of 4.82 for Satisfaction and Learning, most students are overall satisfied with the class. This value is slightly higher than the prior found values for BSG.

With a mean of 5.38 students are very satisfied with their lecturers leading the game. This is a finding one could expect since values for facilitation were also the highest in

Table 2. Descriptive Statistics of HIG and BSG.

Descriptives

	Satisfaction and Learning		Facilitation		SG_Reality/ Relevance		SG_Compre- hension	
	HIG	BSG	**HIG**	BSG	**HIG**	BSG	**HIG**	BSG
N	54	968	56	975	56	976	56	976
Missing	9		7		7		7	
Mean	4.82	4.59	5.38	5.33	4.15	4.44	5.30	5.00
Median	4.92		5.40		4.00		5.33	
Std. Dev	0.81	1.06	0.62	0.82	0.84	1.05	0.61	0.81
Min	3		4		2		3.33	
Max	6		6		6		6	

All values relating to BSG (grey) are taken from a previous study with the same questionnaire [15].

prior studies. We also find a very high value (5.3) for Simulation Game Comprehension. Obviously, students were able to understand how to interact with the game and how to interpret results. With a delta of 0.30 students rate the HIG to be more understandable than BSG. With a delta of 0.29 students rate the relation to reality of the HIG to be lower than in a variety of BSGs.

3.2   RQ2: Do Students Learn Basic Economic Concepts of Health Insurance Markets When Playing the HIG?

As described before, test-scores could range between -13 and 16. Looking at the data from the pre-test (N = 63) in Table 3 we see that students did not exhaust the poles. Minus three was the lowest and twelve was the highest score. We also see a concentration of results between minus one and six with a mean of 3.17, a median of 3.0 and a standard deviation of 3.31.

At least one pole was exhausted in the post-test (Table 4): One participant achieved a result of 16 points while the lowest score was still -3 as in the pre-test. Overall, the distribution tends more towards the higher scores compared to the pretest with a peak at 10 points reached by 16 participants (compared to only two in the pre-test). This is also reflected in the higher mean of 7.68 and the higher median of 9.00. The standard deviation also increased by 1.23 points to 4.54. The increased standard deviation and the gap between the mean and the median indicate that not all students could benefit from the game in the same way. Some individual high performers are especially responsible for the increased mean compared to the pre-test.

Table 3. Frequencies and Distribution: Scores Pre-Test

Score Pre-Test	Counts	% of Total
-3	1	1.6 %
-2	1	1.6 %
-1	11	17.5 %
0	1	1.6 %
1	3	4.8 %
2	13	20.6 %
3	10	15.9 %
4	1	1.6 %
5	1	1.6 %
6	13	20.6 %
7	3	4.8 %
8	1	1.6 %
9	1	1.6 %
10	2	3.2 %
12	1	1.6 %
		100%

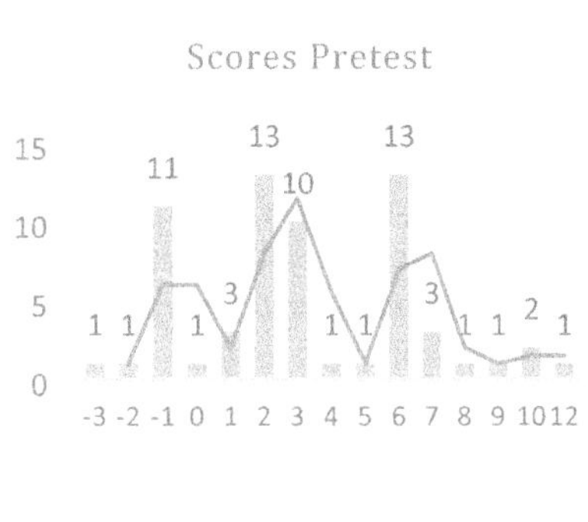

Table 4. Frequencies and Distribution: Scores Post-Test

Score Post-Test	Counts	% of Total
-3	2	3.6 %
-1	1	1.8 %
0	1	1.8 %
1	2	3.6 %
2	3	5.4 %
3	3	5.4 %
4	1	1.8 %
5	2	3.6 %
6	6	10.7 %
7	4	7.1 %
8	3	5.4 %
10	16	28.6 %
11	2	3.6 %
12	3	5.4 %
14	6	10.7 %
16	1	1.8 %
		100%

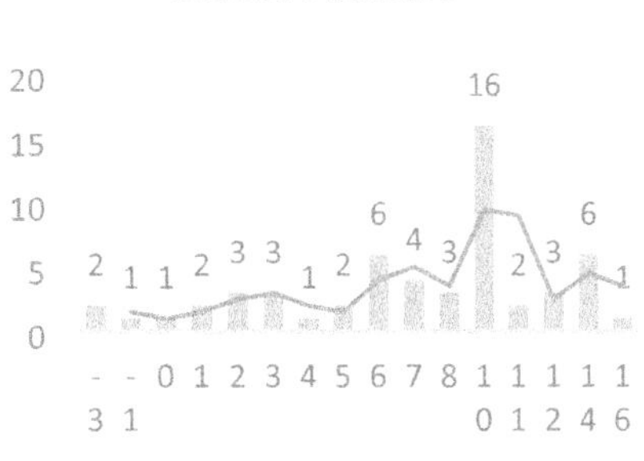

A paired sample T-Test comparing the scores of the pre-test (3.17) and the post-test (7.68) reveals a highly significant result of $p < .001$ with an effect size of 0.917 (Cohen's d) which is a very large effect. RQ1 can therefore be answered as such: What we have seen in the descriptive statistics was confirmed by the statistical test: By playing and debriefing the HIG students can significantly improve their knowledge of health insurance markets.

3.3 RQ3: Does Learning Differ Between Roles Taken Over in the Game (Insurer/consumer)?

To evaluate RQ3 we use a difference-in-differences approach [16]. This means that we compare the differences between pre-test and post-test results between different roles in the game (customers and insurances). One could expect that students who volunteer for insurers, the role that requires a little more mathematical understanding, would score higher in the pre-test. The descriptive statistics show that this is not the case. Scores of students playing insurances were a little lower than scores of those being customers (Table 5). Comparing the results of the post-tests we find both roles on almost the same score meaning that students playing the insurance role had improved more than students playing customers.

Table 5. Role Differences

Descriptives

	Role in the game	Score Pre-Test	Score Post-Test	Learning Gain
N	Customer	38	38	38
	Insurance	17	17	17
Mean	Customer	3.66	7.68	4.03
	Insurance	2.59	7.82	5.24

We have calculated t-tests for the following constellations:

- Comparison of pre-test scores between roles ($p = 0.274$)
- Comparison of post-test scores between roles ($p = 0.918$)
- Comparison of the learning gain between roles ($p = 0.400$)

Even though we see slight differences in the descriptive statistics these are not significant. Students taking the insurance-role do not score significantly different than students taking the customer-role, neither in the post-test nor in the pre-test. And even though the insurance-students have a slightly higher learning effect, this difference is not significant either. We conclude that learning does not differ significantly between the roles taken over in the game.

3.4   RQ4: Does the Health Economics Experiment Work?

Representative of the investigation of the health economics experiment respectively the question, whether the expected effects can be observed, the risk scores of those consumers insured and those not insured are analyzed.

In the data comprising 91 evaluable consumers of five different courses, we find such a statistically significant difference using a t-test in scenario 3 (mean risk score insured 3.16; uninsured 1.76; p $=$ 0.00) and scenario 4 (3.33 vs. 2.08; p $=$ 0,00). In contrast, the difference in scenario 1 (2.77 vs. 2.15; p $=$ 0.169) and scenario 2 (2.74 vs. 2.25; p $=$ 0.186) is much smaller and not statistically significant at the 95% level (Flaschberger, 2022).

4   Discussion

4.1   RQ1 - Student Evaluation

Under RQ1 we compared evaluation results on the HIG game with results on a variety of business simulation games. Asking for Satisfaction and Learning on the one hand and Facilitation on the other hand students rate classes taught with the HIG slightly better than classes taught with other business simulations. The results show that the game is well appreciated by students and can continue to be used in teaching. Of more interest might be the two variables evaluating the simulation game: Comprehension on the one hand and the games' relation to reality: regarding Comprehension the HIG is rated better than a variety of business games, meaning that students can follow the information and results provided by the game well. But students rate the HIG to be not as close to reality as other business simulation games. This finding corresponds with the actual idea of the HIG as outlined in the introduction. In a rather abstract and simplified way the HIG introduces some of the very complex dynamics of health insurance markets under different regulations governments can use to regulate the market. The students' assessment that the game is less close to reality than other simulation games is therefore understandable and plausible.

4.2   RQ2 - Learning Effects

To answer RQ2 we applied a knowledge test to evaluate whether students learn basic economic principles on health insurance markets when playing the game. The results clearly show that students learn about health insurance markets with the HIG. We found highly significant differences between the pre- and the posttest with an effect size of 0.917 (Cohen's d), which is very large. We can state that the HIG is a suitable intervention to learn about health insurance markets in higher education. The surprisingly high effect size might also be explained by the novice status of students. None of them had a lecture on health insurance markets before even though at least some of them work at health insurance companies during their internships. Further evaluation should also include classes with some more prior knowledge to be able to interpret the results of the learning test in a more differentiated way.

Having prior studies on learning with simulation games in mind our findings are not surprising. They are in line with the results of the meta-analysis of [17], which shows that simulation-based learning is among the most effective means to facilitate learning of complex skills in higher education. The influential meta-analysis of Abrami et al. [18] investigates the effect of different teaching strategies on students' learning of critical thinking. This meta-analysis shows a significant effect for "Authentic or Anchored Instructions" which includes besides three other categories "Simulations" and "Playing games" on generic critical thinking skills ($g^+ = 0.25$)[1]. So, we may assume, that the HIG besides supporting the learning of health economic aspects of health insurance also supports to enhance more general skills like critical thinking.

4.3   RQ3 - Role-Specific Learning Effects

To play the game students choose either the role of an insurer or the role of a customer. As mentioned in the introduction, the role of an insurer might be somewhat more demanding, since insurers must calculate premiums (in real life as in the game). In the classes evaluated the facilitators have asked students if they feel confident to take over the outlined insurance-role and assigned especially students who volunteered for the role. Therefore, one could imagine that students playing the insurance-role would score better in the pre-test. The opposite is the case. The results of insurers in the pretest are somewhat under the results of customers (but the difference is not significant). With the post-test we find that insurers and customers reached almost the same results (7.68 and 7.82), meaning that insurance-students were able to learn relatively more and catch up with the customers. Comparing the gain in learning of customers (4.03) and insurances (5.24) we find a descriptive difference but no significant result in the t-test. The slight effects we observe could be coincidence – for more reliable statements in this context we must wait for a larger sample size.

Overall, this is a pleasant result because independent from the roles taken over in the game students learn about the relevant concepts of health insurance markets. These results should be interpreted with caution: $N = 38$ for customers and $N = 17$ for insurers are rather small sample sizes for statistical comparisons. Further data collection with the HIG might reveal clearer and more reliable results.

4.4   RQ4 - Observed Simulation Effects

The HIG is not only a simulation game, but at the same time a kind of health economic experiment. So, from a health economics perspective, it is interesting to see to what extent the effects expected from health economic theory can actually be observed in the results of the game. This is exemplified here by the health economic concept of "adverse selection". Adverse selection can occur in (health) insurance markets when asymmetric information between insurer and consumer is given: the insured person knows his or her health status better than the insurer. If an insurer does not know the risk level of a

---

[1] For content specific critical thinking skills Abrami et al. find an even higher significant effect over all approaches, but due to lower sample size, there is no differentiation of the effect by teaching strategies.

consumer, it may offer something like a medium premium. For low risks this could be a too high premium, and they waive health insurance. If the insurer anticipates that low-risk persons are less likely to insure themselves, it will take this into account in the premium calculation. This prevents even more consumers (medium risks) from subscribing an insurance contract and so on. The same happens if regulation does not allow premium differentiation and health insurance is not obligatory. Consequently, low-risk individuals may not get an opportunity to insure themselves at an adequate premium [19, 20].

According to this concept of adverse selection we expect a higher risk score for insured people than for uninsured people, especially in scenarios 2 and 3, where insurers do not know the risk score of the consumers respectively could not even use this information for risk-rated premiums. For scenario 4 we do expect a higher average risk score for insured consumers than for uninsured as well, but for different reasons. For scenario 1 we do not expect a significant difference in the risk score, because there is symmetric information, meaning insurers *and* consumers know the risk scores of the consumers in this scenario. Therefore insurers can calculate risk-rated (a kind of tailor-made) premiums. The results in Sect. 3.4 show highly significant differences in the expected direction for risk scores between insured and uninsured in scenario 3 and 4. The differences in scenarios 1 and 2 are a lot smaller, what is expected for the first case, but not for the second. There may be some disturbing effects in very similar description of scenario 1 and 2. So it may be a good idea to change the sequence of all the scenarios in one of the next simulations. For a bigger sample, perhaps the difference for (current) scenario 2 gets significant as well, whereas that for (current) scenario 1 stays insignificant.

This phenomenon of adverse selection is systematically analyzed and discussed in the debriefing based on the data produced by the participants of the respective simulation.

5 Conclusion

The goal of this study is to evaluate the HIG in terms of student evaluation (RQ1), learning effects (RQ2), differences in learning effects according to the roles assumed in the game (RQ3) and the validity of the game (does it really represent health insurance markets? RQ4).

We can state that students are very satisfied with the game and the facilitators leading it. Students also rate the HIG as a very understandable game, they can follow the information and results provided by the game. Compared to other business simulations the game is rated slightly lower with respect to its relation to reality. This is plausible because it is the game's idea to demonstrate very complex markets in a simplified way to make basic economic phenomena in these markets transparent for students. In this sense, the example of adverse selection speaks for its' validity and the HIG is able to represent effects of real markets.

In line with prior educational studies on simulation games we find that students significantly increased their knowledge on health insurance markets by playing the HIG. This effect is independent of the roles taken over in the game. T-tests comparing insurers and customers on test results were not significant. As an overall conclusion we can recommend using the HIG in higher education in the field of health insurance, health economics or insurance economics. It is a valid simulation game displaying real market effects. The "active learning" approach of the HIG helps to support deeper learning instead of pure surface learning. According to the results of our test, participants learn details of health insurance systems, and they experience how health insurance markets work – or do not work. At the same time, they have fun competing for best performing insurance company or for best citizen spending least money on health care over four different regulatory phases.

References

1. Blötz, U. (ed.) (with Bundesinstitut für Berufsbildung). Planspiele und Serious Games in der beruflichen Bildung: Auswahl, Konzepte, Lernarrangements, Erfahrungen—Aktueller Katalog für Planspiele und Serious Games 2015 (5., überarbeitete Auflage), BIBB Bundesinstitut für Berufsbildung; W. Bertelsmann Verlag GmbH & Co. KG (2015)
2. Beranic, T., Hericko, M.: Introducing ERP concepts to IT students using an experiential learning approach with an emphasis on reflection. Sustainability **11**(18), 1–17 (2019). https://doi.org/10.3390/su11184992
3. Ney, M., Gonçalves, C., Balacheff, N.: Design heuristics for authentic simulation-based learning games. IEEE Trans. Learn. Technol. **7**(2), 132–141 (2014). https://doi.org/10.1109/TLT.2014.2316161
4. Riegger, M.J.: Planspiele an der Hochschule in der Theologie – ein problemgeschichtlich-systematischer Überblick. Zeitschrift Für Hochschulentwicklung **18**(Sonderheft Planspiele), 61–78 (2023). https://doi.org/10.21240/zfhe/SH-PS/04
5. Kadel, J., Buschmann, C., Haas, S., Meßner, M.T., Adl-Amini, K.: Planspiele und simulative Methoden in der Lehrkräftebildung – ein Literaturüberblick. Zeitschrift Für Hochschulentwicklung **18**, 19–39 (2023)
6. Engartner, T., Meßner, M.T.: Tarifverhandlungen als Gegenstand von Planspielen in der arbeitnehmer- und gewerkschaftsorientierten Bildung. In: Petrik, A., Rappenglück, S. (eds.) Handbuch Planspiele in der politischen Bildung, vol. Band 81, pp. 69–76. Wochenschau Verlag (2017)
7. Krathwohl, D.R.: A revision of bloom's taxonomie: an overview. Theory Pract. **41**(4) (2002). https://www.depauw.edu/files/resources/krathwohl.pdf
8. Meadows, D.H.: Thinking in Systems: A primer. Earthscan (2009)
9. Monat, J.P., Gannon, T.F.: What is systems thinking? A review of selected literature plus recommendatios. Am. J. Syst. Sci. **4**(1), 11–26 (2015)
10. Duke, R.D., Geurts, J.: Policy Games for Strategic Management: Pathways to the Unknown. Dutch University Press (2004)
11. Rappenglück, S.: Planspiele in der Praxis der politischen Bildung: Entwicklung, Durchführung, Varianten und Trends. In: Petrik, A., Rappenglück, S. (eds.) Handbuch Planspiele in der politischen Bildung, vol. Band 81, pp. 17–34. Wochenschau Verlag (2017)
12. Klabbers, J.H.G.: A framework for artifact assessment and theory testing. Simul. Gaming **37**(2), 155–173 (2006)
13. Trautwein, F., Alf, T.: Theory-based development of an inventory for the evaluation of simulation game lectures. In: Harteveld, C., Sutherland, S., Troiano, G., Lukosch, H., Meijer, S. (eds.) Simulation and Gaming for Social Impact. ISAGA 2022. Lecture Notes in Computer Science, vol. 13622, pp. 3–21. Springer, Cham (2023). https://doi.org/10.1007/978-3-031-37171-4_1
14. Flaschberger, S.: Funktionsprobleme im Krankenversicherungsmarkt. Eine empirische Analyse anhand des Krankenversicherungsspiels "The Health Insurance Game". Master thesis. Fachhochschule Kärnten (2022)

15. Alf, T., Trautwein, F.: Simulation games on sustainability – a comparative study. In: Harteveld, C., Sutherland, S., Troiano, G., Lukosch, H., Meijer, S. (eds) Simulation and Gaming for Social Impact. ISAGA 2022. Lecture Notes in Computer Science, vol. 13622, pp. 121–133. Springer, Cham (2023). https://doi.org/10.1007/978-3-031-37171-4_8

16. Schwerdt, G., Woessmann, L.: Empirical methods in the economics of education. In Econ. Educ., 3–20 (2020). Elsevier. https://doi.org/10.1016/B978-0-12-815391-8.00001-X

17. Chernikova, O., Heitzmann, N., Stadler, M., Holzberger, D., Seidel, T., Fischer, F.: Simulation-based learning in higher education: a meta-analysis. Rev. Educ. Res. **90**(4), 499–541 (2020)

18. Abrami, P.C., Bernard, R.M., Borokhovski, E., Waddington, D.I., Wade, C.A., Persson, T.: Strategies for teaching students to think critically: a meta-analysis. Rev. Educ. Res. **85**(2), 275–314 (2015). https://doi.org/10.3102/0034654314551063

19. Einav, L., Finkelstein, A.: Selection in insurance markets: theory and empirics in pictures. J. Econ. Perspect. **25**(1), 115–138 (2011). https://doi.org/10.1257/jep.25.1.115

20. Rothschild, M., Stiglitz, J.: Equilibrium in competitive insurance markets: an essay on the economics of imperfect information. Q. J. Econ. **90**(4), 629 (1976). https://doi.org/10.2307/1885326

Conceptualizing Embodied Debriefing
in Simulation and Gaming Studies

Weronika Szatkowska[1,3](✉) ⓘ, Małgorzata Ćwil[1] ⓘ, and Willy Christian Kriz[2] ⓘ

[1] Center for Simulation Games and Gamification, Kozminski University, Warsaw, Poland
`Weronika.szatkowska@im.uu.se`
[2] FH Vorarlberg, Dornbirn, Austria
[3] Human-Computer Interaction, Uppsala University, Uppsala, Sweden

Abstract. This theoretical study discusses a novel approach to debriefing that incorporates embodiment into the traditional debrief process. Debriefing is a key activity for processing game experiences, as it enables clarification, the transfer of game learnings from working memory to long-term memory, and the integration of new knowledge with existing cognitive schemas. Embodied debriefing can offer a new perspective on designing debriefing for simulation games, taking into account human bodily predispositions and environmental influences. We conceptualized it as a process that occurs after a simulation game session (or its parts), when participants reflect on their experiences and analyze the outcomes, deploying modes of embodied cognition—bodily movements, gestures, and interactions with the environment. In the paper, we discussed three modes of embodied debriefing: role-play exercise, creative process, and bodily representations within space. Therefore, when designing debriefing sessions, it is valuable to allow participants to engage in embodied modes of representing thoughts and reflections, such as gestures, pointing, touching, tracing, drawing, and larger body movements, which support the learning process.

Keywords: Debriefing · Embodiment · Embodied Cognition · Cognitive Load Theory · Embodied Cognitive Load Theory · Simulation Games

1 Traditional Approach to Debriefing

In the context of simulation and gaming, debriefing refers to the process that takes place after a simulation game session (or its parts), when participants reflect on their experiences and analyze the outcomes [1, 2, 3]. The debriefing process aims to turn the reflections into valuable learning [4]. It provides an opportunity for players to discuss the actions they took (game analysis), the decisions they made, and the results that followed (game reflection), with the goal of extracting lessons and insights for future improvement or real-world application (transfer of knowledge and learning outcomes) [1, 5, 6]. The process should be conducted with a consideration for the learners' needs [6].

David Crookall [7] highlights that the core aspect of any serious game is the debriefing, and that one key debriefing element is participant engagement. It is fueled by a range

F. Trautwein et al. (Eds.): ISAGA 2025, LNCS 16439, pp. 148–161, 2026.
https://doi.org/10.1007/978-3-032-20129-4_11

of emotions—such as joy, frustration, satisfaction, or sadness—therefore, players' feelings should always be considered and processed at that point. Besides, debriefing serves multiple purposes in simulation educational games. For example, it provides an opportunity for de-roling, allowing players to safely step away from their in-game roles [7]. This is the time for players to reflect on their individual or group performance during the simulation. Debriefing provides participants with an opportunity to reflect on their progress and to carry away lessons that enhance their knowledge and skills [8]. During debriefing sessions, participants can share their thoughts, feelings, and reactions to the game. This often includes discussing challenges faced during the simulation, any surprises, and the strategies employed. Debriefing is a critical moment for players to connect their in-game experiences to real-world applications. It is also a time for a facilitator to provide constructive feedback on performance and decisions made during the simulation. This feedback encourages growth and can help players understand areas that need improvement. Nevertheless, these two aspects —feedback and debriefing—should be distinguished.

Debriefing is a crucial part of the simulation experience, allowing players to critically evaluate their performance, learn from their mistakes, and solidify their understanding of key concepts. Many game researchers claim that good debriefing is crucial for a successful learning experience [1, 8–14]; however, the components of successful debrief and hands-on practices are still subjects of ongoing discussions [9, 15, 16]. We can distinguish some examples of comprehensive works addressing this challenge, for instance *Debriefing: A Practical Guide* by David Crookall [4] or a chapter *Debriefing as a Leverage Point for the Transfer of Simulation Game Learning Outcomes to Reality: Building Blocks Before and During Debriefing That Enhance Learning Transfer* by Marieke de Wijse-van Heeswijk et al. [16] in *Transferring Gaming and Simulation Experience to the Real World* book. However, it still happens that debriefing takes the form of a non-involving discussion or even a lecture, showing PowerPoint slides [9, 18]. Some of the educational games do not include debriefing activities at all [18]. No matter how experienced the teacher is, facilitating a debrief involves challenges related to participant dynamics and managing contributions [8]. Proper debriefing must be structured, in-depth, given the time it requires, sometimes in iterations, facilitated with care, and a host of other things [7] to have a beneficial impact on learning, attitudes, and performance [19].

There are various types of debriefing, i.e., reflection-in-action and reflection-on-action [21, 22]. In the first approach, reflective opportunities are made available during gameplay, usually between rounds or stages [23, 24]. The other approach is to stimulate reflection after gameplay [21]. Debriefings can be expert-led, self-led, or group-led [4], and can take an oral or written form, performed individually or collaboratively [21]. Quite often, debriefing involves discussion [14, 15], which, of course, can be successful when well executed.

Debriefing is an interactional space that can be designed and adapted in real time [24]. It is not a static construct—the facilitator responds to the participants' needs and dynamics [6], contributing in real time to the meaning-making process. Interactions during debriefing are characterized by varying social dynamics and patterns [25], with the facilitator, structures, and tools used playing a key role in this process. Therefore, we acknowledge that debriefing is an interactive, dynamic, and designable space. From a cognitive perspective, this approach opens avenues for designing new, promising learning environments.

2 Cognitive Load Theory and Debriefing

Cognitive Load Theory (CLT), developed by John Sweller [26], explains how the limitations of human memory impact learning and problem-solving. The theory distinguishes between three types of cognitive load: *intrinsic load*, which arises from the inherent complexity of the material; *extraneous load*, which results from ineffective instructional design; and *germane load*, which relates to the mental effort dedicated to building schemas that facilitate learning [27]. By understanding these components, educators and designers can create materials that optimize cognitive processing and improve learning outcomes. This is also relevant for simulation and gaming, which are used to explain complex processes as part of a learning experience.

Several instructional design principles stem from CLT. For example, the *worked example effect* suggests that providing step-by-step solutions reduces extraneous load, helping learners focus on schema acquisition [28]. Similarly, *the modality effect* emphasizes that presenting information through multiple sensory channels, such as visual and auditory modes, can reduce overload and enhance comprehension [29]. Another key principle, the *split-attention effect*, highlights the importance of integrating related information sources to minimize unnecessary cognitive effort [30].

These insights have broad applications, particularly in instructional design, multimedia learning, and Human-Computer Interaction (HCI). By reducing extraneous cognitive load and enhancing germane processing, well-designed materials can significantly improve learning efficiency. This makes CLT a valuable framework for educators, instructional designers, and interface developers seeking to create effective and cognitively efficient learning environments [31].

From the perspective of Cognitive Load Theory, debriefing is a crucial moment when knowledge stored in working memory is processed and transferred to long-term memory. It serves as an external stimulus, evoking new cognitive mechanisms. This situation is illustrated by the human memory processing model presented in Fig. 1. In this scheme, information is acquired by humans through a variety of channels associated with the different senses, commonly referred to as sensory memory. Working (short-term) memory is the part of our memory where we briefly store and actively process new information to help us think, learn, and understand. For learning to happen, information must first be processed in working memory before it can be stored in long-term memory. Long-term memory works unconsciously and holds information nearly permanently once we have truly learned it.

In simplified terms, this information is organized into mental structures called schemas [32]. When we encounter familiar information, these schemas are automatically retrieved from long-term memory and processed in working memory. This process is natural and effortless because it is a fundamental cognitive ability. More experienced learners can easily transfer large amounts of well-organized knowledge from long-term memory to working memory, helping them solve complex problems more efficiently than those with less knowledge [33]. Importantly, external stimulus can be a self-reflection, reflections of others, or the game experience itself.

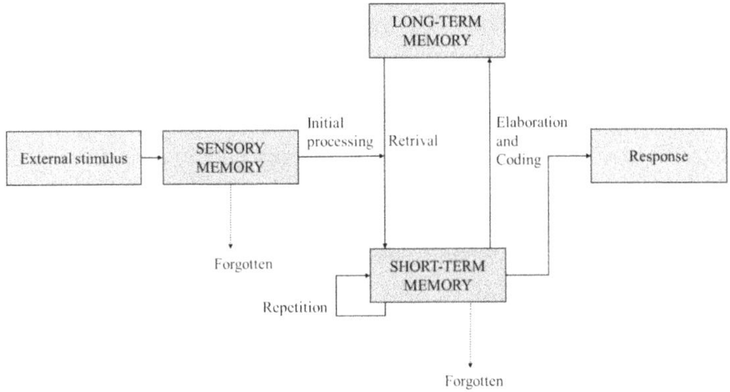

Fig. 1. Human memory processing based on Alasraj et al. [34]. Human memory processing model from the CLT perspective.

From this perspective, debriefing is a means of reinforcing the transfer of information from short-term to long-term memory. Information – i.e., new facts, skills, or opinions - in the form of game experiences and reflections, is processed in short-term memory, in reference to the existing knowledge. Participants' statements result from analyzing game experiences through the lens of cognitive schemas stored in long-term memory. Asking typical debriefing questions about the connection between the game experience and real life [35] or lessons learned [5] allows for a more effective integration of the game experience with existing cognitive schemas that the individual has developed so far, as well as the creation of completely new connections. Thus, debriefing is not only an important social and reflective process but also a cognitive one.

3 Embodied Cognitive Load Theory and Games as Embodied Experiences

Embodied cognition is a research paradigm within the cognitive sciences that explores the relations among humans' bodies, the external environment, and cognitive processes [38, 39, 40]. Emerged from this field, Embodied Cognitive Load Theory (ECLT) extends traditional Cognitive Load Theory by incorporating the role of the body and physical interactions in cognitive processing. While CLT primarily focuses on working memory limitations and instructional design, ECLT suggests that cognition is deeply influenced by bodily movements, gestures, and interactions with the environment [41–43]. According to this view, cognitive load is not only a function of mental effort but also of how learners physically engage with their surroundings. By distributing cognitive processing across the body and external tools, ECLT proposes that learning can be optimized by designing activities that integrate physical actions with cognitive tasks [42].

Numerous studies support the idea that embodied learning can reduce cognitive overload, enhance comprehension, and significantly improve learning effectiveness [43]. For example, using hand gestures while solving math problems has been shown to improve problem-solving efficiency by offloading cognitive demands [44] and enhancing individual learning [45]. Hosetter [46] argued that humans in general are genetically predisposed to engage in nonverbal communication, including gestures.

Similarly, interactive learning environments that involve movement, such as virtual reality or tangible user interfaces, can facilitate deeper understanding by leveraging multiple sensory and motor channels [47], a support claim widely confirmed by research on simulations and gaming. These findings suggest that instructional design should consider not just the complexity of the material but also the embodied aspects of learning, ensuring that physical actions complement cognitive processing rather than impose additional load. Beilock [48] summarized it by stating that *the way we move affects our thoughts, decisions, and preferences*, citing the example of kids who absorb more when they use their bodies as a learning tool.

Klabbers [49] stated that *a mixture of sensory-motor capacities is required to perform a game*. In the macro learning cycle, the game phase primarily fosters hands-on engagement, whereas structured reflection afterwards enables players to make broader connections to real-world applications. Games thus function within a *magic circle*, a temporary space where real-world dynamics and rules are suspended, yet the experiences within this space often transcend its boundaries, influencing players' behaviors, social structures, and cognitive development in meaningful ways. Through these mechanisms, simulation games not only provide immersive experiences but also serve as learning tools that integrate different cognitive processes and contextual social interactions.

Therefore, simulation games constitute an embodied experience as they typically involve some form of physical representation, whether through tangible components or digital interfaces that players interact with. Even when the game exists solely within the shared reality of its participants' minds, it has real-time effects on their relationships and interactions in the physical world, within the *magic circle*. It aligns with Kolb's [50] experiential learning cycle, where games serve as a medium for active experimentation and a basic experience, engaging players in direct action and decision-making. This concept is widely used in simulation and gaming literature to integrate debriefing and experience across the macro and micro cycles of simulation games.

Embodiment in games is achieved through game elements or bodily interactions imposed by the rules [53, 54]. In board games, embodiment emerges through tactile mechanics, such as manipulating objects or making specific moves [53]. Board games also involve spatial decision-making, or audio-based mechanics. In video games, embodiment is supported through interface design, mechanics such as motion-controlled gameplay (e.g., keyboard or pad), first-person perspective or head-tracking, and force feedback in controllers, enhancing sensory immersion and physical engagement [56, 57]. In VR, haptic gloves and controllers simulate object weight and texture, while full-body tracking in games encourages kinesthetic engagement [58–60]. Spatial awareness is heightened through 360-degree environments, while 3D spatial audio enhances auditory immersion. Even scent and taste can be integrated, using olfactory recognition as a gameplay mechanic [59]. Although these elements and mechanisms are present in studies on game design, HCI, or UX, their application to the debriefing phase is a relatively new idea.

4 Embodied Debriefing

Actions during the game and the related embodied experiences fuel the debriefing, which is a process of abstracting the individual's bodily experience into a shared conceptual understanding [49]. However, debriefing, as a key element in processing knowledge gained from a game, can also be an embodied experience. Therefore, when designing debriefing sessions, it is possible to engage participants in representing their thoughts and reflections through embodied modes—gestures, pointing, touching, tracing, drawing, and larger body movements [60]—which support the learning process.

For the purpose of this theoretical paper, we thus define embodied debriefing as:

a process that takes place after a simulation game session (or its parts), when participants reflect on their experiences and analyze the outcomes deploying modes of embodied cognition — bodily movements, gestures, and interactions with the environment.

This means that the traditional discussion is expanded with means to engage the senses and movement in the process of generating and processing reflections, reducing cognitive load, and facilitating the integration of game-based learning into mental schemas. Although the term embodied debriefing is not widely recognized, some simulation game designers intuitively apply practices that support embodied cognition.

For instance, Kriz and Nöbauer [61] discuss using physical mood indicators as part of debriefing or using physical positioning within a space to express feelings and the degree of agreement with given statements expressed by the facilitator or participants. Besides, Kriz [5] further suggests debriefing through expressive art techniques such as drawing, making sculptures with tangible materials, or using the human body as a living sculpture to express deeper meaning. Lastly, embodiment should be considered as a part of a recognized tradition of reflection in psychological studies, giving as an example systemic constellation work [62], art therapy [63], gestalt therapy [64], as well as some traditions of psychotherapeutic work [65] or psychodrama [66]. In the following section, we would like to discuss several examples of techniques used for embodied debriefing, along with practical case studies.

4.1 Case Study – Marketplace

Marketplace is a business simulation game, usually used for higher education purposes [69, 70], in which non-traditional debriefing approaches can be introduced. Students are involved in the process of making business decisions in conditions that mimic a real-life economic environment. The Marketplace business simulation game is an educational tool where players take on the role of entrepreneurs. The game simulates real-world marketplace dynamics and allows players to manage various aspects of running a business, including accounting, marketing, human resources, sales, and production.

The gameplay usually lasts 6 or 8 decision rounds (6 for part-time students and 8 for full-time students), each representing a quarter in the company's life. After each round, there is time for a reflective, debriefing session. During the formative assessment moments, a facilitator presents general information about the market and about what has happened in the last decision round. They discuss the situation with the students, representatives of all the companies. The facilitator asks how they feel about the results, and if anything surprised them during this round.

Debriefing as a Role-Play

Once during the gameplay, in the middle of the course, the debriefing session takes a different form. When students know how to interpret their company's results, they can secure additional financing from the investor. To do so, they are expected to engage in a role-playing exercise where they take on roles of entrepreneurs and the facilitator takes on the role of an investor. For the purpose of preparing to the role-play exercise, students analyze their results from the previous rounds and develop a strategy for the next quarters. This allows players to reflect on their decisions during the game and helps teams discuss their performance as a group. It helps them understand why certain choices lead to success or failure and encourages critical thinking. Additionally, students have the opportunity to participate in simulations of real business negotiations. They prepare all the documents needed, decide what to wear, and how to behave during such a meeting. Each participant must introduce themselves as a board member and describe their area of responsibility. The facilitator can ask questions about students' virtual companies, and it is also a great opportunity to provide feedback. The investor can ask about any issues that seem problematic in the company and offer advice and hints.

4.2   Case Study - The People

"The People" is a simulation game by Szatkowska, Ćwil and Wardaszko [35] that illustrates the complexity of social and political relationships during the migration crisis at the Polish-Belarusian border. It is a simulation board game incorporating elements of role-playing and collective storytelling. The game is played mostly by high school students as part of the social science curriculum.

During the game, participants observe the consequences of the crisis from various perspectives and learn about the dilemmas arising from the on-site legal framework, as seen through the viewpoints of borderland residents with varying attitudes towards refugees. Since the game can be a challenging experience—both emotionally and cognitively—it requires careful debriefing. The post-game debriefing follows a classic model of questions addressing emotions, in-game events, and their interpretations.

Debriefing as Creative Exercise

After the initial discussion, players engage in an exercise in which they create new rules and cards for the game to make it "legit". This activity facilitates reflection on what is missing in real life—whether in terms of legal solutions, social mechanisms, or political structures. Participants illustrate new cards and share their ideas. The artistic component supports reflection on these issues, while the creative process helps mitigate feelings of helplessness, which often affect teenagers who do not yet have jobs or a sense of influence on the world [69].

By first engaging with the current state of affairs in the game, participants are encouraged to explore potential solutions through a creative, reflective process. Research on the game's impact has demonstrated that after playing and participating in the exercises, ¼ more participants (61%) expressed a willingness to engage in volunteer work related to the issue.

4.3   Case Study – ICHIBA

The ICHIBA (marketplace in Japanese) exercise, conceptualized by Junkichi Sugiura and the author at the ISAGA Summer School in 2006, is an embodied debriefing technique that integrates dynamic group interaction and reflective discourse [70]. The core methodology involves participants moving around a designated space, referred to as the "marketplace," followed by a series of group-based discussions prompted by specific reflection questions. This technique facilitates interpersonal exchanges and encourages participants to reflect upon shared experiences and learning insights.

Participants begin by walking around the room for approximately 30 s to simulate navigating a marketplace. After this brief period, a facilitator signals participants to stop and form small discussion groups. These groups, typically consisting of three to four individuals, are expected to engage in short, focused dialogues concerning a specific question posed by the facilitator. These interactions resemble informal encounters in a marketplace where individuals engage in brief, spontaneous conversations. This phase is typically repeated several times (three to five rounds), with the groups being reshuffled after each round to foster diverse interactions and reflection on different topics.

To initiate engagement, the facilitator may pose simple, light-hearted questions designed to help participants get to know one another, such as "When was the last time you felt genuinely happy?" Alternatively, these questions may be directly relevant to the training context, such as "What was your most valuable team experience to date?" These prompts create an environment conducive to both initial bonding and meaningful reflection on the training themes. As the activity progresses, participants may reflect on their experiences within the exercise itself, with debriefing questions such as, "What insights can you apply to your professional practice based on the simulation?" or "Which aspect of today's workshop was most valuable to your learning process?".

Debriefing as Bodily Representations
The term *ICHIBA* also serves as an acronym, representing the following interpersonal integration framework:

- **I**: Interpersonal
- **C**: Comparison
- **H**: Horizontal
- **I**: Integration
- **B**: Border
- **A**: Awareness

This model incorporates interpersonal comparison and horizontal integration by recognizing boundaries within group interactions. In contrast to the basic "Marketplace" method, *ICHIBA* involves a deeper, more continuous reflective process in which participants remain focused on a single reflection question throughout multiple rounds.

In the *ICHIBA* exercise, participants initially form groups based on shared responses to the reflection question, such as "What significant learning experience did you have today?" If participants identify common insights, they physically connect (e.g., by holding hands) and proceed to walk around the room together in subsequent rounds. The continuous focus on a single reflection question promotes sustained interpersonal comparison. As the rounds progress, groups merge based on commonalities in their learning experiences, enabling the integration of diverse perspectives. However, certain boundaries may emerge as some groups or individuals may not find common ground, thus preserving the concept of "Border Awareness".

The objective of *ICHIBA* is not necessarily to achieve full group cohesion but to encourage awareness of both similarities and differences within the group. As participants interact, they navigate these boundaries, resulting in diverse group configurations—ranging from complete integration to fragmented, smaller groups. The end of the exercise involves a final reflection on these group dynamics, with participants sharing insights into their learning experiences.

ICHIBA is particularly effective when repeated with different reflective questions, allowing facilitators to explore how participants' opinions evolve over time. This iterative process offers insights into the collective distribution of opinions and the degree of consensus or divergence within the group. It provides valuable data on whether participants can unify under a common understanding or if distinct "blocks of opinion" emerge, illustrating the complexities of group decision-making and learning. Finally, it involves the whole body in the information processing and spatial distribution of opinions.

4.4   Limitations and Future Directions

Embodied cognition theories are a relatively new field of research in the context of simulation and games. The interdisciplinary nature of this approach means that our understanding of how specific environmental elements, design choices or bodily movements influence learning processes remains ambiguous, with knowledge scattered across various disciplines—including pedagogy, cognitive studies, adult education, HCI, and neurology. Besides, the effectiveness of embodied learning can be moderated by various factors [71], which requires an in-depth understanding of the broad context of the experience.

Currently, research on embodied cognition requires an experimental approach to determine the applicability of particular techniques in learning different types of material. For instance, teaching hard and soft skills through games may require entirely different debriefing strategies. Embodied cognition is also challenging to study due to the inherent complexity of the phenomenon, which does not easily fit into simple survey questions or interviews, as subjective experiences are difficult to quantify. This challenge may call for alternative research methods that consider physiological parameters or qualitative materials produced during experimental debriefing sessions. Finally, integrating new elements with well-established, documented debriefing techniques should be studied to ensure they complement each other, effectively supporting pedagogical goals and fostering long-term changes in participants.

5 Conclusion

Debriefing is a key activity for processing game experiences, as it enables clarification, the effective transfer of game learnings from working memory to long-term memory, and the integration of new knowledge with existing cognitive schemas. Embodied debriefing can offer a new perspective on designing debriefing for simulation games and game-based learning, accounting for human bodily predispositions and environmental influences. We conceptualized it as a process that takes place after a simulation game session (or its parts), when participants reflect on their experiences and analyze the outcomes, deploying modes of embodied cognition—bodily movements, gestures, and interactions with the environment.

In the paper, we discussed three forms of embodied debriefing - role-play, creative process, and bodily representations within space. However, this is not an enclosed list - it is rather an indication of the existing approaches and their connection to embodied cognitive studies. These cases deployed various means—dramatic expression, drawing, or movements —that complemented the learning goals of the games. The choice of these techniques was informed by the content participants would acquire and the nature of the core game exercises. We hope that this perspective will inform the design of debriefing as a rich and meaningful interaction space, grounded in its intrinsic connection to embodied learning processes.

Disclosure of Interests. Authors have no competing interests.

References

1. Kriz, W.C., Sugiura, J., Kikkawa, T.: Gaming simulation: terminology and fundamentals. In: Kikkawa, T., Kriz, W.C., Sugiura, J. (eds.) Gaming as a Cultural Commons. Translational Systems Sciences, vol. 28, pp. 3–23. Springer, Singapore (2022). https://doi.org/10.1007/978-981-19-0348-9_1
2. Nakamura, M.: Participants' perceptions of gaming simulation. In: Kaneda, T., Kanegae, H., Toyoda, Y., Rizzi, P. (eds.) Simulation and Gaming in the Network Society. Translational Systems Sciences, vol. 9, pp. 53–63. Springer, Singapore (2016). https://doi.org/10.1007/978-981-10-0575-6_5
3. Tipton, E.J., Leigh, E., Kriz, W.C., Crookall, D.: Debriefing: the real learning begins when the game stops. In: Simulation and Gaming in the Network Society, pp. 473–475 (2016)
4. Crookall, D.: Debriefing: a practical guide. In: Angelini, M.L.; Muñiz, R. (eds.) Simulation for Participatory Education: Virtual Exchange and Worldwide Collaboration, Springer Texts in Education, pp. 115–214 (2023)
5. Kriz, W.C.: A systemic-constructivist approach to the facilitation and debriefing of simulations and games. Simul. Gaming **41**(5), 663–680 (2010)

6. Schwägele, S., Zürn, B., Lukosch, H.K., Freese, M.: Design of an impulse-debriefing-spiral for simulation game facilitation. Simul. Gaming **52**(3), 364–365 (2021)

7. Crookall, D.: Engaging (in) gameplay and (in) debriefing. Simul. Gaming **45**(4–5), 416–427 (2014)

8. Deason, E.E., Efron, Y., Howell, R.W., Kaufman, S., Lee, J., Press, S.: Debriefing the debrief. Ohio State Public Law Working Paper (202) (2013) (2008)

9. Cantrell, M.A.: The importance of debriefing in clinical simulations. Clin. Simul. Nurs. 4(2), e19–e23

10. Crookall, D.: Serious games, debriefing, and simulation/gaming as a discipline. Simul. Gaming **41**(6), 898–920 (2010)

11. Shinnick, M.A., Woo, M., Horwich, T.B., Steadman, R.: Debriefing: the most important component in simulation? Clin. Simul. Nurs. **7**(3), e105–e111 (2011)

12. Barreteau, O., Le Page, C., Perez, P.: (2024): Contribution of simulation and gaming to natural resource management issues: an introduction. Simul. Gaming **38**(2), 185–194 (2007)

13. Zhang, J., Hu, Z.: Advancing game-based learning in higher education through debriefing: social constructivism theory. J. Educ. Gift. Young Sci. **12**(1), 15–27

14. Dufrene, C., Young, A.: Successful debriefing—Best methods to achieve positive learning outcomes: a literature review. Nurse Educ. Today **34**(3), 372–376 (2014)

15. Roungas, B., de Wijse, M., Meijer, S., Verbraeck, A.: Pitfalls for debriefing games and simulations: theory and practice. In: Naweed, A., Wardaszko, M., Leigh, E., Meijer, S. (eds.) Intersections in Simulation and Gaming. ISAGA SimTecT 2016 2016. Lecture Notes in Computer Science, vol. 10711, pp. 101–115. Springer, Cham (2018). https://doi.org/10.1007/978-3-319-78795-4_8

16. de Wijse-van Heeswijk, M., et al.: Debriefing as a leverage point for the transfer of simulation game learning outcomes to reality: building blocks before and during debriefing that enhance learning transfer. In: Kikkawa, T., Kriz, W.C., Sugiura, J., de Wijse-Van Heeswijk, M. (eds.) Transferring Gaming and Simulation Experience to the Real World. Translational Systems Sciences, vol. 43, pp. 39–71. Springer, Singapore (2025). https://doi.org/10.1007/978-981-96-2755-4_4

17. LeBaron, M., Alexander, N.M.: Death of the role-play. In: Honeyman, C., Coben, J., De Palo, G. (eds.) Rethinking Negotiation Teaching: Innovations for Context and Culture. DRI Press (2009)

18. Nicholson, S.: Completing the experience: debriefing in experiential educational games. In: Proceedings of the 3rd International Conference on Society and Information Technologies, pp. 117–121 (2012)

19. Kikkawa, T., Kriz, W.C., Sugiura, J.: Differences between facilitator-guided and self-guided debriefing on the attitudes of university students. In: Wardaszko, M., Meijer, S., Lukosch, H., Kanegae, H., Kriz, W.C., Grzybowska-Brzezińska, M. (eds.) Simulation Gaming Through Times and Disciplines. ISAGA 2019. Lecture Notes in Computer Science, vol. 11988, pp. 14–22. Springer, Cham (2021). https://doi.org/10.1007/978-3-030-72132-9_2

20. Lederman, L.C., Kato, F.: Debriefing the debriefing process: toward an expanded look. In: Crookall, D., Kiyoshi, A. (eds.) Simulation and Gaming Across Disciplines and Cultures. Sage, Thousand Oaks (2005)

21. Van Der Meij, H., Leemkuil, H., Li, J.L.: Does individual or collaborative self-debriefing better enhance learning from games? Comput. Hum. Behav. **29**(6), 2471–2479 (2013)

22. Alf, T., de Wijse, M., Trautwein, F.: The role of reflection in learning with simulation games–a multi-method quasi experimental research. Simul. Gaming **54**(6), 621–644 (2023)

23. Koops, M., Hoevenaar, M.: Conceptual change during a serious game: Using a lemniscate model to compare strategies in a physics game. Simul. Gaming, 1–18 (2012). https://doi.org/10.1177/1046878112459261

24. Krogh, K., Bearman, M., Nestel, D.: "Thinking on your feet"—a qualitative study of debriefing practice. Adv. Simul. **1**, 12 (2016)
25. Abegglen, S., Greif, R., Balmer, Y., Znoj, H., Nabecker, S.: Debriefing interaction patterns and learning outcomes in simulation: an observational mixed-methods network study. Adv. Simul. **7**, 28 (2022)
26. Sweller, J.: Cognitive load during problem solving: effects on learning. Cogn. Sci. **12**(2), 257–285 (1988)
27. Sweller, J., van Merriënboer, J.J.G., Paas, F.G.W.C.: Cognitive architecture and instructional design. Educ. Psychol. Rev. **10**(3), 251–296 (1998)
28. Sweller, J., Cooper, G.A.: The use of worked examples as a substitute for problem solving in learning algebra. Cogn. Instr. **2**(1), 59–89 (1985)
29. Mousavi, S.Y., Low, R., Sweller, J.: Reducing cognitive load by mixing auditory and visual presentation modes. J. Educ. Psychol. **87**(2), 319–334 (1995)
30. Ayres, P., Sweller, J.: The split-attention principle in multimedia learning. In: Mayer, R.E. (ed.) The Cambridge Handbook of Multimedia Learning, pp. 135–146. Cambridge University Press, Cambridge (2005)
31. Chandler, P., Sweller, J.: Cognitive load theory and the format of instruction. Cogn. Instr. **8**(4), 293–332 (1991)
32. McVee, M.B., Dunsmore, K., Gavelek, J.R.: Schema theory revisited. Rev. Educ. Res. **75**(4), 531–566 (2005)
33. Sweller, J.: Evolution of human cognitive architecture. Educ. Psychol. Rev. **15**(1), 1–55 (2003)
34. Alasraj, A., Freeman, M. B., Chandler, P.: Considering cognitive load theory within E-learning environments. In: Pacific Asia Conference on Information Systems (2011)
35. Szatkowska, W., Ćwil, M., Wardaszko, M.: Awareness over knowledge: an exploratory study on a refugee crisis game. Simul. Gaming **56**(2), 210–236 (2025)
36. Kontra, C., Goldin-Meadow, S., Beilock, S.L.: Embodied learning across the life span. Top. Cogn. Sci. **4**(4), 731–739 (2012)
37. Shapiro, L.: Embodied Cognition. Routledge, New York (2010)
38. Wilson, M.: Six views of embodied cognition. Psychon. Bull. Rev. **9**(4), 625–636 (2002)
39. Borghi, A.M., Cimatti, F.: Embodied cognition and beyond: acting and sensing the body. Front. Psychol. **1**, 1–14 (2010)
40. Hutto, D.D., Kirchhoff, M.D., Myin, E.: Extended, embodied cognition: a review. Cogn. Process. **16**(4), 319–332 (2015)
41. Skulmowski, A., Rey, G.D.: Embodied cognitive load theory: towards combining bodily and mental load factors. Educ. Psychol. Rev. **30**, 347–365 (2018)
42. Choi, H.H., van Merriënboer, J.J.G., Paas, F.: Effects of physical and mental practice on cognitive load and learning performance. Educ. Psychol. Rev. **26**, 225–244 (2014)
43. Lyu, S., Deng, L.: A meta-analysis of embodied learning in digital environments. Comput. Educ. **205**, 105–113 (2024)
44. Goldin-Meadow, S., Nusbaum, H., Kelly, S.D., Wagner, S.M.: Explaining math: gesturing lightens the load. Psychol. Sci. **12**(6), 516–522 (2001)
45. Dargue, N., Sweller, N., Jones, M.P.: When our hands help us learn: a meta-analysis of the effects of gesture on learning. Learn. Instr. **58**, 110–121 (2019)
46. Hostetter, A.B.: When do gestures communicate? A meta-analysis. Psychol. Bull. **137**(2), 297–315 (2011)
47. Johnson-Glenberg, M.C., Megowan-Romanowicz, C., Birchfield, D.A., Savvides, S.: Embodied games, next-gen simulations, and motoric-cognitive scaffolding: contributions to learning in STEM domains. Education Tech. Research Dev. **62**(4), 575–592 (2014)
48. Beilock, S.L.: How the Body Knows Its Mind: The Surprising Power of the Physical Environment to Influence How You Think and Feel. Atria Books, New York (2015)

49. Klabbers, J.H.G.: The Magic Circle: Principles of Gaming & Simulation. Sense Publishers, Rotterdam (2009)
50. Kolb, D.A.: Experiential Learning: Experience as the Source of Learning and Development. Prentice-Hall, Englewood Cliffs, NJ (1984)
51. Gee, J.P.: Video games and embodiment. Games Cult. **3**(3–4), 253–263 (2008). https://doi.org/10.1177/1555412008317309
52. Gregersen, A., Grodal, T.: Embodiment and interface. In: Perron, B., Wolf, M.J.P. (eds.) The Video Game Theory Reader 2, pp. 87–106. Routledge, New York (2008)
53. Arnab, S., et al.: Mapping learning and game mechanics for serious games analysis. Br. J. Educ. Technol. **46**(2), 391–411 (2015)
54. Farrow, R., Iacovides, I.: Gaming and the limits of digital embodiment. Philos. Technol. **27**, 221–233 (2014)
55. Kim, S.Y.S., Prestopnik, N., Biocca, F.A.: Body in the interactive game: how interface embodiment affects physical activity and health behavior change. Comput. Hum. Behav. **36**, 376–384 (2014)
56. Kilteni, K., Groten, R., Slater, M.: The sense of embodiment in virtual reality. Presence: Teleoperators Virtual Environ. **21**(4), 373–387 (2012)
57. Vázquez, C., Xia, L., Aikawa, T., Maes, P.: Words in motion: Kinesthetic language learning in virtual reality. In: Proceedings of the 2018 IEEE 18th International Conference on Advanced Learning Technologies, (ICALT), pp. 272–276. IEEE, New York (2018)
58. Johnson-Glenberg, M.C.: Immersive VR and education: embodied design principles that include gesture and hand controls. Front. Robot. AI **5**, 375272 (2018)
59. Davis, S.B., Davies, G., Haddad, R., Lai, M.K.: Smell me: engaging with an interactive olfactory game. In: Bryan-Kinns, N., Blanford, A., Curzon, P., Nigay, L. (eds.) People and Computers XX – Engage, pp. 27–39. Springer, London (2007). https://doi.org/10.1007/978-1-84628-664-3_3
60. Way, A., Ginns, P.: Embodied learning and cognitive load: a meta-analysis and theoretical integration. Educ. Psychol. Rev. **36**, 1–28 (2024)
61. Kriz, W.C., Nöbauer, B.: Teamkompetenz. Konzepte, Trainingsmethoden, Praxis, 4th edn. Vandenhoeck & Ruprecht, Göttingen (2008)
62. Schneider, J.R.: Family Constellations: Basic Principles and Procedures. Carl-Auer-Systeme Verlag, Heidelberg, Germany (2007)
63. Edwards, D.: Art Therapy. Sage, London (2013)
64. Brownell, P.: Gestalt Therapy: A Guide to Contemporary Practice. Springer Publishing, New York, NY (2010)
65. Fugate, J.M., Macrine, S.L., Hernandez-Cuevas, E.M.: Therapeutic potential of embodied cognition for clinical psychotherapies: from theory to practice. Cogn. Ther. Res. **48**(4), 574–598 (2024)
66. Kedem-Tahar, E., Felix-Kellermann, P.: Psychodrama and drama therapy: a comparison. Arts Psychother. **23**(1), 27–36 (1996)
67. Cadotte, E.R.: How to use simulation games in the classroom? J. Entrepreneurship **31**(2_suppl), S90–S134 (2022)
68. Lokhande, M., Cadotte, E.R., Agrawal, B.: Molding conscious leaders. South Asian J. Bus. Manag. Cases **8**(3), 262–275 (2019)
69. Szatkowska, W.: The people: a serious role-playing game designed to address a humanitarian crisis. Int. J. Role-Playing IJRP **14**, 9–21 (2023). Full Issue
70. Kriz, W.C.: Time capsule of gaming simulation: back to the future of ISAGA. In: Kaneda, T., Kanegae, H., Rizzi, P., Toyoda, Y. (eds.) Hybrid Simulation and Gaming in the Networked Society, pp. 4–31. Jasag, Kyoto (2015)
71. Lyu, Y., Deng, L.: Embodied cognitive load theory: a systematic review and research agenda. Educ. Psychol. Rev. **36**, 1–25 (2024)

Developing an Evaluation Design
for a Simulation-Based Team Training Series
with Global Virtual Teams: A Virtual Action
Learning Approach

Nick Ludwig[(✉)] [iD]

Friedrich Schiller University Jena, Jena, Germany
`Nick.ludwig@uni-jena.de`

Abstract. Global Virtual Teams (GVTs) show great potential and importance in a globalised and digitally connected world. Research on how to train GVTs and how to evaluate training impact remains underexplored, especially for simulation-based training interventions. Virtual Experiential Learning (VEL) offers a promising approach, yet its impact is rarely assessed through rigorous evaluation. This study develops an evaluation design using Virtual Action Learning (VAL), an iterative methodology integrating participants into the evaluation process to enhance relevance and accuracy.

The study addresses two key research gaps: the limited implementation of digital simulation-based team training for GVTs and the lack of thorough evaluations for such training approaches. By developing a longitudinal, mixed-methods evaluation design for simulation-based team training series, this research aims to bridge these gaps.

Following an Action Research approach, two GVTs from an international energy and mobility organization participated in a VEL team training series, followed by four iterative evaluation cycles to develop a formative and summative evaluation design. A mixed-methods framework was used, measuring training impact across four levels—reaction, learning, behaviour, and organisational results—adapting Kirkpatrick's model to digital, intercultural team environments.

Findings highlight the need for a multi-layered evaluation framework. Balancing summative and formative approaches ensures both immediate feedback and long-term impact assessment. Integrating participant-driven adaptation enhances evaluation validity, while the mixed-methods design captures both quantitative and qualitative insights.

This study contributes to evaluation research by offering a structured yet flexible model for assessing VEL interventions in GVTs, advancing methodological discussions on training effectiveness and impact measurement.

Keywords: Evaluation · Simulation-based Team Training · Virtual Action Learning · Virtual Experiential Learning · Global Virtual Teams

F. Trautwein et al. (Eds.): ISAGA 2025, LNCS 16439, pp. 162–176, 2026.
https://doi.org/10.1007/978-3-032-20129-4_12

1 Introduction

Evaluating a training serves two purposes: first, it allows for the establishment of a "link" between the intervention and an impact on participating individuals, their teams and organizations, thus proving its effectiveness [1]. Second, by proving this effectiveness training can be legitimized [2]. Conducting an evaluation, however, has several pitfalls to overcome. Mainly but not only, improper interpretation and inappropriate use of results, as well as inappropriate data-gathering instruments, cause evaluations to fail [2]. However, studies call for increasingly sophisticated evaluation designs: Individual satisfaction, knowledge improvements, or behavioral changes are less of interest than organizational or societal impacts. Next to the evaluation's content, an elaborate design is increasingly requested [3–5]. Thus, longitudinal studies measuring impact at multiple points in time and reflecting not only individual outcomes but also impacts on a group, organization, or societal level are, on the one hand, called for; on the other hand, they highlight the problem of conducting an evaluation.

The intricacy of conducting an evaluation can be seen in the scarcity of evaluations in the field of trainings focusing on cross-cultural competence in general, but especially in the field of Global Virtual[1] Team training [1, 5–7]. The three intertwined trends of globalization, digitization, and the increasing use of teams as the most preferred form of collaboration have caused a rise in Global Virtual Teams [8–10]. GVTs promise great potential for solving challenges caused by these developments: they bundle expertise [11], save resources [12] and lead to innovation [8]. Thus, they have become the center of attention in the practice of large, multinational organizations and research: GVTs "are becoming the norm, rather than an exception" [9]. However, the characteristics that lead to this potential cause several pitfalls: GVTs face challenges in dealing with complexity, digital communication and intercultural interaction. Even though knowledge, skills, abilities and others (KSAOs) needed for GVTs have been theoretically and methodologically analyzed [8, 9], interventions aiming at training and developing these KSAOs are scarce but suggest that Virtual Experiential Learning holds promise for methodologically fostering this competence [13–16]. Nevertheless, evaluation within this domain remains an underdeveloped yet significant area of research.

Evaluations in the field of simulation-based training focuses on the one hand on theoretical considerations, debating on what and how exactly to evaluate [17, 18]. On the other hand, empirical findings and meta-analyses focus either only on the simulation and not the whole program [19], on methods of how to asses a simulation's effectiveness [20] or evaluate programs for students in specialized areas [21].

Thus, three sub-fields of evaluation studies emerge, to which this study aims to contribute: although a few evaluation studies for digital simulations exist [22–24], this

---

[1] Concerning the question of whether to use the term "virtual" or "digital": Even though the notions of the two concepts seem too entangled to call for the dominance of one over the other, I speak of digital, whenever I am not referring to a specific concept that has been coined as "virtual" by the original author, due to three reasons. Firstly, the term digital implies that something is created or stored using computer technology rather than a simulation of reality. Secondly, it implies that it can be physical or digital instead of not physically presented, and lastly, because it can be tangible or intangible rather than existing only in the mind.

research area is yet to be explored in-depth, as the same is true for team training via simulations (however, mainly conducted in the field of medicine) [25–27] and the combination of both areas, digital team training through simulations.

The study aims to bridge these resulting research gaps. First, with GVTs increasing in their existence, the resulting need for developing and training them is, although apparent, scarcely researched. Second, sophisticated longitudinal evaluation designs reflecting team and/or organizational impact of trainings are generally scarce. Specifically, the evaluation of virtual experiential learning interventions in the form of online simulation-based training for GVTs is underexplored [16], making this a research gap of high importance for researchers and practitioners. The developmental process is based on an Action Research approach, thus catering to the appropriateness and adequateness of methods for measuring this construct by involving participants in reflecting on this appropriateness [28–31].

2 Theory

2.1 Global Virtual Teams

A Global virtual team can be described as an "interdependent virtual team whose members are geographically and time-dispersed across cultural and national boundaries" [9] The definition of GVTs as a sub-form of Virtual Teams (VTs), however, relies on the concept of virtual teams, which are „groups of geographically, organizationally and/or time dispersed workers brought together by information and telecommunication technologies to accomplish one or more organizational tasks" [9]. The difference between virtual teams (VTs) and GVTs then lies in "cultural [...] boundaries": Members of GVTs are not only separated by geographic and thus temporal distance, but their main characteristics are differences in language, cultural values, and daily experiences [8, 9]. The individual members of these teams are then united in a team-based structure facilitated by telecommunication technologies to complete organizational tasks interdependently and achieve desirable task and organizational outcomes. [9].

2.2 Developing Global Virtual Teams

On the one hand, several potential promising factors, such as bundling expertise [11], saving resources [12], and leading to innovation [8], provide strong legitimacy for the increasing appearance of GVTs. On the other hand, challenges like dealing with a complex, dynamically evolving environment, intercultural interactions and digital communication [8, 9] prove that working in GVTs successfully demands requirements. These two sides demonstrate the necessity for appropriate development measures to improve GVTs in the areas of intercultural interaction, digital communication, and complex problem-solving. Three trends have emerged in the field of team training, serving as guidelines for developing GVTs appropriately: Conducting the interventions digitally [32–34], the call for appropriateness of an approach to teaching and learning styles of the team, especially when working with heterogeneous groups such as GVTs [35, 36] and lastly, using simulations [19–21; for the case of GVTs see 22].

Simulations create immersive, relatable, and authentic experiences that closely mimic work environments without replicating them exactly [40, 41]. These simulations offer three key advantages: they foster acceptance through authenticity and immersion, integrate gamification to enhance engagement, and provide freedom of action by maintaining a safe distance from real-world tasks [18]. Simulations and well-designed games create a model of the reality participants need to learn about, before a reflective debriefing of the experience transfers these learnings back into reality. By simulating a version or an extract of reality, computer-based simulations provide a "playing field" for the experience that is later reflected and transformed into learning with three main advantages: it is accepted by team members firstly due to its authentic, thick, and complex representation or simulation of an artificial environment. Secondly, the developments in the simulation, combined with an overarching goal and subtasks, lead to gamification, causing another point explaining the acceptance and, thus, legitimacy of using Experiential Learning for team development. Thirdly, since the simulated reality is not the actual reality, the distance to the actual task they work on leads to the freedom of action that makes it a highly reliable and valid instrument [18, 42].

The form of (virtual) Experiential Learning [43, 44] offers characteristics matching the requirements of an appropriate way to design and implement development measures for GVTs, catering to their uniqueness [45] and allowing to conduct simulation-based training approaches. Kolb's Experiential Learning Theory (ELT) conceptualizes learning as a dynamic and holistic process in which knowledge is created through the transformation of experience [46–48]. It is structured around a learning cycle involving four interrelated modes—Concrete Experience, Reflective Observation, Abstract Conceptualization, and Active Experimentation—driven by the resolution of the dialectics experience/abstraction and action/reflection [46, 48]. ELT emphasizes that learning is not a linear outcome, but a recursive process shaped by the interaction between individuals and their environment. Rooted in the work of scholars like Lewin and Follett, ELT also provides a foundational link to action research by integrating scientific inquiry with practical experience [48].

The digital character of GVTs and the necessity of authenticity concerning the simulation cause a digital implementation of Experiential Learning. This is reflected in the sub form of virtual Experiential Learning (VEL) [43–45, 49]: "Virtual experiential learning is achieved through the integration of different motivating technologies like virtual reality, augmented reality, games and simulations in an active learning context" [43]. Thus, virtual Experiential Learning as a subform of Kolb's experiential learning [46] matches the team-development intervention's demands for a GVT.

2.3 Evaluating Developing Global Virtual Teams

In the evaluation of simulations for team development, most studies adopt a summative approach, focusing on assessing the overall effectiveness of a finished simulation in comparison to alternative teaching methods [21]. While such evaluations are useful for making final judgments about merit or impact, they often overlook the underlying mechanisms and contextual factors that contribute to a simulation's success [17, 21]. In contrast, formative evaluation approaches aim to support the ongoing development and refinement of simulation-based learning tools. By examining how and why simulations work, formative evaluations provide a scientific basis for program improvement and enhance their effectiveness in specific learning contexts.

One summative model guiding evaluation research for several decades has been Kirkpatrick's model of four levels: "It has helped focus training evaluation practice on outcomes […], fostered the recognition that single outcome measures cannot adequately reflect the complexity of organizational training programs, and underscored the importance of examining multiple measures of training effectiveness" [3]. The model includes four levels on which a training's impact can be evaluated: *"reaction"*, *"learning"*, *"job performance"*, and *"organizational impact"* [50].

With the first level, learners' *reactions* to the intervention are investigated. How satisfied were they with, e.g. the training's content, material, facilitators, methods, etc.? [51–53].The second level serves the evaluation of the content, examining what employees learned from participating in the training program. *Learning* then can be constituted as "the extent to which participants change attitudes, improve knowledge, and/or increase skill as a result of attending the program" [53]. *Performance* is the degree to which participants apply their newly acquired knowledge and skills on the job [51]. This constitutes level three. Finally, the *organizational impact* includes all attempts to measure actual relevant organizational changes due to the training intervention, such as increased sales, lowered turnover, decreased costs, or increased production [52, 53].

Formative evaluation, particularly in the form of theory-based approaches [17, 21], offers a structured alternative to summative methods by focusing not only on outcomes but on the underlying processes that lead to those outcomes. Such approaches—also known as theory-driven, program theory, or theory-oriented evaluations—seek to clarify and test the assumptions that guide how a simulation is expected to produce its effects. Instead of referring to grand theories, these evaluations often use logic models to map the intended pathways between inputs, processes, and outcomes in a specific educational context. In simulation-based learning, this involves distinguishing between the simulation's internal model and a second-level logic model that represents its educational application, including, e.g. hypotheses about success factors. Reynolds [54] outlines a seven-step process for using logic models as one form of theory-based evaluation approach [17, 21], from model development and outcome measurement to testing causal mechanisms and identifying improvements in both the simulation's design and implementation.

Compared to outcome-oriented "black-box" evaluations, formative approaches reveal why a simulation works by identifying key mediating factors such as learner characteristics or group interactions. This is particularly valuable when transferring simulations to new contexts or target groups [17, 18, 21]. Ultimately, logic models serve as a conceptual backbone for formative evaluation: they guide the design of evaluation strategies, support interpretation of results, and help optimize simulation-based learning environments.

Thus, this study balances summative and formative approaches: by using the four levels as evaluation areas for a simulation-based team training series and involving the teams in their analysis via an Action Research approach, the foundation for a logic model for the complete training series is prepared.

3 Research Design and Methods

3.1 The Participating Global Virtual Teams

The two participating GVTs are both part of the same international organization in the energy and mobility sector. Team A, consisting of 13 people from four countries (Germany, India, China, and Romania) on two continents, works in the field of agile software development. One main part of the team is located in Germany, sometimes conducting sub-team meetings in person. The person holding the role of the Product Owner played a key role, providing input on team challenges three times before the start of the training series and analyzing the evaluation design and its results together with the Scrum Master after each evaluation, thus contributing to the planning phases.

Team B is comprised of seven people from three countries (Germany, Poland, India) on two continents and works together for the same organization in the form of traditional project management. The team, even though working together to reach a shared goal, has less of a shared working environment since its members mostly fulfil the roles of leading sub-teams and coming together only for specific meetings. The leader of the team, together with his manager, provided insights on the team's challenges twice before the training series started. The evaluation results were analyzed by these two, together with one sub-team leader, resulting in feedback applicable to adjusting the training and evaluation concept.

3.2 The Research Design: Applying Virtual Action Learning to a Virtual Experiential Learning Intervention

By applying a Virtual Action Learning (VAL) [28, 30, 31] design of *action*, *investigation* and *adaptation* to the specific context of the two developed GVTs, the research design for developing an evaluation design emerges. The research design followed the circle of *action* (implementation of the training session), *investigation* (follow-up evaluation), and *adaptation* (training choices for the next session). For each team, four Action Research cycles of *action*, *investigation*, and *adaptation* were conducted, informing the final evaluation design.

The analysis of the first evaluation *investigated* the question of where the training evaluation did and did not evaluate an impact. This resulted in an *adaptation* of the evaluation design, trying to solve the recurring problem of different impact areas that require special, appropriate methods of conducting and analyzing data to evaluate impact appropriately. This *adapted* approach was then again *acted* on, restarting the *action*, *investigation*, and *adaptation* process of Action Research [28, 31, 55]. This was repeated for another two training sessions and their evaluation, which concluded in a final analysis and resulting adaptation of the evaluation concept.

***Action*: The Conducted Team Training Series**

The four-session training series aimed at facilitating knowledge, skills and attitudes (KSA) for the GVT-specific topics of intercultural interaction (session 1), dealing with complexity (session 2), digital communication (session 3), and the interdependency of these three challenges (session 4). For each session, objectives on all three levels

(KSA) were stated, serving as referring frames for the success and thus evaluation of the training's impact [2, 56, 57].

Each session had a similar (but due to necessary *adaptations* not identical) procedure based on Kolb's Experiential Learning Cycle (ELC) [46]. The session started with a *concrete experience* after a brief introduction. The team participated in the online simulation "Eternal Ice"[2], a mid-fidelity simulation designed for virtual experiential learning. Developed in 2020, it entails up to four different sessions, in which the participants have to solve different challenges, corresponding to the topic of the session while also relating to their everyday work: operating under time pressure, communicating via videoconference and exchanging chat messages with the simulated team manager while making critical in-game decisions. By managing tasks and visualizing communication processes, participants experience realistic team dynamics, decision-making, and problem-solving in a virtual environment [58].

The subsequent *reflection* was implemented via a joint debriefing [59], focusing on topics identified prior to the session, together with the team or based on the facilitator's observations. This reflection was enriched with theories and models building on the previously identified problems corresponding to the session's topic, constituting the *theoretical integration* of Kolb's ELC [46, 48]. The sessions concluded with the *active experimentation part*, consisting of the attempt to transfer key learnings via self-reflective methods (e.g., letter to oneself, construction of resolutions, etc.).

Investigation: The Conducted Evaluation

As the evaluation of the training itself was based on Kirkpatrick's evaluation model, *reactions* of the participants, their *learning*, possible *behavioral* changes and the *organizational* impact of the simulation-based team training series were evaluated.

The level of *reaction* was measured with a 5-point Likert scale asking for satisfaction with the following items: *Facilitator knowledge, facilitator behavior, simulation, debriefing, theoretical input, and tools used during the session.*[3] The scale ranged from *very dissatisfied* to *dissatisfied, neutral*, and *satisfied* to *very satisfied*.

Learning was evaluated via tests and self-disclosure. The test contained multiple single-choice components. Here, aspects and main takeaways of the discussed theories and models of the session's topic were investigated. The self-disclosure was conducted with another 5-point Likert scale asking for the satisfaction with and amount of learning, and open-text responses [60].

Performance evaluation was conducted observantly via a self-developed Behavioural Marker System (BMS) [6, 61, 62] applied for the same kind of meetings over 6 months. Interviews with the team leaders validated the observation results. The BMS consisted of three sub-systems, each one focusing on one topic addressed in a session: Sub-system IC for intercultural interaction, sub-system C for dealing with complexity, and sub-system DC for digital communication. The content and scope (number of categories and

---

[2] More information about the simulation can be found on the developers' website (https://tea mera.me/methods/) and in the explanatory video (https://youtu.be/ZYcuuo6R8fc).

[3] This and all other surveys, as well as the following behavioral marker systems and the final evaluation design can be requested from the author, as they can't be provided here for limitations of space.

corresponding elements) of the sub-systems varied according to the investigation and adaptation of the corresponding session (see discussion below).

Evaluating *organizational impact* relied on the one side of data made accessible by the organization of the participating GVTs. For one team, quantitative organizational performance data was provided, focusing on the *quality* and *quantity of communication* via measuring *meeting duration, velocity of work*, and *fluctuation*. On the other side, a questionnaire evaluated the constructs of *psychological safety* [63] and *job satisfaction* [64] at the beginning and end of the Action Research process.

***Adaptation*: The Conducted Virtual Action Learning Approach**

After analyzing the evaluation results, they were discussed with the team leaders. Next to these interviews, notes by the facilitator during the session and a field diary after the session were analyzed, thus forming a second source for the adaptation. Lastly, team members either gave indirect feedback via the team leaders or reached out to the facilitator via email. The content of this feedback served as the third foundation for a revision of the training and evaluation design.

4 Data and Results

The collected and analyzed data can be presented according to the Action Research process. The implementation of the four simulation-based trainings per team, making up the *action* part, was recorded, thus eight videos of the 2:30h training sessions were obtained.

The *investigation*, informed by Kirkpatrick's evaluation model, included data about all four levels: *reactions* were collected via the survey eight times in total (after each of the four sessions for both teams). *Learning* was investigated 18 times in total: three times per topic (baseline/before the training, after the session, after the whole series concluded) on the three topics of the training for both teams. *Behavior* and possible behavioral changes were analyzed through the observation of ten recorded meetings: five per team (baseline / before the meeting, and after each of the four sessions). Data on the *organizational results*, constituting the training impact on the organization, was collected through a survey before and after the training series per team (4 surveys), and additional quantitative data on meeting duration and velocity of work was provided by one team.

Data concerning the *adaptation* consists of eight interviews with the team leaders for validating the evaluation/investigation results and the resulting changed approaches, a field diary of the facilitator containing thoughts on the training, the evaluation of the training and possible solutions or thoughts on new approaches, as well as several emails of participants with feedback on the evaluation design. Analyzing these data and subsequently *adapting* the evaluation's content and form of the applied methods is intended by Action Research inquiries [30, 31, 55].

4.1 Adaptations to the Evaluation Design

To evaluate participants' *reactions*, the survey's content was adapted, as well as semi-structured interviews focusing on the impressions of the team leaders, and the offer to provide "informal" feedback via email was added. A question specifying what tools the satisfaction was related to was appended, as multiple tools were used, and the question by itself was perceived as confusing. Next, the items *"general atmosphere"* and *"teammates"* were added as team members attributed a high relevance to these aspects concerning overall satisfaction with the training. Lastly, the language of the survey was smoothed out, as participants perceived some questions as too complicated.

The original design for collecting data concerning *learning* did not include an open-text response for stating key learnings about the topic, only relying on quantitative self-disclosure about the satisfaction with the learnings. The author perceived this as limiting insights into precise pieces of learning content, therefore also limiting hypotheses about learning mechanisms. Thus, the open-text item *"Please reflect on the session about [e.g. intercultural competence]: What did you take out of that session?"* was added. After having conducted the first training sessions, another source for evaluating learning became evident: The transfer part at the end of each VEL-based session includes the manifestation of key takeaways.

Evaluating *learning* in a VEL intervention presents a pragmatic dilemma: precise assessment requires stable, time-robust testing, yet the flexibility inherent in VEL and VAL approaches demands adaptability. As theoretical input may shift in response to team reflections during the simulation, using the same test pre- and post-intervention becomes problematic. In this study, an extensive initial test allowed for post-hoc adaptation—omitting irrelevant items while retaining enough data to draw meaningful conclusions about participants' *learning*.

The analysis of how *performance* was evaluated results in two findings. First, interviews proved insightful for validating observations or for adjusting hypotheses and understanding the observed behavior of team members. Second, observing behavior and behavioral changes possibly caused by the training via a behavioral marker system is an insightful and fruitful approach. However, the quality of its insights depends on the quality of the marker system. Thus, the systems were repeatedly redefined by adding categories and elements inductively to the original theory-based marker systems. The resulting number of categories and elements caused a scope of the systems that included more than 60 elements in total, making them too extensive and unmanageable. Following the remarks of the interviewees, the systems were reduced. Each system consists of five different categories, resulting in a different number of elements. System C (Complexity) includes eleven elements, system IC (intercultural interaction) contains 18 elements, and system DC (digital communication) holds 16 elements.

Data concerning *organizational impact* was collected at the beginning and end of the Virtual Action Learning process, with the analysis results presented in the last session to the team. Therefore, this part of the evaluation design underwent only one *action, investigation,* and *adaptation* cycle in contrast to the four cycles the other three levels went through. Investigating this part of the evaluation indicates the necessity to have continuous access to organizational performance data and the clarity of possible *organizational impact* areas. Only then can the content and form of the data allow for a coherent analysis of the training's impact on the organizational performance.

4.2 The Final Evaluation Design

As Action Research [31, 55] and its sub-form of Virtual Action Learning [28, 30] understand research as an ongoing inquiry in which method and results are constantly interdependent, the evaluation design was adapted in content and methods.

After four Virtual Action Learning cycles, evaluating *reactions* via a survey including 10 items (see above), semi-structured interviews and "informal" channels such as e-mail proved appropriate. Even though raising research-pragmatic challenges, evaluating team members' *learning* through VEL interventions can be conducted, as shown after several VAL cycles. Tests focusing on the addressed theories and models, quantitative and qualitative self-disclosure about learning, and the consideration of in-training takeaways were developed as appropriate methods for evaluating *learning*. Investigating and adapting the design to evaluate *performance* led, on the one hand, to a behavioral marker system, including three sub-systems (see above). On the other hand, validating the observational results by interviewing the team leaders and focusing on changes in the team behavior was sometimes perceived as laborious, but never as unnecessary. Lastly, the *investigation* and *adaptation* of how to evaluate *organizational impact* indicated a strong connection between the training objectives and related areas of organizational performance. The Virtual Action Learning cycle concluded in a two-fold approach: on the one side, easily accessible data about more general aspects of working in a GVT (such as fluctuation, job satisfaction and psychological safety) were collected with a survey designed by the author. On the other side, team-specific aspects of organizational impact were conducted (for an agile team, e.g. velocity, meeting duration, quality of communication).

5 Conclusion: Discussion of Results and Implications

The evaluation of simulation-based team development interventions remains a complex challenge, often resulting in a scarcity of rigorous assessments. This study addresses this gap by developing a comprehensive evaluation design for simulation-based Virtual Experiential Learning (VEL) interventions within Global Virtual Teams (GVTs) using Virtual Action Learning (VAL). Given the increasing reliance on GVTs due to globalization and digital collaboration, effective evaluation models that measure training impact at individual, team, and organizational levels are crucial.

Key findings underscore the need for a sophisticated and adaptable evaluation framework for VEL interventions in GVTs. Effective evaluation must consider the complexity of the didactic design and the specific characteristics of virtual teams. This includes capturing the quality and subjectivity of participants' *reactions*, assessing the type of knowledge gained while balancing pre- and post-intervention data collection, and accounting for how digital media mediate both *behavior* and its observation. Evaluating *organizational impact* further requires thoughtful operationalization of goals and careful collection of contextual data. Ultimately, the effectiveness of the evaluation relies on the quality of its instruments. These findings can flow into an overarching theory-based approach for evaluation and thus inform the development of a "program model" [17, 21].

The integration of VAL ensures a methodological match between the methodological approaches of conducting the training via VEL and evaluating the training, thus expanding the recent claim and approach by other simulation evaluation studies of applying theory-oriented approaches for the evaluation of gaming and simulations in their context of use [17, 21]. This provides a first foundation for a formative approach, also catering to developing a "program model" through reflecting on inputs and processes influencing the training outcome and thus its impact. Moreover, the fact that the content of each session and between sessions is accordingly adjusted from the reflection and investigation part requires a comprehensive instrument that filters out according to how each training was carried out. VAL, with its transparent and reflective character, promises to be such an instrument. Thus, participants actively contribute to shaping evaluation methods, thereby enhancing the validity and applicability of the assessment tools.

The proposed evaluation model offers contributions to both theory and practice in the field of simulation and gaming. Theoretically, it enriches existing evaluation research in the field by integrating Virtual Action Learning (VAL), thereby bridging a connection between Experiential Learning Theory (ELT) and Action Research (AR) that, while conceptually established for non-virtual scenarios, has rarely been applied in digital contexts. Furthermore, the suggested design combines summative and formative approaches to evaluate digital, simulation-based team trainings. Practically, the model supports team developers and trainers in designing effective interventions for global virtual teams (GVTs) by addressing their unique challenges. For evaluation practitioners, it provides principles and methods not only to assess training impact, but also to critically examine the validity of the evaluation process itself.

The study may be limited in its external validation due to the number of evaluated GVTs. However, this limitation is addressed through an expert panel (as asked by Action Research approaches) of academics and practitioners who critically review findings and the final evaluation model.

By combining different approaches (e.g. summative approaches as suggested by Kirkpatrick and formative approaches such as theory-based evaluation), the emerging independent field of simulation evaluation is strengthened through this study.

Disclosure of Interests. The authors have no competing interests to declare that are relevant to the content of this article.

References

1. Mendenhall, M.E., Stahl, G.K., Ehnert, I., Oddou, G., Osland, J.S., Torsten, M.K.: Evaluation studies of cross-cultural training programs - a review of the literature from 1988–2000. In: Handbook of Intercultural Training, pp. 129–143. SAGE Publications, Thousand Oaks, Calif (2004)
2. Topno, H.: Evaluation of training and development: an analysis of various models. IOSRJBM. **5**, 16–22 (2012). https://doi.org/10.9790/487X-0521622

3. Bates, R.: A critical analysis of evaluation practice: the Kirkpatrick model and the principle of beneficence. Eval. Program Plann. **27**, 341–347 (2004). https://doi.org/10.1016/j.evalprogplan.2004.04.011

4. Njah, J., et al.: Measuring for success: evaluating leadership training programs for sustainable impact. Ann. Glob. Health **87**, 63 (2021). https://doi.org/10.5334/aogh.3221

5. Wang, M.L., Gomes, A., Rosa, M., Copeland, P., Santana, V.J.: A systematic review of diversity, equity, and inclusion and antiracism training studies: Findings and future directions. Transl. Behav. Med. **14**, 156–171 (2024). https://doi.org/10.1093/tbm/ibad061

6. Salas, E., Reyes, D.L., Woods, A.L.: The assessment of team performance: observations and needs. In: von Davier, A., Zhu, M., Kyllonen, P. (eds.) Innovative Assessment of Collaboration. Methodology of Educational Measurement and Assessment, pp. 21–36. Springer, Cham (2017). https://doi.org/10.1007/978-3-319-33261-1_2

7. Salas, E., et al.: Does team training improve team performance? A meta-analysis. Hum. Factors **50**, 903–933 (2008). https://doi.org/10.1518/001872008X375009

8. Schulze, J., Krumm, S.: The "virtual team player": a review and initial model of knowledge, skills, abilities, and other characteristics for virtual collaboration. Organ. Psychol. Rev. **7**, 66–95 (2017). https://doi.org/10.1177/2041386616675522

9. Scott, C.P.R., Wildman, J.L.: Culture, communication, and conflict: a review of the global virtual team literature. In: Wildman, J., Griffith, R. (eds.) Leading Global Teams, pp. 13–32. Springer, New York, NY (2015). https://doi.org/10.1007/978-1-4939-2050-1_2

10. Wang, R., Rechl, F., Bigontina, S., Fang, D., Günthner, W.A., Fottner, J.: Enhancing intercultural competence of engineering students via GVT (Global Virtual Teams)-based virtual exchanges: an international collaborative course in intralogistics education. In: Proceedings of the International Association for Development of the Information Society (IADIS) International Conference on E-Learning (Lisbon, Portugal, July 20–22, 2017), pp. 137–146. International Association for the Development of the Information Society, Lisbon, Portugal (2017)

11. Goettsch, K.L.: Working with global virtual teams: a case study reality check on intercultural communication best practices. Glob. Adv. Bus. Commun. Conf. J. **5**, 26 (2016)

12. Cagiltay, K., Bichelmeyer, B., Kaplan Akilli, G.: Working with multicultural virtual teams: critical factors for facilitation, satisfaction and success. Smart Learn. Environ. **2**, 11 (2015). https://doi.org/10.1186/s40561-015-0018-7

13. Ferreira-Lopes, L., Elexpuru-Albizuri, I., Bezanilla, M.J.: Developing business students' intercultural competence through intercultural virtual collaboration: a task sequence implementation. JIEB. **14**, 338–360 (2021). https://doi.org/10.1108/JIEB-06-2020-0055

14. Syzenko, A., Diachkova, Y.: Building cross-cultural competence in a foreign language through technology-enhanced project-based learning. AI. 9, 411–418 (2020). https://doi.org/10.34069/AI/2020.27.03.45

15. Wiggins, B.E.: Toward a model for intercultural communication in simulations. Simul. Gaming **43**, 550–572 (2012). https://doi.org/10.1177/1046878111414486

16. Zwerg-Villegas, A.M., Martínez-Díaz, J.H.: Experiential learning with global virtual teams: developing intercultural and virtual competencies. MG. **9**, 129 (2016). https://doi.org/10.11144/Javeriana.m9-18.elgv

17. Kriz, W.C., Hense, J.U.: Theory-oriented evaluation for the design of and research in gaming and simulation. Simul. Gaming **37**, 268–283 (2006). https://doi.org/10.1177/1046878106287950

18. Peters, V., Vissers, G., Heijne, G.: The validity of games. Simul. Gaming **29**, 20–30 (1998). https://doi.org/10.1177/1046878198291003

19. Faizan, N.D., Löffler, A., Heininger, R., Utesch, M., Krcmar, H.: Classification of evaluation methods for the effective assessment of simulation games: results from a literature review. Int. J. Eng. Ped. **9**, 19–33 (2019). https://doi.org/10.3991/ijep.v9i1.9948

20. Bas, N., Löffler, A., Heininger, R., Utesch, M., Krcmar, H.: Evaluation methods for the effective assessment of simulation games. In: Auer, M., Tsiatsos, T. (eds.) The Challenges of the Digital Transformation in Education. ICL 2018. Advances in Intelligent Systems and Computing, vol. 916, pp. 626–637. Springer, Cham (2020). https://doi.org/10.1007/978-3-030-11932-4_59

21. Kriz, W.C., Auchter, E.: 10 years of evaluation research into gaming simulation for German entrepreneurship and a new study on its long-term effects. Simul. Gaming **47**, 179–205 (2016). https://doi.org/10.1177/1046878116633972

22. Verkuyl, M., Djafarova, N., Mastrilli, P., Atack, L.: Virtual gaming simulation: evaluating players' experiences. Clin. Simul. Nurs. **63**, 16–22 (2022). https://doi.org/10.1016/j.ecns.2021.11.002

23. Mousavi Baigi, S.F., Norouzi Aval, R., Sarbaz, M., Kimiafar, K.: Evaluation tools for digital educational games: a systematic review. ACTA (2022). https://doi.org/10.18502/acta.v60i8.10835

24. Ivens, S., Oberle, M.: Does scientific evaluation matter? Improving digital simulation games by design-based research. Soc. Sci. **9**, 155 (2020). https://doi.org/10.3390/socsci9090155

25. Rice, Y., DeLetter, M., Fryman, L., Parrish, E., Velotta, C., Talley, C.: Implementation and evaluation of a team simulation training program. J. Trauma Nurs. **23**, 298–303 (2016). https://doi.org/10.1097/JTN.0000000000000236

26. Weaver, S., et al.: Simulation-based team training at the sharp end: a qualitative study of simulation-based team training design, implementation, and evaluation in healthcare. J. Emerg. Trauma Shock **3**, 369 (2010). https://doi.org/10.4103/0974-2700.70754

27. Gjeraa, K., Møller, T.P., Østergaard, D.: Efficacy of simulation-based trauma team training of non-technical skills. A systematic review. Acta Anaesthesiol. Scand. **58**, 775–787 (2014). https://doi.org/10.1111/aas.12336

28. Dickenson, M., Burgoyne, J., Pedler, M.: Virtual action learning: practices and challenges. Action Learn. Res. Pract. **7**, 59–72 (2010). https://doi.org/10.1080/14767330903576978

29. Cho, Y., Egan, T.: The changing landscape of action learning research and practice. Hum. Resour. Dev. Int., 1–27 (2022). https://doi.org/10.1080/13678868.2022.2124584

30. Coghlan, D., Coughlan, P.: Effecting change and learning in networks through network action learning. J. Appl. Behav. Sci. **51**, 375–400 (2015). https://doi.org/10.1177/0021886314540210

31. Pedler, M., Burgoyne, J.: Action learning. In: Bradbury, H. (ed.) The SAGE Handbook of Action Research, pp. 179–187. SAGE Publications, Los Angeles (2015)

32. Barsom, E.Z., Graafland, M., Schijven, M.P.: Systematic review on the effectiveness of augmented reality applications in medical training. Surg. Endosc. **30**, 4174–4183 (2016). https://doi.org/10.1007/s00464-016-4800-6

33. Gegenfurtner, A., Quesada-Pallarès, C., Knogler, M.: Digital simulation-based training: A meta-analysis. Brit. J. Educ. Tech. **45**, 1097–1114 (2014). https://doi.org/10.1111/bjet.12188

34. Graafland, M., Schraagen, J.M., Schijven, M.P.: Systematic review of serious games for medical education and surgical skills training. Br. J. Surg. **99**, 1322–1330 (2012). https://doi.org/10.1002/bjs.8819

35. Arthur, W., Bennett, W., Edens, P.S., Bell, S.T.: Effectiveness of training in organizations: a meta-analysis of design and evaluation features. J. Appl. Psychol. **88**, 234–245 (2003). https://doi.org/10.1037/0021-9010.88.2.234

36. Ergashevich, E.A., Mado, A.: Methodology of organizing and implementing training activities. Acopen. **9** (2023). https://doi.org/10.21070/acopen.9.2024.8363

37. Eppich, W., Howard, V., Vozenilek, J., Curran, I.: Simulation-based team training in healthcare. Simul. Healthc. J. Soc. Simul. Healthc. **6**, S14–S19 (2011). https://doi.org/10.1097/SIH.0b013e318229f550

38. Merién, A.E.R., Van De Ven, J., Mol, B.W., Houterman, S., Oei, S.G.: Multidisciplinary team training in a simulation setting for acute obstetric emergencies: a systematic review. Obstet. Gynecol. **115**, 1021–1031 (2010). https://doi.org/10.1097/AOG.0b013e3181d9f4cd
39. Weaver, S.J., Dy, S.M., Rosen, M.A.: Team-training in healthcare: a narrative synthesis of the literature. BMJ Qual. Saf. **23**, 359–372 (2014). https://doi.org/10.1136/bmjqs-2013-001848
40. Alexander, A.L., Brunyé, T., Sidman, J., Weil, S.A.: From gaming to training: a review of studies on fidelity, immersion, presence, and buy-in and their effects on transfer in PC-based simulations and games. DARWARS Train. Impact Group **5**, 1–14 (2005)
41. Andreatta, P.B., Bullough, A.S., Marzano, D.: Simulation and team training. Clin. Obstet. Gynecol. **53**, 532–544 (2010). https://doi.org/10.1097/GRF.0b013e3181ec1a48
42. Strohschneider, S.: Human Factors und interkulturelle Teamentwicklung. In: Interkulturelle Personal- und Organisationsentwicklung : Methoden, Instrumente und Anwendungsfälle, pp. 129–144. Verl. Wissenschaft & Praxis, Sternenfels (2010)
43. de Carvalho, C.V.: Virtual experiential learning in engineering education. In: 2019 IEEE Frontiers in Education Conference (FIE), pp. 1–8. IEEE, Covington, KY, USA (2019). https://doi.org/10.1109/FIE43999.2019.9028539
44. Santos, L., Escudeiro, P., de Carvalho, C.V.: Evaluating virtual experiential learning in engineering. In: International Society for Engineering Education (ed.) 2013 International Conference on Interactive Collaborative Learning (ICL), pp. 42–48. IEEE, Piscataway, NJ (2013)
45. Majgaard, G., Weitze, C.: Virtual experiential learning, learning design and interaction in extended reality simulations. In: Proceedings of the 14th European Conference on Game Based Learning, pp. 372–379. ACI (2020). https://doi.org/10.34190/GBL.20.010
46. Kolb, D.A.: Experiential Learning: Experience as the Source of Learning and Development. Pearson Education, Inc, Upper Saddle River, New Jersey (2015)
47. Kolb, D.A.: Experiential Learning: Experience as The Source of Learning and Development. Prentice Hall, Englewood Cliffs, N. J. (1983)
48. Kolb, A.Y., Kolb, D.A., Passarelli, A., Sharma, G.: On becoming an experiential educator: the educator role profile. Simul. Gaming **45**, 204–234 (2014). https://doi.org/10.1177/1046878114534383
49. Nix, S.O.: Team development for the virtual workspace. The role of debriefing in experience-based learning - a case study (2023)
50. Krumm, S., Terwiel, K., Hertel, G.: Challenges in norm formation and adherence: the knowledge, skills, and ability requirements of virtual and traditional cross-cultural teams. J. Pers. Psychol. **12**, 33–44 (2013). https://doi.org/10.1027/1866-5888/a000077
51. Kirkpatrick, D.L. (ed.): Evaluating Training Programs: The Four Levels. Berrett-Koehler Publishers, San Francisco, Calif (1998)
52. Kirkpatrick, D.L.: Techniques for evaluating training programs. J. Am. Soc. Train. Directors **13**, 3–9 (1959)
53. Kirkpatrick, D.L., Kirkpatrick, J.D.: Implementing the Four Levels: A Practical Guide for Effective Evaluation of Training Programs. Berrett-Koehler, San Francisco, Calif (2007)
54. Kirkpatrick, D.L., Kirkpatrick, J.D.: Evaluating Training Programs: The Four Levels. Berrett-Koehler Publishers, San Francisco, Calif (2006)
55. Reynolds, A.J.: Confirmatory program evaluation: a method for strengthening causal inference. Am. J. Eval. **19**, 203–221 (1998). https://doi.org/10.1177/109821409801900204
56. McNiff, J., Whitehead, J.: All You Need to Know About Action Research. Sage Publications, Thousand Oaks, CA (2006)
57. Weisbrod, B.A.: Conceptual Issues in evaluating training programs. Mon. Labor Rev. **89**, 1091–1097 (1966)
58. Fantini, A.E.: Assessing intercultural competence - issues and tools. In: The Sage Handbook of Intercultural Competence. SAGE Publications, Thousand Oaks, Calif (2009)

59. Ludwig, N., Strohschneider, S.: Debriefing für die interkulturelle Teamentwicklung – methodische und beziehungstheoretische Überlegungen. interculture journal – Online J. Intercultural Stud. **22**, 107–124 (2023). https://doi.org/10.24403/JP.1342175
60. Baskin, C.: Using Kirkpatrick's four-level-evaluation Model to explore the effectiveness of collaborative online group work (2001)
61. Crichton, M.T., Moffat, S., Crichton, L.: Developing a team behavioural marker framework using observations of simulator-based exercises to improve team effectiveness: a drilling team case study. Simul. Gaming **48**, 299–313 (2017). https://doi.org/10.1177/1046878117693266
62. Manser, T., Perry, J., Schmutz, J.: Verhalten ist messbar: Behavioural Marker Systeme und Kompetenzentwicklung. In: St.Pierre, M., Breuer, G. (eds.) Simulation in der Medizin. Springer, Berlin, Heidelberg (2013). https://doi.org/10.1007/978-3-642-29436-5_15
63. Edmondson, A.C., Lei, Z.: Psychological safety: the history, renaissance, and future of an interpersonal construct. Annu. Rev. Organ. Psychol. Organ. Behav. **1**, 23–43 (2014). https://doi.org/10.1146/annurev-orgpsych-031413-091305
64. Gurtner, A., Kolbe, M., Boos, M.: Satisfaction in virtual teams in organizations (2007). https://doi.org/10.24451/ARBOR.19202

Simulation, Education and Ethics – What a Mix!

Elyssebeth Leigh[1] (✉) ⓘ, Heemi Ateremu McNeill[2] ⓘ, and Derek Wade[3] ⓘ

[1] University of Technology Sydney, Ultimo, Australia
elyssebeth.leigh@icloud.com
[2] University of Canterbury, Christchurch, New Zealand
[3] Kumido Adaptive Strategies, Illinois, USA

Abstract. Public statements about ethics declare individual, group, or organisational beliefs, values, and principles to the world. They are intended to be clear statements about how their owners will interact with the real world. Of necessity, simulations, and games used for learning, warp and bend reality to generate replications of aspects of the real world creating opportunities to generate new insights and knowledge. Because of this it is difficult to imagine a text that could declare a clear and absolutely ethical boundary applicable to every setting. In this paper we examine how a complex web of forces informs the actions of individual simulationists as they design and choose activities to further education and research goals. While we use educational contexts as our primary lens, our aim is to initiate a broader discussion about ethical considerations across all simulation domains. We explore how different ethical frameworks interact with various simulation types, potentially leading to very different participant experiences. We propose that making implicit ethical stances explicit is essential for responsible simulation practice in any field. This work challenges simulationists to either demonstrate that they know, understand, and apply in practice their own espoused ethical stance, or are willing to spend time learning how to do so consistently and then share their experiences. Our aim is to foster a more nuanced understanding of the ethical dimensions shaping the field of simulations and games for learning.

Keywords: Simulation Ethics · Education Theories · Categorising Simulations · Ethical Frameworks · Simulationists

1 Introduction

Public statements about ethics are a means of declaring individual, group, or organisational beliefs, values, and principles to the world. Such statements may be provided as a "Best Practice" guidelines [12], a "Code of Conduct" [7], or a Statement of Values and Code of Ethics [6]. Whatever their title, their goal is to provide a clear and concise account of intentions, ensure transparency and develop trust between those avowing the statement and those with whom they interact. While these intentions are clear enough, attempts to enact them can be complex to navigate. Nuances in values and beliefs, specific contextual requirements or differences in understanding about word meanings can lead to unintentional offence or triggering participants' anxieties or concerns.

© The Author(s) 2026
F. Trautwein et al. (Eds.): ISAGA 2025, LNCS 16439, pp. 177–193, 2026.
https://doi.org/10.1007/978-3-032-20129-4_13

In this paper we challenge the notion that an ethics statement alone is sufficient to ensure ethical behaviour and participant safety and explore several problems associated with developing ethics guidelines for users in the field of simulation and games. While our examples draw primarily from learning and research contexts, the principles we explore extend to all domains where simulation is employed.

Simulationists must be able to state and live their own ethical stances using language contextualising their intentions and actions regarding impending experiences. They must become skilled at avoiding reliance on potentially inappropriate generic ethics statements. This requires a nuanced understanding of how ethical frameworks interact with simulation design and facilitation choices.

Two particular factors make the facilitation of simulations and games an especially risky endeavour. The first is that facilitators with different ethical frameworks operate honestly within their own ethical framework yet may still inadvertently cause participant harm. The second is the difficulty of categorising simulation activities in such a way as to understand how they perform as tools. The extremely variable nature of simulations and games, the various roles of people using them, the purposes to which they can be put, and societal expectations about purposes and intended results all influence their effectiveness as contexts and tools.

While we use educational contexts as our primary lens for exploring these issues, our goal is to initiate a broader conversation about ethical frameworks across all simulation domains. By examining how ethical stances manifest in educational simulations, we offer a starting point for practitioners in other contexts to consider their own ethical frameworks and how these might influence simulation design and facilitation. The challenges we identify concerning the alignment of ethical stance, simulation type, and theoretical framework are relevant for a broad range of simulation contexts.

Throughout this paper, we encourage readers to consider how the frameworks and principles we discuss might manifest in their own specific domains. The examples we provide from educational settings can serve as analogues for similar ethical considerations in other contexts, with appropriate translation to domain-specific concerns. Our goal is not to prescribe a single ethical approach–but rather to stimulate reflection on the ethical dimensions of simulation practice across all domains.

2 Diversity in Ethical Frameworks

Ethics is central to the process of deciding what should be done. Choices made by simulationists, such as specific activities to be experienced by participants and the content of learning programmes, reflect the ethical nature of their practice. Simulations that are characterised by ambiguity and conflicting values prevent practitioners from applying standardised principles as solutions. Instead, they must make choices based on their beliefs about the ways things ought to be. However, such choices are frequently made without paying any attention to the value judgements and assumptions implicitly operating throughout the decision-making process.

In their exploration of ethical practice in adult education Brockett and Heimstra [2] developed a model of three layers of consideration within which actions are located, as shown in Fig. 1. An individual's *Personal Values System* is a unique amalgamation of factors, based on application of values and beliefs that are constantly being re-enacted within each new setting. On entering a new context, they are (more - or less) aware of expectations for achieving a balance among multiple responsibilities as they work.

Having located educators within this framework Brockett and Heimstra suggest that the way forward is through self-reflection via exploration of values and contextual obligations and analysis of possible consequences of various options for action. Asking themselves: *"What are my beliefs? How committed am I to them?"* and then *"What are my obligations? How will I respond to ethical dilemmas if I encounter them at work?"* and finally *"How well do I understand the consequences of my values-informed actions?"* All these questions apply to consideration of ethical actions on the part of those using simulations and games.

2.1 Eight Ethical Frameworks

So, what ethical frameworks are available to educators? How do they differ? And what are their implications? The following brief review introduces eight ethical frameworks which each make their own assertions as to 'rightness'. We don't endorse any of them, intending to simply introduce them as possible tools for readers to use when considering their own Personal Values System. The eight frameworks are.

Moral realism	*Social contract*
Legal positivism	*Feminist ethics*
Natural law tradition	*Deontological (duty) ethics*
Relativism	*Consequentialism*

Perhaps the most familiar ethical framework in Western environments is *moral realism* which upholds a belief in the impartial and universal nature of ethics and admits of no deviation from *'sacred truths.'* This approach is often found in religious contexts where *'absolute'* and *'invariate'* statements abound. Facts are objective and what is *'right'* and *'correct'* is seldom subject to argument since they are considered to exist independently of human emotions and beliefs.

In contrast *legal positivism* is based on the belief that laws regulating human behaviour are created by human authorities and are not necessarily 'morally' based. However, rather than seeing laws as made by humans the stance of the *natural law tradition* in ethics holds that laws should be founded on universally recognised fundamental moral principles. But this in turn is challenged by the ethical stance of *relativism* whereby laws and ethics are held to be unique to each culture and therefore highly variable across the globe.

Each has had varying degrees of support and development through centuries of human social development. More recent contemporary approaches to the *social contract* consider that ethical principles and behaviour emerge from agreements by members of societal groupings wanting to achieve social order and for mutual benefit. In contrast, *feminist ethics* challenge traditional theories and practices that overlook or exclude the experiences of women and other marginalized groups.

Deontological (duty) ethics, hold that actions which adhere to known rules are right, regardless of the outcome. In opposition to this is the concept of *consequentialism* which judges the moral rightness of an action based on its outcome or consequences. And finally, for our purposes there is the comment from USA Supreme Court Justice Potter Stewart that *"ethics is knowing the difference between what you have the right to do and what is right to do"*. His words indicate a belief in the importance of knowing the boundaries between one's own rights and what others in your context might considered to be wrong.

Each stance has self-referential clarity, meaning their adherents consider their own stance to be most valid. Any group gathered for a simulation activity could have members who are adherents to any of them. Since language and behaviour discloses beliefs, how a facilitator frames the briefing of a simulation will be influenced by their own ethical stance – no matter how much they strive for ethical neutrality at such moments.

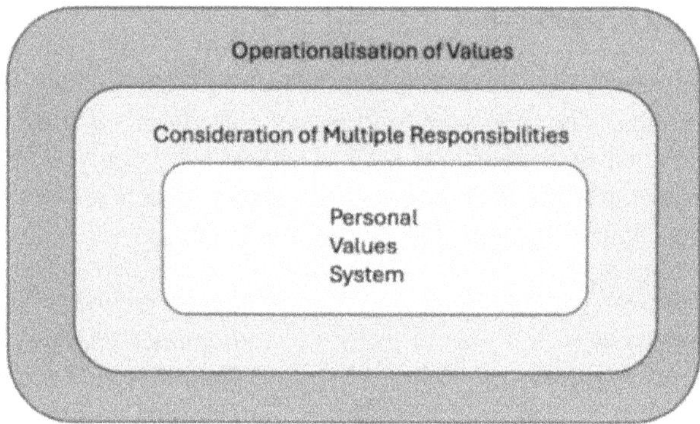

Fig. 1. Dimensions of Ethical Practice in Adult Education (Brockett and Heimstra 2004)

3 Ethics in Action

To illustrate the difficulties involved in navigating ethical frameworks in simulation contexts, we present two hypothetical cases. Our purpose is to demonstrate how different theoretical and ethical frameworks can produce valid learning outcomes while employing very different perspectives and stances and yet may still create significant breaches in relation to participant safety.

In the following cases, the behaviour of facilitators is inevitably influenced by a range of factors, including personal values, social context, educational experiences, and organisational expectations. The behaviour in each case represents a specific amalgamation of such factors creating unique responses to unique conditions, which means those behaviours may change when conditions do. However, the cases also represent patterns of behaviour that are identifiable and repeatable by the particular actor described as well as others. Such patterns can be equally ethical within given contexts and yet may also be seen to be unethical when the framework or perspective changes.

3.1 Case I – Teaching for Inclusion

Scenario. In a professional development workshop for higher education facilitation, participants engage in a simulation designed to explore inclusive teaching principles.

Twenty faculty members from diverse disciplines are divided into small groups, with each group representing a fictional academic department facing challenges related to student equity and inclusion. The simulation presents specific scenarios where faculty must make decisions about curriculum design, classroom management, and address student concerns around representations and accessibility.

During the simulation, a heated debate emerges in one group when some participants begin questioning the fundamental premise of the exercise. They express discomfort with what they perceive as ideological framing of the scenarios and argue for greater emphasis on academic rigor rather than inclusion. This creates tension as other participants feel their colleagues are dismissing important equity considerations. The facilitator must decide how to address this conflict while maintaining the educational integrity of the simulation and respecting diverse viewpoints.

Facilitator A Response – – this facilitator identifies the conflict as a deviation from the intended learning path. They view the disagreement as a barrier to participants achieving the predetermined learning outcomes about inclusive practices. They redirect the conversation firmly back to the simulation parameters, they clarify evidence-based rationale for inclusive based teaching practices, and its positive impact on academic rigour. Reflective feedback is introduced to established benchmarks and clarify assessment rubrics that measure progress towards predefined inclusive teaching behaviours.

The facilitator explains that competency in inclusive teaching requires the practice of specific skills that have been validated through research. The focus of the workshop is the mastering of these techniques, not debating their validity.

Facilitator B Response – this facilitator recognises the disagreement as an authentic expression of different educational values and sees the conflict as a valuable learning opportunity rather than a disruption to be managed. They pause the simulation to acknowledge the emerging tension and create space to discuss the divergent viewpoints. The conversation gets reframed as an exploration of how academic rigour and inclusion might complement rather than oppose each other. Participants are given the opportunity to collaboratively develop scenarios that would address both values, and reflective questioning is used to help participants uncover their underlying assumptions about teaching and learning.

The facilitator explains how such a disagreement reflects real tensions that exist in academia, and suggests that including diverse perspectives allows for exploration of how to balance authentic yet contrasting educational values.

Unanticipated Participant Impact. *Participant X* is a senior lecturer experiencing increasing psychological distress during the session. His teaching style is influenced by his undiagnosed neurodiversity, and he has recently faced a formal complaint from students claiming his teaching was "inaccessible". The complaint was eventually dismissed; however, the experience was humiliating and triggered a depressive episode. As the scenarios explored and critiqued various "inaccessible teaching practices" which mirrored his own teaching style, he felt implicitly accused and retraumatised.

Facilitator A perceives his quietness as resistance to the prescribed inclusive techniques and attempts to provide concrete examples of "proper" inclusive teaching inadvertently reinforced his sense of inadequacy.

Facilitator B misreads his withdrawal as thoughtful reflection and later invites him to share insights during the open dialogue about tensions between different educational values, unintentionally putting him on the spot when he's least emotionally equipped to engage.

3.2   Case II – Navigating Autonomy

Scenario.   A professional development programme for experienced healthcare practitioners focuses on developing innovative approaches to patient-centred care. A workshop brings together 30 senior clinicians from various specialities who are already experts in their fields. The programme is designed as a self-directed learning environment where participants identify their own learning needs and collaborate to develop solutions to complex healthcare challenges. The facilitators have prepared simulation activities involving standardized patients presenting with multifaceted care needs, but the structure intentionally allows for significant autonomy in how they approach and learn from these encounters.

During the first simulation, several participants become visibly frustrated with the lack of clear direction. A divide emerges in the group, where some participants embrace the self-directed approach and begin organising their own learning agenda, while others push for more structured guidance to make better use of their time. The simulation stalls as participants debate the structure of the simulation rather than engaging with the patient scenario. In responding to the resistance, the facilitators must balance the programme's learning approach and the legitimate concerns of participants.

Facilitator C Response –   this facilitator recognises that some of the participants' expectations about learning relationships are being challenged, creating legitimate tension that needs to be addressed. They pause the scenario to discuss the educational approach and its rationale, acknowledging the discomfort as a natural part of transitioning from traditional pedagogical approaches. They propose a modified social contract, where the facilitators will provide clearer signposts at key points, and participants will commit to working outside their comfort zones between these points.

The facilitator explains this as a necessary renegotiation of the roles in the learning process and that they see their role as creating conditions where collective wisdom can emerge rather than relying on 'external experts' to direct learners to preset outcomes. However, even experts need varying levels of support in unfamiliar spaces sometimes, and the facilitator acknowledges expressions of discomfort as part of a learning process.

Facilitator D Response –   this facilitator views the resistance as a natural stage in the evolution of self-directed learners and sees working through this discomfort as an essential part of the learning process itself.

They maintain the original learning approach without significant modification and respond to requests for direction by asking reflective questions such as *"What would help you move forward? How might you discover that for yourself?"* Just-in-time resources are provided as participants identify specific learning needs, and the emerging group dynamics are used as a learning opportunity about healthcare teams needing to function with uncertainty.

Unanticipated Participant Impact. *Participant Y*, an experienced emergency physician, begins experiencing acute anxiety symptoms during the unstructured simulation activity. Six months earlier, she was the lead physician during a mass casualty incident where insufficient protocols and unclear leadership contributed to preventable deaths. Though cleared of any wrongdoing, she has been struggling with post-traumatic stress and self-doubt. The ambiguity and lack of clear direction in the scenario unintentionally mirrors the chaos of that traumatic event. Her distress increases as participants debate how to proceed without clear guidance.

Facilitator C misinterprets the participant's discomfort as typical resistance to the learning approach. The revised "learning contract" fails to address her specific trauma response to ambiguity.

Facilitator D encourages embracing discomfort as part of the learning process, inadvertently reinforcing the participant's sense she should "push through" rather than acknowledge her distress. The commitment to the process unintentionally creates conditions that replicate elements of her trauma without providing psychological safety.

Effective management of such conflicts between learning intentions and actual experiences requires thoughtful understanding of the nature of an activity and its potential for generating both learning – and harm. This involves understanding the nature of each activity and preparation, by the facilitator, for a potentially limitless array of actual outcomes. One way to achieve such understanding involves awareness of how categorising activities can help forecast their impact on learners.

4 Categorising Simulations and Games

Categorising simulations and games is a complex – and sometimes conflicted – process [8, 12] with indications that factors of context and intent will always impede efforts to arrive at an all-encompassing categorisation. Because of this it is important for educators to have as rich as possible an understanding of the diversity of simulation formats and applications. And since there is no single, easy way to summarise all that information, we offer three models that provide different perspectives on understanding simulations and games. The three models are respectively a spectrum approach, a hierarchical one, and a relational one. For ease of reading what follows, we use the term 'activities' to cover what could be included in the very broad spectrum of simulations and games used for education and research.

Choices about forms of activity will be made in accord with the facilitator's own perceptions of what is *'right'* and *'what works'*. Their implicit (or explicit) ethical considerations, in terms of beliefs and values, will then shape the way the activity is used.

4.1 Categorising on a Continuum from 'Open' to 'Closed'

With all this in mind we have chosen to employ Christopher and Smith's dichotomy of 'open' and 'closed' categories [4] which identifies activities according to the nature of their initiating proposition and the extent to which the ending is predictable. Table 1 provides key facets which characterise open vs closed categorisations.

A 'closed' activity begins with the initiating proposition of *"this is the problem how will you solve it?"* Whatever lies ahead is a puzzle for which there is at least one known solution. Conversely an 'open' activity begins from the proposition that *"you are entering an unknown situation – what will you do?"* Whatever lies ahead is created by participants as they address an unsolved problem. *"What will happen?"* asked one designer of such activities and answered, *"We don't know – you have not done it yet."*

In both of the Cases described above it seems likely that the participants were expecting to engage with a 'closed' format activity while the facilitators were employing an 'open' format without sufficient awareness of the possible impact on participants of its attendant uncertainties. If this distinction was not made explicit, participants were entering an environment where their sense of certainty in what they knew would be disturbed. While this is part of the ethos of simulations and games for learning, in these cases it created problems for those involved, as decisions based on personal ethics led to discomfort and dismay.

Table 1. Characteristics of 'open and 'closed' activities. (Adapted from Christopher and Smith 1987).

Characteristics of 'Open' Simulations	Characteristics of 'Closed' Simulations
• Feeling of separateness	• Feeling of togetherness
• No clarity about what to assume	• Shared assumptions about the process
• Leader is unlikely to direct or intervene	• Leader is seen as benevolent and in control
• Differences are personal *not functional*	• Differences are *functional*
• This is a journey rather than a crisis, multiple routes and sub-plots	• There is a 'crisis' to be solved
• Constraints are approximate 'real life' not imposed by the process	• Constrained by detail and role instructions
• Focus is on chance happenings and multiple lines of action	• Focus is on a moment of 'crisis' or 'solving the problem'
• Conflict and uncertainty *"real problems don't have clear answers"*	• Conflict is conciliatory *"puzzles have answers"*

4.2 Categorising Within a Hierarchy of 'Realness'

The second model positions activities in a hierarchical arrangement progressing from "most real" to "most abstract" [11]. This identifies activities according to their degree of 'fidelity' with real life moving through incremental levels of abstraction. Table 2 summarises the sequence with reference to specific forms of activity and the likelihood of degree of emotional engagement.

Taylor's arrangement begins with case studies which he considers to be versions of actual events recreated as narrative reports and then arranges various activities along a continuum as their format move further towards abstraction until reality is represented by the algorithms of machine code.

Such a categorisation can help facilitators decide on 'how much' realism to introduce into a simulation or game-based activity based on the extent to which they want participants to engage emotionally with the events within the activity. This will help generate awareness of the likely causes for any emergent disturbances so that they can be prepared for in advance. Given this, it is possible that these activities were 'too emotionally loaded' for those participants affected and that choosing a 'less real' format could have generated desired learning outcomes with less emotional engagement.

4.3   Categorising as a Set of Relationships

This relational model uses a Venn diagram to represent the interconnection of key features of three core modes of activity [5]. Figure 2 shows how key modes of 'game', 'simulation' and 'case study' combine in various ways to create four sub-categories, of which the most complex is 'simulation game used as case study'. Table 3 illustrates key features of these modes of activity. While the activities in each Case were clearly intended to 'simulate' reality for the purpose of objective analysis, participant reactions suggest that some 'game' elements were unintentionally present. For example, a sense of 'competing' (win/lose) in regard to professional capability and status seems to have been triggered by the activity (however unintentionally).

Table 2. Simulations and Games from Most Real to Most Abstract. (Adapted from Taylor 1977).

Activity	Emotional state	Relationship to reality
Case study	Observations of the real world. No requirement to become involved	**Most "Real"** Least emotionally involving
In-basket or In-tray	Non-interacting, one-to-one depiction. Some emotional attachment to quality of decision making	
Incident process "action maze"	Interacting one-to-one representation. Emotional engagement as "panel member"	
Role playing	Formally structured group portrayal using one-to-one interactions. Interactions are potentially very engaging	**Least "Real"** Most emotional and highly involving
Gaming simulation or game simulation	Informally structured group or one-to-one portrayal of interactions. May evoke strong emotions because of intersections between prior events and current experiences	

(continued)

Table 2. (*continued*)

Activity	Emotional state	Relationship to reality
Machine simulation or computer simulation	Data and decisions embedded in mathematical representations. Perhaps group interactions about decisions. No expectation of emotional engagement with a 'machine' but the likelihood of strong emotional reactions to decisions and actions required	

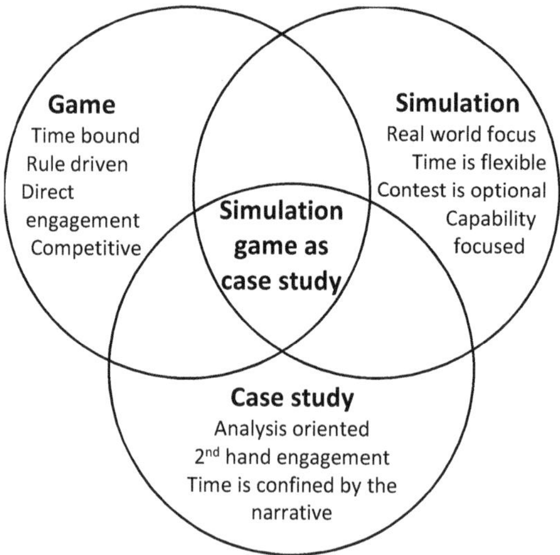

Fig. 2. Simulation, Game and Case Study as a Venn Diagram of Key Features. (Adapted from Ellington et al. 1982)

Table 3. Three Basic Modes of Simulated Activity (Eddington et al. 1982 adapted)

Activity	Features	Essential Characteristics	Facilitator Actions
Games	Time-limited Rule driven Scored (win/lose)	• Must involve overt competition of some sort, either between individuals or teams • Must have rules • Examples include football, poker and Scrabble	Introduces rules, umpires and monitors rules, has the role of judge during debriefing

(*continued*)

Table 3. (*continued*)

Activity	Features	Essential Characteristics	Facilitator Actions
Simulations	Open-ended Behaviour oriented Real-life focused Process-driven	• Represent actual simulations drawn from real life, or hypothetical approximation • Operational – participants enact all, or part of, a • process • Examples include mechanical computer-driven devices (simulators)	Introduces scenario, rules, and roles, then stands aside during the action; uses the debriefing to guide reflective analysis on participants performances. Judgement offered if the learning objectives necessitate comparison to performance standards or processes
Case studies	In-depth analysis Detail-oriented Focus on results	• Analysis of a problem or situation • Users identify characteristics of the situation, and/or develop appropriate responses • Examples include decision-focused scenarios	Guides learners through a series of questions and analytical approaches to achieve insights related to key decisions. Pushes for exploration of ideas and application of concepts related to learning objectives

4.4 Choosing a Convenient Dichotomy for Exploration

Given the current insolubility of achieving a single classification/categorisation format we have chosen to focus particularly on the Christopher and Smith [4] dichotomy of 'closed' and 'open' categories as a framework for considering the application of personal preferences for employing simulations for learning and research. This is because it provides a convenient way of exploring ethics and therefore enables exploration of associated educational theories and models of the contexts in which simulations and games are being used. However, we invite readers to keep in mind the existence of all those alternative models.

Using the dichotomy of a 'closed/open' model for learning activities provides two ends of a spectrum for ways of thinking about personal beliefs and stances and the 'either/or' choices that routinely face every educator. In the next section we briefly introduce relevant educational theories arraying them along a spectrum to inform a discussion of the values informing them.

5 Educational Theory as a Contextual Lens

Having explored various ethical frameworks and simulation types, we now turn to educational theory as an example of a contextual lens through which the ethics of using simulations and game-based learning can be examined. We emphasise that while education is our primary domain of expertise, similar theoretical frameworks exist in other domains where simulation is employed.

5.1 A Dichotomy from 'Traditional' to 'Progressive'

Educational theorists have been examining the nature of learning for millennia, such that the 21st century has a plethora of viewpoints from which to choose. With the closed/open dichotomy in mind we chose to begin our exploration by arranging contemporary theories along a continuum that has 'traditional' at one end and 'progressive' at the other. For our purposes we include the following features as characteristic of traditional education –

- Teacher is in control of all activity
- Learners' work is chosen and directed by the teacher
- Classrooms are 'formal' – work is highly structured, and assessment is centralized
- Curricula / learning benchmarks are set by teacher or higher authority
- Ordering / sequencing information – set by teacher or higher authority
- Uniformity of expectations about learner progress is the norm
- Learning progress is assessed in a standardised manner

  Progressive education, on the other hand –

- Is learner-oriented
- Uses experience as a key learning strategy and tool
- Classrooms are 'informal' – tasks may be individualised with assessment devolved to individual goals
- While curricula may be centrally formulated, learner progress may be highly individualised with benchmarks developed with the learner
- Expectations about learners' progress is individualized
- Learners encouraged to identify their own goals and progress targets

  In the two Cases it is possible to surmise that the facilitators were attempting to operate towards the 'progressive' end of this spectrum while the participants expectations may have been lodged at its 'conservative' end.

5.2 Adult Education Strategies

In effect the dichotomy of traditional versus progressive approaches divides opinion and practices across all aspects of education in formal, informal and non-formal settings. We focus on adult education contexts and introduce four approaches as summarised in Table 4.

Table 4. Four Approaches to Educating Adults

Strategy	Characteristics	Values and judgement	Focus
Pedagogy	• Training and efficiency in learning • Freedom *from* distraction in learning • Mager, Davies, Gagne	• Values are hierarchical • Testing as judgement	**Teacher driven**
Humanistic	• Learner-centred • Freedom *to* learn • Rogers, Heron, Perls, Egan	• Unconditional positive regard • Respect for learner's goals	
Andragogy	• Self-directed learning • Freedom *as* learners • Knowles, Brookfield	• Learners' goals are central • Personal judgements of success	
Social action	• Critical pedagogy • Freedom *through* learning • Boal, Friere, Illich	• Collective personal action • Learning is not value free • Acceptance of criticism	**Learner focused**

In this arrangement 'Training and Efficiency in Learning' – as a Teacher Driven approach – equates to 'traditional' education while the other three align along a continuum towards 'progressive' becoming increasingly Learner Focused. The 'Training and Efficiency in Learning' approach rests on a belief in hierarchical arrangements of knowledge, and of its owners.

There are clearly delineated roles of 'student' and 'teacher/trainer' and, for the learner, knowledge is acquired through concentrated attention to pre-set content and processes. Control and authority over teaching processes are recognisable to anyone emerging from traditional 'school' environments and will be readily accepted by adults as a familiar way of acquiring new information, as will the values and beliefs which inform it.

The remaining three frameworks incrementally shift the locus of control and authority away from the teacher giving it progressively to the learner – who is no longer considered to be a submissive 'student' but instead is seen to be an adult taking charge of their own approaches to learning.

5.3 Where is the Learner in All of This?

Looking at education from the perspective of the learner, Jack Mezirow's exploration of the *Transformative Dimensions of Adult Learning* [9] drawing on the work of Jurgen Habermas (a German philosopher and social theorist) differentiated three ways in which human beings generate knowledge. Habermas called these technical/instrumental, practical, and emancipatory and defined each one as employing distinctly different means of experiencing learning, methods for discovering knowledge, and ways of validating assertions about it.

In this framework, the *'technical'* is the domain of instrumental learning, while the *'practical'* concerns communicative learning and the *'emancipatory'* dimension is one of critical reflection and as such has implications for each of the other two. For Habermas there is a fundamental distinction between "… the dynamics of learning to control and manipulate the environment (instrumental/technical learning) and the dynamics of learning to understand others (communicative learning)." [9, pp. 72–73].

Technical learning concerns ways humans control a context (including people in it), emphasises the primacy of empirical knowledge and employs technical rules. For this type of learning the central focus is on cause-effect relationships and task-oriented problem solving. A review of the characteristics of 'closed' simulations reveals that they are well suited to this environment.

Communicative learning involves building consensual social norms grounded in "the intersubjectivity of the mutual understanding of intentions and secured by the general recognition of obligations" [9, p. 75]. We see this behaviour in action when groups need to agree on the validity of such things as choices for action, explanations of behaviour, or excuses and recommendations. There are no pre-set solutions such that individuals and/or groups must decide what is right or wrong, ethical or not, nice or nasty. All such considerations are "moments in an ongoing process of talk; responses to what has been said before as well as remarks about a world outside the speakers." [9, p. 77]. Here again a comparison with the characteristics of 'open' simulations reveals they are well suited to providing the means of simulation-based hypothetical explorations of such environments. Mezirow's own focus on transformative learning is summarised by him as.

> The emancipation in emancipatory learning is emancipation from [all those] forces that limit our options and our rational control over our lives. But have been taken for granted or seen as beyond human control. [9, p. 87]

And while achieving such emancipation may be an admirably aspirational goal it is impeded by expectations created by 'traditional education' via inculcation of a mindset of reliance on experts with higher authority. Users of emancipatory learning must first expressly challenge such embedded habits of 'being done to' which is a familiar challenge for simulation. By its very nature simulation activities remove (at least during the action phase) familiar sources of dependency on which traditional education has taught us to rely. And, as so clearly demonstrated in Snowden et al.'s [11] work on the Cynefin domains of knowledge, removing these props can generate deep confusion in participants and an urgent demand to return to familiar ground well removed from expectations of independence.

6 Practical Considerations for Ethical Simulation Practice

Having examined the intersection of ethical frameworks, simulation types, and educational theory (as a conceptual example), we now turn to practical considerations for practitioners across all simulation domains. While the specific manifestations may differ, these core principles can guide ethical practice in any context where simulation is employed.

Self-Reflection and Ethical Awareness. The first step in ethical simulation practice is self-reflection. As Brockett and Heimstra [2] suggest, practitioners should:

- Examine personal beliefs and values about what constitutes "good" practice
- Consider the extent to which these beliefs influence their design and facilitation choices
- Reflect on how their ethical stance might align with one of more of the frameworks discussed earlier
- Explore how (and if) their beliefs and values align with their various contexts

This self-reflection is not a one-time activity but rather an ongoing process of examining how one's ethical stance evolves over time and in response to different contexts. For example, practitioners might consider keeping a reflective journal to document ethical dilemmas they encounter and how they resolve them.

Communicating Ethical Boundaries. Once practitioners have clarified their own ethical stance, they must consider how to communicate this to participants. Clear communication about the nature and purpose of a simulation helps set appropriate expectations and reduces the risk of psychological harm. Consider:

- How much information should participants receive before engaging in the simulation?
- What assumptions about "good" participation are embedded in the design?
- How are power dynamics managed within the simulation?
- What safety mechanisms are in place for participants who experience distress?

Designing for Ethical Alignment. Simulation design should align with the ethical framework most appropriate to the context and goals. This might involve:

- For closed simulations with clear "right answers": ensuring the standards being taught are ethically justifiable and avoiding implicit bias in what is considered "correct"
- For open simulations with multiple pathways: creating conditions where diverse perspectives can be expressed while maintaining psychological safety.
- For high-fidelity simulations: considering the ethical implications of realism, including the risk of re-traumatisation.
- For game-based simulations: examining how competition and reward structures might reinforce or challenge existing power dynamics.

Responding to Ethical Dilemmas in Real-Time. As our Cases illustrated, ethical dilemmas can unexpectedly emerge during even the most carefully designed and facilitated simulations. Practitioners can prepare for managing these dilemmas by:

- Developing a decision-making framework for addressing unexpected situations
- Creating protocols for responding to participant distress
- Establishing boundaries about when to intervene versus allowing a simulation to continue
- Building in reflection points to allow participants to communicate about their experience.

Debriefing with Ethical Sensitivity. The debriefing phase of simulation offers a crucial opportunity to address ethical dimensions of the experience. Effective ethical debriefing might include:

- Creating space for participants to express emotional responses before moving to cognitive analysis
- Acknowledging multiple perspectives on what constitutes "good" or "effective" practice
- Exploring the values and assumptions that informed decisions made during the simulation
- Connecting the simulation experience to real-world ethical considerations
- Providing resources for participants who may need additional support.

7 What Next for Ethics for Simulation and Games Organisations and Facilitators?

In this paper, we have explored the complex interplay between ethical frameworks, simulation types, and contextual theories. While we have drawn our examples primarily from educational contexts, the principles we have discussed extend to all domains where simulation is employed.

The ethical frameworks that guide simulation design and facilitation often remain implicit, yet they profoundly shape participant experiences. We challenge the simulation community across all domains to examine their ethical assumptions, articulate their values, and engage in dialogue about how these influence simulation practice. Just as we have explored educational contexts, we invite practitioners in healthcare, policy, business, military, and other domains to examine the ethical dimensions of their work.

Some questions we invite the community to consider include:

- How do your ethical beliefs influence your design and facilitation choices?
- What ethical frameworks best align with the simulation types you employ?
- How do you navigate ethical dilemmas that emerge during simulation activities?
- What mechanisms do you have in place to ensure participant safety and psychological well-being?
- How might an increase in ethical awareness enhance effectiveness of your practice?

We assert that ethical considerations have always been part of simulation practice, whether explicitly acknowledged or not. The challenge now is to make these considerations explicit, to engage in critical reflection about the values that inform our work, and to share our experiences with the broader community.

Only through such critical reflection can we ensure that our simulations serve the intended purposes while respecting the dignity and safety of all participants. We hope this paper serves as a catalyst for ongoing dialogue about ethics across the diverse world of simulation practice.

Acknowledgements. We thank Katherin Coster, Libby Cassey and [1] Michaela (Micky) Fenakel Fiedelman for their invaluable help in completing this article.

Disclosure of Interests.   There are no competing interests in writing this article.

References

1. Argyris, C., Schön, D.A.: Organizational learning: a theory of action perspective. Reis **77**(78), 345–348 (1997)
2. Brockett, R.G., Hiemstra, R.: Toward ethical practice (2004)
3. Cervero, R.M.: Becoming more effective in everyday practice. New Dir. Contin. Educ. **44**, 107–113 (1989)
4. Christopher, E.M., Smith, L.E.: Leadership Training Through Gaming: Power, People and Problem-Solving. Kogan Page, London (1987)
5. Ellington, H., et al.: A Handbook of Game Design. Kogan Page, UK (1982)
6. IAF: Statement of values & code of ethics. https://www.iaf-world.org/site/pages/statement-values-code-ethics. Accessed 18 Apr 2025
7. IEEE: IEEE code of conduct. https://www.ieee.org/content/dam/ieee-org/ieee/web/org/about/ieee_code_of_conduct.pdf. Accessed 18 Apr 2025
8. Leigh, E.E., Levesque, L.L.: Facilitating Simulations. Edward Elgar Publishing, USA (2024)
9. Mezirow, J.: Transformative dimensions of adult learning. ERIC (1991)
10. Snowden, D.J., Boone, M.E.: A Leader's Framework for Decision Making, pp. 69–76. Harvard Business Review, November 2007. https://hbr.org/2007/11/a-leaders-framework-for-decision-making. Accessed 11 Feb 2025
11. Taylor, J.: Instructional gaming procedures in planning education. Asp. Simul. Gaming, 103–115 (1977)
12. Watts, P.I., et al.: Onward and upward: introducing the healthcare simulation standards of best practice. Clin. Simul. Nurs. **58**, 1–4 (2021). https://doi.org/10.1016/j.ecns.2021.08.006
13. de Wijse-van Heeswijk, M., Leigh, E.: Ethics and simulation games in a cultural context: why should we bother? And what can we learn?. In: Kikkawa, T., Kriz, W.C., Sugiura, J. (eds.) Gaming as a Cultural Commons. Translational Systems Sciences, vol. 28, pp. 149–167. Springer, Singapore (2022). https://doi.org/10.1007/978-981-19-0348-9_9

Securing Implicit Experiential Knowledge with Applied Games in Industry 4.0

Joshua Birenheide[1]($\boxtimes$) , Julia Arlinghaus[2] , and Maria Freese[1]

[1] Otto von Guericke University Magdeburg, Universitätsplatz 2, 39106 Magdeburg, Germany
joshua.birenheide@ovgu.de
[2] University of St. Gallen, Dufourstr. 40a, CH-9000 St. Gallen, Switzerland

Abstract. The ongoing digitalization processes in the industrial context, within the framework of Industry 4.0, enable more efficient and innovative working conditions. However, the framework of Industry 4.0 comes with manifold challenges and demands, including new skills, competencies and knowledge assurance. Applied games can be used as such a training tool, as they can facilitate learning processes by allowing workers to experience real-world problems in a safe environment. For successful game design and implementation in the industrial sector, it is important to understand how applied games contribute to the demands of Industry 4.0. In order to explore the current state of the usage of applied games in the industrial context, a structured literature review was conducted. The results show that in this context, applied games are mostly designed as a digital singleplayer game used for education purposes and played by students or operators. Furthermore, the main goal of these applied games was the acquisition of procedural skill or declarative knowledge. Especially implicit experiential knowledge is an important asset in the industrial context. The transfer of this knowledge from experienced to unexperienced workers is only possible through practical involvement. Applied games can make an important contribution to this, and are thus able to address several difficulties in the ongoing digitalization and in Industry 4.0. To ensure effective game design and the use of applied games in future, research will have to focus on the evaluation of applied games and validate their benefits in a quantifiable manner.

Keywords: Applied Games · Digital Transformation · Human Centricity · Industry · Serious Games

1 Introduction

To ensure competitiveness of companies through increased efficiency and innovation, the integration of technology into human labor is crucial [1–3]. This integration of technology is the core of Industry 4.0, which focuses mostly on digitalization and the use of technologies to make (work) processes more productive and efficient. To realize this digital transformation, ongoing adaptation processes that integrate new technologies into everyday work are needed [2]. These come with additional challenges that must be overcome [4–6]. One of these challenges is that workflows are becoming more complex

F. Trautwein et al. (Eds.): ISAGA 2025, LNCS 16439, pp. 194–213, 2026.
https://doi.org/10.1007/978-3-032-20129-4_14

and therefore more demanding, but also more vulnerable to risks, requiring sufficient management [7, 8]. These developments in digitalization result in new demands for the workers which in turn requires the acquisition of new skills [9]. At the same time, implicit experiential knowledge, which is understood as "an intuitive grasp on intricate or difficult situations" [10, p. 249] and can only be learned through experiencing events in work situations, is becoming increasingly important due to the increasing complexity of the work environment [11, 12]. Implicit experiential knowledge enables workers to efficiently assess situations and make correct decisions and is therefore particularly important in situations of uncertainty and complex, interrelated processes [10]. Nowadays, experienced workers are retiring faster than new workers can be trained which leads to a shortage of skilled workers in the industry [13, 14]. Especially with regard to the ongoing demographic change and the resulting shift in the age structure it is evident that securing implicit experiential knowledge is a critical objective in the digitalized working place [10, 15]. Traditional knowledge management approaches in form of lectures, handouts or videos tend to focus on explicit knowledge, do not recreate realistic working conditions and are largely incapable of capturing experience-based knowledge [16]. To secure implicit experiential knowledge and thus support the process of continuous learning, interactive and experience-based methods are needed [17, 18]. Applied games, defined as "games that have been applied to a purpose other than pure entertainment" [19, p. 15], make use of the concept of experiential learning and therefore appear to be suitable as a tool for implicit knowledge transfer [20, 21]. Applied games could provide a basis for knowledge acquisition in Industry 4.0 due to their ability to make work scenarios experienceable while using motivating and playful mechanics [22]. To further exploit the capabilities of applied games to secure implicit knowledge and foster continuous learning in industry, it is important to understand how applied games can be used more efficiently in the industrial context. This would lay the basis for better knowledge transfer and therefore knowledge retention [16]. To realize this, it is necessary to analyze their current application within Industry 4.0 as this helps to understand whether the potential benefits are already being realized, where there are gaps or problems, and what recommendations can be made. This knowledge can help to fully exploit the potentials of applied games securing implicit knowledge in the industrial sector. On this basis, the main question in this paper is: *How have applied games been used as a method to support knowledge transfer and learning in Industry 4.0 contexts?*

The remainder of this article is structured as follows. First, we highlight the theoretical background regarding the challenges in digital transformation with a focus on implicit experiential knowledge, the role of the human factor and applied games in the context of Industry 4.0. Second, the methodology used in this publication (structured literature review, SLR) is described. The aim is to provide an overview of state-of-the art usage of applied games, especially how they are used to secure implicit experiential knowledge in Industry 4.0. Third, the results of the SLR are reported and discussed. With this systematic qualitative approach, we contribute to current research regarding the classification of applied games in the context of Industry 4.0 while identifying areas for future research.

2 Theoretical Background

During the last decade, industrial transformation in Europe was determined by the transition towards Industry 4.0, emphasizing the digital progress [23]. This digitalization in particular can enhance the efficiency, growth potential, and innovative capacity of companies, ensuring competitiveness [24, 25]. However, the European Commission [26] identified shortcomings of Industry 4.0 that prevent systemic transformations in the spirit of Europe's 2030 goals for sustainable growth. As a result, a new framework (Industry 5.0) has been proposed that builds on the idea of Industry 4.0, with a focus on environmental and economic sustainability, resilience, and human-centricity [26]. With this transition to Industry 5.0, the role of humans is given a central significance in the context of digital transformation, adding social aspects to technical organizational systems [27]. With this change from technical towards socio-technical systems, the work requirements become more complex and demanding, as an additional emphasis is placed on forward planning and decision-making [28]. To fulfill these higher demands, new skills and competencies are required which is why companies not only face the challenge of appropriate training but also of securing this new knowledge for unexperienced workers [9]. Two-thirds of companies rate experiential knowledge as a qualification requirement in a digital working world [15]. Experiential knowledge consists of explicit (learning, based on rules) and implicit (based on learned causal relationships and functional dependencies) knowledge; implicit knowledge is therefore foremost inhabited by older and more experienced workers [12]. Through demographic change it becomes necessary to transfer this implicit experiential knowledge to younger, less experienced workers [29, 30]. As this knowledge can only be gained by experiencing the associated relevant systems, simulations of these situations might be useful to facilitate implicit experiential knowledge acquisition while providing a secure environment with room for mistakes [12, 31]. In the course of digitalization it was shown that implicit experiential knowledge is an important asset that cannot be formalized and automated and therefore needs to be learned and inhabited by the human labor force [32]. To ensure adequate securing of implicit experiential knowledge, methods have to result in high knowledge retention, facilitate engagement through interactivity, be motivating, and be accessible for all workers, also with regard to low literacy or language proficiency [16].

Although traditional learning formats like technical manuals or video instructions may be somewhat effective regarding the density of learned information, they are lacking practical involvement and application of the newly learned contents [33, 34]. They are oftentimes strictly structured and include only a limited amount of interaction which can result in lower (long-term) engagement which in turn leads to lower knowledge retention [35]. Real-world practices and learning through trial and error in a safe environment are missing in traditional learning methods resulting in low effectiveness of this learning practice [35, 36]. In contrast to traditional learning formats, applied games can be used as a simulation and training tool to mimic challenges and their real-world representations [37]. They offer the opportunity for experiential learning through the simulation of real-world scenarios while using motivating game mechanics [37]. Since implicit experiential knowledge can be built through experiential learning, experiencing these events through applied games, which are a tool for experiential learning, can lead to the generation of implicit experiential knowledge [17, 18]. Unlike pure entertainment games, applied games always pursue a defined goal while still following traditional game mechanics [22, 38, 39]. The objectives of these games can be many-sided, such as knowledge transfer, help with decision-making processes or a cost-efficient training for building expertise [29]. Applied games take into account different modalities while creating an abstracted model of reality. They can therefore include both digital and/or non-digital parts as well as social or individual experiences [22, 40–42]. Evidently, the use of applied games is beneficial for companies in the industrial sector, especially when compared to traditional learning formats [16]. Analyzing the current use of applied games in the industrial sector leading to an overview of their potentials and possible shortcomings gives the opportunity to draw conclusions regarding future game design and further implementation of applied games in the industrial context. To the best of the authors' knowledge such a comprehensive overview is missing in literature resulting in a missing quantifiability of the use of applied games in Industry 4.0.

To answer the research question of how applied games are used in Industry 4.0 to secure implicit experiential knowledge, the following sub-questions were formulated, leading to four coding criteria in total (see Table 1). As implicit experiential knowledge preservation may be particularly relevant in certain application areas, especially in highly complex organizational systems, it is important to get a contextualized understanding of practices across different application domains. Implicit experiential knowledge transfer seems to be most relevant in the context of demographic change to ensure that workers are adequately trained. It is therefore essential to identify the target groups in which applied games are currently used, to analyze whether the potentials of applied games are already utilized for certain target groups. Knowing the target groups of applied games can also help to guarantee user-centered design. Although multiple possible goals of applied games are known [22, 43], there is no quantifiable information about the objectives of applied games that are used in the context of Industry 4.0. Both user-centered and goal-orientated game design are important assets for the effective use of applied games and therefore for securing implicit experiential knowledge as they ensure that needs of target groups and for reaching a predefined goal are met.

Table 1. Overview research questions

Question	Motivation	Specification
What are the application areas of applied games in Industry 4.0?	Quantification of utilization areas	(1) Application areas
Who are the target groups of applied games in Industry 4.0?	User-centered game design	(2) Factual user groups, not necessarily the intended target groups
What are the objectives of applied games in Industry 4.0?	Goal-orientated game design	(3) Objective of the applied game
What type of applied games are being used in Industry 4.0?	Quantification of game typification	(4) singleplayer/multiplayer; competitive/cooperative; digital/analogue

In order to obtain an overview of state-of-the-art usage of applied games in the industrial sector, a review of current research is necessary. Systematic approaches are commonly used to find relevant literature while minimizing biases [44, 45]. For this reason, the SLR methodology was used as it provides transparency and traceable research steps [45].

3   Method

According to Tranfield et al. [45], a SLR process is based on three stages: planning, conducting, and reporting and dissemination. In the first stage, relevant literature is identified. This was done using the two databases 'Scopus' and 'Web of Science'. Both of them were chosen because they are internationally recognized due to the spectrum of included journals, conferences and other sources of high scientific standard [46]. To find relevant literature in the two databases, a search string consisting of the dimensions applied gaming and industry was used. To account for the synonymous use of terms for applied games, the search term was extended with commonly used synonyms, namely serious games, simulation games and game-based learning [e.g. 19]. The emerging idea of Industry 5.0 adds the human factor into the framework of Industry 4.0, focusing on the wellbeing of the human workers in complex systems during the interaction with technology. As applied games are a tool used for analyzing these complex systems, the term "Industry 5.0" was included in the search string, additionally to "Industry 4.0". Earlier drafts of the search string revealed that in current literature, applied games are rarely explicitly mentioned as a tool for securing implicit experiential knowledge, especially with a connection to a certain application domain, even if this is effectively their goal. To account for this, a broader search was conducted focusing on the use of applied games in Industry 4.0 and 5.0 and not including the term "implicit experiential knowledge". This also enables a broader exploration of industrial application areas. The final search string was (("applied gam*" OR "serious gam*" OR "game based learning") AND ("industry 4*" OR "industry 5*")). The search included English-written conference papers, journal articles, book chapters and reviews published in the period from 2016 to 2024. Duplicates and conference proceedings were excluded (n = 22). Papers not written in English (n = 1) or without access to the full paper (n = 4) were also excluded from the analysis. Additionally, publications that did not provide any relevant information to answer the research question, specifically without relation to the industrial sector or applied games (n = 16), were not included in the analysis of the full papers. Finally, publications about games that were not yet in the development status and therefore not yet tested, were excluded (n = 13). If several papers were written about the same game, only the first publication was used (n = 1). This resulted in a total of 26 publications. In a second step, all 26 full papers were coded with "MAXQDA" based on a deductive qualitative approach [47]. After identifying relevant sub-research-question (see Table 1), the analysis followed the three-level codes of the grounded theory methodology by Strauss and Corbin [48]. The third step, reporting the results, is described in the next section.

4   Results

Firstly, the results of the specific sub-research questions are reported descriptively. Secondly, the overlapping coding criteria of the included applied games are analyzed and reported. The included papers were all published between 2016 and 2024 (n = 26). A significant amount of the papers was published by researchers located in Europe, especially in Germany (n = 7) and Italy (n = 7). All papers explicitly use the term "Industry 4.0" while the term for applied games varies, as indicated by the search string.

4.1   Current Use of Applied Games in Industry 4.0

In the industrial context, applied games are used in a multitude of different application domains (see Appendix 2.1). There are examples of applied games used in the big sector of Architecture, Engineering & Construction (AEC), for instance to simulate highly complex real-world port operations [49, 50]. There are also applied games dealing with industrial safety training or analyzing stress and perceived workload to ensure a safe work environment [e.g. 51, 52]. It is important to note that a majority of the included applied games are primarily used in education. A more detailed overview of the analyzed games and their classification can be found in Appendix 3. Most of the included applied games are either played by students or operators (see Appendix 2.2). Ten of the included applied games in the industrial sector are played solely by students. Seven of the included applied games are played by trainees or operators in the industry. The target groups of other games were not as specific and were either used for both students and employees [53, 54] or learners of the intended topic in general [55, 56]. It has to be noted that in some cases students were the only users of the applied game, although the authors intend for a different or additional target group [e.g. 57, 58]. The objectives of applied games in the industrial sector can be generally divided into two distinct groups, as can be seen in Appendix 2.3: specific declarative knowledge acquisition and specific procedural skill acquisition. In the first category, knowledge about the particular domain or target topic is learned, in some cases as a basis before further training [56, 59] and in other cases just for knowledge transfer [60–62]. Applied games are also used to gain procedural skills in either a particular domain of the industry like sustainable manufacturing [63] or port operations [49, 50] or as a tool for enhancing decision-making skills in the industrial context [51, 64, 65]. Applied games are typically typified according to the social component (single-/multiplayer) and the game medium (digital/analogue; see Table 2). Additionally, games can be classified regarding the competitiveness or the need for cooperation. About two thirds of all included games were designed as a singleplayer game with no social interaction with other human actors as part of the game. Of the eight multiplayer games, six can be classified as cooperative [59, 61, 66, 67], while two are competitive [55, 68]. One of the singleplayer games can also be seen as competitive, as a leaderboard is presented to the players that enhances competitiveness through comparison [64]. Only three of the 26 games are analogue, including a board game [55] and two roleplaying games that simulate different actors in a production context [59, 61], all others are digital-based.

Table 2. Types of applied games in an industrial context.

Type	Sub-category	Number of publications
Number of players	Singleplayer	18
	Multiplayer	8
Form	Analogue	3
	Digital	23
Interaction mode	Competitive	3
	Cooperative	6

Note. With regard to the interaction mode, all other games did not contain similar interactions.

4.2 Context-Dependent Use of Applied Games for Securing Implicit Experiential Knowledge

To get further knowledge about the potentials of applied games as a tool for securing implicit experiential knowledge in Industry 4.0, it is not only important to assess the goals, application domains and target groups individually, but also to put them in relation to each other. In order to get an understanding of this context-dependent use of applied games in the industrial context, the relations between the sub-research questions were analyzed.

Five of the games that are played solely by students are used in the education domain, sometimes specifically used for examinations in an academic context [69], other times as a learning tool for distinct topics in science, technology, engineering and mathematics (STEM) or logistics [51, 57, 60]. In contrast to this, none of the games played by operators are used in the education domain (see Table 3). Port operators [49, 50], crane operators [52], and workers in industrial plants [70] use applied games to simulate their respective working environment and to train particular required skills. These applied games used for trainees or operators mostly have a focus on procedural skill acquisition, for example on soft skills like leadership and team-working in a high-stress environment [70]. The applied game of [52] includes an immersive virtual reality environment for training occupational risk prevention in the operation of bridge cranes. Through the applied game, crane operators can train procedural skills to gain implicit knowledge about risk prevention in their occupational field.

Contrary to this, games designed for students are oftentimes used to gain declarative knowledge. Students learn about cybersecurity in manufacturing systems or about industrial plants through dynamic virtual representations [57, 71]. Furthermore, decision-making skills are prioritized by some of the games. The logistic simulator used by [64] exposes the players to increasingly difficult scenarios with an increasing number of decisions that the players have to make to maximize the outcome of the fictional logistics operations. Both objectives can be used for securing implicit experiential knowledge as long as the specific simulated situations are connected to the domain in which the knowledge should be learned.

Table 3. Applications of applied games for operators and students compared.

Target group	Trainees/Operator		Students	
Application domain/Objective	Procedural Skills	Declarative Knowledge	Procedural Skills	Declarative Knowledge
AEC	2	0	1	1
Manufacturing	1	1	1	1
Industrial Safety	1	1	0	0
Education	0	0	2	3

5 Discussion and Contribution

Digitalization enables more efficient workflows, enhancing companies' competitiveness while also presenting them with new demands. Requirements for workers get increasingly complex, resulting in the need for appropriate training for skill and knowledge acquisition. Simulating complex work environments to engage in experiential learning might be beneficial. To achieve this, new tools capable of adequate simulation will be required. As applied games are one of these tools, this paper addressed the question of how applied games are used to secure implicit experiential knowledge as a mean for meeting the challenges of digital transformation and the demands of Industry 4.0, focusing on the identification of industrial application domains, target groups, objectives and modalities. Furthermore, shortcomings of current applied games were identified. To achieve this, a structured literature analysis was conducted.

A substantial challenge in the industrial sector is nowadays appropriate training. Traditional training methods oftentimes do not address the need for real-world application and flexibility. Moreover, they can be unengaging, resulting in inattentive learners which would lower the knowledge retention [16]. In line with this, the most prominent application within the industrial context is applied games used in education in the context of industry 4.0. In learning contexts in the industrial sector, applied games empower an interactive and more motivating learning mode [55, 69, 72]. Applied games used in the education domain seem to be most relevant for students as evident by the number of games played by students (n = 6) in this application area. In contrast, none of the applied games played by trainees or operators were used in the education domain but rather in AEC, manufacturing or industrial safety. Teaching safety awareness through occupational hazards simulation [52] or decision-making skills in the logistics sector [51, 64] are examples of the use of these applied games. Therefore, the analysis showed that applied games are already in use in the context of Industry 4.0 in a multitude of application domains. This shows that applied games have further potential to be used as a training tool in these areas. In an industrial context, applied games are either used for declarative knowledge or procedural skill acquisition. Complex tasks can be simulated to gain specific knowledge about processes, for example in port operations or the construction of offshore windmills [50]. Giving support in form of learning experiences in a simulated environment before being confronted with the real-world situation, gives the opportunity to bring out already skilled workers while being cost-effective [29]. The transfer of implicit experiential knowledge is seen as an important asset in the industrial context. Succeeding in transferring this knowledge from experienced to unexperienced workers is only possible through practical involvement. Applied games realize this practical involvement and therefore experience-based learning by simulating tasks and their real-world representations, such as the inspection of wheel loader [12, 31, 37]. Learning procedural skills directly related to the work experience seems to be most relevant for trainees and operators, as this is the most prominent objective of the applied games developed for this target group. These broad applications lead to the conclusion that applied games are a suitable and flexible tool to simulate complex scenarios in Industry 4.0, to obtain implicit experiential knowledge and therefore enable more human-centered innovations. This flexibility enables applied games to fit to target groups and their needs that are just as broad. When focusing on the group of trainees and operators, the developed applied games are foremost used for procedural skill acquisition through simulating real-work scenarios in the respective industrial domain, which implies further potential for the use of applied games for this purpose.

Although workers in some industrial areas are "traditionally [...] quite conservative with taking up new technologies" [50, p. 1], analogue games are rarely used. Analogue games catalyze social interactions and emotional reactions, making them especially suitable for multiplayer components. All included analogue games were designed for multiple players, with two of them being cooperative and one competitive [55, 59, 61]. Of the included digital games, only five of the 18 are intended for multiplayer use. The data collection during analogue game sessions might be challenging, as data should be collected without disturbing the game play [73]. This is one of the advantages of digital games – data collection can be done during the gameplay without the players noticing. This also enables quantitative research, as outcomes can easily be tracked, even with high player numbers. It might be advantageous to use digital games for the simulation of highly complex systems, as it allows for a more realistic representation of the real-life environment. Industrial work environments like port operations, industrial sites of the metalworking industry, or wheel loader of mining companies are often complex and require similarly complex simulations [31, 49, 58]. In line with this finding, 23 of the 26 games included in the review are digital. The decision to design a singleplayer or multiplayer game has to be determined by the system that is to be simulated and by limitations in resources or other challenges [74]. A multiplayer game enables the observation of human-human interactions while a singleplayer game might simulate these interactions through non-player characters.

Based on these findings it has been highlighted that applied games contribute to securing implicit experiential knowledge through their ability to simulate real-world scenarios in a multitude of application contexts and are therefore a suitable and beneficial tool for meeting the challenges of digital transformation and the demands of Industry 4.0.

6 Future Research

The conducted SLR revealed some shortcomings of the existing literature. Due to the availability and willingness of student participants to test the games, they are the most reported target or test group. In some cases, this shows limits of the game as it has never been tested in the field or with the intended target group [e.g. 31]. It is important to note, that almost none of the reviewed papers included a form of validation other than user experience questionnaires. The need for quantitative data regarding the use of applied games in general cannot be understated as it will highlight the most effective use cases and forms of applied games in the industry. Therefore, it is crucial to explore the evidence-based effects and benefits of applied games. Evaluating the learning outcomes of applied games resulting in meta-reviews assessing the effectiveness of applied games in the industrial sector would enhance the significance of the results immensely. To further validate the results of this analysis, the use of case studies would be beneficial.

The methodology of the SLR has some limitations. Overall, only a limited number of papers were included in the SLR. First, a significant number of the described games have been developed and tested by European researchers. This might limit the generalization of the results. The search string focus on Industry 4.0 and Industry 5.0 was deliberately chosen, to get an overview on to which extend applied games are already used in this particular context. As the term Industry 5.0 was coined by the European commission in 2021 [26], a geographical bias is plausible and could explain the prevalence of papers originated in Europe. The same applies for the term Industry 4.0 which was established by a working group commissioned by the German government [75]. To avoid the possible geographical bias, the search string of this SLR could be extended in the future to include more papers about games that are used in adjacent application domains. The use of additional search terms that are less biased will broaden the selection of papers. Advanced forward and backwards search of papers will support this as well. In addition to this, it must be noted that only one of the papers explicitly used the term "Industry 5.0" [51], although 12 papers were published after the introduction of the concept of Industry 5.0, seven of which were by European researchers. Thus, the search string of this SLR could be refined in the future to include more papers that accurately depict the use of applied games in an industrial context. Finally, a significant amount of conceptional papers (n = 13) had to be excluded during the review process. These papers explained the need and theoretical approach for applied games in the industrial sector without presenting a game themselves. Repeating a similar SLR in the future could include these papers, once the described games are realized.

This also shows, that the need for applied games is already identified and that there are development ideas regarding games in the industrial sector. The missing advancement of the games' design, further emphasizes the importance of applied game development as a tool in Industry 5.0. Applied games enable the simulation of the interaction of human and technology in highly complex systems, making it highly recommendable using them in future research. Further validation using quantifiable data and the addressing of shortcomings will be needed to further enhance the benefits of applied games in the context of Industry 4.0 and beyond.

Acknowledgments. The authors have received funding from the European Union.

Disclosure of Interests.   The authors declare that they have no known competing financial interests or personal relationships that could have appeared to influence the work reported in this paper.

Appendix

Appendix 2.1

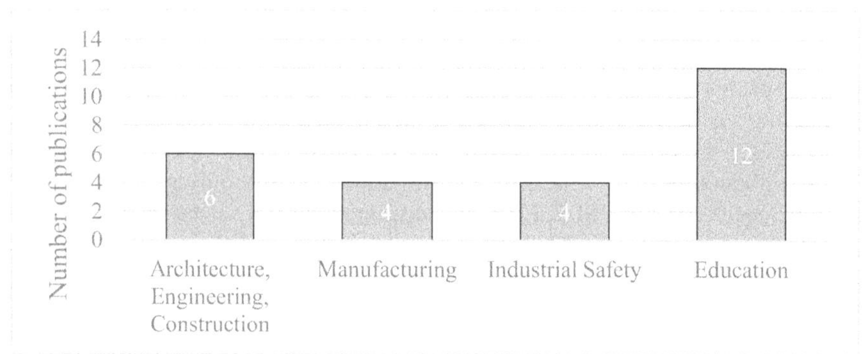

Application domains of applied games in an industrial context.

Appendix 2.2

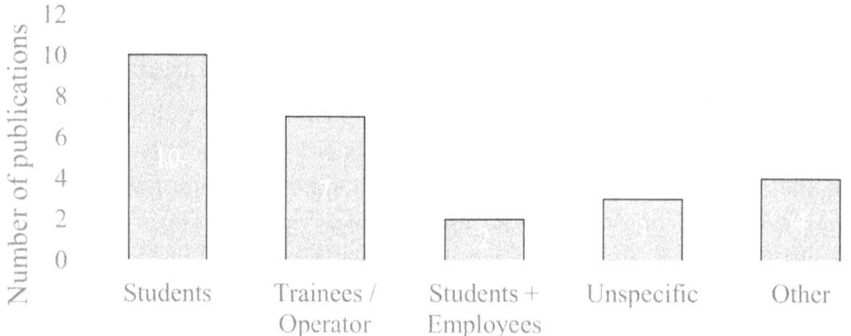

Target groups of applied games in an industrial context. "Unspecific" means not a specific target group. In the "other" category single entries were summarized.

Appendix 2.3

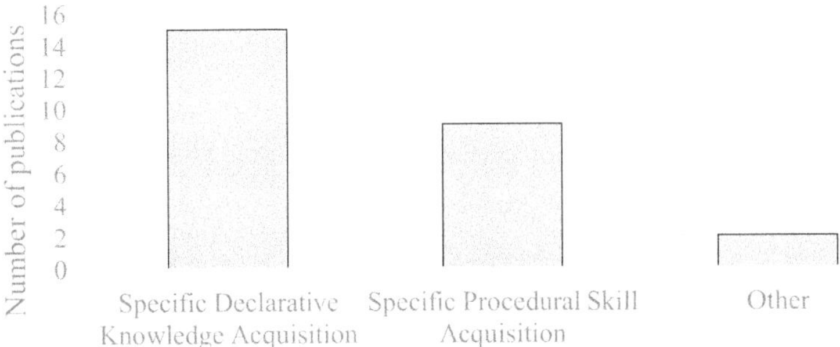

Objectives of applied games in an industrial context. In the "other" category, single entries were summarized.

Appendix 3

Author	Year	Used application	Application domain	Target group	Objective	Classification
Abed et al.	2016	Oculus rift as training tool for bridge operators in a steel factory; based on the Learning Adventure 3D serious game environment	Manufacturing	Trainees/Operator	Specific knowledge acquisition	digital, multiplayer, cooperative
Baalsrud Hauge et al.	2022	Mixed reality application for education of engineers and students using sensors on a forklift	Education	Students + Employees	Specific knowledge acquisition	digital, singleplayer
Benitez et al.	2022	Logistic business game focussing on decision making in logistics operations	Education	Students	Specific procedural skill acquisition	digital, singleplayer, competitive
Blöchl et al.	2017	"From Job Shop Production to One-Piece-Flow", simulating assembly lines of a company producing logistics trolleys	AEC (lean logistics)	Other (management staff)	Specific knowledge acquisition	analog, multiplayer, cooperative

(continued)

(continued)

Author	Year	Used application	Application domain	Target group	Objective	Classification
Brauner et al.	2016	Simulation of decision-making tasks in a supply chain environment	Manufacturing (DSS)	unspecific	Specific procedural skill acquisition	digital, singleplayer
Bruzzone et al.	2024	Simulation of container terminal operations with extended reality for port operator training	AEC (port operations)	Trainees/Operator	Specific procedural skill acquisition	digital, singleplayer
Cazzola et al.	2019	Augmented reality application for use in educational contexts	Education	Other (pupils)	Specific knowledge acquisition	digital, singleplayer
Checa et al.	2021	Immersive virtual reality environment for occupational risk prevention in the operation of bridge cranes	Industrial safety	Trainees/Operator	Specific procedural skill acquisition	digital, singleplayer
Dallasega et al.	2020	Use of virtual and augmented reality in a project simulation game for lean construction methodologies	AEC (lean construction)	Students	Specific knowledge acquisition	digital, multiplayer, cooperative
Duin et al.	2017	ArKoH Port game for training operators in a port environment	AEC (port operations)	Trainees/Operator	Specific procedural skill acquisition	digital, singleplayer
Eckardt & Robra-Bissantz	2019	Serious game for learning information literacy	Education	Students	Specific knowledge acquisition	digital, singleplayer
Gordan et al.	2024	Serious game for resilience of critical infrastructure, simulating physical or cyber-attacks on a system	Industrial safety	Trainees/Operator	Other (critical infrastructure resilience)	digital, multiplayer, competitive
Gutiérrez-Rodríguez et al.	2021	3D environment used to learn about safety elements to lower occupational accident rates	Industrial safety	Trainees/Operator	Specific knowledge acquisition	digital, singleplayer

(continued)

(continued)

Author	Year	Used application	Application domain	Target group	Objective	Classification
Koch et al.	2021	Immersive virtual scenario for sensor placement within an industrial environment	Education	Students	Other (evaluation tool)	digital, singleplayer
Mortensen et al.	2019	Serious game for creating Industry 4.0 awareness using stakeholder roleplay	Education	Other (non-experts)	Specific knowledge acquisition	analog, multiplayer, cooperative
Mystakidis et al.	2021	Virtual reality escape room for education	Education	Other (teacher)	Specific knowledge acquisition	digital, singleplayer
Nicoletti & Padovano	2019	Serious game for learning emergency responses on an oil storage plant as an emergency manager	Industrial safety	Trainees/Operator	Specific procedural skill acquisition	digital, multiplayer, cooperative
Oliveira et al.	2022	First-person serious game in virtual reality for inspection and training in wheel loader	AEC (mining operations)	Students	Specific procedural skill acquisition	digital, singleplayer
Oliveri et al.	2019	Serious game for evaluation of various technologies to improve warehousing operations	Education	Students	Specific knowledge acquisition	digital, multiplayer, cooperative
Perini et al.	2017	Serious game for learning about the Life Cycle Assessment for sustainable manufacturing	Manufacturing	Students	Specific procedural skill acquisition	digital, singleplayer
Ramirez-Montoya et al.	2024	Serious game for designing logistics networks, including customizable real-world logistics scenarios	Education	Students	Specific procedural skill acquisition	digital, singleplayer

(continued)

(continued)

Author	Year	Used application	Application domain	Target group	Objective	Classification
Riera & Vigário	2020	Dynamic 3D virtual serious games for building a virtual representation of industrial plants (FACTORY I/O)	Education	Students	Specific knowledge acquisition	digital, singleplayer
Rossano et al.	2020	Simulation game for training to build car engine configurations with specific characteristics	Education	Students + Employees	Specific knowledge acquisition	digital, singleplayer
Teichmann et al.	2020	Serious board game for education on Industry 4.0 and the modernization of factory workshops, using loop-based learning	Education	unspecific	Specific knowledge acquisition	analog, multiplayer, competitive
Tharot et al.	2023	3D virtual game for training cybersecurity in manufacturing systems	Manufacturing	Students	Specific knowledge acquisition	digital, singeplayer
Vassigh et al.	2024	VR game prototype for industrial robotics training	AEC (robotics)	unspecific	Specific knowledge acquisition	digital, singleplayer

References

1. Cimini, C., Pirola, F., Pinto, R., Cavalieri, S.: A human-in-the-loop manufacturing control architecture for the next generation of production systems. J. Manuf. Syst. **54**, 258–271 (2020). https://doi.org/10.1016/j.jmsy.2020.01.002
2. Moeuf, A., Lamouri, S., Pellerin, R., Tamayo-Giraldo, S., Tobon-Valencia, E., Eburdy, R.: Identification of critical success factors, risks and opportunities of Industry 4.0 in SMEs. Int. J. Prod. Res. **58**, 1384–1400 (2020)
3. Tomašević, A.N.: Reshaping the future of work: navigating the impacts of lifelong learning and digital competences in the era of 5.0 industry. Soc. Inform. J. (2023). https://doi.org/10.58898/sij.v2i1.01-06
4. Arlinghaus, J., Antons, O.: Management für digitalisierung und industrie 4.0. In: Frenz, W. (ed.) Handbuch Industrie 4.0: Recht, Technik, Gesellschaft. pp. 1121–1145. Springer, Heidelberg (2020). https://doi.org/10.1007/978-3-662-58474-3_58
5. Bekkhus, R.: Do KPIs used by CIOs decelerate digital business transformation? The case of ITIL. DIGIT 2016 Proc. (2016)

6. Vial, G.: Understanding digital transformation: a review and a research agenda. J. Strateg. Inf. Syst. **28**, 118–144 (2019). https://doi.org/10.1016/j.jsis.2019.01.003
7. Kessler, M.: The human factor in operations management - understanding the influence of cognitive biases in production and risk management (2023)
8. Vilko, J., Ritala, P., Edelmann, J.: On uncertainty in supply chain risk management. Int. J. Logist. Manag. **25**, 3–19 (2014). https://doi.org/10.1108/IJLM-10-2012-0126
9. Kolade, O., Owoseni, A.: Employment 5.0: the work of the future and the future of work. Technol. Soc. **71**, 102086 (2022). https://doi.org/10.1016/j.techsoc.2022.102086
10. Büssing, A., Herbig, B.: Implicit knowledge and experience in work and organizations. In: International Review of Industrial and Organizational Psychology 2003, pp. 239–280. Wiley, Hoboken (2003). https://doi.org/10.1002/0470013346.ch7
11. Wang, Z., Ren, S., Chadee, D., Liu, M., Cai, S.: Team reflexivity and employee innovative behavior: the mediating role of knowledge sharing and moderating role of leadership. J. Knowl. Manag. **25**, 1619–1639 (2021). https://doi.org/10.1108/JKM-09-2020-0683
12. Mättig, B., Kretschmer, V.: Einsatz digitaler assistenzsysteme in der logistik 4.0. In: ten Hompel, M., Vogel-Heuser, B., Bauernhansl, T. (eds.) Handbuch Industrie 4.0: Produktion, Automatisierung und Logistik, pp. 1–25. Springer, Heidelberg (2019). https://doi.org/10.1007/978-3-662-45537-1_114-1
13. Brucker Juricic, B., Galic, M., Marenjak, S.: Review of the construction labour demand and shortages in the EU. Buildings **11**, 17 (2021). https://doi.org/10.3390/buildings11010017
14. Acemoglu, D., Restrepo, P.: Demographics and automation. Rev. Econ. Stud. **89**, 1–44 (2022). https://doi.org/10.1093/restud/rdab031
15. Placke, B., Schleiermacher, T.: Anforderungen der digitalen Arbeitswelt: Kompetenzen und digitale Bildung in einer Arbeitswelt 4.0. IW Consult (2018)
16. Gao, Y., Gonzalez, V., Yiu, K.T.W.: Serious games vs. traditional tools in construction safety training: a review (2017). https://doi.org/10.24928/JC3-2017/0070
17. Kolb, D.: Experiential learning: experience as the source of learning and development (1984)
18. Armstrong, S.J., Mahmud, A.: Experiential learning and the acquisition of managerial tacit knowledge. Acad. Manag. Learn. Educ. **7**, 189–208 (2008). https://doi.org/10.5465/amle.2008.32712617
19. Kniestedt, I.: Engagement in applied games (2023). https://doi.org/10.4233/e6fedd21-5130-4311-a4bd-e1d5a87b89ec
20. Alrehaili, E.A., Al Osman, H.: A virtual reality role-playing serious game for experiential learning. Interact. Learn. Environ. **30**, 922–935 (2022). https://doi.org/10.1080/10494820.2019.1703008
21. Gouveia, D., Lopes, D., de Carvalho, C.V.: Serious gaming for experiential learning. In: 2011 Frontiers in Education Conference (FIE), pp. T2G-1-T2G-6 (2011). https://doi.org/10.1109/FIE.2011.6142778
22. Schmidt, R., Emmerich, K., Schmidt, B.: Applied games – in search of a new definition. In: Chorianopoulos, K., Divitini, M., Baalsrud Hauge, J., Jaccheri, L., Malaka, R. (eds.) ICEC 2015. LNCS, vol. 9353, pp. 100–111. Springer, Cham (2015). https://doi.org/10.1007/978-3-319-24589-8_8
23. Schumacher, A., Erol, S., Sihn, W.: A maturity model for assessing industry 4.0 readiness and maturity of manufacturing enterprises. Procedia CIRP **52**, 161–166 (2016). https://doi.org/10.1016/j.procir.2016.07.040
24. Milošević, I.M., et al.: Digital transformation in manufacturing: enhancing competitiveness through industry 4.0 technologies (2024). https://doi.org/10.56578/pmdf010104
25. Romero, D., Bernus, P., Noran, O., Stahre, J., Fast-Berglund, Å.: The operator 4.0: human cyber-physical systems & adaptive automation towards human-automation symbiosis work systems. In: Nääs, I., et al.(eds.) APMS 2016. IFIPAICT, vol. 488, pp. 677–686. Springer, Cham (2016). https://doi.org/10.1007/978-3-319-51133-7_80

26. Directorate-General for Research and Innovation (European Commission), et al.: Industry 5.0, a transformative vision for Europe: governing systemic transformations towards a sustainable industry. Publications Office of the European Union (2021)
27. Sony, M., Naik, S.: Industry 4.0 integration with socio-technical systems theory: a systematic review and proposed theoretical model. Technol. Soc. **61**, 101248 (2020). https://doi.org/10.1016/j.techsoc.2020.101248
28. Mattsson, S., Fast-Berglund, Å., Li, D., Thorvald, P.: Forming a cognitive automation strategy for operator 4.0 in complex assembly. Comput. Ind. Eng. **139**, 105360 (2018). https://doi.org/10.1016/j.cie.2018.08.011
29. Brauner, P., Ziefle, M.: Beyond playful learning – serious games for the human-centric digital transformation of production and a design process model. Technol. Soc. **71**, 102140 (2022). https://doi.org/10.1016/j.techsoc.2022.102140
30. Eriksson, K., et al.: Experiences in running a professional course on digitally-enabled production in collaboration between three Swedish universities. In: Advances in Transdisciplinary Engineering (2022). https://doi.org/10.3233/ATDE220184
31. Oliveira, T.R., et al.: Virtual reality system for inspection and training in wheel loader. ACM Int. Conf. Proceeding Ser. (2022). https://doi.org/10.1145/3604479.3604503
32. Huchler, N.: Grenzen der Digitalisierung von Arbeit – Die Nicht-Digitalisierbarkeit und Notwendigkeit impliziten Erfahrungswissens und informellen Handelns. Z. Für Arbeitswissenschaft **71**, 215–223 (2017). https://doi.org/10.1007/s41449-017-0076-5
33. Maunsell-Terry, J., Taşkin, N.: A comparative analysis on employee training: competency-based vs traditional. Ege Akad. Bakis Ege Acad. Rev. (2023). https://doi.org/10.21121/eab.980800
34. Chao, C.-J., Wu, S.-Y., Yau, Y.-J., Feng, W.-Y., Tseng, F.-Y.: Effects of three-dimensional virtual reality and traditional training methods on mental workload and training performance. Hum. Factors Ergon. Manuf. Serv. Ind. **27**, 187–196 (2017). https://doi.org/10.1002/hfm.20702
35. Rodriguez, H.M.R., Ribon, V.L.B., Viñas, L.B.P., Santiago, C.S., Malabag, B.A.: Enhancing corporate and factory training through game development: a comparative review. In: Bhateja, V., Dey, M., Senkerik, R. (eds.) FICTA 2024 2024. SIST, vol. 422, pp. 201–212. Springer, Singapore (2025). https://doi.org/10.1007/978-981-96-0147-9_17
36. Sadeghi, B., Richards, D., Formosa, P., Hitchens, M.: Experiential learning or direct training: fostering ethical cybersecurity decision-making via serious games. In: Baghaei, N., Ali, R., Win, K., Oyibo, K. (eds.) PERSUASIVE 2024. LNCS, vol. 14636, pp. 262–272. Springer, Cham (2024). https://doi.org/10.1007/978-3-031-58226-4_20
37. Jansen, R.J.G., van Zelst, M.: The multiple facilitator: scientists, sages and rascals. Simul. Gaming **52**, 273–289 (2021). https://doi.org/10.1177/1046878121989376
38. Kinitzki, M., Hertweck, D., Kühfuß, P., Kinitzki, V.: How SMEs can use games to assess the innovation potential of new technologies. In: Proceedings of the Central European Conference on Information and Intelligent Systems (2018)
39. Ma, M., Oikonomou, A., Jain, L.C. (eds.): Serious Games and Edutainment Applications. Springer, London (2011). https://doi.org/10.1007/978-1-4471-2161-9
40. Bartalucci, L., et al.: A Kinaesthetic hand exoskeleton system toward robot-augmented rehabilitation therapies in the health 4.0 era. In: Proceedings of the 2023 10th International Conference on Bioinformatics Research and Applications, New York, NY, USA, pp. 135–142. Association for Computing Machinery (2024). https://doi.org/10.1145/3632047.3632068
41. Irhadtanto, B., Rohmah, I.I.T., Junarti, Cuhanazriansyah, M.R., Cahyaningrum, Y.: Implementation of educational technology based on gamification in interactive monopoly games in the 4.0 Era. Int. J. Interact. Mob. Technol. IJIM. **18**, 157–166 (2024). https://doi.org/10.3991/ijim.v18i18.50549

42. Roukouni, A., Lukosch, H., Verbraeck, A., Zuidwijk, R.: Let the game begin: enhancing sustainable collaboration among actors in innovation ecosystems in a playful way. Sustainability **12**, 8494 (2020). https://doi.org/10.3390/su12208494

43. Connolly, T.M., Boyle, E.A., MacArthur, E., Hainey, T., Boyle, J.M.: A systematic literature review of empirical evidence on computer games and serious games. Comput. Educ. **59**, 661–686 (2012). https://doi.org/10.1016/j.compedu.2012.03.004

44. Durach, C.F., Kembro, J., Wieland, A.: A new paradigm for systematic literature reviews in supply chain management. J. Supply Chain Manag. **53**, 67–85 (2017). https://doi.org/10.1111/jscm.12145

45. Tranfield, D., Denyer, D., Smart, P.: Towards a methodology for developing evidence-informed management knowledge by means of systematic review. Br. J. Manag. **14**, 207–222 (2003). https://doi.org/10.1111/1467-8551.00375

46. de Groote, S.L., Raszewski, R.: Coverage of Google Scholar, Scopus, and Web of Science: a case study of the h-index in nursing. Nurs. Outlook **60**, 391–400 (2012). https://doi.org/10.1016/j.outlook.2012.04.007

47. Gilgun, J.F.: Deductive qualitative analysis and grounded theory: sensitizing concepts and hypothesis-testing. In: The SAGE Handbook of Current Developments in Grounded Theory, pp. 107–122. SAGE Publications Ltd., 1 Oliver's Yard, 55 City Road London EC1Y 1SP (2019). https://doi.org/10.4135/9781526485656.n7

48. Strauss, A., Corbin, J.: Basics of Qualitative Research: Techniques and Procedures for Developing Grounded Theory, 2nd edn. Sage Publications, Inc., Thousand Oaks (1998)

49. Bruzzone, A.G., et al.: Promoting safety, security, awareness and productivity in port plants. Procedia Comput. Sci. **232** (2024). https://doi.org/10.1016/j.procs.2024.01.035

50. Duin, H., Gorldt, C., Thoben, K.-D., Pawar, K.: Learning in ports with serious gaming. In: 2017 International Conference on Engineering, Technology and Innovation Engineering, Technology & Innovation Management 2020 New Challenges, New Approaches ICEITMC 2017 – Proceedings, January 2018 (2017). https://doi.org/10.1109/ICE.2017.8279917

51. Ramirez-Montoya, M.S., Rodes-Paragarino, V., Pacheco-Velazquez, E., Ramirez-Etcheverry, S.: Transforming logistics education by a virtual logistics simulation generator: UX pilot study. In: 2024 IEEE Gaming Entertainment and Media Conference GEM 2024 (2024). https://doi.org/10.1109/GEM61861.2024.10585758

52. Checa, D., Martínez, K., Osornio-Rios, R.A., Bustillo, A.: Virtual reality opportunities in the reduction of occupational hazards in industry 4.0. Dyna Spain **96**, 620–626 (2021). https://doi.org/10.6036/10241

53. Baalsrud Hauge, J., Basu, P., Sundus, F., Chowdhury, A., Schurig, A.: Design of a mixed reality game for exploring how IoT technologies can support the decision making process. In: Auer, M.E., Bhimavaram, K.R., Yue, X.-G. (eds.) REV 2021. LNNS, vol. 298, pp. 281–288. Springer, Cham (2022). https://doi.org/10.1007/978-3-030-82529-4_27

54. Rossano, V., Lanzilotti, R., Roselli, T.: A simulation game to acquire skills on industry 4.0. In: HCI International 2020 - Late Breaking Papers: Cognition, Learning and Games, pp. 730–738 (2020). https://doi.org/10.1007/978-3-030-60128-7_53

55. Teichmann, M., Ullrich, A., Knost, D., Gronau, N.: Serious games in learning factories: perpetuating knowledge in learning loops by game-based learning. Procedia Manuf. **45** (2020). https://doi.org/10.1016/j.promfg.2020.04.104

56. Vassigh, S., Bogosian, B., Peterson, E.: Performance-driven VR learning for robotics. In: Computational Design and Robotic Fabrication, pp. 356–367 (2024). https://doi.org/10.1007/978-981-99-8405-3_30

57. Riera, B., Vigário, B.: HOME I/O and FACTORY I/O: a virtual house and a virtual plant for control education. IFAC-Pap. **50** (2017). https://doi.org/10.1016/j.ifacol.2017.08.1719

58. Gutiérrez-Rodríguez, Á., López-García, J.D., Sanabria, R.A., Acevedo-Zapata, S.: Industry 4.0 and digital transformation in higher education through the perspective of smart cites. In: CEUR Workshop Proceedings, vol. 2992 (2021)
59. Blöchl, S.J., Michalicki, M., Schneider, M.: simulation game for lean leadership – shopfloor management combined with accounting for lean. Procedia Manuf. **9**, 97–105 (2017). https://doi.org/10.1016/j.promfg.2017.04.031
60. Eckardt, L., Robra-Bissantz, S.: EGameFlow in a serious game: gaming experience with the same game design but different learning content. In: Proceedings of the 23rd Pacific Asia Conference on Information Systems Secure ICT Platform for the 4th Industrial Revolution. PACIS 2019 (2019)
61. Mortensen, S.T., Nygaard, K.K., Madsen, O.: Outline of an industry 4.0 awareness game. Procedia Manuf. **31**, 309–315 (2019). https://doi.org/10.1016/j.promfg.2019.03.049
62. Mystakidis, S., Papantzikos, G., Stylios, C.: Virtual reality escape rooms for STEM education in industry 4.0: Greek teachers perspectives. In: 6th South-East Europe Design Automation, Computer Engineering, Computer Networks and Social Media Conference SEEDA-CECNSM 2021 (2021). https://doi.org/10.1109/SEEDA-CECNSM53056.2021.9566265
63. Perini, S., Luglietti, R., Margoudi, M., Oliveira, M., Taisch, M.: Training advanced skills for sustainable manufacturing: a digital serious game. Procedia Manuf. **11** (2017). https://doi.org/10.1016/j.promfg.2017.07.286
64. Benitez, A.F., Herrera, L.M., Pacheco, E., Espinosa, J.M.M.: Visualization, serious games and decision making. In: Proceedings of the European Conference on Games Based Learning, October 2022
65. Brauner, P., Valdez, A.C., Philipsen, R., Ziefle, M.: Defective still deflective – how correctness of decision support systems influences user's performance in production environments. In: HCI in Business, Government, and Organizations: Information Systems, pp. 16–27 (2016). https://doi.org/10.1007/978-3-319-39399-5_2
66. Abed, H., Pernelle, P., Carron, T., Ben Amar, C.: Scenario modeling for serious games: an approach for industry sector. In: Chiu, D., Marenzi, I., Nanni, U., Spaniol, M., Temperini, M. (eds.) ICWL 2016. LNCS, vol. 10013, pp. 185–194. Springer, Cham (2016). https://doi.org/10.1007/978-3-319-47440-3_21
67. Dallasega, P., Revolti, A., Sauer, P.C., Schulze, F., Rauch, E.: BIM, augmented and virtual reality empowering lean construction management: a project simulation game. Procedia Manuf. **45**, 49–54 (2020). https://doi.org/10.1016/j.promfg.2020.04.059
68. Gordan, M., et al.: Protecting critical infrastructure against cascading effects: the PRECINCT approach. Resilient Cities Struct. **3**, 1–19 (2024). https://doi.org/10.1016/j.rcns.2024.04.001
69. Koch, J., Gomse, M., Schüppstuhl, T.: Digital game-based examination for sensor placement in context of an Industry 4.0 lecture using the Unity 3D engine - a case study. Procedia Manuf., 563–570 (2021). https://doi.org/10.1016/j.promfg.2021.10.077
70. Nicoletti, L., Padovano, A.: Human factors in occupational health and safety 4.0: a cross-sectional correlation study of workload, stress and outcomes of an industrial emergency response. Int. J. Simul. Process Model. **14**, 178–195 (2019). https://doi.org/10.1504/IJSPM.2019.099912
71. Tharot, K., Duong, Q.B., Riel, A., Thiriet, J.-M.: A cybersecurity training concept for cyber-physical manufacturing systems. Procedia CIRP **120** (2023). https://doi.org/10.1016/j.procir.2023.09.179
72. Cazzolla, A., Lanzilotti, R., Roselli, T., Rossano, V. (eds.): Augmented reality to support education in industry 4.0. In: Presented at the 2019 18th International Conference on Information Technology Based Higher Education and Training, ITHET 2019 (2019). https://doi.org/10.1109/ITHET46829.2019.8937365

73. Cooper, D.F., Klein, J.: Board wargames for decision making research. Eur. J. Oper. Res. **5**, 36–41 (1980). https://doi.org/10.1016/0377-2217(80)90071-5
74. Freese, M., Bekebrede, G.: Game research by design in project management and beyond. Proj. Leadersh. Soc. **6**, 100174 (2025). https://doi.org/10.1016/j.plas.2024.100174
75. Kagermann, H., Wahlster, W., Helbig, J.: Securing the future of German manufacturing industry: recommendations for implementing the strategic initiative industrie 4.0. Final report of the Industrie 4.0 Working Group (2013)

Sustainability, Climate, and Urban Resilience

The World Climate Game© as a Tool for Change
- Solving World Problems Through Play -

Rouven Kaiser[1]([☒]) [iD] and Matthias Mittelberger[2]

[1] Center for Climate Resilience, University of Augsburg, 86153 Augsburg, Germany
r.kaiser@uni-a.de
[2] Weitblick GmbH, Bruno-Marek-Allee 5/7, 1020 Viena, Austria
matthias.mittelberger@weitblick-gmbh.org

Abstract. Climate change is one of the greatest global challenges of the 21st century and requires innovative educational approaches to convey complex inter-relationships and promote the ability to act sustainably. This article presents the World Climate Game as a best-practice example of interactive learning methods. The game simulates international climate negotiations and allows participants to slip into different roles such as political decision-makers, economic actors or civil society organisations. The aim is to promote both cognitive and emotional learning processes and to create a deep understanding of the dynamics of the global climate crisis. The World Climate Game is based on a hybrid simulation that integrates scientifically sound climate and economic data. It visualises the impact of human activities on ecosystems and global politics. Empirical surveys with over 700 participants show that the game not only strengthens environmental awareness and political insight, but also promotes social skills such as cooperation and negotiation skills. Methodologically, the concept is characterised by approaches from transformative education and global citizenship education. The qualitative and quantitative results of the study confirm that the game motivates participants to reflect critically and develop sustainable solutions. Overall, the World Climate Game makes a significant contribution to environmental education and personal development by combining knowledge, emotional involvement and the ability to act. The findings emphasise the relevance of interactive learning formats for overcoming complex global challenges and offer suggestions for the further development of serious games in an educational context.

Keywords: Serious Games · Climate Change · Transformative Learning

1 Introduction

Climate change is one of the most pressing global challenges of the 21st century and requires interdisciplinary approaches to sensitize, educate and motivate people to act. Against this background, the use of simulation games has become increasingly established as a didactic tool to make complex topics in the context of climate science and political decision-making accessible. This paper looks at the World Climate Game as a

F. Trautwein et al. (Eds.): ISAGA 2025, LNCS 16439, pp. 217–232, 2026.
https://doi.org/10.1007/978-3-032-20129-4_15

best-practice example of linking education and interactive learning methods. The World Climate Game simulates global climate negotiations and enables participants to experience different stakeholder roles and perspectives on climate policy. Both the scientific foundations of climate change and the challenges of international climate policy are addressed. The aim of this study is to work out the didactic potential of the World Climate Game and to evaluate the benefits of the method in educational work. The paper is structured as follows: Firstly, the theoretical foundations and the methodological framework of the World Climate Game are explained. Empirical data on the effectiveness of the method is then presented and analyzed. Finally, the central research questions for analyzing the effectiveness of the game in educational work are discussed and answered.

2   Theoretical Approach

The World Climate Game sees itself embedded in several theories and traditions of thought, which characterize and shape it both methodologically and didactically as well as in terms of content. First and foremost, the humanistic and existential-philosophically influenced existential pedagogy was a guiding principle in its development. This theory by Kolbe [1], Waibel [2] and Bollnow [3] was particularly influential in terms of the attitude of the game facilitator and the design of the entire game experience regarding people's basic motivations. This involves a holistic consideration of the human being in all its dimensions and respect for the dignity of the participants, especially about their free choice, their orientation towards personal values as a source of motivation and the experience of meaning as a condition for a fulfilled existence. The resulting teaching attitude for game facilitators is characterized by phenomenological openness, a deep appreciation of the person and the dignity of the human being, a fundamental process orientation (as opposed to a goal orientation), the consideration of a good relationship between the involved participants and the facilitators as a didactic methods, and the learning of social behavior based on the living model of the teacher [4]. In addition, the post-colonial theories surrounding the subject area of Global Citizenship Education GCE, as well as the considerations surrounding the topic of Education for Sustainable Development (ESD) based on the UN's Agenda 21 [5], played a major role in the development of the content. The SDGs of the United Nations [6] were also used as a framework model. This results in a strong emphasis on critical reflection, systemic thinking, participation and sustainability of the dominant narratives [7, 8]. Regarding political education, the reference to democracy education and the Frankfurt Declaration [9] is essential and trendsetting for critical-emancipatory political education. The World Climate Game is therefore also committed to human rights and children's rights in accordance with the United Nations.

3   The World Climate Game

3.1   The Idea

The basic idea of the World Climate Game is to make the complex challenges of the global climate crisis understandable in a playful way and to serve as a counterweight to the growing fear of climate crisis. It offers participants the opportunity to slip into different roles and experience the impact of their actions on the environment, economy and society. A combination of scientifically based simulation, social interaction and haptic elements creates an interactive learning environment in which participants can collaboratively develop sustainable solutions. The game promotes both cognitive and emotional learning experiences and creates a deeper understanding of global interrelationships. The aim of the World Climate Game is to teach action skills, develop empathy for different stakeholder groups and emphasize the importance of international cooperation for climate protection.

3.2 What It is About

The World Climate Game offers a comprehensive and multi-layered approach to the global climate crisis. The content is based on the latest scientific findings and covers the ecological, economic and social dimensions of the climate problem. The focus is on the causes and consequences of global warming, particularly the anthropogenic greenhouse effect, the loss of greenhouse gas sinks and the damage to ecosystems. The players experience how emissions from various sectors such as industry, transport and agriculture contribute to global warming. The degradation of landscape tiles on the game board illustrates the progressive loss of biodiversity, carbon sinks and natural resources. The economic context of the climate crisis is illustrated by simulating global markets and resource flows. Production costs, wage levels and tax systems influence the players' strategies for action. The dynamic between sustainable investments, promoting innovation and reducing emissions can be experienced, while at the same time the need for economic stability takes center stage. A central component of the game is the link between climate crisis and social issues. Population growth, social inequalities, climate justice and political instability are an integral part of the game mechanics. Players must work together to develop solutions that combine social justice and environmental sustainability. The game materials include both physical and digital elements. These include a detailed game board, game pieces and markers as well as a digital platform that integrates the latest scientific data. Interactive scenarios and event cards illustrate the interactions between humans, nature and the economy. The overarching aim of the Game is to convey a deep understanding of the global climate crisis and to emphasize the complexity and urgency of the issue to participants. The playful approach stimulates both cognitive and emotional learning processes to develop sustainable options for action and strengthen a sense of responsibility.

3.3 Gameplay

The World Climate Game is designed as a multi-day simulation game. A playthrough usually takes three days with seven hours of play per day. The course of the World Climate Game is divided into several phases that build on each other and provide a comprehensive learning experience. At the beginning, the participants receive an introduction to game mechanics. The game facilitator explains the different factions, the respective game elements and the basic course of the game rounds. The roles are then assigned, with the participants representing different groups of actors in the climate crisis, such as political decision-makers, economic actors or NGOs. The game board, which shows an abstract world map with regions, resource deposits, emission sources and ecosystems represented by hexagonal tiles, is placed in the center of the room. The round indicator runs over ten decades, starting in the year 2000. The main reason for starting in 2000 is that players can play from the past to the future. The first round is mainly to familiarize players with the game. After that, they will understand the key mechanics, the setup and the round sequences. Each round consists of three phases. In the event phase, the game facilitator presents global challenges based on real data, such as natural disasters, political crises or climatic developments, that reflect the current state of the climate crisis. During the subsequent negotiation phase (2), the players exchange ideas within and between the factions. They develop strategies, decide on climate protection measures, negotiate trade agreements and plan political alliances. Economic decisions and innovation processes can also be initiated here. They can then implement these at the same time. This is followed by the announcement phase (3), in which the respective factions inform each other about their actions, plans and findings. Then the next decade begins as an event phase again, in which the digital platform updates the global changes based on the decisions made. Emission values, economic data and environmental conditions are displayed transparently, and the consequences and results of the game decisions are visualized in figures and graphics. Thus, each round of the game has an arc of suspense that begins with confronting the negative aspects of the climate crisis and continues through a process of self-directed learning to effectively overcome the challenges. A moderated reflection phase takes place after each game day. Here, the participants reflect together on the impact of their decisions on the environment, economy and society. The game facilitator supports this process by asking specific questions and emphasizing key learning moments. The game ends either after the last decade or when the playing time has expired. At the end of the game, there is a comprehensive debriefing that covers both the results achieved and their transferability to real-life contexts. The cooperation processes, individual and collective options for action and the learning success are discussed. The structured process of the World Climate Game not only ensures a sound transfer of knowledge, but also promotes social skills, critical thinking and cooperative problem-solving approaches.

3.4 The Three Dimensions of the World Climate Game

The World Climate Game is a hybrid board game combining digital, simulation and analogue elements. These three dimensions provide a multi-layered gaming experience, stimulating cognitive, emotional and social learning processes. Thematically, it focuses on the climate crisis; methodologically, it focuses on the development of soft skills and self-empowerment. In the simulation dimension, the aim is to begin with a setting that is almost real, based on scientific data and scenarios. From there, development is oriented towards real-world development, especially in the first decades, but necessarily deviates from the real-world situation. The three dimensions are explained in detail below.

The Climate and Economic Simulation

At the heart of the game is a database-supported climate and economic simulation. This is based on scientifically sound models and realistic data sources, particularly the emissions data from the IPCC [10], the HDI data [11] and the data sets from the 'Gapminder' website [12]. The setting is clearly oriented towards real-world data and must reduce the complexity at certain points to ensure smooth gameplay. The focus is on climate and economic data from well-known global organizations. The hexagonal landscape tiles on the game board exist in three states: healthy nature, degraded nature and destroyed ecosystem. This visualization illustrates the influence of human activities on greenhouse gas sinks and biodiversity. The political regions are labelled with specific production costs, wage levels and tax rates. Socio-economic aspects such as population growth, housing construction, population supply and infrastructure are also depicted. The game objects such as factories, energy plants and infrastructure elements are linked in the database with emission values, construction costs and resource utilization. Players can manage their resources, make investments, trade goods and track emission values via a browser-based application. The game facilitator can moderate the course of the game and intervene if necessary. The aim of the simulation is to make the complex interactions between the ecosphere, the economy and human activity understandable. The design of the database and the climate-economy model is inspired by Jay Forrester's work 'World Dynamics' [13] and the book 'Limits to Growth' [14]. The main difference is that Forrester's system is controlled by algorithms, whereas in the World Climate Game the decisions of the individual players define the state of the complex system. After each round of the game, graphical reports on the global state of the environment and economy are presented to visualize the effects of the players' decisions.

The Socio-Economic Simulation

The socio-economic simulation game of the World Climate Game comprises 12 factions, each representing specific groups of actors in the global climate crisis. The factions are not individuals, but collective actors such as governments, economic sectors and civil society organizations. Five of the factions are governments, which reflect large, imagined regions of the world in an abstract form. They have the task of enacting laws, managing budgets and conducting diplomatic negotiations. A further five factions represent global economic players in selected functional sectors with the aim of producing goods, trading and pursuing economic interests. Civil society forms an independent faction that acts as a critical body. It can exert influence through protests and civil society involvement or act as a mediator in conflict situations. This is complemented by an international organization that takes on the role of diplomatic mediator and peacekeeper. Each section could define personal roles for each player. Ultimately, each player can play their role as freely as possible. The gameplay allows for a wide range of known or unknown acting options. The only limitations are the players' creativity and at some points the gameplay itself. This simulation game places great emphasis on the dynamics of social interaction. Players not only take on roles but also experience the effects of and take responsibility for global crises. Through immersion and identification, the game achieves an emotional understanding of the characters' perspectives, complementing and deepening the cognitive and behavioral aspects of the learning content. Faction roles promote the ability to recognize and negotiate political, economic, and social contexts. It is very important to keep the following in mind when talking about the game: Players have a great deal of freedom in their choice of actions. The role of the game facilitator should be interpreted as very hands-off. Their focus should be on the simulation and rule-keeping level. Interventions should be kept to a minimum.

The Board Game Dimension

The third dimension is the haptic-visual board game component. The central game board measures 150 cm × 150 cm and has an aesthetically pleasing design to focus the group's attention and symbolize the common center of the game. The game board visualizes the planetary effects of the climate crisis and makes them physically tangible through game pieces, markers and landscape tiles. It supports the adoption of a global perspective on the causes of and solutions to the climate crisis, which embeds the regional or individual challenges of the factions in a larger context. The round scoreboard depicts the course of a century in decades and shows the long-term developments of the climate crisis. The board game dimension not only serves to visualize, but also to motivate through classic game elements such as resource management, strategy development, negotiation, crisis management and the element of chance. The physical game materials also support the learning process by making abstract content such as emissions and biodiversity loss concrete and tangible.

By combining these three dimensions - the data-based simulation, the social interaction and the physical board game dimension - the World Climate Game succeeds in creating an immersive and motivating learning environment. Participants experience the complexity of the global climate crisis on a cognitive, emotional and practical level and are encouraged to develop solutions together.

4   General, Pedagogical and Didactic Considerations

4.1   Key Aspects of Game Modelling

The World Climate Game's modelling system is based on several central assumptions that shape the game's design and functioning. Firstly, the system recognizes that the global climate crisis is a complex, interconnected problem that cannot be solved by technical innovations or individual political decisions alone. Rather, it requires an interplay of ecological, economic, and social factors. Secondly, the model assumes that human activity, particularly economic activity, is the cause of current climate developments, and that collective decisions can significantly influence emissions, resource consumption, and environmental conditions. Thirdly, the game assumes that global actors have different interests, areas of responsibility and scope for action, and that conflicts and cooperation between these actors are decisive for the success of climate policy measures. These assumptions form the basis of a three-dimensional game system in which a data-based climate and economic simulation operates with realistic parameters (e.g. emission factors and production costs). This assumes that systemic changes are quantifiable and can be depicted through model-based interventions. The socio-economic simulation game reflects the assumption that political and economic governance takes place through a discursive and often conflictual negotiation process, in which rational, normative, power-related and emotional aspects all play a role. The physical board game dimension assumes that haptic-visual representations promote cognitive and emotional processing of complex contexts, thus intensifying learning.

4.2 Intended Effects

The World Climate Game has a multi-layered intended effect that encompasses cognitive as well as emotional and social learning objectives. The focus is on conveying a comprehensive understanding of the causes, effects and possible solutions to the global climate crisis. The combination of simulation, role play, and board game makes it possible to experience complex interrelationships in an understandable way. Participants are given the opportunity to experience and reflect on the dynamics between economic activities, political decisions and ecological consequences within the protected framework of a game. The key aim of the game is to promote a holistic awareness of the problem. It is not just about imparting specialist knowledge, but also about strengthening the realization that the climate crisis is a systemic problem that affects different groups of actors in different ways and can only be overcome through interdisciplinary and cooperative approaches. It is emphasized that both individual behavioral changes and structural measures are necessary. It is essential that the clarification of responsibility leads to orientation and relief for the participants and counteracts a one-sided shift of responsibility to the (consumption) decisions of the individual. Another important aspect of the intended effect is the promotion of emotional involvement and empathy. By taking on roles and actively experiencing challenges, an emotional connection to the topic is created that enables lasting learning experiences. Participants not only gain cognitive knowledge but also develop compassion and a deeper understanding of the global inequalities and impacts associated with the climate crisis. In addition, the World Climate Game aims to help young people to become aware of and subsequently integrate the complex emotional dimensions of the climate crisis. The aim is to counteract the phenomena of 'climate change grief', which were empirically proven for example in the SOS Children's Villages Youth Study [15]. The World Climate Game is also intended to teach action-oriented and personality-building skills. These include skills such as critical thinking, problem-solving, communication and negotiation skills and teamwork. The WHO framework model of life skills [16] and the 'Inner Development Goals' [17] have been relevant in defining the learning objectives. Participants learn to develop viable compromises in complex negotiation situations, to resolve conflicts constructively and to work together to develop strategies for overcoming the climate crisis. These skills are not only relevant for dealing with the climate crisis but are also transferable to other social challenges and have a universal preventative effect in the context of psychosocial health promotion. The game also aims to strengthen the experience of self-efficacy. Participants should learn that they are able to bring about change and make constructive contributions. Recognizing the direct impact of their decisions on the course of the game makes them aware of their ability to act and counteracts feelings of powerlessness. The opportunity to be creative and playful in their roles opens the game up to unexpected outcomes and complex learning processes. Ultimately, the World Climate Game aims to make players more aware of global justice issues. It makes it clear that the climate crisis affects people in different regions of the world to varying degrees and that historical inequalities play a role. This change of perspective makes topics such as climate justice, social responsibility and intergenerational justice comprehensible. Overall, the World Climate Game aims not only to impart knowledge, but also to create a profound learning experience that combines knowledge, emotions and the ability to act. In this way, it contributes to transformative education that aims to empower people to actively and thoughtfully work towards a sustainable future.

4.3 Personal Development in Modern Times

In view of the increasing complexity and dynamics of global challenges, personal development in the late modern global age is a key educational task. The World Climate Game addresses these challenges by confronting participants with the multi-layered aspects of the climate crisis in an interactive learning setting and encouraging them to reflect on their own values, abilities and options for action. A central goal of the personal development process is to develop a reflective self-awareness. Participants should learn to critically scrutinize their own points of view, perceive a variety of perspectives and grasp complex issues in their entirety. The world climate game supports this by putting the players in different roles and confronting them with realistic global challenges. This promotes the ability to empathize with other positions and develop social empathy. The promotion of action competence and self-efficacy is another focus of personality development in the World Climate Game. By taking responsibility for decisions and experiencing the consequences of their own actions during the game, participants learn that their actions can have an impact on global processes. This experience not only strengthens their awareness of their own effectiveness, but also motivates them to actively participate in shaping social transformation processes. The World Climate Game also contributes to the development of moral judgement. The confrontation with ethical dilemmas, such as the distribution of global resources or the balancing of economic and ecological interests, requires a reflective examination of value conflicts. The facilitator supports this process with targeted questions and reflection phases that enable participants to reflect on their decisions about justice, solidarity and sustainability. Another key aspect of personal development is the promotion of critical thinking. The World Climate Game encourages participants to critically question information, analyses narratives and develop alternative solutions. This is achieved through the simulation-based examination of global crisis scenarios in which there are no simple solutions and interdisciplinary approaches are required. Finally, the global climate game supports the development of team and communication skills. Joint decision-making in groups, negotiating compromises and dealing with conflicts are an integral part of the game. Participants learn to argue their own positions, but also to respect the perspectives of others and develop joint solutions. Overall, the World Climate Game makes an important contribution to personality development in the global late modern age thanks to its holistic approach. It combines cognitive, emotional and social learning processes and creates a learning environment that encourages participants to respond to global challenges in a reflective, empathetic and action-orientated way.

The World Climate Game aims to promote self-efficacy, responsibility and cooperative action in the context of climate crisis. The game is designed for experiential learning rather than for the faithful reproduction of real systems. The simulation operates with simplified parameters and focuses on central interdependence. Complex feedback and non-linear dynamics are only partially represented. Systemic depth is limited in favor of clear feedback and controllability. The management game level enables players to change their perspective, design creative processes and take on decision-making responsibility. However, it is based on abstracted roles with limited reference to reality. This results in asymmetrical gaming experiences and normative settings (deliberately so). The board game dimension supports immersion and vividness but can hinder cognitive depth and content-related reflection by introducing gaming elements. These methodological settings are deliberate didactic reductions designed to make complex issues accessible and enable transformative learning processes.

Overall, these assumptions imply that education for sustainable development cannot be achieved through knowledge transfer alone, but rather through experience-based, interactive and cooperative action. The World Climate Game is therefore an expression of a transformative approach to education based on systemic thinking, multi-perspective understanding, and participatory problem solving.

5 Results from Impact Assessment Through Qualitative and Quantitative Data Collection

A classic survey analysis approach was used to record the impact to shed light on both qualitative and quantitative dimensions of the data. A total of 740 questionnaires were analyzed as part of the study, which were collected following 35 different games. The surveys were conducted among the participants immediately after the end of the respective games as a mandatory part of the event. The wide range of survey settings, which reflect the broad diversity of the sample, is particularly noteworthy. The data was collected from an age group of 13 to 62 years and covers all school types in the Austrian education system. In addition, the survey was also conducted in the context of cooperation with extracurricular educational institutions, which further increases the significance of the results. The structure of the survey and the results obtained are presented in detail below, with transparent analysis. This paper does not focus on analyzing the players' game results or comparing them with real-world data. The aim of this paper is to demonstrate the effectiveness of the game from a general perspective.

5.1 Quantitative Analysis of the World Climate Game Learning Effects

Method

This section is dedicated to the quantitative analysis of the data collected, with the aim of systematically presenting and interpreting key trends and distributions of the variables recorded. The first analysis is based on simple statistical key figures. All relevant data sets relating to the content aspects of the survey are considered. The focus is therefore on the data that enables statements to be made about the participants, their perceptions and experiences within the analyzed contexts. The relevant questions are: 1.'How did you like the World Climate Game overall?'; 2.'How did you like your role in the game?'.

Results

The results of the evaluation provide exciting insights into the general gaming experience of the participants. The first question deals with the overall distribution of the participants' respective roles in the game and their specific evaluation. The observations made previously can be confirmed here. Only a small proportion of participants found the game experience less good or bad. Just under 50% rated their own role experience as very positive. Overall, almost 90% of players were satisfied with the game. Only around 9 per cent had a less positive experience. 2.4% even had a bad experience. (see Fig. 1) In absolute numbers: around 380 people felt their role in the game was very good and 277 felt it was good. 70 participants perceived it as less good and 17 people even though they were not positive at all. A very clear majority were satisfied to very satisfied with the game experience. In the next step, a more in-depth analysis in the sense of an individual case evaluation would be interesting. However, this would require a more in-depth qualitative survey.

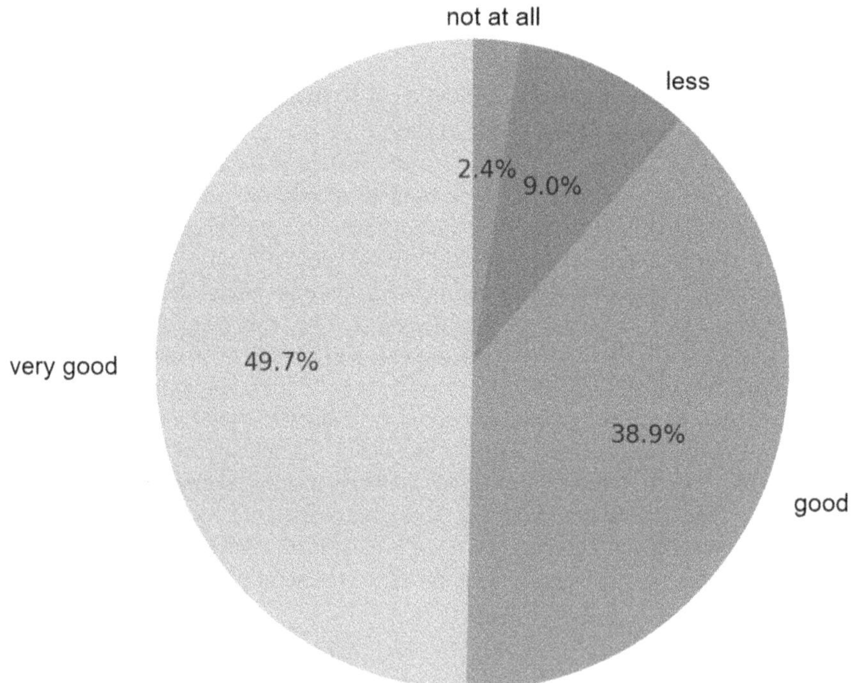

Fig. 1. Overall distribution of responses by evaluation category (Source: Own illustration)

The second question provides an insight into the respective role-specific categorization. It allows a more precise analysis of which faction rated their own role experience as good or bad and how well they perceived it to be playable. The question is first summarized and analyzed about the overarching categories of cooperation, government, UIO and civil society. The data was weighed accordingly. The results show clear differences in the perception of role experiences between the various groups, as can be seen in Fig. 2. The cooperation category has a high number of positive responses. Most of the ratings are in the 'very good' category, followed by 'good'. Nevertheless, there is also some negative feedback in the categories 'less' and 'not at all', which indicates a mixed, but overall, very positive perception. The government category also shows a high dominance of the categories 'very good' and 'good'. Negative feedback is less common here than in the Cooperation group, which indicates an overall very positive perception of the role experience in government contexts. The UIO role also shows a very positive distribution of responses with a clear focus on 'very good'. However, negative assessments are also recorded here. Civil society shows a balanced distribution. 'Very good' and "good" are predominantly represented, but it is clearly recognizable that a larger proportion is accounted for by negative assessments. This indicates an overall more differentiated perception compared to the other groups. To summarize, the results show that most participants rated their role experience as positive, particularly in the Government, Cooperation and UIO groups. The civil society players must be assessed in a more differentiated way. This data suggests that the role design could be partially optimized to ensure a consistently positive gaming experience.

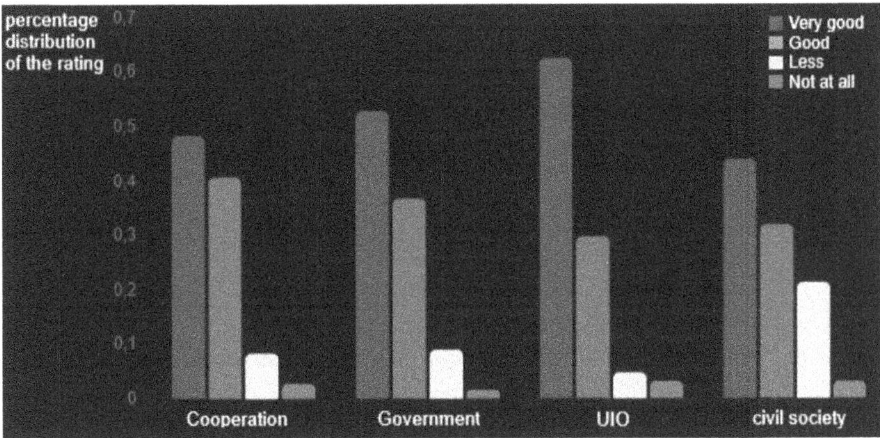

Fig. 2. Game rating by category (Source: Own illustration)

To be able to answer the relevant questions in more detail and better, the same questions were analyzed again on a role-specific basis, as can be seen in Fig. 3. The most common response category was 'very good', which was dominated by most roles. In particular UIO, Pasgana, Zentari, Sekon, Industrial Corp. and UIO recorded high scores in this category, indicating an overall positive perception of the role experience in these groups. Most of the other roles are also perceived by the participants as predominantly positive and well-integrated. At the same time, it is noticeable that roles such as Elatrien, Stone Corp. and civil society show a greater dispersion in the ratings. For these roles, there is not only a lower proportion of 'very good' ratings, but also a strikingly high number of responses in the 'less' and 'not at all' categories, which could indicate possible dissatisfaction with the role experience. Overall, the corp. roles tend to be in the middle of the distribution and show a relatively balanced rating. They have a solid proportion of 'good' and 'very good' responses, but also some critical ratings, which somewhat diminish the overall impression. The Government category also performs well, with an overwhelming majority of positive responses, but a slightly higher proportion of average and negative ratings than Cooperations. The existing variance indicates a need for optimization, but first and foremost a good design of the role definitions. This requires a precise analysis of the text responses.

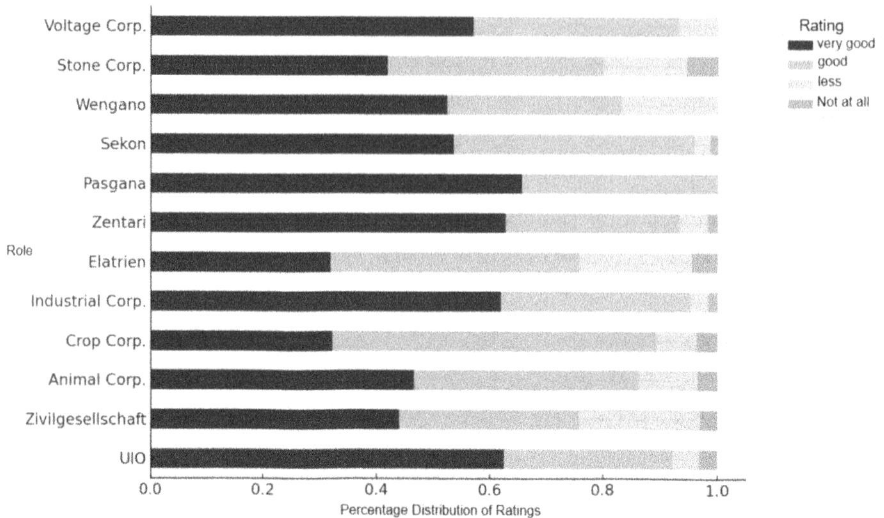

Fig. 3. Game rating by role (Source: Own illustration)

Overall, the role-based analysis shows that most participants rated their role experience as predominantly positive, but with slight variations between the individual roles. The data suggests that some roles may require more intensive engagement with the game mechanics or role design to ensure an equally positive experience for all participants.

5.2 Qualitative Analysis of the World Climate Game Learning Effects

Method

The analysis was carried out with the help of content-structuring qualitative content analysis according to Philipp Mayring [18]. The aim was to systematically categorize the answers documented in the data collection to make the main points and tendencies of the learning experiences visible. The study was based on inductive categorization, which was developed from the material. This was followed by an in-depth semantic analysis, including a simple sentiment analysis, to identify overall tonality and thematic clusters. The categorization was carried out iteratively, supplemented by a manual review of random samples of the comments. The questionnaire comprises three questions: 1) 'What did you learn from the World Climate Game?'; 2) 'What did you particularly like about the World Climate Game?'; 3) 'What did you not like about the World Climate Game?'.

Results

After reviewing the data for question 1, it was categorized into the following main categories: Environmental Awareness, Political Insights, Social Dynamics, Financial

Insights and Other. The category Other was further differentiated into general statements, provocative/resignative statements and incomprehensible statements to improve interpretability. Most responses could be categorized as Environmental Awareness and Political Insights. Statements such as 'I have learnt how harmful CO2 can be' illustrate an increased environmental awareness. Political insights were reflected in statements such as 'It is difficult to make decisions that are fair to everyone'. The social dynamics category included statements on group processes and power relations, such as 'It is important to work together as a group'. Here it became clear that the participants recognized the need for cooperation and negotiation skills. Financial insights were evident in statements such as 'I understood how to budget with limited resources'. This illustrates that the game was also able to emphasize aspects of resource management and economic decision-making. The Other category was less frequent but showed interesting trends. General statements such as 'learnt a lot' remained unspecific. Resignative statements, including 'I don't care about the environment' or 'Nothing new learnt', indicate frustration or rejection of the game. Incomprehensible statements were not significantly represented in the data collection. The results indicate that the World Climate Game fundamentally helps to promote environmental awareness and political connections. At the same time, the resignative statements point to possible challenges during the game or the emotional reaction of the participants. Superficially formulated answers in the 'Other' category could indicate insufficient cognitive processing of the game content or a lack of opportunities for reflection during the game. This analysis shows that the World Climate Game is potentially effective in promoting learning processes in the areas of environmental awareness and political decision-making, but in certain cases is met with resistance and little reflection.

The results regarding the second question can be summarized as follows: 1. Participants emphasized the different aspects of negotiation and discussion. Participants particularly appreciated the negotiation dynamics and the opportunity to interact. 2. They also mentioned the good immersion. Visible through enjoyment of the game, personal attachment to the role and emotional involvement. Some appreciated the resulting closeness to reality and the knowledge gained through the game. 3. Justice and fairness were also relevant. Although less frequently mentioned, some emphasized the good handling of conflict situations and their solutions within the game. 4. Their own independence and assumption of responsibility was perceived positively. Participants emphasized the opportunity to act independently and take responsibility. 5. The game mechanics were also praised: technical aspects and the complexity of the game design were emphasized, including the structure of the game world and the use of digital tools. This point was mentioned by almost all participants. The analysis shows that the game mechanics, followed by interactive elements, particularly the negotiation processes, were perceived as particularly positive. While aspects such as fairness were only mentioned sporadically, it was found that personal responsibility and emotionality also played a role. The high weighting of the game mechanics can be attributed to the immersive design of the world climate game, which obviously made a strong impression.

The third question deals with aspects of the game that could be improved. The aim of the question was to identify key points of criticism and make suggestions for improvement. The qualitative analysis revealed five central points of criticism: 1. Game mechanics, especially the long explanation phases (76 mentions), too frequent repetitions in the gameplay (41 mentions) and great complexity of the game mechanics (10 mentions). 2. Negative social dynamics and unsupportive group behavior such as a lack of cooperation (7 mentions) and other behaviors (3 mentions) were also discussed, albeit much less frequently. 3. Content-related aspects, such as insufficient depth and coverage of topics, were only mentioned sporadically. 4. Inadequate conflict management, in particular differently perceived threat scenarios and undifferentiated conflict presentations (28 mentions) were also mentioned. 5. An unclear allocation of roles (8 mentions) was mentioned sporadically. The sentiment analysis showed that most of the feedback was formulated neutrally, which indicates a differentiated perception of the participants. Based on the results, there is potential for the following improvements: optimization of the game mechanics, including by shortening the explanation phases and reducing repetition, clearer allocation of roles through more precise role descriptions, expansion of the depth of content through optional inclusion of additional topics, particularly geographical aspects, and further promotion of group interaction to improve cooperation.

The qualitative evaluation shows that the World Climate Game predominantly provides (very) positive learning experiences in environmental awareness, political insights and social dynamics. While aspects such as the negotiation dynamics and game mechanics were largely rated positively, there was criticism of the length of the explanation phases and the complexity.

The impact assessment of the World Climate Game is primarily based on subjective evaluations of the gaming experience, particularly in terms of role satisfaction. There is limited systematic measurement of cognitive or affective learning outcomes. Pre/post measurements and control groups are lacking. Expanding the instruments to record impact dimensions such as self-efficacy or system understanding would validate the data further. It would also be interesting to conduct a broader and deeper analysis of the participants' backgrounds to enable more comprehensive differentiation. Using standardized scales and a pre/post design to record concrete changes is recommended to improve the assessment. Additionally, qualitative analysis could be carried out in a more systematic, broader and deeper methodological manner to increase the significance and comprehensibility of the results.

Overall, the game promotes environmental education and political reflection but shows potential for optimization in the game design.

6   Conclusion

The results of this study show that the World Climate Game, as an innovative educational tool, is highly effective in promoting environmental awareness, social responsibility, and political reflection. The game succeeds in making complex global interrelationships tangible in a way that appeals to cognitive, emotional, and social learning processes. The combination of simulation, business game, and board game dimensions enables an immersive learning experience in which knowledge acquisition, empathy, and action orientation are interrelated. It is particularly noteworthy that the game contributes to holistic personality development through its multi-layered forms of interaction. Participants experience themselves as active players in a global system, recognize the consequences of their actions, and reflect on social and ecological responsibilities. This achieves the central educational goals of transformative education: systemic thinking, empathy development, responsibility-taking, and self-efficacy. At the same time, the findings should be viewed with an awareness of certain limitations. Methodologically, the impact analysis is based on subjective assessments by participants, which may be influenced by individual perceptions and situational factors. No objective measurement of learning progress or long-term effects was carried out as part of this study. The lack of pre-post surveys and comparison groups also limits the significance of the findings with regard to sustainable competence development. The results show clear trends, but do not allow any causal conclusions to be drawn about actual learning success. Furthermore, the World Climate Game is based—for didactic reasons—on a reduced model complexity that simplifies real political, economic, and ecological processes. Although this reduction facilitates comprehensibility and action orientation, it is accompanied by a certain abstraction of real system dynamics. As a result, structural power asymmetries, historical inequalities, and cultural differences can only be considered to a limited extent. Likewise, the role design remains normatively framed, which emphasizes certain perspectives more than others. Despite these limitations, it can be said that the World Climate Game has a remarkable educational impact. It promotes key competencies for education for sustainable development by establishing the connection between knowledge, emotion, and practical experience. The results show that learning processes are particularly effective where emotional involvement, reflection, and social interaction converge. For future research, it seems sensible to expand the empirical recording of learning effects and to deepen it through combined qualitative and quantitative methods. Pre-post designs, standardized scales for measuring self-efficacy and systemic thinking, and longitudinal studies could better reflect the long-term impact. Cross-cultural studies would also be valuable in testing the adaptability of the game in different educational contexts. Overall, the World Climate Game shows that education on complex global challenges is particularly effective when it is experience-based, participatory, and emotionally embedded. This makes it possible to address learners holistically and empower them not only to understand global responsibility, but also to actively shape it.

Acknowledgments. Rouven Kaiser is grateful for financial support of the Young Researchers Travel Scholarship Program of the University of Augsburg.

Disclosure of Interests. Matthias Mittelberger works for Weitblick GmbH as a game developer. Weitblick is the owner of the game. He was also game master by some of the games. Rouven Kaiser was also game master by some of the games and received an honorarium from Weitblick GmbH for these games. His main salary is paid by the university. The questionnaire was not influenced by the two authors. It was anonymous and independently integrated in the evaluation process.

References

1. Kolbe, C.: Existenzielle Kommunikation im Horizont der Zumutungen des Daseins – Zugänge aus Existenzanalyse und Logotherapie. In: Büssing, A., Giebel, A., Roser, T. (eds.) Spiritual

Care & Existential Care interprofessionell, pp. 93–104. Springer, Heidelberg (2024). https://doi.org/10.1007/978-3-662-67742-1_10

2. Waibel, E.M.: Erziehung zum Sinn - Sinn der Erziehung: Grundlagen einer Existenziellen Pädagogik, 1st edn. Beltz Juventa, Weinheim (2017)

3. Zirfas, J.: Otto Friedrich Bollnow: Existenzphilosophie und Pädagogik, 1st edn. Brill/Schöningh, Paderborn (2009)

4. Bandura, A.: Social Learning Theory, 1st. edn. Prentice-Hall, Englewood Cliffs (1977)

5. United Nations: Agenda 21. https://sdgs.un.org/goals. Accessed 02 Feb 2025

6. United Nations: The 17 Goals | Sustainable Development. https://sdgs.un.org/goals#icons. Accessed 02 Feb 2025

7. Andreotti, V.D.O., de Souza, L.M.T.M.: Postcolonial Perspectives on Global Citizenship Education, 1st edn. Routledge, New York (2012)

8. Banks, J.A.: Diversity, group identity, and citizenship education in a global age. In: Educational Researcher, pp. 129–139. Sage Journals (2008)

9. Frankfurter Erklärung. https://akg-online.org/sites/default/files/frankfurter_erklaerung.pdf. Accessed 02 Feb 2025

10. Intergovernmental Panel on Climate Change: Climate Change 2021 – The Physical Science Basis: Working Group I Contribution to the Sixth Assessment Report of the Intergovernmental Panel on Climate Change, 1. eds., Cambridge (2023)

11. United Nations: Human Development Index, New York (2022)

12. Gapminder: Gapminder. https://www.gapminder.org/. Accessed 02 Feb 2025

13. Forrester, J.W.: World Dynamics, 2nd edn. Wrigt-Allen Press, Cambridge (1971)

14. Club of Rome: Die Grenzen des Wachstums: Bericht des Club of Rome zur Lage der Menschheit, 17th edn. Dt.-Verlag, Stuttgart (1972)

15. Rohrer, M., Gferer, N.: SOS-Kinderdorf Jugendstudie 2020. https://www.sos-kinderdorf.at/getmedia/c94b3a03-89d4-4560-a994-98c257ebe04c/Ergebnisbericht_SOS-Kinderdorf_J ugendstudie_2020.pdf. Accessed 02 Feb 2025

16. World Health Organisation: Life skills education for children and adolescents in schools. https://iris.who.int/handle/10665/63552. Accessed 02 Feb 2025

17. Ankrah, D., Bristow, J., Hires, D., Artem Henriksson, J.: Inner development goals: from inner growth to outer change. In: Field Actions Science Reports, pp. 82–87. Open Edition Journal (2023)

18. Mayring, P.: Qualitative Inhaltsanalyse. In: Flick, U., Kardorff, E. von, Steinke, I. (eds.) Qualitative Forschung: Ein Handbuch, 12. edn. Reinbek bei Hamburg, Rowohlt, pp. 468–474 (2017)

Defend the Delta: Prototyping and Testing a Tower Defense Game on Salt Intrusion

Robert-Jan den Haan[1]([envelope]) [iD] and Paran Pourteimouri[1,2] [iD]

[1] University of Twente, Drienerlolaan 5, 7522 NB Enschede, The Netherlands
r.j.denhaan@utwente.nl
[2] Deltares, Boussinesqweg 1, 2629 HV Delft, The Netherlands

Abstract. Shaping climate resilient futures is a key challenge faced all around the globe. To support this, games are used to bring people together, experience plausible future climatic conditions, and experiment with possible courses of action. In this study, we present the Delta Management Game, a simulation game designed for stakeholders to explore the impact of and courses of action against historic and plausible future salt intrusion events. In the game, players are challenged to defend critical locations in the Dutch Rhine-Meuse delta against salt water during multiple droughts. A novel approach is that the game builds on the tower defense subgenre and its characteristic mechanisms in combination with a physical board to represent the delta, prepare its defense, and show augmented simulations. We organized four sessions with a game prototype to evaluate to what extent the game is applicable to support policy-making around fresh water availability in the Netherlands. The formative evaluation showed that the game and its design was overall received positively and, at least conceptually, aligned well with relevant policy questions faced in Dutch fresh water management. We discuss key improvements that players highlighted to increase alignment with policy-making like including further trade-offs. We additionally discuss the game's design and how building on the tower defense subgenre enabled capturing both short-term and long-term climate change effects. We end with offering a main benefit of expanding experimentation potential through the game's physical board in combination with computation-based simulations.

Keywords: Simulation game · climate change · salt intrusion · tangible interaction · augmented reality

1 Introduction

Worldwide, we increasingly experience the effects of climate change through intensified weather events such as last year's historic drought in South America [1] or the extreme flooding in the Valencia region [2]. It is therefore not surprising how considerable work is focused on using simulation games to contribute to addressing climate change and increasing climate resilience [3–6]. Such games are designed for a variety of purposes, like in education to teach international climate politics [7], but a particular subset of these games focuses on supporting stakeholders in shaping climate resilient futures (see

F. Trautwein et al. (Eds.): ISAGA 2025, LNCS 16439, pp. 233–247, 2026.
https://doi.org/10.1007/978-3-032-20129-4_16

[8–18] as only a selection of examples). In the Nexus Game for example, players explore competing interests for water resources in transboundary river management, with climate change diminishing available resources [17]. Lawrence and Haasnoot [15] used a simulation game to raise awareness on how taking decisions may limit options in the future by challenging players to develop a sustainable water management plans for a stylized river in four turns, facing new climatic conditions in each. Onencan [14] used the WeShareIt game to support policy makers in considering how to reduce climate induced disaster risk in the Nile river basin. What these and other games generally have in common is that they capture dynamics of an (environmental) system or spatial area and engage players in future scenarios that include climatic conditions. As simulation games, they seek to establish an environment in which players can learn from experimenting with actions and experiencing simulated effects and trade-offs [19, 20]. The main assumption is that (social) learning from such games is transferable and contributes to change processes needed to shape climate resilient futures [21].

Our focus in this paper is on using a game to explore future fresh water management in delta systems. Particularly, we focus on salt intrusion, that is the process of salt water propagating further in-land when counter pressure from rivers is low (i.e. droughts). Salt intrusion is a concern in deltas globally, with the frequency of extreme salt intrusion events likely to increase [22]. In the Netherlands, salt intrusion is becoming a pressing issue that threatens fresh water availability [23]; its extent and impact are expected to increase driven by lower river flows and sea level rise as a result of climate change [24]. From a policy perspective, a main focus is on maintaining the function of key freshwater intake points, keeping the delta's waterways navigable, and sustaining aquatic nature [25]. In this context, we are developing the Delta Management Game to support players in exploring ways to increase resilience against salt intrusion during droughts events in the Rhine-Meuse Delta under climate change.

In this study, we present the Delta Management Game and evaluate a work-in-progress prototype. A novel approach of the game is that it builds on the tower defense subgenre using a physical board with augmented simulations. Following the subgenre, players are challenged to cooperatively prepare their defense in anticipation of an attack wave – a historic or possible salt intrusion event – which is subsequently simulated using a physics-based computational model that captures chloride concentrations (indicating salinity) in a networked delta. The prepared defense on the board is taken as input for the simulation and serves as the basis for preparing the defense for the next, more challenging attack wave.

Using the prototype, our goal was to evaluate the main concept of the game and its applicability in policy-making guided by the research questions: to what extent the game enables players in exploring salt intrusion mitigation measures and in the context of fresh water management and climate change; and to what extent the game is seen as well aligned to support exploring relevant policy questions. To that end, we organized four game sessions with stakeholders from diverse backgrounds to play the game prototype. Player actions were recorded to see what players did during these sessions and players completed a post-game questionnaire with open and closed questions to get their feedback on the game and suggest improvements.

In the next sections, we first briefly discuss relevant work on games to support shaping climate resilient futures and tower defense games. We then present the Delta Management Game including a description of the evaluated prototype. Subsequently, we describe the sessions, data collection and analysis, and report the results. We end with a brief discussion of the results and the game's tower defense inspired design using a physical board before reaching conclusions and presenting our intended next steps.

2 Related Work

To include future climatic conditions in simulation games, a common approach is to include a temporal scale that covers multiple years as part of the game. Particularly a turn-based approach where a certain amount of time is simulated between turns is employed widely [8–16]. The total simulated time and time between turns varies, which has a consequence on how climatic conditions are captured. For example, the Sustainable Delta Game [8] uses four turns of 25 years each, with simulations in between following long-term climate projections. The Invitational Drought Tournament [9] in turn simulates five years in 20 turns to capture one or multiple types of drought based on climate modelling, capturing how climate change can intensify such events. In FARMORE, players play three years with varying climatic conditions in 13 turns per year to explore how climate variability affects livestock forage production and animal diet regimes [16]. In the Delta Management Game, we build on these works by exploring the use of the tower defense subgenre and its game mechanisms to include simulated short-term events as attack waves and long-term climate change projections as time between attack waves.

Tower defense games can be seen as a subgenre of strategy games, in which players aim to defend locations or resources from enemy attack waves. Players build defensive structures next to or on lanes where enemies move through, possibly adding a mazing structure to increase the length of the enemies' path. In serious gaming, tower defense games are mainly explored in education contexts around two topics: (1) (personal) health [26–32]; and (2) cybersecurity [33–37]. On (personal) health, examples include LiverDefense, where players build liver cells that produce enzymes specialized to deal with incoming waste materials to learn about the basic functions of the human liver [27]. In InfecBlock, focused on teaching public health knowledge, players among others place defensive structures like disinfectant towers to protect characters against viruses [28]. On cybersecurity, players need to protect their servers by building structures that defend from waves of various types of cyber-attacks in the Cyber Defense Tower Game [35]. McGregor [34] presents a game where players need to organize and maintain a defense against enemies that try to access the systems of a bank, teaching players about secure programming and vulnerabilities. What these games have in common is that they build on a metaphor of protecting something of interest from outside influences. We too were drawn to the tower defense subgenre from the metaphorical idea of protecting a delta from increasingly difficult drought events that cause salt intrusion. We extend on the above games by exploring the use of the tower defense subgenre into the environmental domain, additionally adding a physical board to support cooperation.

3   Delta Management Game

The Delta Management Game focuses on salt intrusion and how it threatens a variety of delta functions. When salt intrusion events occur, delta areas which normally have fresh water become brackish as a result of saline sea water reaching these areas, leading to water quality problems like inability to produce drinking water and damage to (aquatic) nature [24]. Our rationale for looking at the tower defense subgenre for inspiration is that salt intrusion events occur on the short-term – droughts lasting weeks to months – while expected to intensify and/or last for a longer duration in the long-term – changing climatic conditions in the next decades (see [24] for an outlook on the Dutch Rhine-Meuse delta). Such interplay between and compounded effects of two temporal scales is captured in the concept of resilience, that is the capacity of a system to cope with sudden or gradual disruptions [38, 39]. Enabling players to experience the impact of salt intrusion in the future therefore needs to include both temporal scales.

Following the tower defense subgenre, the main concept for the Delta Management Game therefore evolves around using attack waves as simulating (future) droughts resulting in a lack of fresh water flowing down the delta's waterways and leading to salt water entering the delta system from the sea side. Focusing on supporting policy-making, intended players are stakeholders that range from national policy-makers to drinking water companies and water management experts to ecologists. By playing the game, we aim for players to increase their understanding of the delta system and how it functions, learn about the effects and trade-offs of salt intrusion mitigation measures, and learn about the interests and perspectives of other stakeholders. Players need to cooperate to protect key locations in the delta by for example ensuring that chloride concentrations at freshwater intake points do not exceed location specific threshold values for an extended duration in simulated historic or future projected drought events. To do so, they adapt the delta before each next attack wave by for example changing the width or depth of waterways as a way of limiting salt water propagating further in-land, effectively defending the key locations. Each next attack wave represents a jump in the future, simulating a drought event that is based on climate change projections. In the next subsections, we present the game and its mechanisms in more detail. Where applicable, we include what parts were not fully implemented in the evaluated game prototype.

3.1   Rhine-Meuse Delta Abstraction

The Rhine-Meuse delta is situated in the western part of the Netherlands, where sub-branches of the Rhine and Meuse rivers connect with the North Sea. The area is densely populated with the city of Rotterdam as the main metropolitan area, includes various important industry locations, and has extensive agri- and horticultural activity. Each of these connect to specific freshwater intake points, which consequently have different threshold values depending on what chloride concentrations are acceptable. For these locations, salt intrusion thus concerns a water quality issue. The Rhine-Meuse delta is also a main transportation hub, driven largely by the Port of Rotterdam. Navigability of the delta's waterways is therefore an important economic consideration. During salt intrusion events, the water level in waterways generally drops as a results of low river flows, which can be seen as a water quantity issue. This can directly introduce trade-offs as one main way of mitigating salt intrusion is changing the bathymetry of waterways (like undeepening or narrowing), which affects navigability.

To be able to explore such actions and trade-offs, our aim was to make the Rhine-Meuse delta playable in such a way that: (1) it includes the main waterways, freshwater intake points and important land-based activities connected to these; (2) show the bathymetry of waterways; and (3) abstract the delta in such a way that it is recognizable on the system level yet enables local changes. We created the game on a previously developed system that builds on principles of tangible interaction, that is adding physical representations to digital information [40]. The system uses a physical board that was originally designed to include different elevation levels and spatial augmented reality to project simulations on the game board [41]. A touchscreen monitor presents additional feedback and offers players controls to run a simulation or to switch visualizations. It uses a hexagonal tile-based board to capture a spatial area, with each tile filed by one or a combination of game pieces. The system detects the pieces placed in each tile through color coded markers via a webcam placed underneath the board. The system and an impression of the Delta Management Game is shown in Fig. 1. Using this system enabled us to use stackable pieces to represent different depths in combination with embossed pieces to represent different widths directly on the game's board. These and other game pieces were 3D printed.

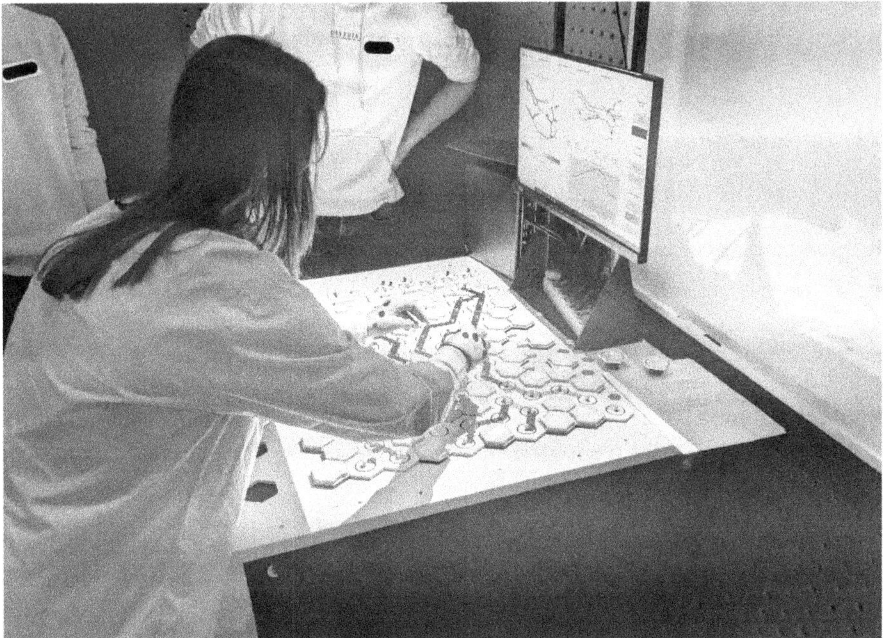

Fig. 1. Impression of the Delta Management Game using the tangible interaction-based game system to support the use of a physical board to take actions on an abstracted Rhine-Meuse delta, simulation results augmented on the game board, and a touchscreen monitor to show additional effects and offer player controls.

To represent the Rhine-Meuse delta, we drew an equal number of polygons on its map as the number of tiles on the physical board to in effect reproject the delta on the system's regular grid (Fig. 2). We drew these polygons to align with the delta's waterways while including tiles in between waterways where freshwater intake points and land-based activities can be placed. All waterways (junction to junction) have at least two tiles on the board. Longer waterways have more tiles that players can separately adapt as actions, which is further explained in the next subsection.

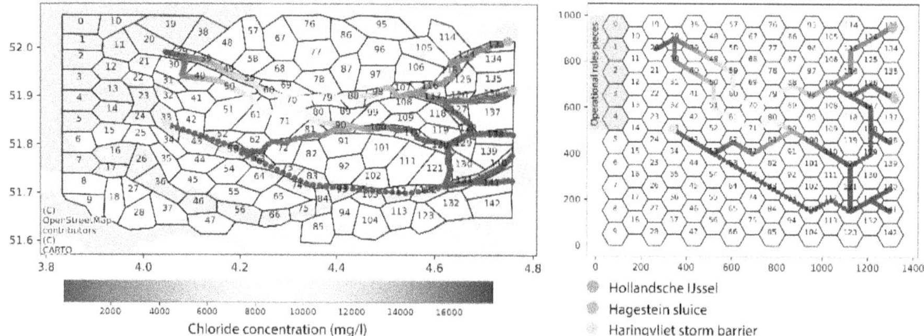

Fig. 2. Abstraction approach using polygons drawn on the Rhine-Meuse delta map with EPSG:4326 coordinates (left) linked to the hexagons of the tile-based game board in pixel coordinates (right). The colored dots on both sides indicate the location where operational rules apply.

3.2 In-Game Actions

In the game, the delta's waterways are essentially the lanes through which the salt intrusion attack waves pass. Players can prepare their defense in three main ways. Firstly, players can adapt the waterways itself, changing the game pieces in the tiles where the waterways are located. Options are changing depth (deepening or undeepening), changing width (widening or narrowing), or blocking waterways (temporary closure or permanent closure with a lock). The tiles where these game pieces are changed directly reflect the action; to deepen a waterway, the tile on the board is lowered. While the blocking waterways option was implemented, it was not made available to players in the evaluation sessions as the main trade-off is with navigability, on which the effects were not yet implemented.

Secondly, players can change operational rules, which reflect the options water managers have to steer river discharge in the Rhine-Meuse system during drought. For example, sluices can be opened more or less to send additional water towards one waterway, diverting it from another. Players can set operational rules for three locations, sluice Hagestein, Haringvliet storm barrier and Hollandsche IJssel (see Fig. 2 for locations), in line with the amount of water that can go through these in reality. In addition, for the Haringvliet and Hollandsche IJssel locations, players can set a threshold value for the Rhine river discharge, which determines the discharge level when that location's operational rule takes effect. Pieces for these operational rules were placed in hexagons with IDs 0 to 4 (see Fig. 2), which all correspond to the sea domain on the map and are not otherwise used during gameplay.

Thirdly, players need to protect freshwater intake points which are located in hexagon tiles adjacent to waterways. The freshwater intake points were stationary in the game prototype, but one not yet implemented option is to move these points further in-land at the expense of adapting infrastructure. Moving these further from their original location incurs higher, non-linear costs.

3.3 Drought Simulations

As attack waves, players face multiple scenarios in the form of salt intrusion events resulting from droughts. In the current game prototype, players face month-long droughts simulated with daily time steps, with the extent and impact of salt intrusion dependent on the players' actions. To simulate these droughts, we incorporated the IMSIDE model [42] which simulates time-dependent, tidally and width-averaged estuarine flow and salinity for a simplified, abstracted delta network, as shown in Fig. 2. IMSIDE was originally developed for modeling salt intrusion as a physical process and has been calibrated for the Rhine-Meuse Delta [43]. Though it was not initially designed for a gaming application, its computational efficiency allows incorporating in-game actions as input parameters and dynamically adjusting boundary conditions to reflect game scenarios.

The game scenarios reflect the two main drivers of salt intrusion: river discharge and sea level [24]. We developed two types of game scenarios. Firstly, scenarios based on measurements from historical drought events, such as those in 2018 and 2022 [44]. Historical droughts are commonly used as reference points in policy-making. Secondly, scenarios based on future climate projections derived from the KNMI'23 scenarios [45], which is a translation of the IPCC 2021 scenarios to the Netherlands. In particular, the high emission-dry (Hd) scenarios, used in Dutch policy-making as part of the Deltascenarios [46], are integrated into the game to simulate future conditions. For both types of scenarios, we derived the required boundary conditions needed in the IMSIDE model, checking the approach and assumptions with water management experts. From the developed game scenarios, players navigate through three distinct turns in the game: (1) the 2018 historic drought, (2) a 2050 Hd scenario drought, and (3) a 2100 Hd scenario drought, each requiring strategic responses to mitigate the impacts of salt intrusion under evolving climate conditions. Players have the option to run multiple simulations within each turn – maximum of three in the game prototype – allowing experimentation with alternative strategies. The result of all actions from the final run of a turn is the starting situation for the next turn.

3.4 In-Game Feedback

The impact from a salt intrusion events are generally determined by chloride concentrations (indicating salinity) at specific locations in combination with the number of (consecutive) days these are above sector specific thresholds. To give feedback on this and subsequent effects, the game incorporates an Integrated Assessment Model (IAM) to evaluate the effects of player actions to mitigate salt intrusion. The IAM consists of seven modules, each assessing key indicators: salinity, hydrodynamics, system signaling, drinking water supply, nautical traffic, ecology and costs. In the game prototype, only the salinity and signal modules were fully implemented as the remaining modules are still under development. The salinity module utilizes the IMSIDE model to compute chloride concentrations along the delta waterways and at freshwater intake points. The signal module shows a traffic light system for all freshwater intake points, capturing if chloride concentrations are below point-specific, normal threshold values (green), between normal and drought threshold values (orange), and above drought threshold values (red). Players can use the information from this module to assess risk in real time and adjust their actions accordingly. Other IAM modules, such as the hydrodynamics module, will provide insights into tidally varying water depths, while the drinking water, nautical traffic, nature, and cost modules will add further complexity by showing socio-economic and ecological trade-offs.

4 Game Sessions and Data Collection

To evaluate the game prototype, we organized four game sessions with seven, six, eight and four players, respectively (25 players total). The sessions were organized within a large research consortium on salt intrusion, which this study is also part of. Player backgrounds included scientists, national and regional water managers, hydraulic engineers, and other stakeholders from drinking water companies or nature organizations. All players signed informed consent forms that included the focus of the study, data collection, and use of data. Each session lasted around 75 min and used an identical setup of a brief introduction by the same dedicated facilitator, playing the same game scenarios, and a questionnaire to collect feedback. The facilitator's main role during gameplay was guiding players when they had questions and ensuring players followed game rules as players were in complete control of taking in-game actions and inspecting feedback using the system. We saved all actions from each session to analyze what actions players – most being experts – experimented with. The self-created questionnaire inspired on previous work [47] had 15 closed and six open questions set up around four topics of interest: (1) overall impression; (2) use of information; (3) presentation of information; and (4) application in policy settings. Each topic had between two and six statements with 5-point Likert scales from totally agree to totally disagree and one or two open questions to explain answers to statements or to offer ideas for improvements. The questionnaire ended with one open question asking players to share any comments not yet covered in other questions (see the Appendix for all open questions asked). To analyze the data from the open questions, we used thematic analysis with a semantic approach [48] to identify common themes and subthemes.

5 Results

With only three runs available per turn, players in all sessions first decided between running a baseline run to first see the turn's scenario or to immediately make changes. Within turns, players experimented mostly with changing depth and width of the northern delta waterways, which have an open connection to the sea. There, players focused mostly on creating less deep and narrower waterways as a way of funneling the salt water and limiting the extent to which salt water propagated in-land. In two sessions, players experimented with very local actions around specific freshwater intake points to decrease the chloride concentrations at these points. The operational rules were only changed in one session, sending more fresh water through the Hagestein sluice to push back salt water in the northern part of the delta.

Overall, players gave positive ratings to the statements in the post-game questionnaire. Figure 3 shows the count of answers and the mean and standard deviation values to each statement. Between topics, especially statements on topic 1 on the overall impression but also topic 4 on the application in policy settings topic had a high share of totally agree answers (between 14 and 22 for these questions). The statements on topics 2 and 3 on the use and presentation of information still had positive answers, with agree as the majority share of answers to statements (between 13 and 15).

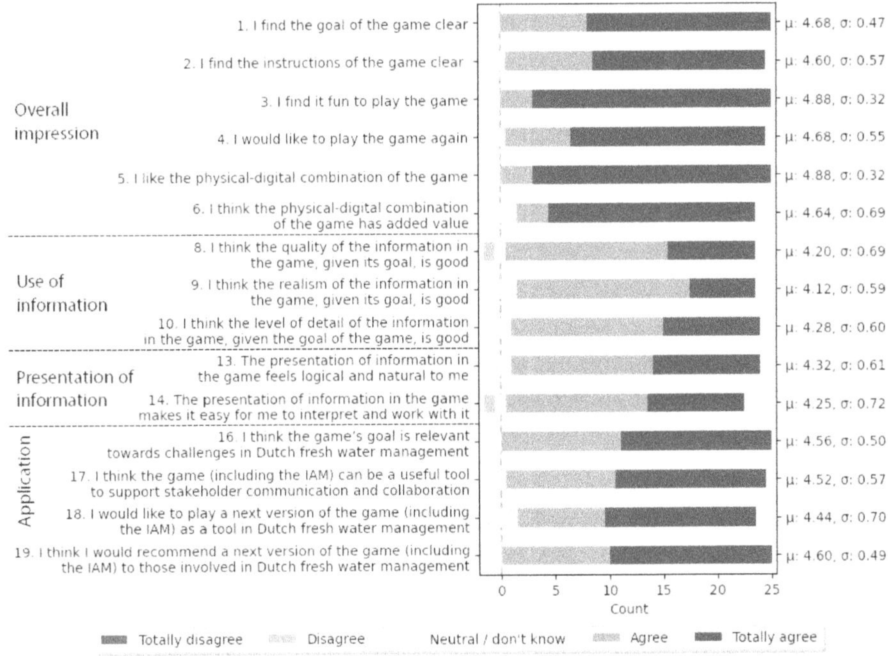

Fig. 3. Answers to the post-game questionnaire statements on four topics of interests (overall impression, use of information, presentation of information and application) following a 5-point Likert scale from totally agree to totally disagree (n = 25). For the descriptive statistics, totally agree is considered as 5, totally disagree as 1. One player did not answer question 14.

In answers to the open questions, players expressed that the game is conceptually aligned with Dutch fresh water management. In answers to the application topic, multiple players mentioned that they expect the game to work well for policy-makers and stakeholders to: (1) gain understanding of the delta system (n = 4); (2) explore possible salt intrusion mitigation strategies (n = 4); (3) offer insights in the effects of mitigation measures (n = 6); and (4) show effects on and interests of other stakeholders (n = 3). Two players suggested specific policy-making settings where they saw the game as a useful exercise.

Answers to the open questions in the other three topics offered a range of possible improvements for the game. Focusing on some recurring mentions, a main point of improvement focused on the in-game feedback to show additional trade-offs by including impacts on other indicators like navigation, nature and costs (n = 13). Other suggestions focused on the delta system, like showing how river discharge is distributed through the waterways following the operation rules (n = 7) and to show additional freshwater intake points relevant to policy-making (n = 7). Quite some answers focused on the game scenarios, with suggestions to also show the Rhine river discharge where it enters the Netherlands (Lobith), a main reference point familiar to the players (n = 4), and to show this information before the next turn rather than after the turn's first run (n = 3). Multiple players indicated they lacked information on how the action deepening would effectively deepen the waterway (n = 6). A final common suggestion focused on explaining the limitations of the game's simulation model (n = 7) and to show uncertainty margins in simulations (n = 2).

6 Discussion

The study presented in this paper should be seen as a formative evaluation, focused on evaluating the overall game concept, its applicability in Dutch fresh water management policy-making, and finding improvements to extend its applicability. Using a work-in-progress prototype, we deliberately did not focus on assessing learning from the game, a summative evaluation we plan to do with a later, more refined version of the game.

In this formative evaluation, the answers to the statements were quite positive, likely influenced by two factors. Firstly, the evaluation was conducted within a research consortium focused on salt intrusion, which this study is part of. The players may therefore have been favorable to the game as it builds on research conducted in the consortium. At the same time, the players were also salt intrusion experts that would likely be critical if the game had major flaws. Secondly, we clearly communicated in each session that the game was a work-in-progress prototype, specifying limitations upfront while refraining from stating future plans until players completed the post-game questionnaires. We speculate that players took the prototype state into account when answering the closed questions. Possibly, players also took their own suggestions into account when answering in particular questions related to the topic of applicability in policy settings (last four questions in Fig. 3). Taking this into account, the ratings of the statements do still show that players valued the overall game concept and saw its applicability to Dutch fresh water management policy-making as aligning well.

We looked to further interpret these ratings and identifying improvements to extend applicability by including the players' answers to the open questions. Particularly in the applicability in policy settings topic where we asked players about what they saw as the game's added value, players provided a variety of comments that align with the game's learning objectives on increasing system understanding ("explaining how the systems works, also for example to executives"), learning about the effects of mitigation measures ("getting a feel of what is needed to keep freshwater intake points fresh"), and learning about other stakeholders ("gaining insights of the interests of and effects on other stakeholders"). There were a substantial number of improvements offered, which can be divided into two categories in line with our questions. Firstly, improvements focused on further aligning with Dutch fresh water management such as the further inclusion of trade-offs and adding additional freshwater intake points important for policy-making. The further inclusion of socio-economic and ecological trade-offs is planned through integrating additional IAM modules. While the game would remain cooperative at its core, including trade-offs would add a competitive element to the game by giving players in-game objectives in line with sectoral interests. Secondly, improvements focused on increasing the game's usability, such as showing information on how freshwater is distributed in the delta system and on how much the (un)deepening action will (un)deepen a waterway. Some suggestions also overlapped between alignment and usability, such as including numbers from key reference points that players are familiar with from policy-making (e.g. Rhine river discharge at Lobith) in game scenarios, even though these locations are outside of the delta's playable area.

From a design perspective, we based the game's concept on the tower defense subgenre, where players need to defend freshwater intake points from multiple attack waves in the form of drought-induced salt intrusion events. Following the concept of resilience [38, 39], we did so to include both the shocks (droughts) and stresses (future climatic conditions). The game's design can therefore also been seen as an exploration of how a tower defense inspired game can be used to support exploring and shaping climate resilient futures. To create a cooperative game, we looked to build on tangible interaction and spatial augmented reality which was initially used in gaming to combine the rich social setting of board games with computation and simulation [49, 50]. There has been limited work on tower defense games using tangible interaction or augmented reality, for example using a digital tabletop surface in combination with physical tokens as towers [51] or using a mobile device to add an augmented reality layer to a graphical user interface on a second device [52]. The Delta Management Game instead uses a spatially augmented all-physical board where players prepare their defense and directly see the resulting simulations. To support shaping futures through games, we see a main benefit of this approach in that it offers additional experimentation potential in a cooperative setting, as players can freely determine the shape, size and location of actions by changing or moving game pieces that are taken as input for simulations.

7 Conclusion and Next Steps

In this paper, we present the Delta Management Game on managing salt intrusion in delta systems under climate change. The game concept is based on the tower defense subgenre, using the metaphorical idea of protecting a delta from increasingly impactful future droughts that cause salt intrusion events. The presented work therefore also extends how a game on climate resilience can build on the tower defense subgenre and its mechanisms. Following the formative evaluation of the game prototype, we conclude that the game as a concept is well received and aligned with policy questions faced in Dutch fresh water management. A refined version is however needed to truly support addressing such policy questions. To do so, we plan to focus on all offered improvements from the evaluation, some already in line with our plans. For example, incorporating additional IAM modules in the game will enable not just showing the mitigating effects on salt intrusion and fresh water availability, but also trade-offs with other sectors. By including these IAM modules and other improvements, the game is intended to be used in Dutch fresh water management to support exploring and shaping climate resilient futures. With a refined version, we plan to evaluate the use of the game in a policy context and to what extent players learn from playing it.

Acknowledgments. This research was supported by the SaltiSolutions program (grant number P18-32), which is partially funded by the Dutch Research Council (NWO) and the Dutch Ministry of Economic Affairs. Ethics approval for this study was obtained from the University of Twente's Natural Sciences and Engineering Science ethics committee under application number 250005.

Disclosure of Interests.   The authors declare that they have no competing interests.

Appendix

List of the open questions asked in the post-game questionnaire (with link to topic):

- If applicable, is there anything you would like to see improved in relation to the overall impression of the Delta Management Game? (1)
- If applicable, what would you change to the information in the game? (2)
- If applicable, what would you want to add to the information in the game? (2)
- If applicable, what would you change to the presentation (or way of presentation) of information in the game? (3)
- If applicable, where do you see the (potential) added value of the Delta Management Game as a tool in Dutch fresh water management? (4)
- If applicable, what do feel needs to be changed or added to the Delta Management Game to use it as a tool in Dutch fresh water management? (4)
- Is there anything else you would like to share that has not come up in this questionnaire?

References

1. Turkewitz, K., Ionova, A., León Cabrera, J.M.: An alarming glimpse into a future of historic droughts. N. Y. Times (2024)
2. Bubola, E., Kwai, I., Bautista, J.: What to know about Spain's devastating floods. N. Y. Times (2024)
3. Flood, S., Cradock-Henry, N.A., Blackett, P., Edwards, P.: Adaptive and interactive climate futures: systematic review of 'serious games' for engagement and decision-making. Environ. Res. Lett. **13**(6), 063005 (2018)
4. Reckien, D., Eisenack, K.: Climate change gaming on board and screen: a review. Simul. Gaming **44**(2–3), 253–271 (2013)
5. Wu, J.S., Lee, J.J.: Climate change games as tools for education and engagement. Nat. Clim. Change **5**(5), 413 (2015)

6. Gerber, A., Ulrich, M., Wäger, F.X., Roca-Puigròs, M., Gonçalves, J.S., Wäger, P.: Games on climate change: Identifying development potentials through advanced classification and game characteristics mapping. Sustainability **13**(4), 1997 (2021)
7. Meya, J.N., Eisenack, K.: Effectiveness of gaming for communicating and teaching climate change. Clim. Change **149**(3), 319–333 (2018)
8. Valkering, P., van der Brugge, R., Offermans, A., Haasnoot, M., Vreugdenhil, H.: A perspective-based simulation game to explore future pathways of a water-society system under climate change. Simul. Gaming **44**(2–3), 366–390 (2013)
9. Hill, H., Hadarits, M., Rieger, R., Strickert, G., Davies, E.G., Strobbe, K.M.: The invitational drought tournament: what is it and why is it a useful tool for drought preparedness and adaptation? Weather Clim. Extrem. **3**, 107–116 (2014)
10. Chew, C., Lloyd, G.J., Knudsen, E.: An interactive capacity building experience–an approach with serious games. In: Serious Games and Social Connect Conference, Singapore (2013)
11. d'Aquino, P., Bah, A.: Land policies for climate change adaptation in West Africa: a multilevel companion modeling approach. Simul. Gaming **44**(2–3), 391–408 (2013)
12. Lamarque, P., Artaux, A., Barnaud, C., Dobremez, L., Nettier, B., Lavorel, S.: Taking into account farmers' decision making to map fine-scale land management adaptation to climate and socio-economic scenarios. Landsc. Urban Plan. **119**, 147–157 (2013)
13. Joffre, O.M., Bosma, R.H., Ligtenberg, A., Ha, T.T.P., Bregt, A.K.: Combining participatory approaches and an agent-based model for better planning shrimp aquaculture. Agric. Syst. **141**, 149–159 (2015)
14. Onencan, A., Van de Walle, B., Enserink, B., Chelang'a, J., Kulei, F.: WeShareIt game: strategic foresight for climate-change induced disaster risk reduction. Procedia Eng. **159**, 307–315 (2016)
15. Lawrence, J., Haasnoot, M.: What it took to catalyse uptake of dynamic adaptive pathways planning to address climate change uncertainty. Environ Sci Policy **68**, 47–57 (2017)
16. Sautier, M., Piquet, M., Duru, M., Martin-Clouaire, R.: Exploring adaptations to climate change with stakeholders: a participatory method to design grassland-based farming systems. J. Environ. Manag. **193**, 541–550 (2017)
17. Mochizuki, J., Magnuszewski, P., Pajak, M., Krolikowska, K., Jarzabek, L., Kulakowska, M.: Simulation games as a catalyst for social learning: the case of the water-food-energy nexus game. Glob. Environ. Change **66**, 102204 (2021)
18. Becu, N., et al.: Participatory simulation to foster social learning on coastal flooding prevention. Environ Model Softw. **98**, 1–11 (2017)
19. Mayer, I.: The gaming of policy and the politics of gaming: a review. Simul. Gaming **40**(6), 825–862 (2009)
20. Kriz, W.C.: Creating effective learning environments and learning organizations through gaming simulation design. Simul. Gaming **34**(4), 495–511 (2003)
21. Rodela, R., Ligtenberg, A., Bosma, R.: Conceptualizing serious games as a learning-based intervention in the context of natural resources and environmental governance. Water **11**(2), 245 (2019)
22. Lee, J., Biemond, B., de Swart, H., Dijkstra, H.A.: Increasing risks of extreme salt intrusion events across European estuaries in a warming climate. Commun. Earth Environ. **5**(1), 60 (2024)
23. Room for sea level rise: An exploration of conceptual perspectives to keep the Netherlands safe and liveable in the long term as sea levels rise, Ministry of Infrastructure and the Environment, p. 48 (2022)
24. van den Brink, M., Huismans, Y., Blaas, M., Zwolsman, G.: Climate change induced salinization of drinking water inlets along a tidal branch of the rhine river: impact assessment and an adaptive strategy for water resources management. Climate **7**(4), 49 (2019)

25. Bakker, F., Hendrickx, G., Keyzer, L., Iglesias, S., Aarninkhof, S., van Koningsveld, M.: Trading off dissimilar stakeholder interests: changing the bed level of the main shipping channel of the Rhine-Meuse delta while considering freshwater availability (2024). SSRN 4967335
26. Brich, J., et al.: LiverDefense: using a tower defense game as a customisable research tool. In: 2015 7th International Conference on Games and Virtual Worlds for Serious Applications (VS-Games). IEEE (2015)
27. Schrader, C., Nett, U.: The perception of control as a predictor of emotional trends during gameplay. Learn. Instr. **54**, 62–72 (2018)
28. Sun, X., Li, T., Miao, K., Zhang, M., Ren, X.: InfecBlock: investigating the effects of a tower-defense serious game for increasing epidemic-related health literacy. Int. J. Hum. Comput. Interact., 1–16 (2024)
29. Matias, B.C., Gomes, V.O., Sarinho, V.T.: "Ultimate food defense": a serious game for healthy eating behavior awareness. In: van der Spek, E., Göbel, S., Do, E.Y.-L., Clua, E., Baalsrud Hauge, J. (eds) ICEC-JCSG 2019. LNCS, vol. 11863, pp. 422–425. Springer, Cham (2019). https://doi.org/10.1007/978-3-030-34644-7_39
30. Andamari, C.S.A., Yong, B., Lee, R.Y.J., Yanfi, Y.: mobile educational game "Imuno" to teach human immune system. In: 2023 6th International Conference of Computer and Informatics Engineering (IC2IE). IEEE (2023)
31. Tan, D.-k.T., et al.: Drug defense: a mobile game for prevention of alcohol abuse. In: International Conference on Computers in Education (2019)
32. Cloude, E.B., Dindar, M., Ninaus, M., Kiili, K.: Synchrony between facial expressions and heart rate variability during game-based learning: insights from cross-wavelet transformation. In: Ferreira Mello, R., Rummel, N., Jivet, I., Pishtari, G., Ruipérez Valiente, J.A. (eds.) EC-TEL 2024. LNCS, vol. 15159, pp. 90–104. Springer, Cham (2024). https://doi.org/10.1007/978-3-031-72315-5_7
33. Straubinger, P., Caspari, L., Fraser, G.: Code critters: a block-based testing game. In: 2023 IEEE International Conference on Software Testing, Verification and Validation Workshops (ICSTW). IEEE (2023)
34. McGregor, L., Chan, S.C., Wlodarczyk, S., Maarek, M.: Aligning a serious game, secure programming and CyBOK-linked learning outcomes. In: 2022 IEEE European Symposium on Security and Privacy Workshops (EuroS&PW). IEEE (2022)
35. Jin, G., Tu, M., Kim, T.-H., Heffron, J., White, J.: Game based cybersecurity training for high school students. In: Proceedings of the 49th ACM Technical Symposium on Computer Science Education (2018)
36. Thornton, D., Turley, F.: Analysis of player behavior and EEG readings in a cybersecurity game. In: Proceedings of the 2020 ACM Southeast Conference (2020)
37. Løvgren, D.E.H., Li, J., Oyetoyan, T.D.: A data-driven security game to facilitate information security education. In: 2019 IEEE/ACM 41st International Conference on Software Engineering: Companion Proceedings (ICSE-Companion). IEEE (2019)
38. Mitchell, T. and K. Harris: Resilience: A risk management approach (2012)
39. Helfgott, A.: Operationalising systemic resilience. Eur. J. Oper. Res. **268**(3), 852–864 (2018)
40. Ishii, H.: Tangible bits: beyond pixels. In: Proceedings of the 2nd International Conference on Tangible and Embedded Interaction. ACM (2008)
41. den Haan, R., et al.: The virtual river game: gaming using models to collaboratively explore river management complexity. Environ. Model. Softw., 104855 (2020)
42. Biemond, B.: IMSIDE, Github repository (2024)
43. Biemond, B., Kranenburg, W.M., Huismans, Y., de Swart, H.E., Dijkstra, H.A.: Dynamics of salt intrusion in complex estuarine networks: an idealised model applied to the Rhine-Meuse Delta. Ocean Sci. **21**(1), 261–281 (2025)

44. Wegman, T.M., Pietrzak, J.D., Horner-Devine, A.R., Dijkstra, H.A., Ralston, D.K.: Observations of estuarine salt intrusion dynamics during a prolonged drought event in the Rhine-Meuse Delta. J. Geophys. Res. Oceans **130**(1), e2024JC021655 (2025)
45. van der Wiel, K., et al.: KNMI'23 climate scenarios for the Netherlands: storyline scenarios of regional climate change. Earth's Future **12**(2), e2023EF003983 (2024)
46. van der Brugge, R., de Winter, R.: Deltascenario's 2024 - Zicht op Water in Nederland, Deltares (2024)
47. Mayer, I., et al.: Integrated, ecosystem-based marine spatial planning: design and results of a game-based, quasi-experiment. Ocean Coast. Manag. **82**, 7–26 (2013)
48. Braun, V., Clarke, V. (eds.) Thematic analysis. In: Cooper, H.E., et al. (eds.) APA Handbook of Research Methods in Psychology, vol. 2, pp. 57–71 (2012)
49. Mandryk, R.L., Maranan, D.S.: False prophets: exploring hybrid board/video games. In: CHI'02 extended Abstracts on Human Factors in Computing Systems (2002)
50. Magerkurth, C., Memisoglu, M., Engelke, T., Streitz, N.: Towards the next generation of tabletop gaming experiences. In: Proceedings of Graphics Interface 2004. Citeseer (2004)
51. Huynh, D.-N.T., Raveendran, K., Xu, Y., Spreen, K., MacIntyre, B.: Art of defense: a collaborative handheld augmented reality board game. In: Proceedings of the 2009 ACM SIGGRAPH Symposium on Video Games (2009)
52. Tolstoi, P., Dippon, A.: Towering defense: an augmented reality multi-device game. In: Proceedings of the 33rd Annual ACM Conference Extended Abstracts on Human Factors in Computing Systems (2015)

A Cooperative Board Game Intervention to Foster High School Students' Conceptual Understanding of the Greenhouse Effect and Climate Change

Sittiched Bunpapanpong and Watcharee Ketpichainarong[(✉)] [iD]

Institute for Innovative Learning, Mahidol University, Salaya, Thailand
`watcharee.ket@mahidol.ac.th`

Abstract. In response to the urgent demands of Sustainable Development Goal (SDG) 13: Climate Action, particularly target 13.3, there is a need for improved education and capacity building to combat climate change. Although several studies indicate that students engage positively with climate change, a significant gap persists in climate change education. High school students, as the next generation facing climate challenges, often lack understanding of fundamental concepts. For example, many misunderstand how the greenhouse effect occurs and impacts climate change. Common misconceptions include beliefs that greenhouse gases cause sunlight to reflect back and forth within the atmosphere, that the greenhouse effect increases global temperature by destroying the ozone layer and allowing more sunlight to enter the Earth, or that it is caused by dust particles covering the atmosphere. This paradox—where concern exists without understanding—highlights the need to enhance students' knowledge of climate change. This preliminary study aims to bridge this gap by developing a cooperative board game to engage high school students with climate change issues while improving their understanding of the greenhouse effect. Eight students participated in a one-group pre-posttest using both quantitative and qualitative methods. Preliminary results revealed that many students held misconceptions before playing the game. However, after engaging with the game, students showed improved understanding of the greenhouse effect and its impact on climate change. These findings suggest that the board game holds promise as an educational tool to engage young learners and improve understanding of climate change.

Keywords: climate change · educational board game · greenhouse effect

1 Introduction

Climate change is one of the most critical challenges of the 21st century, primarily driven by greenhouse gas emissions from various aspects of human activities, such as energy use, transportation, industry, and agriculture [1]. Education plays a vital role in addressing climate change by equipping learners with the knowledge, skills, and values to understand the issue and take action. In alignment with Sustainable Development

F. Trautwein et al. (Eds.): ISAGA 2025, LNCS 16439, pp. 248–263, 2026.
https://doi.org/10.1007/978-3-032-20129-4_17

Goal (SDG) 13: Climate Action, particularly Target 13.3, there is a strong emphasis on improving education and institutional capacity to address climate change [2].

Although young people around the world are increasingly worried about climate change [3], numerous studies indicate that students continue to hold misconceptions about the greenhouse effect and climate change. Common misunderstandings include the belief that greenhouse gases reflect sunlight within the atmosphere, or that they destroy the ozone layer, allowing more sunlight to reach the Earth and thereby increasing global temperatures [4, 5]. This disconnects between concern and understanding highlights the need for innovative educational strategies that address both scientific concepts and social cooperation.

To address this gap, this study developed a cooperative board game designed to enhance high school students' understanding of the greenhouse effect and its role in climate change. The game combines scientific concepts with cooperative gameplay, encouraging learners to explore the causes and consequences of climate change. It also emphasizes that addressing climate change requires collective responsibility and cooperation among individuals.

Accordingly, this study investigates the following research question: What is students' conceptual understanding of the greenhouse effect and its impact on climate change after playing the board game?

The remainder of this paper is organized as follows. The next section presents the theoretical background on SDG 13 and the greenhouse effect, followed by a review of relevant educational interventions and the rationale for using cooperative board games. Subsequent sections outline the methodology, report preliminary findings, and conclude with implications, limitations, and recommendations for future research.

2 Background

In response to this global challenge, Sustainable Development Goal 13 (SDG 13): Climate Action was established to promote urgent measures to combat climate change and its effects. Among its targets, SDG 13.3 specifically calls for improving education, awareness, and human and institutional capacity on climate change mitigation, adaptation, impact reduction, and early warning [2]. A key foundation for understanding climate change is the greenhouse effect—a natural process in which greenhouse gases trap heat by absorbing and re-emitting infrared radiation. However, human activities have intensified this process, resulting in rising global temperatures and altered climate patterns [6].

However, students often misunderstand the greenhouse effect. Gautier, Deutsch and Rebich [7] revealed that many students hold persistent misconceptions—such as confusing the greenhouse effect with ozone depletion or believing that greenhouse gases directly trap sunlight rather than absorbing and re-emitting infrared radiation. These misunderstanding hinder students' ability to understand the scientific concepts underlying climate change. Similarly, Jarrett and Takacs [5] reported widespread misconceptions among secondary students about key scientific concepts related to climate change. Their findings included confusion about the role of greenhouse gases, misbeliefs that greenhouse gases directly destroy the ozone layer. Many students were unable to correctly describe how greenhouse gases interact with infrared radiation—an essential mechanism underlying the greenhouse effect. Schubatzky, Haagen-Schützenhöfer, Wackermann, Wöhlke and Wildbichler [4] analyzed responses from over 600 students and found that while some students selected scientifically correct explanations, the majority demonstrated misunderstandings. A significant portion of students relied on two common misconceptions: the reflection-based explanation, in which students believe that greenhouse gases reflect sunlight back and forth within the atmosphere, and the ozone-depletion-based explanation, which incorrectly attributes global warming to the destruction of the ozone layer, allowing more sunlight to reach the Earth's surface. Such misconceptions pose a significant obstacle to achieving Sustainable Development Goal 13, particularly Target 13.3, which emphasizes the importance of improving education, awareness, and institutional capacity to address climate change. Moreover, when young citizens—despite their motivation to take climate action—lack a sound scientific understanding, their efforts may lead to misinformed mitigation strategies or even maladaptive responses.

Among the strategies for effective climate change education, Monroe, Plate, Oxarart, Bowers and Chaves [8] highlight the importance of directly addressing misconceptions. Several studies have used constructivist approaches to target persistent misunderstandings. For instance, Karpudewan, Roth and Chandrakesan [9] implemented a constructivist-based curriculum integrating hands-on experiments, role-playing, and group discussions to foster conceptual change regarding climate change topics such as the greenhouse effect, global warming, ozone depletion, and acid rain. Their findings showed that students who engaged in these activities demonstrated significantly greater improvements in understanding and a reduction in misconceptions compared to those taught through traditional methods. In another example, Niebert and Gropengiesser [10] found that using simple metaphors and hands-on experiments helps students move from misconceptions to a better understanding of the greenhouse effect and climate change. Similarly, Reinfried, Aeschbacher and Rottermann [11] showed that theory-based, constructivist learning materials significantly improved secondary students' understanding of the greenhouse effect compared to standard textbook instruction, reducing misconceptions and promoting deeper conceptual learning.

However, enhancing conceptual understanding alone may not be sufficient to foster meaningful student engagement with real-world climate issues. To address this gap, the present preliminary study develops a game-based learning intervention grounded in constructivist learning theory [12], enabling students to actively construct knowledge through experience and social interaction. The game aims to improve students' understanding of key scientific concepts—particularly the greenhouse effect—and to connect this understanding to the broader context of climate change.

A wide range of climate change games—both digital and non-digital—have been developed as tools for education and engagement. Wu and Lee [13] describe how these formats vary widely in design, interactivity, and learning potential. Digital games offer dynamic, interactive environments where players can manipulate variables, receive instant feedback, and explore simulated climate scenarios. However, they often require access to technology and may limit face-to-face interaction. In contrast, non-digital games, such as board games, are more accessible and foster cooperation and discussion. Building on these strengths, this study utilizes a non-digital board game format to make abstract concepts more tangible and to support cooperative problem-solving. Its structure also encourages students to recognize the social dimension of climate change, promoting a sense of shared responsibility and stakeholder engagement essential for addressing global challenges.

There are several both commercial and educational board games in climate change education field. Eisenack [14] introduced a commercial board game called KEEP COOL, which is one of the pioneering board games on climate change. Designed to facilitate interdisciplinary communication and education, the game provides a tangible and engaging simulation of global climate negotiations, helping players develop a holistic understanding of climate change issues, encourage active participation, and reflect on complex challenges such as adaptation strategies and power dynamics. Building on this foundation, Fjællingsdal and Klöckner [15] conducted a qualitative study that expanded the investigation to four games—The Settlers of Catan: Oil Springs, Evolution: Climate, Global Warming, and KEEP COOL—and explored how a broader range of board games could make climate issues more accessible, enhance environmental awareness, and encourage players to think critically about both individual and collective actions. Their findings showed that board games not only make complex topics more accessible but also help players visualize the consequences of their decisions.

Vázquez-Vílchez, Garrido-Rosales, Pérez-Fernández and Fernández-Oliveras [16] developed an educational board game named A Planet Near the Abyss, focusing on the impacts of climate change, such as biodiversity loss, ecosystem destruction. The game aims to promote pro-environmental engagement by encouraging players in rescuing endangered species. Another educational board game, Carreira, Aguiar, Onça and Monzoni [17] introduced Celsius: The 2 Degree Challenge. This game was developed to raise awareness of the complexity of climate change and the importance of cooperative action. In the game, players take on the roles of chief executive officers CEOs who must balance creating economic value with the need to reduce carbon emissions, while also influencing public policy to limit global temperature rise to under 2 °C. By combining competitive and cooperative mechanics, the game reflects the real-world tensions between individual interests and collective climate goals. Findings show that Celsius effectively increases players' understanding of climate change, highlights the challenges of balancing economic and environmental priorities, and encourages critical reflection on cooperation for climate action.

Previous studies demonstrate that board games have strong potential to engage students by making complex problems more accessible and enjoyable, while also supporting their understanding of how to address climate change through a focus on mitigation and adaptation strategies. Recognizing these important qualities, this study developed a cooperative board game as an entry point to engage students with climate change issues. The game is designed to immerse players in cooperative problem-solving and to emphasize the use of mitigation and adaptation strategies, while also extending their experience by helping them understand the scientific concept of the greenhouse effect through gameplay. Addressing misconceptions about the greenhouse effect remains a major challenge in climate change education, and this game seeks to bridge that gap by combining scientific knowledge with experiential learning.

3 Intervention

3.1 Development of the Board Game

The board game World in Crisis was developed by the researchers in 2023 and has been refined based on participant feedback and suggestions. Insights from the literature review also informed the design, emphasizing that addressing climate change requires cooperation across various sectors. Therefore, the researchers designed the board game with a cooperative theme to enhance students' understanding of the greenhouse effect and to promote engagement with climate change from both scientific and social perspectives. The game highlights mitigation and adaptation strategies through cooperative gameplay, demonstrating the importance of collective action in real-world climate solutions. Players work together to reduce global greenhouse gas emissions. An overview of the board game is presented below (see Fig. 1).

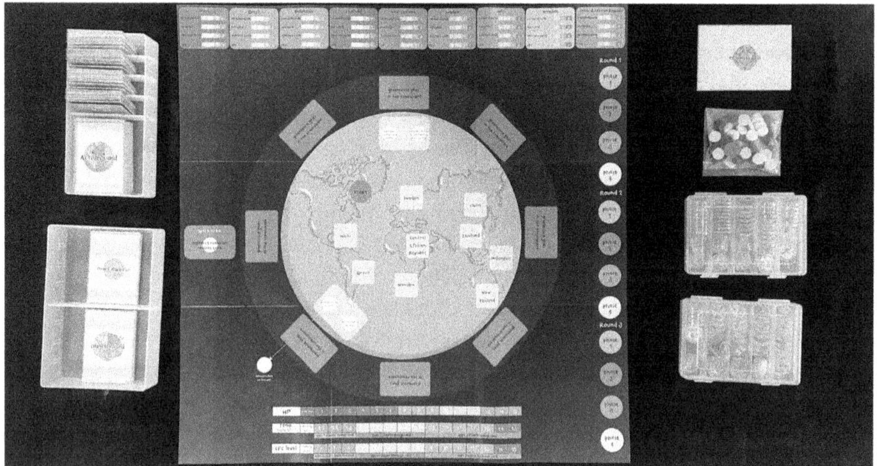

Fig. 1. The overall of "World in Crisis" climate change educational board game

This game were design rely on game base learning by using the input-process-outcome game model [18]. This model proposes significant attributes that engage and learning by playing the game. It consists of three phases: input, game cycle, and outcome as show in the Fig. 2.

Input Phase. Two main components form the game's input. First, the scientific foundation is based on the greenhouse effect, helping students understand how emissions contribute to climate change. Second, the game design emphasizes cooperative play, where students role-play as directors of major sectors—energy, transportation, agriculture, and industry—and cooperate on mitigation and adaptation strategies. Social interaction is essential, fostering communication, shared decision-making, and cooperation, which are critical for addressing real-world climate challenges. The cooperative structure reflects the interconnectedness of global climate issues, where individual actions alone are insufficient.

While playing World in Crisis, players encounter uncertain situations related to the impacts of climate change. The game is designed using a climate change engagement framework proposed by Ouariachi, Olvera-Lobo, Gutiérrez-Pérez and Maibach [19] which incorporates 15 attributes to promote deep engagement (see Table 1). These attributes are further aligned with Chou's gamification framework, integrating core drives such as challenge, strategy, and enjoyment [20]. This design ensures that World in Crisis is not only an educational tool but also a gamified experience that fosters active learning and motivates players to engage meaningfully with climate change issues.

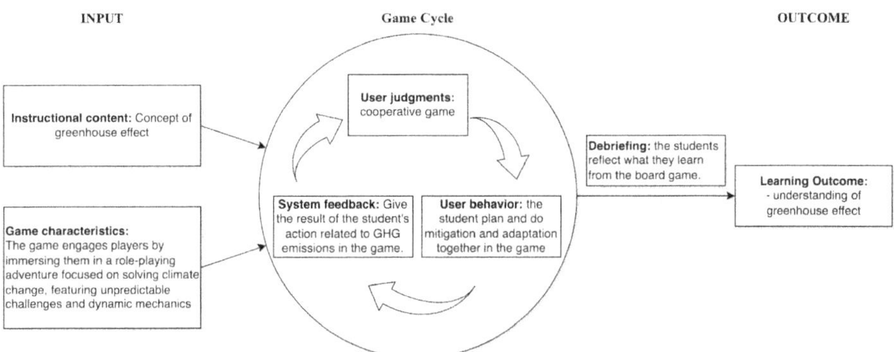

Fig. 2. The game design relies on the input-process-outcome game model

Game Cycle. This phase consists of four components: user judgment, user behavior, system feedback, and the debriefing section.

User Judgment. In this cooperative game, players act as directors of key sectors—energy, transportation, agriculture, and industry—making cooperative decisions under dynamic conditions. Players must use critical thinking to plan and take cooperative actions during each round of the game. They are also required to assess outcomes and adjust their strategies to match the changing situations in each round. This cooperative structure reflects the social dimension of real-world climate action, where addressing climate challenges requires both individual responsibility and coordinated cooperation among all sectors.

User Behavior. The game engages players by challenging them to address climate change. Each round, they use action cards focused on mitigation and adaptation, encouraging engagement as they strategize and cooperate under evolving conditions.

System Feedback. The game provides both positive and negative feedback, rewarding effective mitigation and adaptation with slower climate impacts while ineffective strategies accelerate them, increasing global damage.

Debrief Section. After the game, learners reflect on their experiences and insights gained from the climate change board game.

Table 1. The input phase relies on a climate change engagement framework.

Attributes [19]	Design in "World in Crisis"
Achievable: Encourages players with tasks and changes that are within their capability	To complete the game, players must work together to win the game by reduce greenhouse gases emission and adapt to climate change
Challenging: Engages players with tasks that demand effort and push their limits	The students face the greenhouse effect impact on climate change impacts. The situation will intensify if the students cannot manage greenhouse gas emissions
Concrete: Utilizes simple messages and avoids overwhelming players with text and statistics	The game elements were designed to be easy to play, with minimal text and visuals for better understanding
Credibility: Provides trustworthy information	The game is based on scientific literature, including the greenhouse effect
Efficacy-enhancing: Empowers players or making them feel capable of making a difference	The game encourages students to reduce greenhouse gas emissions through mitigation and adaptation, showing they can help address climate change
Experiential learning: learning through doing rather than through theoretical instruction	Students learn about the greenhouse effect through game mechanics simulating greenhouse gases impacts and can take action using mitigation and adaptation strategies
Feedback-oriented: Offers evaluations of player performance to guide and motivate	The game provides feedback each round. Effective mitigation and adaptation slow climate change, while failure accelerates its impact and increases global damage
Fun: Ensures the gaming experience is enjoyable to keep players engaged	The game engages students by assigning them roles in a sustainability team tackling climate change. As directors of key sectors, they cooperate to complete missions using mitigation and adaptation strategies
Identity-driven: Connects with players on a personal level, relating to their experiences or aspirations	Students role-play as directors of key sectors—energy, industry, agriculture, and transport—working to reduce emissions and manage climate risks, making the experience relatable and meaningful
Levelling-up: Facilitates long-term engagement with clear goals and milestones	Players work to reduce greenhouse gas emissions across all sectors, aiming to bring each emission source to zero, progressing through strategic decisions and challenges

(continued)

Table 1. (*continued*)

Attributes [19]	Design in "World in Crisis"
Meaningful: Evokes strong emotions to make the gameplay and its content significant to the player	The game, rooted in scientific concepts, immerses students in the urgency of climate action, highlighting the significance of solving this global challenge
Narrative-driven: Uses storytelling to engage players emotionally and cognitively	Students take on roles in a sustainability team, brainstorming and planning ways to lower emissions and manage climate impacts, immersing them in the challenge of solving climate change
Reward-driven: Offers incentives for achieving goals or completing tasks within the game	The game rewards students for reducing greenhouse gases, motivating them to take more actions that help combat climate change
Simulating: Creates immersive worlds that model reality, allowing players to explore complex scenarios	The game immerses students in a simulation of climate change, from its causes to its impacts, letting them explore and navigate its challenges
Social: Encourages networking and social interaction within the gaming experience	The game fosters cooperation as students takes on roles with unique responsibilities, requiring teamwork and collective effort to achieve the mission

Outcome Phase. The climate change board game helps students understand the greenhouse effect and the importance of both mitigation and adaptation in addressing climate change.

3.2 Gameplay

Students were asked to play a developed board game in a group of four. The game was designed to complete in three rounds. In the first round, the researcher acts as a facilitator, helping students become familiar with the game. In the following rounds, the students will run the game by themselves. Each round of the game consists of four phases: Solar Radiation Phase, Mitigation and Adaptation Phase, Greenhouse Effect Phase, and Climate Change Phase. The details are as follows.

Phase 1: Solar Radiation Phase. In this phase, the game introduces the visible light token to represent a type of solar radiation that reaches and is absorbed by the Earth's surface. The objective is to help students understand the relationship between solar radiation and the greenhouse effect, which will be explored further in Phase 3.

Phase 2: Mitigation and Adaptation. The student team must work together to reduce greenhouse gas emissions from each country on the main board using action cards, which include mitigation and adaptation cards. This phase helps students experience how cooperation can mitigate climate change and strengthen adaptation efforts.

Phase 3: Greenhouse Effect. The game simulates the consequences of actions taken in the previous phase. Any greenhouse gases the student team fails to mitigate will accumulate in the Earth's atmosphere. Energy absorbed from visible light is re-emitted as infrared radiation, contributing to the greenhouse effect. In this phase, students observe how greenhouse gases interact with infrared radiation and experience the effects of heat accumulation on Earth, leading to rising global temperatures and climate change.

Phase 4: Climate Change. In this phase, students experience the consequences of climate change This phase also corrects misconceptions about the greenhouse effect. To distinguish it from ozone depletion, the game includes Ozone Depletion cards. If CFCs exceed a threshold, players draw a card, reinforcing that ozone depletion is separate from the greenhouse effect and that not all greenhouse gases harm the ozone layer.

The game's four-phase structure is designed to help players experience climate change issues through gameplay. The Solar Radiation Phase introduces the entry of solar radiation into the Earth's system, which relates to the greenhouse effect. In the Mitigation and Adaptation Phase, players represent sectors and take actions that contribute to greenhouse gas emissions. The Greenhouse Effect Phase shows how these gases absorb and re-emit infrared radiation, and the Climate Change Phase reveals the resulting climate change impacts. This phased structure scaffolds learning by clearly linking human activities, the greenhouse effect, and climate-related consequences.

4   Method

This research employs a mixed methods design [21] to integrate quantitative and qualitative data in addressing the research question: What is students' conceptual understanding of the greenhouse effect and its impact on climate change after playing the board game?

4.1   Sample and Implementation Process

This preliminary study implements eight volunteer high school students in public school, Thailand. The procedure and data collection tools use in this study were approves from Institutional Review Board (IRB). Before game implementation, the written consent was obtained from student participants and their guardians. Table 2 presents the details of this board game implementation.

Table 2. Board game implementation

Procedure	Objective	Time
Pretest	Explore students' prior understanding of the greenhouse effect and climate change	30 min
Board game activity	Engage students in learning about climate change through gameplay	60 min
Debriefing section	Facilitate students reflect on their learning and provide feedback	20 min
Posttest	Explore students' understanding after playing the board game	30 min

4.2 Data Collection and Analysis

This preliminary study employed a mixed-methods approach. The conceptual test consisted of six multiple-choice questions and one open-ended question, all developed by the authors based on relevant literature and validated by three experts to ensure content validity. The items were specifically constructed to assess students' conceptual understanding in alignment with the research question.

The multiple-choice questions were designed to assess students' understanding of two core concepts: three questions focused on the greenhouse effect, and the remaining three examined how the greenhouse effect contributes to climate change. The total score for each participant was used to calculate descriptive statistics, including the mean and standard deviation for both the pretest and posttest. An example of a multiple-choice question is presented in Table 3.

Table 3. Example of a multiple-choice question

Question	The Earth receives different types of radiation from the Sun in varying proportions, consisting of visible light, ultraviolet radiation (UV), and infrared radiation. Greenhouse gases are released from human activities around the world. Which of the following scenarios correctly describes the interaction between greenhouse gases and solar radiation that leads to the greenhouse effect?
Option A	Greenhouse gases do not react with visible light, allowing it to reach the Earth's surface. However, they absorb infrared radiation emitted from the Earth's surface
Option B	Greenhouse gases destroy the ozone layer in the atmosphere, allowing a greater amount of UV radiation from the Sun to reach the Earth's surface
Option C	Greenhouse gases absorb visible light from the Sun and directly convert it into heat in the Earth's atmosphere
Option D	Greenhouse gases destroy the ozone layer, allowing more sunlight to enter the Earth's atmosphere, and then absorb visible light and convert it into heat in the atmosphere

Students were also asked to respond to an open-ended question designed to assess their conceptual understanding: "How does the greenhouse effect occur?" Responses collected before and after gameplay were analyzed using content analysis. Answers were categorized into five levels based on Haidar framework [22]: sound understanding, partial understanding, understanding with misconceptions, misconceptions, and no understanding. The criteria for content analysis are shown in Table 4. Both forms of data analysis provide evidence of students' enhanced understanding after playing the board game.

Table 4. Content Analysis Criteria for Open-Ended Responses

Question	How does the greenhouse effect occur?
Sound understanding	The student explains the greenhouse effect accurately and completely, covering all essential points: (1) Greenhouse gases released from human activities cause the anthropogenic greenhouse effect; (2) Greenhouse gases absorb infrared radiation emitted from the Earth surface and re-emit it into the atmosphere; (3) The increased accumulation of infrared radiation in the atmosphere leads to a rise in global temperatures
Partial understanding	The student explains the greenhouse effect correctly and links it to rising temperatures, but the explanation is incomplete or misses some essential aspects compared to a sound understanding
Understanding with misconceptions	The student partially explains the greenhouse effect correctly but also includes misconceptions. Misconceptions may include: (1) Incorrect ideas about how the greenhouse effect occurs, or (2) Mixing up concepts, such as confusing it with ozone layer destruction
Misconception	The student provides an explanation that is incorrect and based on misconceptions about the greenhouse effect
No understanding	The student does not respond to the question

5 Preliminary Result

This study examines the impact of an educational board game on high school students' understanding of the greenhouse effect. The preliminary results suggest that playing the game enhances students' understanding of the greenhouse effect within the context of climate change. After participating in the board game activity, students' understanding was assessed using a test consisting of multiple-choice and open-ended questions. The results indicate a positive progression in their understanding. For the multiple-choice section, which had a maximum score of six points, the mean score increased from 1.50 (SD = 1.32) on the pretest to 3.63 (SD = 1.49) on the posttest. While multiple-choice questions captured overall improvements in students' knowledge, deeper insights were obtained through analysis of the open-ended question, "How does the greenhouse effect occur?" Students' written responses revealed improved understanding of the greenhouse effect, consistent with the positive shift observed in the multiple-choice scores. The findings related to students' understanding are presented below.

5.1 Before Engaging with the Educational Board Game

Among the students' responses, three students' answers were categorized as misconceptions, student's responses reveal that they conflate the greenhouse effect with ozone depletion or general environmental pollution. An analysis of these responses reveals the following misunderstanding.

Misconception Group. Two students (student03 and student06) incorrectly linked the greenhouse effect to damage to the ozone layer, suggesting that greenhouse gases are responsible for ozone depletion and that this process allows more sunlight to reach the Earth. The excerpts from students' responses are as follows.

"Greenhouse gases cause damage to the ozone layer in Earth's atmosphere, allowing more sunlight to pass through to the Earth." (student03)

"Greenhouse gases contribute to the Earth's temperature rise and damage the ozone layer, significantly thinning the layer that once helped reduce the impact of sunlight." (student06)

One of the misconceptions observed in this study was the incorrect belief that greenhouse gases contribute to ozone layer depletion, thereby increasing sunlight penetration and global temperatures. Two students explicitly stated that greenhouse gases damage the ozone layer, allowing more sunlight to reach the Earth's surface. Andersson and Wallin [23] similarly reported that a significant proportion of students incorrectly link ozone depletion to increasing global temperature, assuming that the greenhouse effect is directly influenced by changes in the ozone layer.

One student (student08) provided a response that broadly attributed the greenhouse effect to human pollution, including waste in both water and air, rather than identifying the specific role of greenhouse gases in trapping infrared radiation. The excerpts from students' responses are as follows.

"It is caused by humans releasing waste into nature, both in water and in the air." (student08)

The misconception that the greenhouse effect comes from general pollution rather than greenhouse gas buildup is common in both this pilot study and past research. Student08 claimed it is caused by human pollution, including waste in water and air, rather than understanding how greenhouse gases trap infrared radiation. This aligns with Gautier, Deutsch and Rebich [7], who found that many students confuse the greenhouse effect with air pollution and fail to distinguish greenhouse gases from other pollutants like aerosols. As a result, students may believe that reducing all pollution will stop climate change, whereas in reality, the key lies in mitigating greenhouse gas emissions.

Five students were categorized as having partial understanding with misconception. They recognized that greenhouse gases play a role in increasing Earth's temperature; however, they could not explain the process of the greenhouse effect. Additionally, their explanations contained misconceptions, indicating that while they understood some aspects of the concept, they also held an incorrect understanding. The identified misconception was as follows:

Understanding with misconception group. Five students incorrectly believed that greenhouse gases form a distinct "layer" that reflects heat back and forth, preventing it from escaping, rather than recognizing their role in absorbing and re-emitting infrared radiation. The excerpts from students' responses are as follows.

"The emission of a large amount of greenhouse gases causes the greenhouse layer to become thicker, leading to the reflection of light back and forth, making it difficult for heat to dissipate effectively." (student01)

"The increasing layer of greenhouse gases prevents sunlight entering the Earth from escaping, causing it to be reflected and trapped within the Earth." (student07)

These responses indicate a common misconception that greenhouse gases act as a reflective barrier rather than as absorbers and re-emitters of infrared radiation. Chang and Pascua [24] identified similar misconceptions among Singaporean students, who often explained heat trapping as a result of greenhouse gases forming a "blanket" or "shield" over the Earth, preventing heat from escaping. Their study emphasized that students frequently failed to recognize the role of infrared radiation in the greenhouse effect and instead assumed that sunlight, often in the form of ultraviolet radiation, was directly responsible for warming the Earth.

5.2 After Engaging with the Educational Board Game

Students demonstrated improved understanding of the greenhouse effect. Posttest analysis showed that none of the students held misconceptions. Four students achieved sound understanding, and four demonstrated partial understanding. The details are presented below.

Partial Understanding Group. Students in this group demonstrated an improved understanding of the greenhouse effect which no students no longer hold misconception which was found in before playing board game. The excerpts from students' responses are as follows.

"The increase of carbon dioxide, nitrous oxide, methane, and CFCs in the atmosphere causes heat to accumulate on Earth." (student04)

In addition, students were able to identify major greenhouse gases, as presented in the game. However, their explanations of the greenhouse effect process remained simplified, as they only mentioned the accumulation of heat on Earth rather than detailing the process of infrared radiation interactions with greenhouse gases. Varela, Sesto and García-Rodeja [25] similarly noted that the greenhouse effect is an abstract and complex concept, making it difficult for students to integrate causal and functional relationships into their understanding. Even though students no longer held misconceptions, they did not fully articulate the role of infrared radiation absorption and re-emission, which is central to the scientific explanation of the greenhouse effect.

Sound Understanding Group. Students in the sound understanding group demonstrated scientifically accurate explanations of the greenhouse effect, correctly describing the absorption and re-emission of infrared radiation by greenhouse gases. They no longer held common misconceptions, such as confusing the greenhouse effect with ozone depletion or misunderstanding the heat-trapping process.

"It is caused by visible light from the Sun being absorbed by the Earth's surface and then emitted as infrared radiation. As the infrared radiation rises into the

atmosphere, greenhouse gases absorb it and reemit some of the radiation into space while redirecting the rest back to Earth. This accumulation of infrared radiation leads to an increase in Earth's temperature." (student05)

This explanation demonstrates conceptual clarity, distinguishing visible light from infrared radiation, a common misconception. Their response accurately describes the absorption and re-emission of infrared radiation, explaining how greenhouse gases contribute to heat accumulation on Earth. This aligns with Varela, Sesto and García-Rodeja [25] highlight that board games as effective tools for understanding complex scientific concepts through tactile engagement and simulation. Physical interaction helps visualize abstract processes, reinforcing learning and correcting misconceptions. Games create microworlds, where players experiment with decisions and observe consequences, deepening conceptual understanding.

6 Conclusion and Future Development

Overall, the preliminary findings support the effectiveness of the board game in enhancing students' understanding of the greenhouse effect. Most students progressed from misconceptions to more accurate conceptions, highlighting the potential of game-based learning in climate change education. Future research will collect interview data and gameplay recordings to gain deeper insights and will expand the study to examine not only conceptual understanding but also climate change engagement with a larger group of participants.

Acknowledgments. This research was supported by The Scholarship for Thesis Promoting SDGs Policies for the Fiscal Year 2024, provided by the Faculty of Graduate Studies, Mahidol University (MUGR SDGs67-09).

Disclosure of Interests. The authors have no competing interests to declare that are relevant to the content of this article.

References

1. IPCC: Climate Change 2022 - Mitigation of Climate Change: Working Group III Contribution to the Sixth Assessment Report of the Intergovernmental Panel on Climate Change. Cambridge University Press, Cambridge (2022)
2. United Nations General Assembly: Transforming our world: The 2030 Agenda for Sustainable Development (2015)
3. Hickman, C., et al.: Climate anxiety in children and young people and their beliefs about government responses to climate change: a global survey. Lancet Planetary Health (2021)
4. Schubatzky, T., Haagen-Schützenhöfer, C., Wackermann, R., Wöhlke, C., Wildbichler, S.: Navigating the complexities of student understanding: exploring the coherency of students' conceptions about the greenhouse effect. Sci. Educ. (2024)
5. Jarrett, L., Takacs, G.: Secondary students' ideas about scientific concepts underlying climate change. Environ. Educ. Res. **26**, 400–420 (2020)
6. IPCC: Climate change 2021: the physical science basis (2021)

7. Gautier, C., Deutsch, K., Rebich, S.: Misconceptions about the greenhouse effect. J. Geosci. Educ. **54**, 386–395 (2006)
8. Monroe, M.C., Plate, R.R., Oxarart, A., Bowers, A., Chaves, W.A.: Identifying effective climate change education strategies: a systematic review of the research. Environ. Educ. Res. **25**, 791–812 (2019)
9. Karpudewan, M., Roth, W.-M., Chandrakesan, K.: Remediating misconception on climate change among secondary school students in Malaysia. Environ. Educ. Res. **21**, 631–648 (2015)
10. Niebert, K., Gropengiesser, H.: Understanding and communicating climate change in metaphors. Environ. Educ. Res. **19**, 282–302 (2013)
11. Reinfried, S., Aeschbacher, U., Rottermann, B.: Improving students' conceptual understanding of the greenhouse effect using theory-based learning materials that promote deep learning. Int. Res. Geogr. Environ. Educ. **21**, 155–178 (2012)
12. Vygotsky, L.S., Cole, M.: Mind in Society: Development of Higher Psychological Processes. Harvard University Press (1978)
13. Wu, J.S., Lee, J.J.: Climate change games as tools for education and engagement. Nat. Clim. Change **5**, 413–418 (2015)
14. Eisenack, K.: A climate change board game for interdisciplinary communication and education. Simul. Gaming **44**, 328–348 (2013)
15. Fjællingsdal, K.S., Klöckner, C.A.: Green across the board: board games as tools for dialogue and simplified environmental communication. Simul. Gaming **51**, 632–652 (2020)
16. Vázquez-Vílchez, M., Garrido-Rosales, D., Pérez-Fernández, B., Fernández-Oliveras, A.: Using a cooperative educational game to promote pro-environmental engagement in future teachers. Educ. Sci. **11** (2021)
17. Carreira, F., Aguiar, A.C., Onça, F., Monzoni, M.: The celsius game: an experiential activity on management education simulating the complex challenges for the two-degree climate change target. Int. J. Manag. Educ. **15**, 350–361 (2017)
18. Garris, R., Ahlers, R., Driskell, J.E.: Games, motivation, and learning: a research and practice model. Simul. Gaming **33**, 441–467 (2002)
19. Ouariachi, T., Olvera-Lobo, M.D., Gutiérrez-Pérez, J., Maibach, E.: A framework for climate change engagement through video games. Environ. Educ. Res. **25**, 701–716 (2019)
20. Chou, Y.-K.: Actionable Gamification: Beyond Points, Badges, and Leaderboards. Fremont (Calif.): Octalysis Group (2016)
21. Creswell, J.W., Creswell, J.D.: Research Design: Qualitative, Quantitative, and Mixed Methods Approaches. Sage publications (2017)
22. Haidar, A.H.: Prospective chemistry teachers' conceptions of the conservation of matter and related concepts. J. Res. Sci. Teach. **34**, 181–197 (1997)
23. Andersson, B., Wallin, A.: Students' understanding of the greenhouse effect, the societal consequences of reducing CO2 emissions and the problem of ozone layer depletion. J. Res. Sci. Teach. **37**, 1096–1111 (2000)
24. Chang, C.-H., Pascua, L.: Singapore students' misconceptions of climate change. Int. Res. Geogr. Environ. Educ. **25**, 84–96 (2016)
25. Varela, B., Sesto, V., García-Rodeja, I.: An investigation of secondary students' mental models of climate change and the greenhouse effect. Res. Sci. Educ. **50**, 599–624 (2020)

Key Factors for Using Games Such as WhereWeMove in Municipal Flood Risk Communication and Collaboration

Thomas Rehder, Juliette Cortes-Arevalo(✉), and Geertje Bekebrede

Delft University of Technology, P.O. Box 5015, Delft, The Netherlands
v.j.cortesarevalo@tudelft.nl

Abstract. This study identifies key factors for integrating the WhereWeMove game into municipal flood risk communication and collaboration strategies. The game started as a research initiative to support the design of adaptation policy by helping risk management organizations to explore how risk perception and resources shape players' adaptation choices. During the game rounds, players take the role of a homeowner to learn about their choices given the available game resources and adaptation options. After the gameplay, participants discuss the relations between their game and real-life choices to envision strategies to strengthen homeowners' capacities. By considering that government organizations often hesitate to adopt innovations according to their available resources, we carried out semi-structured interviews with two municipalities and a province representative to explore their adoption intentions and needs. Thereby, we identified which factors to finetune in the game prototype or pursue at the adopting organizations to use the game in the municipal communication and collaboration strategies. On one side, successful adoption depends on integrating the game into a broader communication strategy aligned with the adaptation priorities across government levels. Conversely, adequate municipal resources and expertise, as well as the game's ease of use, local relevance, and sufficient data privacy, are required to make the gameplay part of municipal efforts. Adoption is initially considered with a dedicated group contributing to the design of government policies to observe policy-related effects and outputs. Players are conceived as a limited group of professionals and representatives of residents or an advisory organization at the municipality or province.

Keywords: Serious game adoption · Flood risk management · climate adaptation

1 Introduction

Floods due to extreme rainfall and river overflow in (sub)urban areas are becoming more frequent and severe, causing property damage and endangering lives [1]. Flood exposure increases in lowland areas due to the limited capacity to drain excess surface water and the combined effect of land subsidence [2]. The July 2021 floods in Germany, Belgium, and the Netherlands revealed that urban drainage systems may not be built for

© The Author(s) 2026
F. Trautwein et al. (Eds.): ISAGA 2025, LNCS 16439, pp. 264–279, 2026.
https://doi.org/10.1007/978-3-032-20129-4_18

such extremes, and river protective measures like dikes or storage zones are not possible to implement everywhere [3]. Floods often affect public and private property, so flood management strategies should coordinate and share responsibilities accordingly [4]. Therefore, governments increasingly require complementary adaptation measures, for example, by homeowners [5]. Homeowners can move to a better-protected location or take structural measures at the current house to permanently prevent the entry of excess water, such as raising the ground, installing door panels, or temporarily placing sandbags if there is a warning time. They can help increase the drainage capacity by using measures such as green gardens or limiting damage to their private property by repurposing spaces [6]. Designing government policies to strengthen the capacity of homeowners to take action is difficult for various reasons [7]. Technically, private house adaptations depend on factors like house type, flood exposure, and possibilities to provide warnings [8]. Institutionally, municipalities may not have the expertise or resources that national guidelines require for planning adaptations [4]. Climate adaptation strategies could further worsen socio-spatial inequalities [9]. Socially, many residents lack the resources to act or do not know the flood risks and the feasible adaptation options. Such is the case in the Netherlands, where risk perception is low due to the dike protection [10]. With little experience of severe river flooding and increasing rain floods, residents struggle to grasp the potential consequences. Residents need support to strengthen their knowledge or financial capacities to take action [11]. To address these challenges, communication strategies should better consider residents' motivating factors and preferences for action and build trustworthy relationships to share responsibilities accordingly [12]. Clear and actionable communication to residents is essential from all government levels [13]. Particularly, communication from provinces and municipalities towards homeowners helps to make them aware of the flood risks and the measures they can take before, during, and after a flood event [14].

Serious games are increasingly used to support players' decision-making and collective action [15]. Such games further allow players to experience (flood) scenarios and (adaptation) options that are otherwise difficult to try [16]. Serious games are further developed as a communication and collaboration tool for flood risk management [17]. According to the organization and innovation characteristics and capacities, the public sector is generally hesitant in adopting innovations in its day-to-day practice [18]. To plan adoption efforts, this study addresses the question: What factors influence local organizations' adoption of serious games in their communication strategy? The adoption of serious games in educational settings [19] and corporate environments [20] are extensively studied, but not as much in a public organizational setting [21]. To this end, we adapted the framework of innovation adoption and diffusion in the public sector as developed by De Vries et al. [22]. We used WhereWeMove as a reference to identify key factors for using games in municipal flood risk communication and collaboration. To this end, we carried out semi-structured interviews with representatives from two municipalities and one province in the Netherlands.

2   Antecedent Factors Influencing Adoption in the Public Sector

This section outlines the antecedents (i.e., attributes of an innovation or factors that should be present) for adopting innovations, such as a serious game, in the public sector. In theory, the design and implementation of an innovation should *"reduce the uncertainty in the cause-effect relationships involving a desired outcome."* [23(p. 13)]. An individual or organization considers these factors when seeking additional information about the innovation. Then, diffusion is *"the process by which an innovation is communicated through certain channels over time"* (p. 5) among interested actors. To plan adoption and diffusion efforts, one should consider the innovation-decision process, which includes five steps:

(1) Knowing about an innovation through available communication channels.
(2) Raising interest (often through others) to help representatives of intended adopting organizations form an attitude towards the innovation.
(3) Support the adoption decision by recognizing that the decision can be made independently, collectively, by order, or contingent on a first experience.
(4) Facilitating the innovation implementation.
(5) Confirming (or not) the implementation decision and offering alternative options when needed.

To support this process, De Vries et al. [22] identified antecedent factors from a meta-synthesis study, noting that adoption and diffusion depend on the innovation and the organization. Table 1 brings together: First, public management (PM) studies about administrative, technological, service, product, or conceptual innovations. Second, public policy (PP) studies about governance and conceptual innovations. Third, e-government (EG) studies about technological and product service innovations engaging various actors in government practices through Information and Communication Technologies. Although serious gaming does not necessarily contain digital elements, e-governance factors influence those that include them. De Vries et al. [22] further grouped the factors into five categories: environmental, inter-organizational, organizational, innovation, and individual factors. The following sections summarize which factors were expected to be relevant for our case based on a literature search about flood risk management communication and gaming.

2.1   Environmental Factors

We distinguish the site-specific environmental factors from (inter) organizational environmental factors. We further used this category as a selection criterion to approach municipalities to interview. As such, this category refers to the problem relevance and the socio-economic characteristics of the area concerned, such as the area's wealth and urbanization. Moreover, flood risk depends on the geographical exposure and the socio-economic, physical, environmental, and institutional vulnerabilities and capacities of at-risk people. Key environmental flood factors include magnitude, area, and duration, influenced by water channels, drainage, protection, and catchment management [1]. Risk perception further depends on the past experiences, reaction capacity, and hazard awareness of the people at risk [14]. For instance, younger, less experienced, less educated,

Table 1. Factors referred by De Vries et al. [22] from the Public Policy (PP), Public Management or E-government (EG) literature. (*) The factors considered as a selection criterion for the interviews. (**) The factors not considered in the interview protocol due to their limited relevance to this study. In italics, the factors reframed to the scope of the study.

Category	Factors	Source
Environmental	Socio-economic characteristics, *local relevance*	PP
Inter-Organizational	Learning, mimicry**	PP/PM
	High levels of collaboration, regulatory mandates*, competition**, socio-economic characteristics, frequent dissemination, *two-way communication and co-creation opportunities*	EG/PP/PM
Organizational	Training for employees, *ease of training*	EG
	Supportive leadership, organizational structure	EG/PM
	Slack resources, Supportive culture	EG/PP/PM
	Large size*, Intra-organizational networks**	
Innovation	High ease of use, absence of security/privacy issues, low implementation costs	EG
	High compatibility, relative advantage, trialability and observability	EG/PP
Individual	Personality characteristics, perceived peer pressure	EG
	Skills of public servants	EG/PP
	Innovation resistance	EG/PM
	Demographic aspects	EG/PP/PM

and/or less privileged respondents are arguably more hesitant to share their risk perceptions [24]. Low-income homeowners with short tenure in a community may further lack the resources to take action [16].

2.2 Inter-organizational Factors

Inter-organizational factors refer to the collaboration or relations with external stakeholders to carry out the processes that the innovation supports. It includes disseminating information about an innovation. Further, it includes the regulatory aspects (laws or mandates) influencing innovation diffusion or adoption. We interpreted the regulatory aspects as the mandates requiring local government to more actively engage with private actors, such as homeowners, for climate adaptation [4]. We did not consider the competition between organizations when dealing with the innovation process, and the extent to which mimicking the innovative behavior of other organizations as important given the societal aim of the organizations. However, public organizations need to learn from each other on how to improve the effectiveness of government policies and deal with flood risk management challenges [9]. Learning across organizations through inter-organizational networks is also considered a relevant game application factor. According to Janssen et al. [15], games support knowledge about the situation, common values, and learning about each other's perspectives. As such, games can integrate various flood risk management roles or limit the game experience to a few roles. Games can further be part of participatory processes to enable inter- and intra-organisational learning and collaboration. This leads to two-way communication and the co-creation opportunities of flood adaptation policy and capacity-building [7]. This factor is essential for social innovations, encouraging collaboration between actors to address societal problems [25].

2.3 Organizational Factors

Organizational factors refer to the level of resources available inside the organization (slack resources, such as money, employees, and ICT facilities), supportive leadership for the innovation's implementation process, organizational structure, and the dominant organizational risk culture. In flood risk management, governments struggle to engage actors, reframe issues, share responsibility, adapt rules, and manage resources like finances, knowledge, and skills [26]. For the implementation of games, factors such as the possibility of training employees and the difficulty of training and/or use of the games are also relevant. Skilled facilitation from coordinating or collaborating organizations is crucial to support this process [16]. We approached large and small municipalities, regardless of their intra-organizational networks to account for diverse adoption needs.

2.4 Innovation Factors

The innovation factors focus on the characteristics of the innovation itself. These include the ease of use, the compatibility or relative advantage, the perceived usefulness, security and privacy issues, costs, trialability (or possibility to experiment with the innovation), and observability (or the extent to which others can see the innovation being used). Games are increasingly designed to support flood risk management communication. However, there are limitations to overcome in the game design [28]. The game narrative and adaptivity should enhance the experience. Poor evaluation and unclear indicators reduce usefulness and effectiveness. Designers should ensure the innovation is reliable, relevant, and user-friendly by considering the player and contextual characteristics of the gameplay. Focus on enjoyment, usefulness, privacy, and security is further necessary [29]. The ability to experiment and the visibility of an innovation are key to relative advantage [30].

2.5 Individual Factors

The factors include the individual attitude towards the innovation and the necessary ICT skills that can positively or negatively affect the diffusion or adoption. It further includes the perceived peer pressure, and the demographic aspects of individuals adopting the innovation, such as their educational background or tenure. Individual factors are related to both the players and the coordinating organizations [31]. Although there is a trend towards active, collaborative, and technology-rich serious games, the necessary

ICT skills may engage some and limit others from participating, both from the players and coordinating organizations. Players often prefer games that have some personal interaction and facilitation [16]. Though preferences may vary with the familiarity and accessibility of the game technology [17].

3 Research Set up

Through interviews with representatives from two municipalities and a province, we identified which factors from Sect. 2 are to finetune into the current game prototype. This study uses WhereWeMove as a reference game to discuss key factors to pursue for using games in municipal flood risk communication and collaboration strategies.

3.1 The WhereWeMove Game

WhereWeMove is a housing game combining a tabletop board with a website that players access through their phone to track their game choices (Fig. 1). The game started as a research initiative to [32]:

(1) Help risk management organizations to explore how risk perception and resources shape players' climate choices.
(2) During game rounds, support players in learning about their choices given the available game resources and adaptation options.
(3) After the gameplay, facilitate players discussions on the relations between their game and real-life choices to envision strategies accordingly.

Six to eight players representing homeowners sit around a table with a facilitator who manages the game resources available to players. The game aims to achieve the highest score possible by increasing satisfaction or earning points for the available income. To this end, every player receives a welfare-type budget, which determines their financial resources and the satisfaction rating for their desired house. According to the game settings, players can decide each round whether to stay or move between the three-game neighborhoods, each with different protection levels against rain and river floods. Whenever players decide to move, it costs satisfaction points. They should choose a new house from among the available houses or negotiate with another participant to buy his/her house. After making their house choice, players respond to climate events and government announcements by choosing flood adaptation measures to prepare for floods or buy satisfaction measures to increase their satisfaction score. Flood events could occur every round, and, depending on the location and adaptation measures, flood damage reduces the player's satisfaction score.

Fig. 1. Tabletop board and game elements impressions.

3.2 Interview Set up

Table 2 outlines the interview guide that the first author used to explore the factors from Sect. 2 as part of a larger study [33]. As national Dutch mandates require local governments to engage with private actors in climate adaptation more actively, we initially limited our interview participants to municipalities. Similarly, according to the government maps, the environmental category was not used in the interview guidance but as a selection criterion to shortlist nearby municipalities located in high to medium flood-risk areas. The short list included 15 municipalities, which we approached via email to ask for an interview during the week of June 3rd to 10th, 2024. After a week, we sent an email reminder and followed up with a phone call. Finally, three municipalities reacted positively to having an interview. Others declined the invitation referring to their lack of resources and priority or simply did not react. One interview was cancelled one day before the meeting.

Finally, we had two interviews: one with a water safety advisor on a large municipality ($<$650,000 inhabitants), and one with a sustainability climate adaptation advisor on a small one ($<$65,000). A third interview was conducted with a game designer from the province in the region. As interview participants did not have experience playing the game, after the first question, the game materials were placed on the table and introduced in slides, which included key results from some gameplay sessions and the after-game discussions. The following interview questions referred to the organizational and inter-organizational categories by asking about the current practices of flood risk communication, public engagement, and co-creation. Interviews were face-to-face meetings lasting 1 to 1.5 h based on participant availability. The interview was recorded to get the verbatim transcripts. The analysis began by assigning keywords to the line-by-line answers to identify the absence or limiting influence, their presence or driving influence, and their in-between presence or conditional influence. The coding continued by labeling keywords per related category and factor to pursue.

Table 2. Interview parts and questions list

Part	Reference category	Influential factors	Guiding questions
1	(Inter) Organizational	Current practices	How does your municipality communicate flood risks and adaptive measures to residents? How effective have these methods been?
2	Organizational	Culture and structure	How does your municipality currently adopt new technologies or innovations? What changes are needed to integrate the game into communication efforts?
3		Leadership and support	How do municipal leaders support the introduction of innovative tools and technologies?
4		Resources and Training	What resources (financial, personnel, technological) support adopting new technology in your municipality? How are staff trained to use these technologies?
5	Innovation	Technological integration	Would implementing a serious game like "WhereWeMove" face acceptance challenges? What technical factors would ease its integration?
6	(Inter) Organizational	Public Engagement and Co-Creation	How does your municipality involve citizens in solving local challenges? How could "WhereWeMove" improve residents' involvement in flood risk management?
7	Innovation	Trialability and experimentation	What opportunities exist to pilot new technologies in your municipality? How can the game be adapted to fit your community's needs?
8		Security and privacy	How does your municipality address security and privacy when implementing new technologies like "WhereWeMove"? Are there specific protocols in place?
9	Individual	Perceptions and enthusiasm	What is the general attitude of public servants towards adopting new technologies?

4 Results

Results are listed by participant and factor category, including a new "politics" category to reflect (inter)organizational influences beyond formal mandates.

4.1 Large Municipality

The environment-related factors are drivers considering the highly urbanized area with outer dike regions. The government offers subsidies; riverine and rainfall flood scenarios are relevant. Inter-organizational-related factors are also related to drivers. High collaboration is present through ongoing cooperation initiatives with (social) housing associations. There are also various (online) communication channels and seasonal dissemination. Two-way communication is present through visits on-site and planned workshops, incorporating flooding scenarios per neighborhood. Co-creation is possible through discussion events in the neighborhood and by supporting residents' bottom-up initiatives. Inter-organizational learning was not mentioned as an influential factor.

Organizational-related factors are in-between or conditional to politically related factors. The municipality encourages responsibility and leadership with support. Adopting the game depends on outsourcing tasks and fitting costs within the budget. The culture favors clear plans, and short training is welcomed. Innovational-related factors are constraining or conditional. The municipality values equity and inclusivity, requiring the game to be accessible and meet data safety standards. It shouldn't place full responsibility on residents without support. The game would be first for awareness raising, followed by co-creation. It should be tested internally before being shared with residents. Individual-related factors are driving. Enthusiasm depends on outsourcing and maintaining trust between residents and the municipality. With a diverse population and various activities, the game could be included if accessible. Politically related factors are in-between or conditional to the approval of, for example, the municipal councils. The organization must allocate capacity and justify the game's strategic importance. A clear communication strategy and strong framing are needed to gain support.

4.2 Small Municipality

Environmental-related factors are constrained due to local relevance. Medium urbanization fits the socio-economic profile, but the game focuses on rainfall, not riverine flooding, and doesn't address integrated drought and flood measures. It also overlooks residents' priority of lowering energy costs. Good collaboration with water authorities and climate adaptation networks drives inter-organizational factors. Frequent newsletters cover floods, droughts, and national campaigns. Inter-organizational learning and co-creation are key despite communication challenges between departments, especially due to a new law requiring closer interaction with residents. Independent departments and limited resources constrain organizational factors. Leadership is needed to integrate efforts, and the municipal council's support is crucial. The game could be used for internal training (pilot tests) to explore responsibility distribution.

Innovation challenges include ensuring accessibility for all residents, addressing data safety, and keeping implementation costs low due to budget cuts. Gaming offers a new approach but should better reflect local relevance. The interviewee has positive expectations, noting that the municipality has the skills to play the game, though it requires time from everyone. Even if the education level of players is relatively good, limiting complexity and follow-up information is needed. Politically, the priority for playing the game should be aligned with the plans at all government levels. By testing the game internally at first, support from the municipal council could follow for broader implementation.

4.3 Provincial Organization

Environmental factors are like those of a large municipality but constrained by local relevance. The recommendation is to expand the game settings and define whether it's open to all residents or a limited group. Inter-organizational communication with residents is limited, as the province focuses on summer workshops, joint projects with professional organizations, and co-creation with professional stakeholders. Organizational factors drive leadership and cross-collaboration, but the organization's size can slow implementation. Budget and capacity must be allocated, though training capacity may be available in the province. Having unclear the target group constrains innovation factors.

The game's monetary system does not make it playable with all residents. Yet, data safety is not a concern if anonymity is ensured. The game should focus on relevance, raising awareness as the top priority. In either case, a positive effect is expected in players' capacity to make more responsible decisions. The game seems highly versatile and possible to adjust to the context. Individual-related aspects are positive as long as an open community exists for implementation. There are different views on how to best communicate with residents that the game would have to bridge. Politically related factors remain challenging as long as there is no clear strategy behind or priority, and municipal awareness remains low.

4.4 Comparative Overview

Table 3 shows that according to the organization type and managing area, important factors for adoption were relevance and compatibility with government guidance, adequate targeting and game complexity for the intended players, and adequate data privacy management. Low resources may limit adoption. However, regardless of the available resources, all organizations consider it important to have a leader in the organization coordinating and supporting the adoption of innovation. Overall, a primary requirement that may limit or drive adoption is the extent to which the game design and play align with the priorities at all government levels and are supported by relevant decision-makers at a local level.

Table 3. Comparative keywords by category and factor: green (somehow present as drivers), red (lacking as constraints), orange (conditional or in-between influence).

Category	Antecedent factors	Key characteristics influencing adoption		
		Large municipality	Small municipality	Province
Environment	Socioeconomic characteristics	High urbanization and budget	Medium urbanization	Very dense area, Wealthy area
	Local relevance	Similar flooding scenarios	Lack of flood experience	Broaden game. Target players
Inter-Organizational	High levels of collaboration	Local cooperation.	Waterboard collaboration. Residents network	Municipal task, No citizen network.
	Frequent dissemination	Online information. Seasonal dissemination.	Newsletters distribution. National campaigns.	No active communication. Few tools.
Inter-Organizational	Inter-organizational learning		Difficult coordination, but there is a safety department.	Summer workshops for municipalities
	Two-way communication	Citizen feedback through on-site visits. Awareness workshops.	Citizen feedback through field visits. Evening events to simulate scenarios.	Joint projects with municipalities and professionals
	Co-creation	Discussion events. Bottom-up approach	Interest in activating residents. Legal compliance required.	Representatives of local stakeholders
Organization	Supportive Leadership	Responsible leadership	Need for a leader as efforts divided	Innovative leaders
	Organizational Structure	Decentralized by law but defined responsibilities	Decentralized implementation	Size slows down implementation. Interest in cross-collaboration
	Presence of slack resources	Outsourcing tasks. Reasonable costs if there is budget	Small budget. Need for staff	Large financial resources Capacity needs to be allocated
	Supportive culture	Concrete plans and expectations	Political dependence	Slow innovation adoption
	Easy training for employees	Short training necessary	Usage for internal training	Basic training for volunteers

(*continued*)

Table 3. (*continued*)

Innovation	High ease of use	High accessibility, Low complexity	Challenging game	Target group dependence
	Absence of security/privacy issues	Data safety & IT compliance	Data safety concerns	Need for anonymity
	Low implementation costs		Short budget	
	High compatibility	Support in responsibilities, equity/inclusivity	The game frame should fit the relevance	
	High perceived usefulness	First, raise awareness. Then, co-creation	Communicate local risks and actions to take	All three objectives, but awareness at first
Innovation	High relative advantage	High versatility	New working way	Positive effect on players. High versatility
	High trialability	Test possibility	Pilot tests	
Individual	Personality characteristics	Certain enthusiasm	Positive expectations	Positive acknowledgment High enthusiasm
	Public servant skills	Outsourcing	Present skills	
	Innovation resistance	Trust issues	Framing importance	Value conflict
	Demographic Aspects	A diverse population reach with various types of activities	Average education to play, but additional information needed	Open community
Political	Plan-based communication	Strategy importance	Prioritization need	Strategy importance
	Innovation program fit	Framing innovation	Main assignment	No priority

5 Discussion

Three main considerations for adoption emerged, based on which game prototype adjustments and diffusion should be planned. First, a new category emerged—politically related factors—which, despite overlapping with organizational factors, highlights the complexity of adopting innovations to meet social demands [25]. The politics category also shows that the innovation steps proposed by Rogers [23] are framed at the individual level. However, the decision process is more complex as organizations have goals, regulations, and informal practices that shape the process [34]. In this context, WhereWeMove should align the gameplay with the wider guidelines of higher government levels. The gaming approach should further have the endorsement of provinces or large municipalities as early opinion leaders for further adoption. Overall, the municipal councils approve the strategies for communicating with residents and require coordination from municipality staff on the overall process, as supportive leadership, culture, and the internal provision of resources are necessary. Alternatives to experiment with the game and observe some of its effects were found in the learning communities set by the province across municipalities and for the internal training of municipal staff. Second, as much of a government support dependence, having concrete implementation plans was of utmost importance while managing expectations of what is possible (or not with the innovation). These plans should be tailored by the organization. In alignment with the needs for games in flood risk management [17], on one side, the game should include the integrated management needs of the municipality, not focusing only on floods. Conversely, suggestions were to reduce the complexity to make the game as inclusive as possible. This suggestion requires choices about what to include or not to keep the game relevant for the adoption context. Moreover, the game frame should consider strategies to support players in taking responsibility for acting and accounting for equity aspects. Third, interview results show the priority set by all management organizations on raising awareness over co-creation to envision strategies for strengthening residents' action capacities or exploring the effectiveness of possible policies. For such an aim, players are conceived as a limited group of professionals and resident representatives at the municipality or advisory organizations, and with students as future professionals.

6 Conclusions

This study allowed us to identify key factors that should be present or pursued for the WhereWeMove game adoption. There are three main antecedent factors to tackle. First, political support can be obtained through a plan-based communication strategy that aligns with the innovation needs of the municipalities. Second, organizational readiness is considered through the availability of resources to support the implementation or by offering the possibility to outsource when necessary. Lastly, fine-tune the game readiness by critically considering which adaptations can improve its relevance, manage the complexity, and ensure the effectiveness of the game play for players and coordinating organizations. Although the factors considered relevant in this study align with more recent meta-analyses [25], future research should verify their relevance by including more regions and interviewees per municipality, or examining how gameplay experience influences game adoption perceptions.

Acknowledgments. The game was developed by the TUDelft Gamelab with funding from the NWO project "Crossing the Borders at the Grensmaas", the 4TU.DeSIRE Resilience and the TUDelft Climate Action with support of Professors Alexander Verbraeck and Tatiana Filatova. WhereWeMove is part of the Delta Enigma research infrastructure, NWO- filenr. 184.036.008.

Disclosure of Interests. No competing interests to declare relevant to this article's content.

References

1. Kundzewicz, Z.W., Pińskwar, I.: Are pluvial and fluvial floods on the rise? Water **14**(17), Article no. 17 (2022). https://doi.org/10.3390/w14172612
2. Brockhoff, R.C., Koop, S.H.A., Snel, K.A.W.: Pluvial flooding in utrecht: on its way to a flood-proof city. Water **11**(7), Article no. 7 (2019). https://doi.org/10.3390/w11071501
3. Koks, E.E., van Ginkel, K.C.H., van Marle, M.J.E., Lemnitzer, A.: Brief communication: Critical infrastructure impacts of the 2021 mid-July western European flood event. Nat. Hazard. **22**(12), 3831–3838 (2022). https://doi.org/10.5194/nhess-22-3831-2022
4. Mees, H.: Local governments in the driving seat? A comparative analysis of public and private responsibilities for adaptation to climate change in European and North-American cities. J. Environ. Plan. Policy Manag. **19**(4), 374–390 (2017). https://doi.org/10.1080/1523908X.2016.1223540
5. Dillenardt, L., Hudson, P., Thieken, A.H.: Urban pluvial flood adaptation: results of a household survey across four German municipalities. J. Flood Risk Manag. **15**(3), e12748 (2022). https://doi.org/10.1111/jfr3.12748
6. Poussin, J.K., Bubeck, P., Aerts, J.C.J.H., Ward, P.J.: Potential of semi-structural and non-structural adaptation strategies to reduce future flood risk: case study for the Meuse. Nat. Hazard. **12**(11), 3455–3471 (2012). https://doi.org/10.5194/nhess-12-3455-2012
7. Forsyth, W., Roberts, T., Brewer, G.: Conceptualising risk communication barriers to household flood preparedness. Urban Gov. **3**(2), 116–129 (2023). https://doi.org/10.1016/j.ugj.2023.02.001
8. Endendijk, T., Botzen, W.J.W., de Moel, H., Aerts, J.C.J.H., Slager, K., Kok, M.: Flood Vulnerability models and household flood damage mitigation measures: an econometric analysis of survey data. Water Resour. Res. **59**(8), e2022WR034192 (2023). https://doi.org/10.1029/2022WR034192
9. Forrest, S.A., Trell, E.-M., Woltjer, J.: Socio-spatial inequalities in flood resilience: rainfall flooding in the city of Arnhem. Cities **105**, 102843 (2020). https://doi.org/10.1016/j.cities.2020.102843
10. Snel, K.A.W., Witte, P.A., Hartmann, T., Geertman, S.C.M.: The shifting position of homeowners in flood resilience: from recipients to key-stakeholders. WIREs Water **7**(4), e1451 (2020). https://doi.org/10.1002/wat2.1451
11. Kuhlicke, C., et al.: The behavioral turn in flood risk management, its assumptions and potential implications. WIREs Water **7**(3), e1418 (2020). https://doi.org/10.1002/wat2.1418
12. Balog-Way, D., McComas, K., Besley, J.: The evolving field of risk communication. Risk Anal. **40**(S1), 2240–2262 (2020). https://doi.org/10.1111/risa.13615
13. Goldberg, M.H., Gustafson, A., van der Linden, S., Rosenthal, S.A., Leiserowitz, A.: Communicating the scientific consensus on climate change: diverse audiences and effects over time. Environ. Behav. **54**(7–8), 1133–1165 (2022). https://doi.org/10.1177/00139165221129539
14. Ali, A., Rana, I.A., Ali, A., Najam, F.A.: Flood risk perception and communication: the role of hazard proximity. J. Environ. Manag. **316**, 115309 (2022). https://doi.org/10.1016/j.jenvman.2022.115309
15. Janssen, M.A., Falk, T., Meinzen-Dick, R., Vollan, B.: Using games for social learning to promote self-governance. Curr. Opin. Environ. Sustain. **62**, 101289 (2023). https://doi.org/10.1016/j.cosust.2023.101289
16. Flood, S., Cradock-Henry, N.A., Blackett, P., Edwards, P.: Adaptive and interactive climate futures: systematic review of 'serious games' for engagement and decision-making. Environ. Res. Lett. **13**(6), 063005 (2018). https://doi.org/10.1088/1748-9326/aac1c6
17. Forrest, S.A., Kubíková, M., Macháč, J.: Serious gaming in flood risk management. WIREs Water **9**(4), e1589 (2022). https://doi.org/10.1002/wat2.1589

18. Buchheim, L., Krieger, A., Arndt, S.: Innovation types in public sector organizations: a systematic review of the literature. Manag. Rev. Q. **70**(4), 509–533 (2020). https://doi.org/10.1007/s11301-019-00174-5

19. Tsekleves, E., Cosmas, J., Aggoun, A.: Benefits, barriers and guideline recommendations for the implementation of serious games in education for stakeholders and policymakers. Br. J. Educ. Technol. **47**(1), 164–183 (2016). https://doi.org/10.1111/bjet.12223

20. Larson, K.: Serious games and gamification in the corporate training environment: a literature review. TechTrends **64**(2), 319–328 (2020). https://doi.org/10.1007/s11528-019-00446-7

21. Castro-Sánchez, E., Kyratsis, Y., Iwami, M., Rawson, T.M., Holmes, A.H.: Serious electronic games as behavioural change interventions in healthcare-associated infections and infection prevention and control: a scoping review of the literature and future directions. Antimicrob. Resist. Infect. Control **5**(1), 34 (2016). https://doi.org/10.1186/s13756-016-0137-0

22. De Vries, H., Tummers, L., Bekkers, V.: The diffusion and adoption of public sector innovations: a meta-synthesis of the literature. Perspect. Public Manag. Gov. **1**(3), 159–176 (2018). https://doi.org/10.1093/ppmgov/gvy001

23. Rogers, E.: Diffusion of Innovations, 4th edn. (2003)

24. Rufat, S., Botzen, W.J.W.: Drivers and dimensions of flood risk perceptions: revealing an implicit selection bias and lessons for communication policies. Glob. Environ. Change **73**, 102465 (2022). https://doi.org/10.1016/j.gloenvcha.2022.102465

25. de O. Carneiro, D.K., Isidro Filho, A., Criado, J.I.: Public sector innovation ecosystems: a proposition for theoretical-conceptual integration. Int. J. Public Adm. **47**(14), 937–950 (2024). https://doi.org/10.1080/01900692.2023.2213853

26. Dieperink, C., et al.: Flood Risk Management in Europe: An Exploration of Governance Challenges. STAR-FLOOD Consortium (2013). http://www.starflood.eu/documents/2013/06/d1-1-2.pdf

27. Edwards, P., et al.: Tools for adaptive governance for complex social-ecological systems: a review of role-playing-games as serious games at the community-policy interface. Environ. Res. Lett. **14**(11), 113002 (2019). https://doi.org/10.1088/1748-9326/ab4036

28. Mittal, A., Scholten, L., Kapelan, Z.: A review of serious games for urban water management decisions: current gaps and future research directions. Water Res. **215**, 118217 (2022). https://doi.org/10.1016/j.watres.2022.118217

29. Spil, T.A.M., Romijnders, V., Sundaram, D., Wickramasinghe, N., Kijl, B.: Are serious games too serious? Diffusion of wearable technologies and the creation of a diffusion of serious games model. Int. J. Inf. Manag. **58**, 102202 (2021). https://doi.org/10.1016/j.ijinfomgt.2020.102202

30. Antonopoulou, K., Dacre, N.: Exploring diffusion characteristics that influence serious games adoption decisions. SSRN Electron. J. (2015). https://doi.org/10.2139/ssrn.3829185

31. Vlachopoulos, D., Makri, A.: The effect of games and simulations on higher education: a systematic literature review. Int. J. Educ. Technol. High. Educ. **14**(1), 22 (2017). https://doi.org/10.1186/s41239-017-0062-1

32. Cortes Arevalo, V.J., et al.: WhereWeMove: the housing game that supports governments and residents in joining efforts for climate action. Delft University of Technology (2024)

33. Rehder, T.S.: Enhancing municipal flood risk communication and community adaptability through serious gaming [MSc thesis, TUDelft] (2024). https://repository.tudelft.nl/record/uuid:f891ab5c-f8ba-42f0-a57e-82b3e7537566

34. García-Avilés, J.A.: Diffusion of innovation. In: The International Encyclopedia of Media Psychology, pp. 1–8. Wiley, Hoboken (2020). https://doi.org/10.1002/9781119011071.iemp0137

Development of a Disaster Response Headquarters Management Game

Junya Tsukamoto[1(✉)], Kaede Fujita[1], Yuta Yamazaki[1], Shintaro Fujita[2], and Manabu Ichikawa[3]

[1] Shibaura Institute of Technology, Functional Control Systems, Saitama, Japan
mf21082@sic.shibaura-it.ac.jp
[2] Shibaura Institute of Technology, Department of Planning, Architecture and Environmental Systems, Saitama, Japan
[3] Shibaura Institute of Technology, Systems Engineering and Science, Saitama, Japan

Abstract. In recent years, multiple large-scale earthquakes have occurred in Japan, highlighting the need for stronger coordination in disaster response. During the hyper-acute phase following a disaster, rapid rescue operations and medical support are essential. However, differences in command structures and the existence of independent systems among response organizations make information sharing a persistent challenge. To address this issue, the authors have developed the "Disaster Response Headquarters Management Game", which simulates inter-organizational coordination. This board game-style simulation assigns players to the roles of the police, fire department, JSDF, and medical team. Each team must conduct rescue operations, transport disaster victims, and manage hospital resources, all while responding to unexpected events. A key feature of the game is its restricted information-sharing system, replicating real-world communication barriers in disaster situations. A test play was conducted with graduate students, revealing both successes and areas for improvement. Players gained an understanding of the importance of inter-organizational collaboration, but challenges such as complex rules and time allocation were noted. While the game effectively recreated decision-making dilemmas, balancing realism with ease of play remains an area for further refinement. Looking ahead, this game is expected to serve as a training tool for disaster response personnel. We plan to collaborate with local governments and disaster prevention agencies to further refine the game and evaluate its effectiveness through additional testing.

Keywords: Disaster response · Emergency Life-Saving · Hyper-Acute Phase · Information sharing

1 Introduction

1.1 Background

In Japan, multiple earthquakes with a seismic intensity of 7 have occurred in the past 30 years. Following the Great Hanshin-Awaji Earthquake in 1995, many

F. Trautwein et al. (Eds.): ISAGA 2025, LNCS 16439, pp. 280–296, 2026.
https://doi.org/10.1007/978-3-032-20129-4_19

disaster response organizations were established, and disaster response methods were reviewed [1]. Subsequently, large-scale earthquakes such as the Great East Japan Earthquake in 2011, the Kumamoto Earthquake in 2016, the Hokkaido Eastern Iburi Earthquake in 2018, and the Noto Peninsula Earthquake in 2024 have continued to occur. In response, these organizations have identified problems and made continuous improvements. However, experts predict that massive earthquakes, such as the Nankai Trough Earthquake and a directly beneath Tokyo earthquake, could occur within the next few decades [2]. Therefore, disaster response organizations must remain vigilant and further enhance their preparedness for earthquakes.

Disaster response can be divided into four phases: the hyper-acute phase (within 72 h after the disaster), the acute phase (within one week), the subacute phase (two to three weeks after the disaster), and the chronic phase (from several months to years after the disaster) [3]. Among these, the hyper-acute phase is a critical period for ensuring rapid life-saving activities and medical care, making it extremely important. During this phase, disaster response organizations rescue affected residents, transport them to hospitals, and gather information on passable roads. Additionally, medical team prioritize medical care for transported victims through triage and provide necessary treatment. If medical resources are insufficient, patients are transferred to hospitals with adequate capacity. The initial disaster response efforts of each organization are directly linked to the survival of residents, and swift rescue operations and victim support are essential to minimize damage.

To carry out these activities effectively, it is crucial for each organization to cooperate and share disaster-related information through coordinated communication. For example, when an organization removes debris from roads, making them passable for vehicles, sharing this information can significantly impact the rescue efforts of other organizations. Additionally, the destination of rescued victims is an important consideration. If all victims are transported to specific nearby hospitals, those hospitals may quickly become overwhelmed and run out of medical resources. Therefore, selecting appropriate transport destinations in coordination with medical professionals is essential.

In this way, timely reporting of operational status by each organization and coordination with other organizations are indispensable for efficiently rescuing disaster victims. However, sharing information among different organizations is not always straightforward. Each organization may use its own system and follow different chains of command, making it difficult to ensure that all information is shared in real time [4]. Given the limited time available, prioritizing rescue operations over information sharing may sometimes be necessary. However, this can lead to uncoordinated efforts by different teams, resulting in wasted resources and inefficiencies.

1.2 Purpose of This Study

Within a limited time-frame, determining what information to share and what actions to take based on that information can be challenging. To address this issue, we have developed the "Disaster Response Headquarters Management Game" to help overcome the challenges of information sharing and coordination in disaster response, while also emphasizing the importance of inter-organizational collaboration. The Disaster Response Headquarters is a command and coordination body established to prevent further damage and facilitate swift and effective recovery efforts during a disaster. The objective of this game is to learn about specific disaster response actions during the hyper-acute phase and to enable smooth disaster response by placing participants in the roles of different rganizations. Additionally, the game aims to let the players notice the importance of inter-organizational collaboration, rather than having each organization operate independently. In this paper, we introduce the details of this game.

2 Literature Review

To enhance the disaster response capabilities of each organization and strengthen interorganizational collaboration, training during non-emergency periods is essential. Various training methods exist, as summarized in the Table 1. Among them, tabletop exercises, which require participants to control and manage an entire disaster scenario, are particularly effective training methods [5]. Additionally, tabletop training methods such as the Hinanzyo Unei Game (HUG) [6] and the Disaster Imagination Game (DIG) [7] are widely used. These games have been adopted as training tools by several municipalities and have been recognized for their effectiveness [8,9]. As a result, gaming-based training methods are gaining attention as a valuable approach to disaster preparedness.

Table 1. Classification and Contents of Disaster Training.

Classification	Contents
Lecture-based Training	Lectures on disaster preparedness
	Seminars by invited external speakers
Practical Training	Disaster response drills
	Evacuation drills (practical)
	Staff assembly drills (practical)
	Shelter setup and operation drills (practical)
Tabletop Training	Image Training
	Workshops such as DIG and HUG
	Tabletop simulation drills using role-playing methods

In Japan, several training programs utilizing games have been developed. Saito et al. (2012) created a board game designed to enhance collaboration among municipalities [10]. In this game, players collect and share information on a disaster-simulated map, and the game ends when all necessary information has been gathered. Through this gaming experience, participants demonstrated an increased awareness of the importance of information sharing and disaster preparedness. Fujioka et al. (2011) developed gamification software that presents disaster-related knowledge in a quiz format [11]. The software was tested with a wide range of participants, from elementary school students to company employees, serving as a tool to raise awareness of disaster preparedness. Kurose (2020) designed a game called Chronology, which reconstructs the sequence of events from the Kumamoto Earthquake with a maximum magnitude of 7.3 that occurred in 2016 [12]. This game was primarily intended for government officials and was highly regarded as an educational tool for understanding the sequence of disaster response efforts. In addition to these studies, there are several other research papers on disaster-related gaming (e.g., Tsuda et al., 2023 [13]; Hirose, 2015 [14]), indicating that gaming approaches for disaster prevention are becoming increasingly mainstream.

However, existing studies using gaming methods have primarily focused on government officials and residents, with very few studies targeting individuals other than government officials who are active during disasters. Ichikawa (2017) stated that integrating gaming and simulation with public health and crisis management in disaster situations could lead to further advancements [15]. On the other hand, there are no known studies discussing gaming approaches related to the provision and allocation of medical resources during disasters, indicating that this field is still in its early stages of development. Based on this, there is a growing need for new gaming methods that involve not only government officials and residents but also other disaster response organizations.

3   Method

3.1   Modeling and Abstraction

Organization Extraction. This study focuses on the hyper-acute phase of disaster response. Since this phase primarily involves life-saving efforts and medical care, we selected the organizations directly involved in these activities. The key rescue organizations include the police, fire department, and Japan Self-Defense Forces (JSDF). After rescue, transported victims receive medical treatment from dedicated medical team led by doctors. These organizations are closely interconnected, allowing for effective collaboration. When incorporating the actions of each organization into the game, we designed a system concept diagram based on Duke's philosophy [16]. Duke emphasized the creation of system overview diagrams to visually represent the overall structure of a system in the game design process. This diagram helps participants and stakeholders intuitively understand the structure and flow of the game. In addition, when mapping out the various complex activities of these organizations in the concept diagram of the system, we made efforts to simplify the process. This approach follows the ideas of Arakawa (2020), who compiled studies on analog game design and emphasized that simplifying real-world phenomena–after careful observation and analysis–can enhance the dilemma-based nature of a game [17]. Following this principle, we deliberately removed unnecessary elements and focused on extracting the critical aspects related to organizational collaboration during disasters. In reality, organizations such as the police and fire department consist of various divisions and departments, each with distinct roles. While internal communication within each organization does occur during actual disasters, this study focuses on information sharing between organizations. Therefore, the internal roles within each organization have been abstracted.

The police carry out a wide range of activities during disasters, including rescue operations, traffic control, and evacuation guidance [18]. In the case of large-scale disasters, the police from across the country gather and operate as support teams. These teams conduct rescue operations using vehicles and helicopters, manage traffic, and handle the transportation and examination of deceased individuals. They typically remain active for about a week following the disaster. Taking into account the roles of the police in disaster-affected areas, we defined the police actions in this game as rescue and search operations, traffic control, and body transportation. Furthermore, we simplified the police action flow into a structured system, as illustrated in Fig. 1.

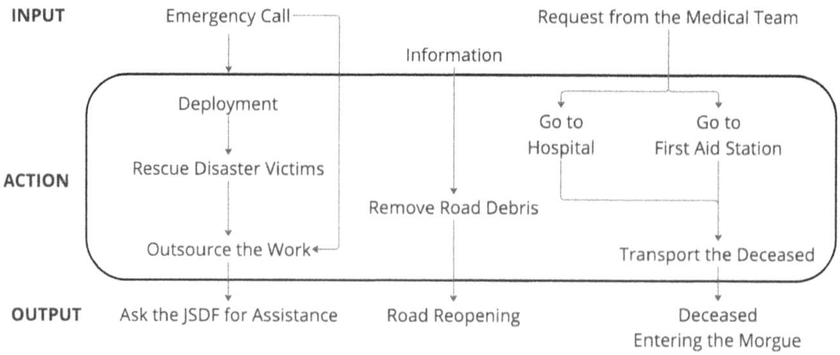

Fig. 1. System Concept Diagram of the Police.

The fire department is responsible for rescue operations and firefighting activities [19]. Rescue operations are primarily conducted based on emergency calls, following a system similar to that of the police. However, in this game, players can control ambulance movements in coordination with the medical team.

If players are unable to handle all transport operations on their own, they can request assistance from the medical team and direct ambulance actions accordingly. We structured this system as illustrated in Fig. 2.

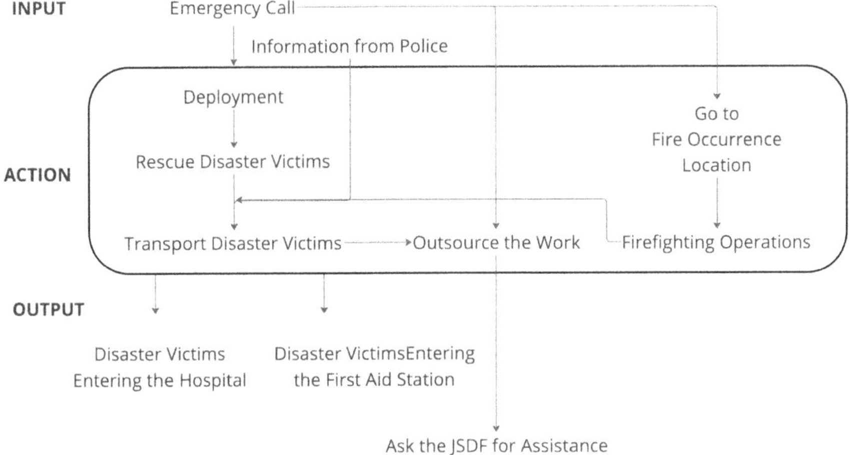

Fig. 2. System Concept Diagram of Fire Department.

The JSDF is Japan's unique defense force. However, its role extends beyond national defense, playing a crucial part in disaster response as well. During disasters, the JSDF is swiftly deployed on request from local governments. Their primary activities include rescue operations, medical support, transportation of supplies, and restoration of the infrastructure. Notably, during the Great East Japan Earthquake in 2011, which caused catastrophic damage across Japan, the JSDF carried out large-scale relief operations and contributed significantly to the recovery of affected areas. Although publicly available resources on their disaster response operations are limited, we have compiled the available information and structured it into the following simplified system [20] (Fig. 3).

The medical team is responsible for managing hospitals and assessing patients' conditions. In terms of hospital management, the medical team adjusts the distribution of patients based on hospital capacity [21]. To ensure adequate medical care for transported disaster victims, they coordinate inter-hospital transfers and arrange for patients to be transported outside the affected area if necessary. In addition, the medical team conducts triage for transported disaster victims (Fig. 4).

Triage is a method used in mass casualty situations, such as disasters, to prioritize treatment and transport based on the urgency and severity of patients' conditions. This approach ensures the effective use of limited medical resources

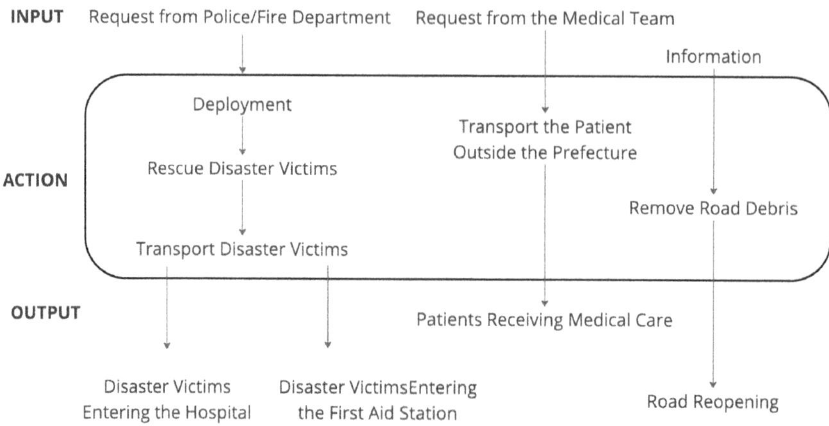

Fig. 3. System Concept Diagram of JSDF.

and maximizes the number of lives saved. In Japan, triage categorizes patients into the following four groups [22]:

- Red (Immediate treatment group): Patients in critical condition requiring immediate treatment to survive.
- Yellow (Delayed treatment group): Patients who are not in immediate danger but require urgent medical attention.
- Green (Minor injury group): Patients with minor injuries who have a low treatment priority.
- Black (Expectant group): Patients who are deceased or have no chance of survival.

Reflection of Organizational Structure. Rescue organizations operate under separate chains of command, making information sharing difficult. Since each organization conducts its own operations independently, there are instances where they may be dispatched to locations where rescue activities have already been completed. To replicate these separate command structures, we implemented a blind format in which each organization's map is hidden from the others. As a result, each organization must gather information on its own board and coordinate with other organizations to share information while constructing its own operational view.

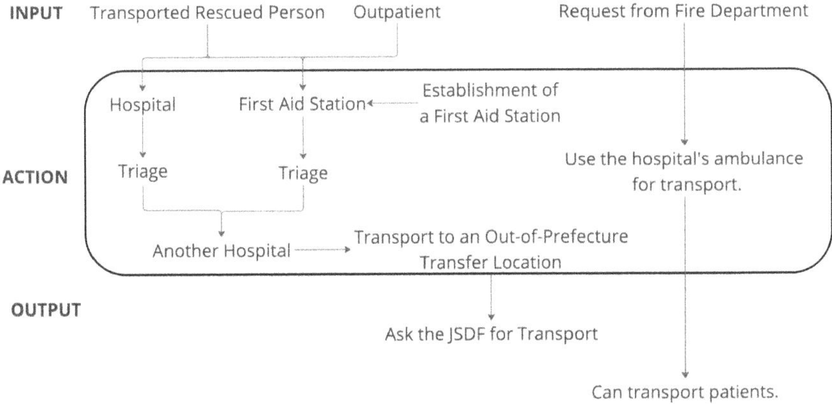

Fig. 4. System Concept Diagram of Medical Team.

3.2   Game Design

Game Overview. The primary target participants are the police, fire department, JSDF, and medical team. However, others can also play to gain a better understanding of how disaster response is conducted. Participants take on one of four roles: the police, fire department, JSDF, or medical team. The game requires at least one participant per role to be playable. Ideally, each role should have two participants, allowing for a maximum of eight players. In addition, one facilitator is required to control the flow of the game.

The game is a board game that utilizes a map, tokens, playing cards, and dice to simulate the rescue and transportation of disaster victims, road restoration, medical demand forecasting, and patient transportation. The map consists of a 4×13 grid (Fig. 5), corresponding to the arrangement of playing cards. The facilitator draws a card, and a rescue request appears at the corresponding location on the board. Players control the police, fire department, and JSDF unit tokens, moving them toward the rescue sites. After rescuing victims, players transport them to hospitals using vehicles or helicopters. The medical team performs triage on the transported victims. To execute the triage action, the medical team rolls a die and converts the rescued token into a corresponding color-coded token based on the result. The game anticipates hospital overcrowding, requiring players to balance patient distribution by directing victims to hospitals with available medical resources. The medical team can also provide instructions to the police, fire department, and JSDF units regarding transport destinations. However, there is still a risk of medical resource shortages. In such cases, the medical team can transport patients outside the prefecture (off the map) to ensure continued medical care.

Fig. 5. Map of This Game.

The medical team has a hospital board that only they can see. The hospital board indicates the maximum capacity for three hospitals: Hospital A, B, and C. Hospital A represents the primary disaster response hospital and has a higher capacity compared to the other hospitals. The medical team is responsible for managing patient numbers to ensure they do not exceed the hospital capacities. If a hospital is already at full capacity when a rescue team transports a victim there, the patient cannot be admitted. If a hospital is full and a victim is transported there, they will not receive medical treatment in time, and as a result, they will be considered deceased at the end of the turn. In addition, the medical team can establish first aid stations at any location on the map. A first aid station serves as a temporary holding area for victims and allows for triage. However, since it does not provide sufficient medical treatment, patients' conditions deteriorate once every three turns.

We have structured each turn into a 2-minute discussion phase followed by a 2-minute action phase. The game consists of 9 turns, after which it ends. During the discussion phase, organizations collaborate to plan their strategy. Then, in the action phase, players execute their planned actions within the given 2-minute time-frame. However, in real disasters, organizations must constantly adapt to unexpected situations, and they are often unable to act exactly as planned. To simulate this reality, the facilitator distributes an event card at the end of each discussion phase. As a result, players must adjust their tactics while still adhering to their initially decided strategy.

Game Objective. At the end of the game, the number of deceased victims is counted, and reducing this number serves as the primary goal for each player. In addition, while all players share the common objective of preventing casualties, each role has its own specific goal. The police have the goal of "Rescue as many requesters as possible.", meaning they must take the lead in rescue operations. The fire department has the goal of "Transport as many rescue requesters as possible.", requiring them to prioritize transporting rescued victims to hospitals.

The JSDF has the goal of "Protect as many citizens' lives as possible.", which is a broader objective that necessitates a wide-ranging perspective on rescue, transportation, and medical care. The medical team has the goal of "Provide medical care to as many disaster victims as possible.", meaning they must anticipate medical needs and ensure patients are transported to appropriate facilities.

Here, we summarize the key points of the game. Each turn begins with a discussion phase where players develop a strategy, and based on this strategy, each organization carries out its actions. However, due to the impact of event cards, players may not always be able to follow their initial plans. In such cases, each organization must reassess its strategy based on both its own objectives and the overall goal, making tactical adjustments and prioritizing necessary actions. The police and fire department primarily focus on rescue and transportation efforts, while the medical team manages patient distribution and hospital capacity. The JSDF must anticipate the overall board situation and provide support to organizations that are lacking resources. Rather than each organization simply processing information based on its own board, effective disaster response is achieved when all players communicate, collaborate, and work toward a unified direction.

Game Preparation. First, the game setup is conducted. Each player receives a board and determines the starting positions for the police, fire department, and JSDF. Players draw one playing card each, and the corresponding location becomes their starting point. Using the same method, players also place Hospitals AC and the morgue. Out-of-prefecture transport spaces are then freely placed in eight spaces adjacent to Hospital A. Next, road debris is placed. Players draw one playing card and one road debris card, then place a road debris token on the corresponding space. After that, players place rescue vehicles, helicopters, ambulances, and doctor helicopters at their respective starting positions. The number of vehicles is set according to the organization's scale:

- the Police: 2 vehicle tokens, 1 helicopter token at the police start location.
- Fire Department: 2 ambulance tokens, 1 fire truck token, 1 helicopter token at the fire department start location.
- JSDF: 2 vehicle tokens, 2 JSDF helicopter tokens at the JSDF start location.
- Medical Team: 1 ambulance token at each emergency hospital, 2 ambulance tokens at the disaster base hospital, and 2 doctor helicopter tokens.

The game setup includes randomized starting positions for units and hospitals. This is designed to enhance replayability. In addition, since actual cities have different layouts for police stations, fire stations, and hospitals, we incorporate randomness to better reflect real-world urban conditions.

Start of Turn. At the beginning of each turn, the facilitator distributes two playing cards to the police and two playing cards to the fire department. These cards represent the random and large-scale occurrence of emergency calls. Additionally, the medical team places one victim token in each of Hospitals AC, representing outpatients and victims transported by entities other than the police, fire department, or JSDF. Once all placements are completed, the 2-minute discussion phase begins. During this phase, players can share information about road debris removal and first aid station placement, synchronizing their maps (this feature does not apply in the first turn). Players can also discuss and strategize for the upcoming action phase. This phase replicates the meetings held at disaster response headquarters in real disaster scenarios.

Once the discussion phase ends, as previously mentioned, the facilitator distributes an event card. Event cards are designed to restrict players' actions. The facilitator draws one event card and hands it to the organization that must respond to it. In addition, the deck of playing cards includes two Joker cards. If the facilitator draws a Joker, additional road debris placement is carried out, simulating road collapses caused by aftershocks.

After the event card is distributed, a 2-minute action phase begins. Each organization reviews its own board and decides on its actions within the 2-minute time-frame, then executes them. During this phase, players cannot see each other's boards. However, since communication between organizations is allowed, players can adjust their tactics in real time while playing. Each player refers to the instruction diagram (Fig. 6, Fig. 7) to select and execute their actions. For example, part of Fig. 6 is the police's mission briefing paper, which describes the police's objectives, basic actions, and rescue methods. Figure 7 is the reverse side of Fig. 6, which is common to all organizations. It describes how to calculate how many people in need of rescue are present after heading to the scene of a call and how to evaluate the game. In addition, the JSDF is the key organization in this game, and advice on how to utilize them is provided in this paper.

4   Results and Discussion

We conducted a test play of this Disaster Response Headquarters Management Game with six master's students majoring in sociology from our research lab. Although they are familiar with playing board games on a regular basis, they have limited experience in disaster response or serious games. To facilitate the gameplay, we provided a 20–30 min briefing covering the background of disaster management in Japan and an explanation of the game. To help players understand the game mechanics, the first turn was conducted as a tutorial with no time limit, which took approximately 10 min. After completing the tutorial, players occasionally asked questions about the rules, such as the number of actions they could take or how to perform rescues in areas with debris. Nevertheless, they generally understood how to play.

There were moments when players acted according to our expectations, as well as instances where their actions deviated from our intended gameplay. One example of expected behavior was the active information sharing and coordinated rescue efforts between the JSDF and the fire department, as well as between the JSDF and the police. Rather than prioritizing individual rescue missions, they focused on the overall number of victims and successfully coordinated their efforts to carry out rescue operations efficiently. On the other hand,

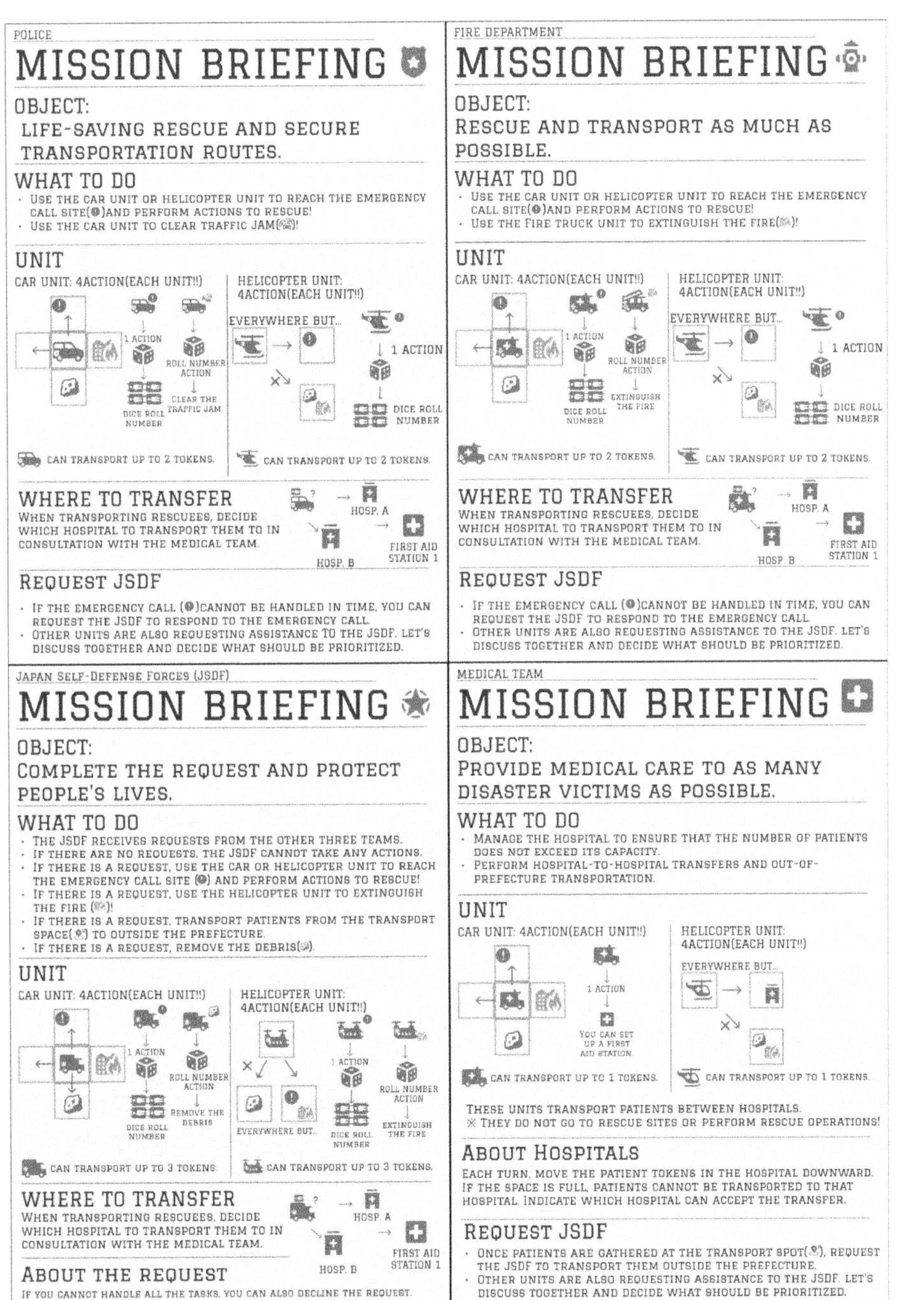

Fig. 6. Mission Briefing Papers for Each Role.

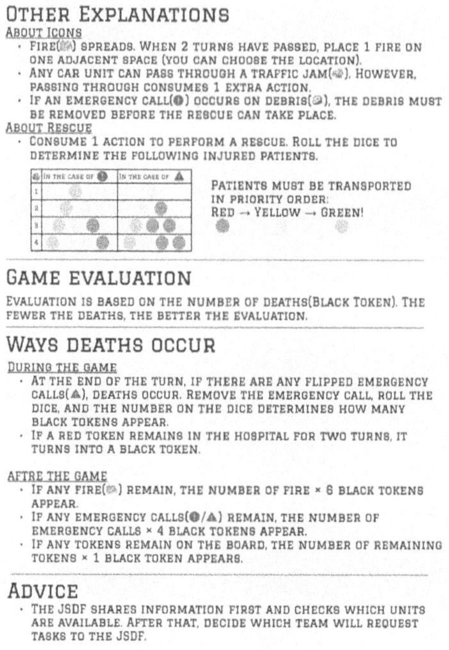

OTHER EXPLANATIONS

ABOUT ICONS
- FIRE(🔥) SPREADS. WHEN 2 TURNS HAVE PASSED, PLACE 1 FIRE ON ONE ADJACENT SPACE (YOU CAN CHOOSE THE LOCATION).
- ANY CAR UNIT CAN PASS THROUGH A TRAFFIC JAM(🚗). HOWEVER, PASSING THROUGH CONSUMES 1 EXTRA ACTION.
- IF AN EMERGENCY CALL(●) OCCURS ON DEBRIS(🪨), THE DEBRIS MUST BE REMOVED BEFORE THE RESCUE CAN TAKE PLACE.

ABOUT RESCUE
- CONSUME 1 ACTION TO PERFORM A RESCUE. ROLL THE DICE TO DETERMINE THE FOLLOWING INJURED PATIENTS.

🎲	IN THE CASE OF ●	IN THE CASE OF ▲
1		
2		
3		
4		

PATIENTS MUST BE TRANSPORTED IN PRIORITY ORDER:
RED → YELLOW → GREEN!

GAME EVALUATION

EVALUATION IS BASED ON THE NUMBER OF DEATHS(BLACK TOKEN). THE FEWER THE DEATHS, THE BETTER THE EVALUATION.

WAYS DEATHS OCCUR

DURING THE GAME
- AT THE END OF THE TURN, IF THERE ARE ANY FLIPPED EMERGENCY CALLS(▲), DEATHS OCCUR. REMOVE THE EMERGENCY CALL, ROLL THE DICE, AND THE NUMBER ON THE DICE DETERMINES HOW MANY BLACK TOKENS APPEAR.
- IF A RED TOKEN REMAINS IN THE HOSPITAL FOR TWO TURNS, IT TURNS INTO A BLACK TOKEN.

AFTRE THE GAME
- IF ANY FIRE(🔥) REMAIN, THE NUMBER OF FIRE × 6 BLACK TOKENS APPEAR.
- IF ANY EMERGENCY CALLS(●/▲) REMAIN, THE NUMBER OF EMERGENCY CALLS × 4 BLACK TOKENS APPEAR.
- IF ANY TOKENS REMAIN ON THE BOARD, THE NUMBER OF REMAINING TOKENS × 1 BLACK TOKEN APPEARS.

ADVICE
- THE JSDF SHARES INFORMATION FIRST AND CHECKS WHICH UNITS ARE AVAILABLE. AFTER THAT, DECIDE WHICH TEAM WILL REQUEST TASKS TO THE JSDF.

Fig. 7. Other explanations of This Game.

there were situations where the medical team's actions did not align with our expectations. During the 2024 Noto Peninsula Earthquake, medical team prioritized transporting patients outside the affected areas. In our game, we had also envisioned that patients would need to be transported to out-of-prefecture spaces to receive medical care. However, instead of following this approach, the medical team focused on setting up first aid stations and performing triage rather than transferring patients out of the area. It was only in the latter half of the game, when hospitals became overwhelmed with patients, that the medical team realized the need for out-of-prefecture transportation and quickly shifted their strategy to prioritize patient transfers. This behavior was in line with the intended game design. We believe that such moments of realization enhance the learning effectiveness of the game and consider them a positive sign.

After completing the tutorial, the game concluded in approximately one hour. Following the session, we collected feedback from the players, and the following comments were observed:

- The game mechanics were challenging, especially in understanding the rules and roles, but as the game progressed, it became enjoyable. Players gained a deeper appreciation of the difficulties of disaster response and learned the importance of information sharing.
- It would be beneficial to clarify the distinction between the discussion phase and the action phase to ensure a smoother game flow.

– During playing game, some players became too focused on their individual
  roles, making it difficult to grasp the overall situation or coordinate with other
  teams. This led to discrepancies in information sharing, causing necessary
  information to be miscommunicated or not conveyed properly.

From this feedback, we identified two key challenges in the game: the complexity
of the rules and the allocation of time between discussion and token movement.
On the other hand, although the number of participants in the test play was
limited, the players found the game enjoyable and successfully achieved its primary objective of information sharing. Therefore, we believe there were no major
issues in the progression of the game.

Through the gameplay sessions involving master's students, these objectives
were generally achieved. Regarding the objective "to learn about specific disaster
response actions during the hyper-acute phase," we believe this was sufficiently
accomplished through gameplay. Understanding and participating in the complex activities involved in disaster response directly contributes to learning about
those activities.

Let us now reflect on the objectives of this game. The goals are as follows:

– To learn about specific disaster response actions during the hyper-acute phase
– To enable smooth disaster response by placing participants in the roles of
  different organizations
– To let the players notice the importance of inter-organizational collaboration

As for "to enable smooth disaster response by placing participants in the
roles of different organizations," this was achieved through active communication
among the students in their respective roles. Furthermore, their collective actions
prioritized the rescue of affected individuals as a whole, indicating that the goal
"to let the players notice the importance of inter-organizational collaboration"
was also fulfilled. Therefore, this game has demonstrated its usefulness in helping
players recognize the importance of coordination in disaster response.

On the other hand, several issues related to the complexity of the game's
rules were identified:

– Players must acquire knowledge from scratch on "disaster response," a topic
  with which they typically have little familiarity
– Each role has significantly different actions and responsibilities.
– Players must understand the actions of other roles in order to determine their
  own.

As a result, even though roles were intended to be separated, players effectively needed to remember the actions of all roles, which may have placed a
cognitive burden on them. Therefore, when developing similar disaster response
games, it is necessary to simplify the game system by reducing the number of
available actions and minimizing role-specific rules.

5 Conclusion

In this study, we developed the Disaster Response Headquarters Management Game. The primary objective is to help players learn the importance of information sharing and inter-organizational coordination during the hyper-acute phase of disaster response. In this game, players take on the roles of the police, fire department, JSDF, and medical team, simulating actual disaster response operations. We aimed to incorporate key elements of disaster response while simplifying gameplay to ensure accessibility. Additionally, by introducing event cards, we were able to create unpredictable situations, effectively replicating the dynamics of real-life disaster response. The game also successfully reproduced the decision-making dilemmas faced in disaster management. In particular, the blind format and time constraints on information sharing accurately reflected the challenges of coordination between different chains of command in actual disaster scenarios.

Through the game, participants were able to learn the importance of information sharing, as well as the challenges and significance of decision-making under constrained conditions. However, some players exhibited behaviors that deviated from actual disaster response scenarios. Therefore, there is room for further refinement in balancing game rules with players' autonomy in decision-making to ensure a more accurate representation of real disaster response operations.

In the future, this game has the potential to be widely utilized as a training tool for disaster response. By incorporating it into the training of disaster response personnel, it is expected to enhance their understanding of inter-organizational coordination and decision-making dynamics. To achieve this, we plan to conduct demonstration experiments in collaboration with local governments and disaster prevention agencies, gathering feedback for further improvements. In addition, it is necessary to present the results quantitatively, such as through surveys.

Acknowledgments. The content of this paper is part of the SIP (Cross-ministerial Strategic Innovation Promotion Program) "Development of a Smart Disaster Prevention Network" (Administrator: National Research Institute for Earth Science and Disaster Resilience).

References

1. Fire and Disaster Management Agency. https://www.fdma.go.jp/publication/ugoki/items/rei_0404_04.pdf?utm_source=chatgpt.com. Accessed 13 May 2025
2. Cabinet Office. https://www.bousai.go.jp/jishin/nankai/taio_wg/pdf/h290825bessatsu.pdf. Accessed 13 May 2025
3. Yoshihara, K.: Emergency medicine; emergency medical system and disaster medicine. The Medical Society of Toho University **66**(1), 32–36 (2019). https://doi.org/10.14994/tohoigaku.2019-015

4. Nakazawa, T.: Addressing natural disasters with the capabilities of the SDF: achieving seamless responses by the relevant organizations. NIDS J. Defense Secur. **18**(1), 75–108 (2015)
5. Iizuka, T.: The study of disaster prevention training targeting local civil servants. Law Politics Rev. **77**, 115–137 (2021). https://doi.org/10.20691/kanhouseiken.7.0_115
6. Hayashi, S.: Learn about shelter management through games - Efforts to spread awareness of HUG developed in Shizuoka Prefecture/Let's learn about shelter management with HUG! - From the dissemination and awareness-raising activities of HUG, an evacuation center management game in Shizuoka Prefecture. Journal of Public Health Nurses, vol. 68, No.10, pp. 835–837, 874–879 (2012). https://doi.org/10.11477/mf.1664101984
7. Komura,T., Hirano,S.: Diagram Training DIG (Disaster Imagination Game). Institute if Social Safety Science, 136–139 (1997)
8. Morimoto, F., Yoshioka, T., Iwai, N.: Local disaster drills using evacuation center management games. J. Japanese Soc. Emergency Med. **20**(1), 36–38 (2017). https://doi.org/10.11240/jsem.20.36
9. Tanigawa, H., Ueta, I., Morita, T.: Results of In-Hospital Educational Training for Disaster Mitigation using Disaster Imagination Games **95**, 29–36 (2018). https://doi.org/10.24596/tokusimabunriu.95.0_29
10. Saito, C., Yamaga, K., Sasaki, I., Iisawa, K.: A board game for sharing the disaster information aimed at cooperation of residents' associations. AIJ J. Technol. Des. **18**(38), 303–308 (2012). https://doi.org/10.3130/aijt.18.303
11. Fujioka, M., Kaji, H., Mihara, J.: Development of Game Software for Earthquake Disaster Education on Portable Game Terminal Bases and Its Application to Educational Exercise. **14**, 133–139 (2011). https://doi.org/10.11314/jisss.14.133
12. Kurose, T.: Development of the Gaming Simulation Through the Usage of The Digital Archives of The 2016 Kumamoto Earthquake. Studies in simulation and gaming **30**(1), 55–63 (2020). https://doi.org/10.32165/jasag.30.1_55
13. Tsuda, M., Yaguchi, T.: A proposal of "inclusive disaster preparedness game" and its ripple effect. AIJ J. Technol. Des. **29**(71), 543–548 (2023). https://doi.org/10.3130/aijt.29.543
14. Hirose, Y.: Development of a risk communication game of common understanding for disaster waste disposal between administration and residents. Stud. Simul. Gaming **25**(1), 3–10 (2017). https://doi.org/10.32165/jasag.25.1_3
15. Ichikawa, M.: Editorial: simulation & gaming in health and medical service. Stud. Simulation Gaming **26**(2), 41 (2017). https://doi.org/10.32165/jasag.26.2_41
16. Richard D.Duke., Nakamura, M., Ichikawa, A.: Gaming Simulation: Dialogue with the Future. ASCII, Japan (2001)
17. Arakawa, A.: The availability of education through analog game design in universities. Studies in Simulation and Gaming **30**(2), 84–94 (2020). https://doi.org/10.32165/jasag.30.2_84
18. National Police Agency. https://www.npa.go.jp/hakusyo/h24/honbun/pdf/05_tokushu.pdf. Accessed 13 May 2025
19. Murota, T.: The National Crisis Disasters and Emergency Fire Response Teams (Enhancing the Disaster Response Capabilities of Emergency Fire Response Teams). 1st edn. Kindaishobo, Japan (2022)
20. J-Rescue Editorial Department.:Document: The Great East Japan Earthquake – On the Frontlines of Rescue. 1st edn. Ikaros Publications, Japan (2014)

21. Ministry of Health, Labour and Welfare. https://www.mhlw.go.jp/stf/shingi/2r9852000001tefj-att/2r9852000001tev6.pdf. Accessed 13 May 2025
22. University hospital Medical Information Network (UMIN) Center. https://plaza.umin.ac.jp/~GHDNet/98/gc29kose.html?utm_source=chatgpt.com. Accessed 13 May 2025

Using Game-Based Research Approaches to Gauge Children's Perceptions: Insights from a Food Education Project

Nicolás Méndez Barreto[1,2](✉) [iD], Lamprini Chartofylaka[2] [iD], Aurélie Maurice[2] [iD], Nicolas Darcel[1] [iD], and Rallou Thomopoulos[3] [iD]

[1] Université Paris-Saclay, Physiologie de la Nutrition et du Comportement Alimentaire, UMR 0914, Palaiseau, France
`nicolas.mendezbarreto@univ-paris13.fr`
[2] Université Sorbonne Paris Nord, Laboratoire Educations et Promotion de la Santé, UR 3412, F-93430 Villetaneuse, France
[3] INRAE - IATE Joint Research Unit, UMR 1208, Montpellier, France

Abstract. This paper provides insight into how gaming can be used to explore the children's experience of food, and to envision possible future transitions in their eating habits. The case study presented is part of the ERMES project, an interdisciplinary initiative funded by the French National Research Agency (ANR-23-CE36-0009), focused on primary school children aged 9–10 in the Île-de-France region. The project aims to develop scientific understanding on how children engage with and relay "food messages" in their daily lives, and how these messages influence their attitudes and eating habits. The paper presents and discusses the use of research game-based workshops to capture children's attitudes, preferences, and understanding of nutrition in a playful and engaging manner. These activities not only facilitate data collection but also foster trust and active participation among children. Additionally, the case study highlights the challenges of conducting action-oriented research in school settings, including minimizing researcher influence and addressing scientific bias. Findings suggest that game-based approaches are effective in exploring complex topics like sustainable eating, offering insights into children's peer culture and food-related behaviors. However, the study emphasizes that game-based activities should complement, rather than replace, traditional methods such as observations and surveys. By integrating games into research, the study provides a novel framework for understanding children's food perceptions, contributing to the development of effective food education strategies.

Keywords: Food Education · School-Food · Children's Perception · Game-Based Research

1 Introduction

Sustainability in nutrition is a complex and challenging field to navigate, particularly when it comes to understanding how individuals perceive, approach, and practice (healthy) eating habits [13]. This complexity becomes even more pronounced when we

© The Author(s) 2026
F. Trautwein et al. (Eds.): ISAGA 2025, LNCS 16439, pp. 297–309, 2026.
https://doi.org/10.1007/978-3-032-20129-4_20

focus on children, whose attitudes and behaviors around food are still in development [5, 27]. Recognizing the need for effective approaches to explore children's understanding of nutrition, this "best practice" paper presents the research facilitation methodology of a qualitative study examining children's perceptions, attitudes, and habits related to food, using game-based activities as an innovative strategy to support data collection and encourage active participation in conversations about their understanding of these concepts.

The elements presented in this paper are drawn from the "ERMES – Children as Recipients and Messengers for Health Education" project (*Enfants Récepteurs et Messagers pour l'Éducation à la Santé*). ERMES is an ongoing interdisciplinary research project funded by the French National Research Agency (ANR-23-CE36-0009). The project fosters a multidisciplinary dialogue by bringing together experts from various fields, including Sociology, Educational Sciences, Informatics, and Economics [25]. ERMES aims to better understand the trajectories of "food messages"—a term we define below—particularly how school children engage with them in their daily lives, how children themselves contribute to relaying them to their entourage, and their impact on attitudes and eating habits.

This paper provides insight into how gaming can be used to explore the children's experience with food, and to envision possible future transitions in their eating habits. Following this introduction, the paper is structured as follows: Sect. 2 provides an overview of the case study, including details on the target audience, location, timeline, objectives, and the tools used in the research. It also highlights some of the key challenges faced during the study, particularly those related to the action-oriented research approach and the use of gaming. Section 3 outlines the design of the research methodology and describes the specific game-based activities that were implemented. Finally, Sect. 4 discusses best practices, drawing on insights from both the case study and relevant literature, and addresses the challenges identified throughout the research process.

2 Case Study Context

2.1 Background

The case study presented is conducted within school settings in France, where canteens play a crucial role in meeting children's nutritional needs [3]. Children typically spend nearly half of their day at school, with most eating there twice a day, for lunch and a snack. Beyond simply addressing nutrition, school meals also influence food choices, shape social norms, and promote an understanding of sustainable eating practices [3]. Recent French policies that encourage organic, quality-labeled products, waste reduction, and vegetarian options emphasize the growing connection between nutrition, sustainability, and education. The school setting provides the advantage of observing how children interact with structured meal environments and school policies, as well as how "peer culture" [10] influences their food-related behaviors, offering valuable insights into the impact of social and institutional factors on dietary habits.

This study is conducted during the school year 2024–2025, across multiple primary schools within the Île-de-France region (Paris and Seine-Saint-Denis). It focuses on *CM1* classes (children aged 9–10), representing a diverse range of socio-economic backgrounds. Data collection takes place throughout the school year and involves observations in canteens, classrooms, and courtyards. The goal of this study is to categorize different types of food-related messages (e.g. informational, normative) and the forms or media through which they are delivered to children (e.g. written, oral, or digital). A food message is defined as any oral or written information related to food, originating from media (e.g. a commercial) or real-life situations (e.g. an event in the schoolyard). These messages may take the form of recommendations, such as "you should eat fruit, it's good for your health," or simple expressions of preference or dislike. They encompass all types of information, advice, or influences related to nutrition, particularly within the school environment. This study aims at exploring their understanding of what defines "good" or "bad" food, the sources of these messages (parents, media, peers.), and specific phrases they recognize or agree/disagree with [1, 24].

2.2 Problem Statement

Observing children in natural settings, such as their schools, is a prolonged task, yet it is essential for understanding their thought patterns regarding food-related issues [23]. This methodological approach raises specific challenges, such as the need for appropriate and intuitive tools to gather children's perceptions, ensuring the right posture to avoid influencing their responses while fostering an atmosphere of trust [14], and addressing privacy concerns. More specifically, this "best practice" paper raises three fundamental research questions:

- RQ1. How can an adult researcher access the ways in which children talk about food?
- RQ2. Can games help to address a complex topic with children?
- RQ3. What challenges regarding scientific bias do we face?

These three Research Questions (RQ) can be detailed as follows:

RQ1. To our knowledge, few researchers have studied the circulation of oral or written information related to food in a school setting. Nevertheless, in Maurice's study [22] on teens' perception and uses of nutritional recommendations, two key discoveries emerged: 1. It is difficult for adolescents to explain why it is "good" to eat fruits or vegetables daily. 2. Even though they don't fully understand them, adolescents use nutritional messages differently based on their understanding of the social interaction they are in. For example, seeking the teacher's approval during a formal lesson reciting food messages like a lesson. This variation of discourses through different contexts and correspondents has also been observed in children [20]. Subsequently, to access and study children's peer culture, we have to be particularly cautious with the ways children perceive us: How can we minimize our influence in children's discourses? How do we engage with them? What language do we use? When and where is our presence pertinent? What is our role as adults in a school setting? When one of the child-participants asks us to play a game with them, do we accept?

RQ2. School-based food education programs often show limited results due to their occasional and top-down nature [16]. In fact, nutrition education schemes are often based on the transmission of educational messages from adults to children. An issue is thus the determination of non-hierarchical education schemes. An option is the use of gaming, while insight into its format and impacts is an ongoing research question [18]. A growing body of research highlights the role of games in nutrition education and behavioural change among children. Serious games and gamification have been shown to enhance learning outcomes and promote healthier dietary habits [2, 8]. In the digital era, educational games come in various formats, including online simulations (ie. *Epidaure Market* [17]), computer games (Pickit!, Cookit! [9]), while physical activities remain a viable option to engage young learners. For instance, the physical game Mestre Chef [15] introduces macronutrient calculation through an engaging, TV-show-inspired format. Beyond education, games serve as research tools by enabling real-time data collection and analysis. Learning analytics track player interactions to assess cognitive and behavioural responses [4], while game-based assessments offer insights into learners' progress and engagement [34]. Does this dual function positions gaming as a powerful approach for both advancing nutrition education and conducting empirical research on dietary behaviours in children?

RQ3. Answering RQ1 and RQ2 demanded a great reflexive effort in terms of research methodology, mostly around the researcher's posture, interactions and attitudes towards children and school personnel. During our observations, we were frequently invited by children to participate in their games. These were excellent opportunities to achieve mutual understanding, according to G.H. Mead's [26] philosophy of action. While taking part in children's activities is a widely accepted research method [7], it is not a common practice to detail how the relationships between participants and researchers are managed [28]. Absence of clarity in methodology construction and application and lack of data surrounding researchers and participants social positions can result in a strong research bias. If games can be useful to enter children's worlds, how can we be aware of the influence we are exercising in our field of research?

Accessing and understanding children's peer culture is undeniably challenging. The discussions briefly presented here have led to the development of several "good practices" that will be further explored in this paper. Before delving into this discussion, the detailed research design is presented to the following questions.

3   Research Design and Methodology

According to the points discussed above, in our case study, we chose to explore various aspects of participants' relationships with their eating habits and discourses, not only through the methodologies outlined in the ERMES project, such as participant observations [23], but also by exploring the dynamics of game-based research workshops as instruments for data collection. The schedule of activities is presented in Fig. 1.

Here, we present in more detail and discuss the first workshop, which took place in October 2024. Two researchers from the ERMES team introduced themselves to all four classes through the ***"Exquisite Food Portraits"*** workshop. This 45-minute/1-hour workshop involved dividing the children into groups of three, with each group tasked with filling in drawings of human-like figures (Fig. 2) with various food illustrations.

Each body part of the figure corresponds to a different question:

Participant observation

October 2024	February 2025	April 2025	June 2025
Workshop 1 : Exquisite food-portraits	Workshop 2 : Your Canteen! Your Rules	Focus Groups	Biographical interviews Surveys "food messages"

Fig. 1. Overview of data collection methods including game-based research workshops

Fig. 2. Human-like figure used for "Exquisite Food Portrait" workshop

- Head (referring to norms, rules, and rational behaviours): For this part, we asked the children to draw a head with foods that are important for "growing strong".
- Body/Heart (referring to emotions, feelings, tastes, and pleasures): For this part, we asked the children to fill the body with their favourite foods or foods they dislike.
- Feet (referring to social grounding and real-life practices): For this part, we asked the children to draw feet with the foods they usually have for breakfast.

We describe our workshops as "game-based" because they integrate core elements of play that foster imaginative interaction and collaborative engagement, key to our research methodology. While not following traditional game structures (e.g., competition, win/lose conditions), they incorporate game mechanics such as goal-setting (assigning foods to body parts), symbolic role-play (imagining what makes a body strong or happy), and co-creation (working in groups to build a shared food portrait). These elements encourage children to approach the activity not as a test, but as a space for personal expression.

Following Sanchez and Romero [30], we understand games not solely by formal rules, but by the player's subjective involvement—what matters is whether the activity is experienced as play. The non-evaluative setting and open-ended task design in our workshop created the conditions for ludic engagement, allowing children to explore personal and cultural meanings of food in ways that were emotionally resonant, creative, and socially co-constructed. This activity served two purposes: it introduced the presence of researchers in the classroom, helping students become familiar with their presence, while also offering a playful and indirect way to gather initial insights into students' perceptions of food. By creating a space for personal expression, the workshop facilitated the collection of rich, qualitative data in a natural and organic manner.

4 Best Practice Discussion

Following the presentation of our game-based research activity, this section discusses our overall methodological approach, returning to our initial questions.

4.1 RQ1. How Can an Adult Researcher Access the Ways in Which Children Talk About Food? Can Games Help? About Participant Observation and Researchers' Positioning

The adult ethnographer that wants to engage in children's games, activities or conversations faces numerous difficulties. First, participant observation in a school setting is only possible thanks to collective work between the participants, the ethnographer and the institutional agents in charge of the school's functioning. To carry out our observations we had to explain who we were, what we wanted to do and what we expected. Logically we had to discuss these things with the children-participants, but we also put a lot of energy and thought into our relationships with schoolteachers and school employees. A crucial point of discussion was the extent of our authority and our legitimacy as adults being present in a school setting. To consider ourselves as responsible for children's "good behavior" or being excessively vigilant of their safety prevents the development of collective action that can allow for mutual comprehension [19]. On numerous occasions we had to explain to children and to the school personnel that we were not there to enforce the school's discipline. In some cases, this means engaging, along with children, in illicit activities (e.g. participating in candy exchanges within school walls or playing with food while we were sitting at the canteen tables).

Being part of a peer-group within a school classroom means for us to spend most of the day with the participants of the study; to share the numerous spaces they navigate during a typical school day. Concretely, we are present, and we engage with the children-participants: In the classroom, in the halls, in the schoolyard or in the school's canteen.

We learned to play with them, but we also learned to eat with them, to work with them, we even learned to joke with them while they joked with us (always between boundaries of complicity and mutual respect). We also discovered that following them in short school trips to museums or cinemas outside of school allowed us to deepen our understanding of in-class relations and interactions. Additionally, during these trips we could grasp their perception of the world outside of school: their "special places" in the neighborhood, their neighbors, their friends, their go-to food-joints, etc. Being with them outside of school meant to share significant moments that deepened not only our scientific comprehension of the situations we observed, it also helps us to remember that through our work we create an emotional and social bond with the participants. This bond is fundamental for our research, it allows us to enter the field, to engage with participants, to understand their perspectives and, most importantly, it is the main reason why participants accept talking to us or why they initiate the interactions themselves.

4.2 RQ2. Gamifying Research: How to Address a Complex Topic with Children?

Discussing complex health-related topics with children like sustainable eating, a topic which is influenced by numerous individual and societal factors [33], can be a challenging task. Incorporating game-based learning seems like an effective approach, as it is particularly valued among Generation Alpha, the target group of our current study. Research consistently shows that game-based learning boosts children's motivation, enhances their performance, and increases their engagement in the learning process [12]. Here, we would like to highlight some good-practices that we discovered through our first game-based activity with the children: The Exquisite Food-Portraits.

This workshop's first objective was to establish good bases for our relation with the student-participants. Because it was our first time encountering the children, we wanted to propose an activity they were already familiar with. After some brief discussions with the class's teachers, we realized that they often used personification as a pedagogical tool with the classes participating in our study. As a method, drawing is both playful and powerful, offering students a unique way to use visual expression as a symbolic "language" to convey ideas, concepts, and complex phenomena [6]. According to Sondergaard and Reventlow [32], drawing not only brings thoughts and emotions to life but also nurtures a sense of "community" between the child and the researcher—an essential bond in research with pupils. In other words, drawing-based activities could also give us an insight into children's perception of the food they eat and the recommendations regarding the food habits they remember. In consequence, if the drawing was structured in different parts, each part referring to an abstract idea associated with food, we could gather more diverse information around children's perception of food. Following the personification idea, it was decided to present a human-like figure separated in three parts, each part making reference to a food-related subject.

The workshop proposed to the participants was ultimately complex in its structure and demanded sustained attention from the participants for a long period of time (45 min to 1 h). To make the activity more dynamic and engaging, drawings were collective. Children were separated into trios, each participant had to draw a section of the human-like figure, fold it (in order to hide their drawing) and, finally, pass it to the participant to their left. This procedure allowed us to not only encourage participant interactions during the workshop but to also give the activity a less demanding rhythm. Instead of one 45 min to 1 h drawing session we had three 10-minute drawing sessions with in-between resting time.

However, we were still facing the problem of participant comprehension to a complex activity. To address this issue, we decided to introduce the activity by giving an example of a portrait in real time. In a short time, with suggestions from the teachers and the students, we made a collective portrait illustrating what was expected at the end of the activity (Fig. 3).

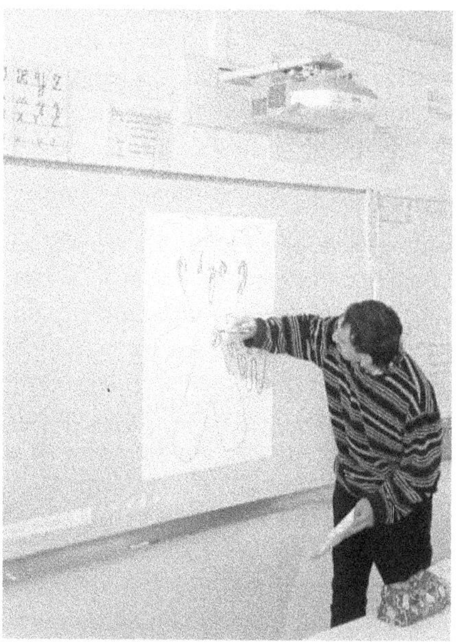

Fig. 3. Explaining the activity

The resulting drawings (Figs. 4, 5, 6) were very appreciated by the children and by the teachers. In one of the classrooms, the participants used these portraits to mark and decorate their assigned school-bag spot.

In addition, these portraits gave us precious information about the children's food habits, food preferences and their knowledge regarding nutritional recommendations. Due to lack of control over potential bias during the experimentation, the information provided by this workshop serves no scientific use. However, it helped us improve our participant observation grid and the focus of the following research-workshops. Although not suitable for formal analysis, the "exquisite food-portrait" game became a crucial point in our research and allowed us to forge the basis of future questioning.

Figs. 4. Three Resulting Food Portraits

4.3 RQ3. What Challenges Regarding Scientific Bias Do We Face? on Researcher's Neutrality and Objectivity

During the planning phase of our methodology, we encountered many approaches concerning the place of an adult researcher working with children. First, we discovered Isabelle Danic, Julie Delalande and Patrick Rayou's [29] perspective. These authors strongly encourage the researcher to refuse engagement in children's activities or games. Even though the ethnographer shares a space with the children-participants, they engage in activities only as a witness or as an assistant, "he rarely takes part in children's games, he avoids (…) introducing himself in children's stories, and by doing so, avoids determining who is right or wrong. By doing otherwise, he would be adopting a point of view in the observed situation, thus losing the neutrality he desires" (p. 117). To maintain researcher neutrality, we had to make significant concessions. It meant hiding our status and our interests from children. It also meant that we were not going to be able to ask children what they think about food in school, thus preventing us from accessing the variety of reasons, symbols or uses they associate with food. Moreover, the reward summoned by this sacrifice wasn't interesting. As Lignier [19] points out in his criticism of Danic, Delalande and Rayou's recommendation, this non-participant ethnographic method defends the "illusion" of a "truth" or an "essence" behind children's activities and discourses. By refusing to engage with children, and maintaining a "neutral" posture, the ethnographer could then access this "truth" that escapes the understanding of the subjects they observe.

In order to hear children talk about food in school we had to ask them about their food, and then ask them again: What do they think of it? Why do they eat it? What memories does this ingredient evoke? Why is this plate disgusting and yesterdays was delicious? Did they read this week's canteen menu? Did you pay attention to the food-related information available? etc. But, by doing so, we were accused by some of our colleagues of exercising excessive influence in our field-work, educating the children and forging our own results. To face this dilemma, we decided to take inspiration from old works in Anglo-Saxon sociology [11, 21] that the "neutrality-oriented" approach completely ignored. In this perspective, interacting and engaging with the participants under study is not a scientific bias but an important research tool that allows for a deeper understanding of children's peer culture and the social dynamics through which they actively contribute in cultural production and change.

However, adopting this participant approach meant paying particular attention to our impact in the field and producing data around this question. In this optic, the trial-and-error approach in our research becomes a fundamental point in our methodology and documenting it becomes one of the main good practices we would like to share. It would be disingenuous to claim that our immersion within the participant group unfolded seamlessly, without any social missteps or moments of discomfort. On numerous occasions we acted in ways that disrupted our engagement with the participants.

An illustrative incident occurred in October 2024, the day following a football match between two prominent teams of the Spanish league. During recess, one of our researchers was approached by Lisa-Marie, a child participant, who informed him that she no longer wished to engage with him for the remainder of the observation period. Surprised, the researcher inquired about her reasoning. Lisa-Marie explained that she had seen him singing a victory song in support of the winning team alongside another participant. Given that the majority of children at the school—including Lisa-Marie—were supporters of the defeated team, this act was perceived as a betrayal. Not fully grasping the depth of her sentiment, the researcher laughed and told her: "it's just a game, it is not that important". However, Lisa-Marie did not share his amusement. She walked away and refused to talk to him for several hours. When the researcher later apologized for not taking her seriously, she replied: "No, I don't accept your apology. You are against me now. Go away!".

Lisa-Marie's strong reaction helped us understand how important being part of a group is for some participants. By laughing and minimizing the importance of the subject, the researcher underestimated the importance of peer groups in daily interactions and the negotiation skills children employ to maintain group cohesion, even "if we don't support the same team". Documenting such "interactional errors" [21] allows us to understand how our own incorporated perceptions find their way into our fieldwork; how little do we know about being a child at primary school. However, through reflection and dialogue, such incidents can inform new approaches to repairing and understanding social exchanges within the research context.

5 Conclusion

While game-based activities can effectively complement traditional data collection methods, they cannot fully replace techniques such as observational studies or surveys. On the one hand, observations, as a direct form of interaction, provide valuable insights into children's behaviors and attitudes towards food [2]. However, observing all children in real-time and capturing the "food messages" they exchange with peers or adults in the school environment—such as teachers or extracurricular activity facilitators—presents a significant challenge for researchers. This challenge is particularly pronounced in crowded, in situ settings like the school canteen, a place where food-related discussions naturally emerge, but where researchers cannot observe the entire population. On the other hand, children's eating behaviors and food choices are influenced by a variety of external factors, such as parental guidance, socio-economic conditions, and peer interactions [31]. These elements play a critical role in shaping children's nutritional attitudes and cannot be fully addressed through game-based activities alone. The insights gathered from the presented workshop will guide the focus of subsequent sessions, ensuring that the most relevant topics are addressed. This will be particularly valuable in refining data collection instruments for the upcoming focus groups, biographical interviews, and surveys with both children and their parents, scheduled for the coming months. Additionally, post-workshop interviews (for example the "draw-and-tell" interviews proposed in the work of Wright-Pedersen et al. [35] could be organized to further enrich the data collection process.

In conclusion, by incorporating game-based activities, an alternative framework for data collection is established—one that creates an engaging space for children to express their thoughts and experiences. The deliberate choice of physical, non-digital games proved to be a valuable methodological strategy, fostering trust and proximity between researchers and participants, while enhancing group cohesion during activities that explore complex issues. However, there is not enough scientific evidence allowing us to conclude that game-based methodologies are in fact more efficient in facilitating children's expression than other methods. Nonetheless, current scientific evidence remains insufficient to determine whether game-based methodologies are more effective than traditional approaches in facilitating children's expression. Further comparative research between game-based and more conventional methods is encouraged.

Acknowledgments. This study was funded by the French National Research Agency within the framework of ERMES - *Enfants Récepteurs et Messagers pour l'Education à la Santé* project (Children as Receptors and Messengers for Health Education, ANR-23-CE36-0009).

Disclosure of Interests. The authors have no competing interests to declare that are relevant to the content of this article.

References

1. Abou Jaoudé, L., Charrier, J., Darcel, N., Maurice, A., Perrin, L., Thomopoulos, R.: Un état des lieux des messages alimentaires à destination des enfants, p. 138 (2022)
2. Adaji, I.: Serious games for healthy nutrition. a systematic literature review. Int. J. Serious Games **9**, 3–16 (2022). https://doi.org/10.17083/ijsg.v9i1.466
3. Avallone, S., Giner, C., Nicklaus, S., Darmon, N.: School Meals Case Study: France. Research Consortium for School Health and Nutrition (2023)
4. Banihashem, S.K., Dehghanzadeh, H., Clark, D., Noroozi, O., Biemans, H.J.A.: Learning analytics for online game-based learning: a systematic literature review. Behav. Inf. Technol. **43**, 2689–2716 (2024). https://doi.org/10.1080/0144929X.2023.2255301
5. Birch, L., Savage, J.S., Ventura, A.: Influences on the development of children's eating behaviours: from infancy to adolescence. Can. J. Diet. Pract. Res. **68**, s1–s56 (2007)
6. Brooks, M.: Drawing as a unique mental development tool for young children: interpersonal and intrapersonal dialogues. Contemp. Issues Early Child. **6**, 80–91 (2005). https://doi.org/10.2304/ciec.2005.6.1.11
7. Christensen, P., James, A.: Research with Children: Perspectives and Practices, 2nd edn. Routledge/Taylor & Francis Group, New York, NY (2008)

8. Dias, J.D., Mekaro, M.S., Cheng Lu, J.K., Otsuka, J.L., Fonseca, L.M.M., Zem-Mascarenhas, S.H.: Serious game development as a strategy for health promotion and tackling childhood obesity. Rev. Lat. Am. Enfermagem **24**, e2759 (2016). https://doi.org/10.1590/1518-8345.1015.2759

9. Dominguez-Rodriguez, A., et al.: Serious games to teach nutrition education to children between 9 to 12 years old. Pickit! and Cookit!. In: Giokas, K., Bokor, L., Hopfgartner, F. (eds.) eHealth 360°. LNICST, vol 181, pp. 143–147. Springer, Cham (2017). https://doi.org/10.1007/978-3-319-49655-9_19

10. Eder, D., Corsaro, W.: Children's peer cultures. Annu. Rev. Sociol. **16**, 197–220 (1990). https://doi.org/10.1146/annurev.so.16.080190.001213

11. Eder, D., Corsaro, W.: Ethnographic studies of children and youth: theoretical and ethical issues. J. Contemp. Ethnogr. **28**, 520–531 (1999). https://doi.org/10.1177/089124199129023640

12. Fernando, P.A., Premadasa, H.K.S.: Use of gamification and game-based learning in educating generation Alpha: a systematic literature review. Educ. Technol. Soc. **27** (2024). https://doi.org/10.30191/ETS.202404_27(2).RP03

13. Herrero, M., Hugas, M., Lele, U., Wirakartakusumah, A., Torero, M.: A shift to healthy and sustainable consumption patterns. In: von Braun, J., Afsana, K., Fresco, L.O., Hassan, M.H.A. (eds.) Science and Innovations for Food Systems Transformation, pp. 59–85. Springer, Cham (2023). https://doi.org/10.1007/978-3-031-15703-5_5

14. Holmes, A.G.D.: Researcher positionality - a consideration of its influence and place in qualitative research - a new researcher guide. Shanlax Int. J. Educ. **8**, 1 (2020). https://doi.org/10.34293/education.v8i4.3232

15. Inamori, P.M.D., Lellis-Santos, C.: MestreChef nutritional game: an alternative method to promote nutrition facts label reading in obesity outreach activities. Adv. Physiol. Educ. **48**, 180–185 (2024). https://doi.org/10.1152/advan.00044.2023

16. Kim, H.S., Park, J., Ma, Y., Im, M.: What are the barriers at home and school to healthy eating?: overweight/obese child and parent perspectives. J. Nurs. Res. **27**, e48 (2019). https://doi.org/10.1097/jnr.0000000000000321

17. Lecêtre, F., Marco, N., Méjean, C., Blanc, N., Cousson-Gélie, F.: Épidaure Market: développement d'un serious game sur l'alimentation durable, une intervention menée en milieu scolaire pour les collégiens. Prat. Psychol. **30**, 247–261 (2024). https://doi.org/10.1016/j.prps.2024.05.001

18. Li, Y., Chen, D., Deng, X.: The impact of digital educational games on student's motivation for learning: the mediating effect of learning engagement and the moderating effect of the digital environment. PLoS ONE **19**, e0294350 (2024). https://doi.org/10.1371/journal.pone.0294350

19. Lignier, W.: La barrière de l'âge. Conditions de l'observation participante avec des enfants: Genèses **73**, 20–36 (2009). https://doi.org/10.3917/gen.073.0020

20. Lignier, W., Pagis, J.: L'enfance de l'ordre: comment les enfants perçoivent le monde social. Seuil, Paris (2017)

21. Mandell, N.: The least-adult role in studying children. J. Contemp. Ethnogr. **16**, 433–467 (1988). https://doi.org/10.1177/0891241688164002

22. Maurice, A.: Les usages sociaux des messages nutritionnels par les adolescents. In: Lhuissier A, Depecker T (eds.) La juste mesure: Une sociologie historique des normes alimentaires. Presses universitaires François-Rabelais, Tours, pp. 317–348 (2013)

23. Maurice, A.: Les préadolescents comme ressorts des actions de santé publique: analyse d'un projet d'éducation alimentaire en collège. Université René Descartes - Paris V (2014)

24. Maurice, A., Berlin, N., Santini, G., Thomopoulos, R.: Symposium: Faire de la recherche interdisciplinaire en promotion de la santé à l'école. L'exemple du projet ERMES, Enfants Récepteurs et Messagers pour l'Éducation à la Santé (2023)

25. Maurice, A., Brière, L., Darcel, N.: Le projet " SPECIALE ": Sciences Participatives pour une Education Citoyenne à l'Alimentation à l'Ecole (2023)

26. Mead, G.H., Morris, C.W., Charles, W., Miller, D.L., Brewster, J.M., Dunham, A.M.: The Philosophy of the Act. The University of Chicago Press, Chicago, Ill (1972)

27. Osera, T., Taniguchi, N., Hashimoto, H., Kurihara, N.: The effect on children's attitudes towards food associated with their non-cognitive skills, and with the nutrition knowledge of their parents. J. Educ. Dev. Psychol. **8**, p54 (2018). https://doi.org/10.5539/jedp.v8n2p54

28. Randall, D.C.: Revisiting Mandell's "least adult" role and engaging with children's voices in research. I Request PDF (2012). https://doi.org/10.7748/nr2012.04.19.3.39.c9058

29. Rayou, P., Danic, I., Delalande, J.: Enquêter auprès d'enfants et de jeunes: objets, méthodes et terrains de recherche en sciences sociales/Isabelle Danic, Julie Delalande et Patrick Rayou. Presses universitaires de Rennes, Rennes (2006)

30. Sanchez, É., Romero, M., Vieville, T.: Apprendre en jouant. Retz (2020)

31. Scaglioni, S., De Cosmi, V., Ciappolino, V., Parazzini, F., Brambilla, P., Agostoni, C.: Factors influencing children's eating behaviours. Nutrients **10**, 706 (2018). https://doi.org/10.3390/nu10060706

32. Søndergaard, E., Reventlow, S.: Drawing as a facilitating approach when conducting research among children. Int. J. Qual. Methods **18**, 1609406918822558 (2019). https://doi.org/10.1177/1609406918822558

33. Varela, P., et al.: Bringing down barriers to children's healthy eating: a critical review of opportunities, within a complex food system. Nutr. Res. Rev. **37**, 331–351 (2024). https://doi.org/10.1017/S0954422423000203

34. Walsh, C., Bokhove, C.: Targeting data collection in games based assessment. Comput. Educ. Open **2**, 100054 (2021). https://doi.org/10.1016/j.caeo.2021.100054

35. Wright-Pedersen, S., Vidgen, H., Gallegos, D.: Children's descriptions of their involvement within everyday food practices. Appetite **200**, 107517 (2024). https://doi.org/10.1016/j.appet.2024.107517

Immersion and Intercultural Perspectives

From Potential to Practice: Applied Immersive Games in Industry

Maria Freese[1]([✉])([iD]), Xianbiao Jiang[1], and Julia Arlinghaus[2]([iD])

[1] Otto von Guericke University Magdeburg, Universitätsplatz 2, 39106 Magdeburg, Germany
`maria.freese@ovgu.de`
[2] University of St. Gallen, Dufourstr. 40a, CH-9000 St. Gallen, Switzerland

Abstract. The successful adoption of digital transformation and the need to use digital technologies in industry to maintain a competitive position requires a socio-technical perspective. The successful and sustainable implementation of such a socio-technical perspective must be accompanied by training programs for employees. Compared to conventional training, game-based approaches are a safe and cost-effective alternative with a particularly high potential. Applied games are generally considered to be a superior tool in training contexts and can increase the effectiveness of immersive technologies through interactivity, feedback, and user involvement, thus applied immersive games take advantage of both immersive technologies and applied games. Given the complex requirements of industrial training, an analysis of the current state of the art in applied immersive games in industry is essential to gain a deeper understanding of their effectiveness. A structured literature review was conducted to systematically assess existing research. The results show that applied immersive games are becoming increasingly popular in a variety of industries, particularly those characterized by hazards. This is also reflected in the main objectives of the applied immersive games, which are often used in the area of safety training. In addition, applied immersive games using VR have been particularly popular. This ensures that users can interact safely and make mistakes in a completely virtual environment without fearing negative real-world consequences. Future research should focus on the long-term effects that applied immersive games could have in industry and beyond.

Keywords: Applied Games · Immersive Technologies · Virtual Reality · Augmented Reality · Extended Reality · Industry

1 Introduction

According to [1: 1], there is "a trend in industries towards adoption of new technologies." The advantages associated with this are the optimization of processes [1], "secure[ing] a competitive advantage" [2: 31] or improving "operational automation, efficiency and maintenance, by interconnecting sensors, devices, machines, and processes, increasing data availability for automation and decision support" [3: 1]. The presence of new digital technologies places additional demands on the industry[1] [4], which must adopt a

---

[1] The term 'industry' is used here in a generic form on purpose to develop an understanding of which industries already use applied immersive games.

© The Author(s) 2026
F. Trautwein et al. (Eds.): ISAGA 2025, LNCS 16439, pp. 313–330, 2026.
https://doi.org/10.1007/978-3-032-20129-4_21

social perspective to address simultaneous challenges such as demographic change. [4] also state that the successful and sustainable implementation of such a socio-technical paradigm must be accompanied by training programs for employees. This is strengthened by the call to combine theoretical and practical knowledge in new training environments [5]. Gaming-based training programs show particularly high potential to achieve this. According to [3: 1], they are "extensively used for instructional and training purposes." In industry, training programs that make use of immersive technologies (e.g., virtual reality, VR) are being implemented. [6: 1] have considered VR-based trainings "as a safe and cost-effective training method that allows workers to be exposed to hazardous tasks with negligible actual safety risks in comparison to existing training methods." This is also confirmed by [7]. Ensuring security and safety in industrial environments is of central importance. [8] describe that industrial security-related incidents have led to substantial financial losses in recent years. Given the rapid development of immersive technologies and the growing demand for game-based applications, the question arises as to what extent applied immersive games – the combination of both applications – are used in industry. Applied immersive games, taking into account a wide range of domains and modalities, aim to use the effective dynamics of applied games and immersive technologies such as VR, augmented reality (AR) or artificial intelligence (AI), using (abstracted) models of reality, to support individuals, teams and/or organizations in pursuing different goals: promoting learning [9], aiding decision-making processes [10], or cost-efficient training [11], however, also analogue games can be immersive. The "increasing attention" has also been highlighted by [12: 252]. The importance of applied immersive games is also growing in the context of the ongoing digital transformation of industry, which involves adopting advanced digital technologies. Understanding the role of applied immersive games in this transformation is essential for assessing their potential to contribute to industrial innovation and performance improvement. All of this leads to the main research question that is addressed in this article: How are applied immersive games currently utilized in industrial contexts?

The remainder of this paper is structured as follows: The second section presents the theoretical background in terms of immersive technologies and applied games. The third section deals with the research method and its implementation. The results are presented in the fourth section. The fifth section is the discussion part. This includes interpreting the results and drawing conclusions. The final section discusses the limitations of this work and suggests ideas for future research.

2 Theoretical Background

2.1 Immersive Technologies and Their Use in Industry

Immersive technologies, such as VR, AR, or mixed reality (MR) play a central role when it comes to enhancing a user experience through immersion [13]. In doing so, they combine physical and digital or virtual components to enable new forms of experience [14]. One crucial feature of immersive technologies is their immersion. Immersion is the subjective feeling that describes an experience in a realistic and complex environment [15]. [16] have shown that there is a significant difference in user experience between viewing 3D data on a screen and exploring the self in the data immersively, navigating and interacting with the body. In addition, there are studies highlighting that immersive technologies provide a more realistic and interactive representation of the reality in a safe environment [17] and thus, help to expand the learning experience.

Research into immersive technologies increases in smart manufacturing [18]. For instance, [19] analyzed 154 publications dealing with VR applications in manufacturing. They (p. 57) state that VR is a useful technology "in achieving rapid understanding and decision-making by visualization and experience" both in product design and production. From the manufacturing industries' point of view, the aim is to maintain and improve competitiveness by combining information technologies with manufacturing. According to [19: 56], "it is now broadly recognized that it is valuable for manufacturing companies to invest in VR." [20: 8] also emphasize the increasing attention of immersive technologies in recent years, but also note that "in depth research on how such technologies can contribute to its users' perceived value has so far been limited." They (p. 9) state clearly that managers who want to implement immersive technologies in their organizations must consider the "importance of end-user experience when choosing hardware and software providers for the intended users." [21] proposed a new approach for representing digital twins of smart factory devices in the development and deployment of industrial extended reality (XR) applications. Their approach is motivated by "the context of human-centric Industry 5.0 towards the Metaverse with immersive digital landscapes to enrich the human experience on factory floors" [21: 13]. To conclude, further research into the use of immersive technologies in industry is needed. In this context, it is crucial to focus on the end user (the human factor), as this is justified by various motivations. Applied games can address this and thus function as a key enabler for a successful human-centered digital transformation in production [22].

2.2 Game-Based Applications in Industry

In the gaming industry, immersive entertainment games become more and more popular, for instance Beat Saber [23] or Pokémon Go [24]. In contrast to entertainment games, which are played for fun, applied games are used for serious purposes (e.g., [25]). [26] designed a digital game for enhancing the learning in lean manufacturing. They [26: 191] state that the gaming-based approach motivates players "to learn through trial and error." This is in line with the consideration of adaptivity in applied games, i.e., the adaptation of tasks according to the skills of the players [27, 28]. [3] developed an applied multiplayer game focused on the Internet of Things. For them, developing a multiplayer game was important to be able to achieve their learning objectives, as these scholars see the multiplayer set-up as a connecting element for social interactions. [29] developed an applied game to teach about Industry 4.0. In their research, they highlight the role of learning loops. These learning loops are created by in-game situations that are challenging but motivating at the same time and are "particularly conducive to efficient knowledge transfer" [29: 264].

To conclude, immersive technologies offer valuable possibilities for industrial applications (e.g., [18]). Applied games can increase the effectiveness of such technologies through interactivity, feedback and user involvement/social collaboration [30]. They are also seen as a superior tool to traditional methods [31] and have demonstrated multiple enhanced learning effects compared to traditional methods (e.g., [32]). According to [33: 1], "most VR training scenarios remain static and do not adapt to users." A non-gamified training making use of immersive technologies can cause low motivation and engagement of the user [34]. Also, [35: 2] stated that "Compared to a VR training without gamified elements, gamified VR training might be able to offer a better approach towards conveying the didactic content and it could simplify the interactions in training scenarios." The requirements of industrial trainings are complex. They demand effective, scalable, and cost-efficient solutions that ensure knowledge transfer and safety compliance [36]. In addition, there are high risk and safety requirements for safety trainings in hazardous industrial sectors (e.g., [37]). [38] stated that a safety training in a real construction environment is dangerous for the trainees. [39] reported that safety trainings in a real environment could consume many resources, such as portable fire extinguishers, and result in environmental pollution and increased training costs. Their research showed that a VR training can reduce costs by 68.13% in comparison to a conventional training. An important objective of safety training is that the relevant knowledge gained from experience during training is internalized by the trainees and can be applied in the real working environment according to the real circumstances. [40] claimed that knowledge transfer losses are due to the weaknesses of traditional safety training modes and learning styles. Applied immersive games have the potential to address these challenges by providing engaging, repeatable, and safe training environments. By examining the current state of the art of the usage of applied immersive games in industry, we can assess their actual impact, identify potential barriers to adoption, and derive recommendations for their effective implementation in industrial settings. The main research question is addressed through six sub-questions that collectively contribute to its comprehensive answer (see Table 1, [41]). The questions cover the topics of immersive technologies, applied games and the evaluation of applied immersive games. To be able to answer them and thus, gain a thorough understanding, a structured literature review has been conducted. This method not only highlights existing research challenges but also identifies future directions, benefiting researchers and practitioners alike.

Table 1. Overview of main research question (RQ), sub-questions (SQ) and motivation.

Research (Sub-)Questions		Motivation
RQ: How are applied immersive games currently utilized in industrial contexts?	SQ1: Which immersive technologies are used in industry as the basis for applied immersive games?	Identification of technologies including soft- and hardware
	SQ2: In which industrial sectors are applied immersive games currently being used?	Identification of relevant industrial sectors to be used for applied immersive games

(continued)

Table 1. (*continued*)

Research (Sub-)Questions		Motivation
	SQ3: What is the motivation of using immersive technologies in industry?	Identification of added value of immersive technologies from an industrial point of view
	SQ4: What are the main objectives of applied immersive games used in industry?	Identification of main objectives of applied immersive games
	SQ5: What are the target groups of applied immersive games used in industry?	Identification of relevant target groups to be considered for applied immersive games
	SQ6: Which methods can be used to measure the impact of applied immersive games in industry?	Identification of participants of evaluations studies and exploration of measurements to evaluate applied immersive games

3 Method

The research protocol can be found in Table 2. 'Scopus' and 'Web of Science' were used to identify relevant publications because of their international reputation [42]. The search string consisted of three key elements. First, as serious games are often used as a synonym for applied games [43], it was decided to include both terms in the search string. Second, as no emphasis should be made on a particular sector of industry, "industr*" was added to the search string. Third, the different forms of immersive technologies mentioned at the beginning of this publication were abbreviated or written out in full and added to the search string. Since developments in technologies should be looked at in the present case, the time span was limited to 5 years [44]. The search included English-written publications from 2020 to 2025. The data was retrieved on January 17, 2025.

This resulted in a total of 117 papers (excluding duplicates). After screening the abstracts, titles and keywords, 18 papers (conference reviews) were removed. When retrieving the full papers, a further three publications were removed due to lack of access to the full paper. The full papers of the 96 publications were then read and screened using the exclusion criteria listed in Table 3. Review papers were excluded to ensure the review focuses on original empirical findings or description of individual applications rather than secondary interpretations, allowing for a direct assessment of primary data and methods. All in all, this led to 31 full papers, which were analyzed in MAXQDA following the grounded theory methodology [46].

Table 2. Protocol of structured literature review [45].

Category	Detailed information
Data bases	Scopus, Web of Science
Search string	("Serious Gam*" OR "Applied Gam*") AND ("Industr*") AND ("VR" OR "Virtual Reality" OR "AR" OR "Augmented Reality" OR "XR" OR "Extended Reality" OR "MR" OR "Mixed Reality")
Time horizon	2020 - 2025
Initial search results	Scopus (n = 103 papers), Web of Science (n = 41 papers)
Number without duplicates	N = 117 papers
Number for full paper screening	N = 31 papers

Table 3. Overview of inclusion and exclusion criteria.

Category	Inclusion criteria	Exclusion criteria	Number of papers
Practical relevance	Relevant to immersive technologies	Not relevant to immersive technologies	10
	Relevant to industry	Not relevant to industry	30
	Relevant to applied games	Not relevant to applied games	11
Paper type	Empirical or conceptional papers	Review papers	14

4   Results

The 31 publications are from the years 2020 (n = 1), 2021 (n = 5), 2022 (n = 12), 2023 (n = 7) and 2024 (n = 6).

4.1   Use of Immersive Technologies in Applied Games Within Various Industry Sectors

Figure 1 shows that VR is the most used immersive technology for applied games in industry (71%). [47] have developed a VR-based simulator for maintenance inspection training of wheel loader for operators. Another example is a VR-based safety training for construction workers for their work at heights [48]. Besides VR, other immersive technologies are rarely used in combination with applied games in industry. [49] did research to train construction engineering students in an MR environment to acquire competencies in the correct use of sensing technologies. These technologies have been used in a wide range of different industry sectors. [50] have identified various industry sectors that are relevant for companies in terms of threats. Although the context is different, this is used as a basis for classifying the different industrial sectors. As nine out of 31 publications could be summarized under 'construction', this category was added. This is also the category in which VR is most frequently used (see Fig. 1). In some industries with hazardous working environments (e.g., construction), applied immersive games are widely used, especially for safety and operational skills training. In the mining industry, [51] proposed a VR game in which a virtual wheel loader was presented with a random set of defects, and the user had to identify the defects and repair them accordingly. [52] focused on an XR simulator to conduct experiments with container terminal operators for safety training to improve their risk awareness and avoid presence in hazardous conditions. [53] constructed a heritage building information model for further interaction in a game-based VR environment.

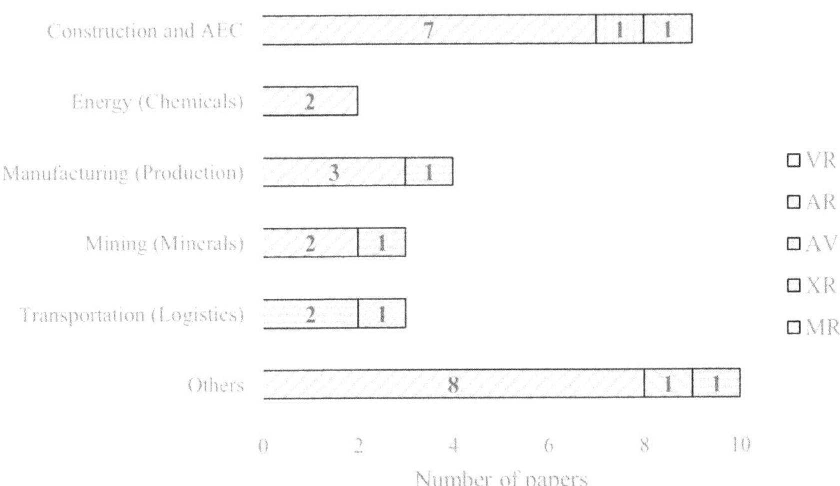

Fig. 1. Distribution of immersive technologies in applied games within various industry sectors. AV = Augmented Virtuality. Further additions to the categories of [50] are in parentheses. The category "others" includes industrial/process safety, software/IT, steel and heavy industry, automotive and education.

Immersive devices can be divided into different groups according to their features. Head-Mounted displays (HMDs) are devices that are worn on the user's head, with the display in front of the user's eyes. There are several mature immersive HMDs in the customer market, like HTC Vive [54] and Meta Quest 2 [55]. Google Cardboard [56] can also be worn on the head, but an additional smartphone is required. In addition, most smartphones with a camera can serve as AR-device. The accessory tracker serves in research as a trackable object in a virtual environment that can be installed or fitted with another target object (e.g., [57]). [57] have integrated an HTC VIVE tracker to create an AV angle grinder as a tool to further enhance immersion in AV training. Table 4 provides an overview of the hardware used as described in the analyzed articles.

Table 4. Overview of used hardware.

Category	Mentioned hardware in the papers
VR	Meta Quest 2, HTC Vive, Oculus Rift, Oculus Rift S, Pico Neo 3 Pro, Google Cardboard, VR Headset
AR	AR-Head-UP
MR	HoloLens 2
Accessories	HTC Tracker, Controller
Others	Sensor, PC, USB6008 DAQ device on ball mill, DisplayPC, Mobile Devices, Headphones

In terms of software, Unity (n = 18) and Unreal (n = 3) were the most common. Both are game engines and are often used to develop immersive applications. They integrate the XR framework, making the development of XR applications more efficient and easier.

4.2 Motivation of Using Immersive Technologies in Industry

The main motivation for using immersive technologies in the publications analyzed is to improve learning and training (see Fig. 2). [58] have mentioned that immersive technologies can simulate a safe training environment and allow mistakes to be made without real-life consequences. This is a key advantage of immersive technologies for use in safety training. Another important feature of immersive technologies is that they can facilitate the learning process by increasing motivation and engagement. This was also one of the main arguments for developing the VR application ScrumVR [59], which is used to teach IT students the Scrum methodology. In addition, compared to the high cost of building real construction in the real world, a virtual world can simulate a real environment at low(er) cost with VR [60]. [11] have developed a VR-based game for training purposes, as it can simulate the underground coal mine environment in a virtual and cost-effective way. Additional motivations for using immersive technologies include the virtual experience of products in advance, providing an immersive user experience, and not being constrained by time and space.

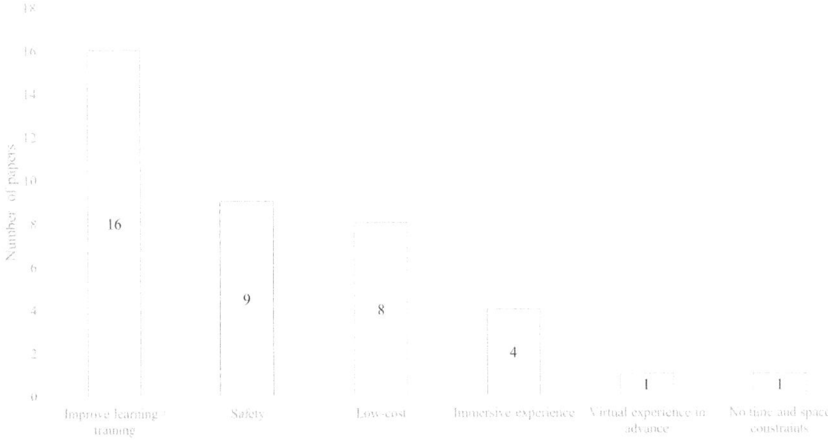

Fig. 2. Motivation to use immersive technologies. In some of the publications, several motivations were mentioned, which is why N > 31.

4.3 Main Objectives of Applied Immersive Games in Industry

The general objective of applications that have made use of applied games and immersive technologies can be summarized as follows: 15 games focused on safety training and eleven addressed knowledge and/or skill acquisition. Three applications set the objectives of the game on maintenance training (see Fig. 3). [17] have presented a 3D simulation model with training sections for filter replacements on a gas-powered plant engine model to provide safety training in a fully immersive virtual environment. Applied immersive games in industry are mainly used to complement or support conventional learning methods, but according to [61], AR head-up display systems can also be designed to attract potential customers by providing an immersive experience of products and services in advance.

4.4 Target Groups of Applied Immersive Games in Industry

Applied immersive games have been developed for different target groups. In 52% (n = 16) of the publications analyzed, the applications were developed directly for industrial workers or operators. For instance, [62] have developed a framework with two VR applications for workers in industrial risk prevention training. [63] described a 3D game environment for workers to learn about industrial safety and included different training steps, such as finding personal protection objects and handling machines properly. Students, students and engineers, students and workers (n = 11) have also often been used as a target group for the applied immersive games developed (e.g., [64]). Other target groups (n = 4) included potential customers, teachers, tourists and professionals in general.

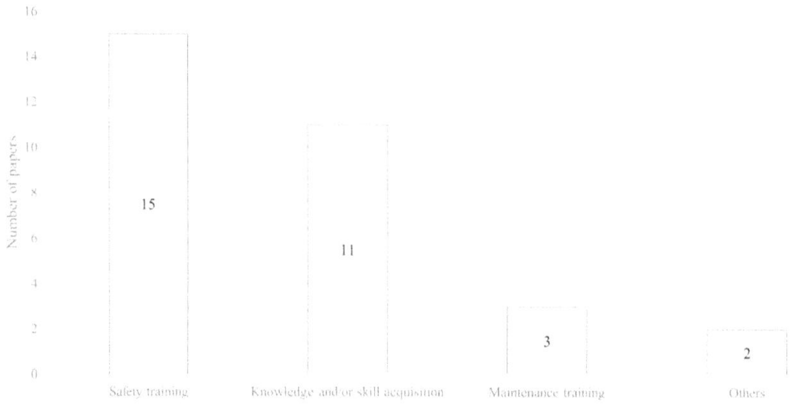

Fig. 3. Main objective of the applied games. The category "others" includes the restoration of cultural values and the attraction of customers.

4.5 Measuring the Impact of Applied Immersive Games in Industry

The publications reporting on empirical studies (n = 24) show a diverse set of participants in their evaluation studies compared to the actual target group of the corresponding applied immersive game (see Table 5). In the study by [59], the evaluation of the applied immersive game used was also done with the target group intended for the game. In detail, the game was developed to teach students knowledge about Scrum. After experiencing this, IT students completed the evaluation questionnaire. In other studies (e.g., [62]), the target group differs from the participant group of evaluation. Questionnaires (n = 18) and user performance data (n = 6) were most frequently used for evaluation purposes. [47] used two standard evaluation questionnaires: NASA-Task Load Index [65] to measure workload and the System Usability Scale [66] to assess the usability. Compared to questionnaires, the collection and analysis of user performance or machine data are also used as evaluation tools. [67] designed a ball mill as part of a digital twin system to share information with the virtual environment and collected test data, such as shaft speeds, for analysis and comparison.

5 Discussion and Contribution

In times of digital transformation and the necessity of using digital technologies in industry in order to maintain a competitive position, there is also a growing demand for game-based applications to meet the challenges of digital transformation, but also to address the general challenges of today's society. Applied games in general can increase the effectiveness of immersive technologies through interactivity, feedback and user involvement/social collaboration [30], thus applied immersive games take advantages of both immersive technologies and applied games. Research has already shown that they have advantages over traditional methods [31, 32] and are considered a superior tool in training contexts [31]. Given the complex requirements of industrial trainings (e.g., safety aspects, domain-specific knowledge, cost-effectiveness, scalability [36]),

Table 5. Overview of the participant groups in reported empirical studies and the number of publications that have referred to these groups

Participants in evaluation studies	Number of publications
Users	7
Students	5
Employees	3
Operators	2
Teachers	2
Engineers	1
Developers	1
Apprentices	1
Research assistant	1

Note. In [68], the number of participants is not specified further.

analyzing the current state of the art of the use of applied immersive games in industry is crucial to understand the contribution that applied immersive games can make in practice. To systematically assess existing research from 2020, a structured literature review has been conducted. This method not only synthesizes the existing body of knowledge, but also provides a foundation for future directions, benefiting researchers and practitioners alike.

According to our results, VR is the most widely used immersive technology for applied games in the industry in the last five years. One of the main reasons may that, unlike other immersive technologies such as AR and AV, the interaction environment in VR is entirely virtual and does not rely on any real-world objects, so that training content for hazardous working environments can be provided at lower costs and used flexibly without location and time constraints. Our research can be seen as a supplement to the study from [41], which analyzed the use of virtual reality-based training systems in the period from 2015 to 2020. Although the role of AR was already discussed there, it is visible that it has not yet been widely implemented in an industrial context since then. Our research also highlights the importance of carefully considering factors such as cost, technical requirements and the specific characteristics of the intended use case when selecting the appropriate immersive technology equipment. That said, it must also be emphasized that there is great potential for the expandability of the software and hardware used in immersive games for special applications [e.g., 65, 69].

Applied immersive games are becoming popular in a variety of industries, particularly those characterized by hazards (e.g., construction, manufacturing, or mining). Training in these hazardous areas is dangerous and risky. Using applied immersive games enables a safe, immersive main objectives of the applied immersive and real-world-like environment. Providing such a safe environment enables users to make mistakes without fearing negative consequences. This is also reflected in the discussed immersive games, which are frequently used in the area of safety training.

Our research confirms the main motivations for using immersive technologies, such as enhancing the learning/training effect, improving safety, and achieving cost-effectiveness [e.g., 41, 70]. In addition to previous studies, this research has identified that experiencing individual products or services is another motivating factor, as it helps customers to decide in favor of a particular product or service. This is also supported by the concept of Retail 4.0, which is based on Industry 4.0. The idea is to use immersive technologies, such as AR, to enhance the customer experience [72].

Research of [73] shows that VR and AR are used in manufacturing, primarily for virtual training. The main purpose of virtual training is to "improve the safety of production systems" (p. 628) and assist employees during assembly processes. Even though our work relates to applied immersive games, our results show that most of these applications are used for safety purposes.

According to our results, the target groups for applied immersive games in different industry sectors can be categorized into two main groups: industry-related employees, such as operators and workers, and potential employees in industry, such as STEM (Science, Technology, Engineering, and Mathematics) students. The focus on students may be due to resource constraints, but it may also be because students are likely to work in industry later on. It is therefore not surprising that Education 4.0 has been established to equip the future workforce of Industry 4.0 with the appropriate skills and competences [74].

Our results show that applied immersive games were not always tested with the intended target group. Access to experts in certain sectors can be critical, so conducting studies with trained students may be an option. Depending on the research question, e.g., if you are testing individual game mechanisms or usability in general, it seems to be a valid approach to expand the initial target group [75].

The successful implementation of digital transformation in industrial contexts requires a socio-technical perspective that places emphasis on both technological innovation and human factors. Applied immersive games put the potential into practice by integrating immersive technologies and game-based learning principles to simulate complex, real-world challenges in a safe and interactive environment. This makes them an essential medium for human-centered innovations in industry. This research summarized the features, motivations, and target users of applied immersive games in various industry sectors and thus, showed how applied immersive games contribute to workforce training, mainly as safety trainings in hazardous industries. In addition, they offer scalable and cost-effective training solutions that align with the operational requirements of industries facing safety risks, skill shortages, and increasing complexity. By providing (virtual) spaces in which users can safely fail, repeat tasks, and receive real-time feedback, these applications can significantly enhance training effectiveness while reducing material costs and safety hazards.

6 Future Research

The approach chosen for this research comes with some methodological limitations. In the context of a structured literature review that analyzes empirical work, the publication bias must be addressed [76]. This means that publications with positive (significant) results are more likely to be published than research papers without such results. Therefore, future research should make use of broader search strategies, such as including grey literature. In addition, the generated data set, taking into account a five-year time period, must be critically viewed. Even if, according to [44], a structured literature review can focus on the last five years when it comes to technology development, the topic of immersive technologies is a very fast-moving one. In this context, such a review provides an overview of the state of art, but it is important to note that, due to the fast pace and dynamic nature of the field, relevant new technologies or trends that have only recently become established are not yet fully reflected in the literature. This means that future research will need to continuously monitor these developments. Furthermore, a different understanding of immersive technologies became apparent in many of the papers analyzed. These ranged from simple PC setups (non-immersive VR) to the use of HMD (fully-Immersive VR, [77]). Making comparisons and drawing general conclusions is difficult in this case. This calls for clear definitions that leave no room for interpretation during implementation. Future research should further explore which immersive technology must be linked to which in-game mechanism to produce the best possible learning outcomes or how the actual motivation influences the use of hardware and software in immersive industrial applications. In this context, it is not always necessary to assume that people are digital natives, because the results of [37: 1] already show that […] beneficial effects can be attributed to the use of gamification in the conducted VR training simulation, particularly for the VR novice participants." As the studies analyzed often examined short-term effects, future research should […] focus on long term effects of using VR serious games on safety performance variables […]" [58: 12]. In conclusion, applied immersive games, which combine the benefits of immersive technologies and applied games, are powerful tools that can form the basis of future research and the development of practical applications in industry and beyond.

Acknowledgments. The authors have received funding from the European Union.

Disclosure of Interests. The authors declare that they have no known competing financial interests or personal relationships that could have appeared to influence the work reported in this paper.

References

1. Baalsrud Hauge, J., Basu, P., Sundus, F., Chowdhury, A., Schurig, A.: Design of a mixed reality game for exploring how IoT technologies can support the decision making process. In: Auer, M.E., Bhimavaram, K.R., Yue, XG. (eds.) REV 2021. LNNS, vol. 298, pp. 281–288. Springer, Cham (2022). https://doi.org/10.1007/978-3-030-82529-4_27
2. Milošević, I.M., Plotnic, O., Tick, A., Stanković, Z., Buzdugan, A.: Digital transformation in manufacturing: enhancing competitiveness through Industry 4.0 technologies. Precis. Mech. Digit. Fabr. **1**(1), 31–40 (2024). https://doi.org/10.56578/pmdf010104
3. Oliveri, M., Baalsrud Hauge, J., Bellotti, F., Berta, R., Gloria, A.D.: Designing an IoT-focused, multiplayer serious game for industry 4.0 innovation. In: IEEE International Conference on Engineering, Technology and Innovation (ICE/ITMC), Valbonne, Sophia-Antipolis, France, pp. 1–9 (2019). https://doi.org/10.1109/ICE.2019.8792680

4. Romero, D., Stahre, J., Taisch, M.: The operator 4.0: towards socially sustainable factories of the future. Comput. Ind. Eng. **139**, 106128 (2020). https://doi.org/10.1016/j.cie.2019.106128

5. Zakrzewska-Bielawska, A., Staniec, I.: Contemporary Challenges in Cooperation and Coopetition in the Age of Industry 4.0. Springer, Cham (2020). https://doi.org/10.1007/978-3-030-30549-9

6. Adami, P., et al.: Effectiveness of VR-based training on improving construction workers' knowledge, skills, and safety behavior in robotic teleoperation. Adv. Eng. Inform. **50**, 101431 (2021). https://doi.org/10.1016/j.aei.2021.101431

7. Ulmer, J., Braun, S., Cheng, C.-T., Dowey, S., Wollert, J.: Gamified virtual reality training environment for the manufacturing industry. In: 19th International Conference on Mechatronics - Mechatronika (ME), Prague, Czech Republic, pp. 1–6 (2020)

8. Gasiba, T.E., Lechner, U., Pinto-Albuquerque, M.: Cybersecurity challenges: serious games for awareness training in industrial environments. arXiv:2102.10432 (2021)

9. Riedel, C.K.H.J., Baalsrud Hauge, J.: State of the art of serious games for business and industry. In: Thoben, K.-D., Stich, V., Imtiaz, A. (eds.) Proceedings of the 2011 17th International Conference on Concurrent Enterprising (2011)

10. Berg, L.P., Vance, J.M.: An industry case study: investigating early design decision making in virtual reality. J. Comput. Inf. Sci. Eng. **17**(1), 011001 (2017). https://doi.org/10.1115/1.4034267

11. Gürer, S., Surer, E., Erkayaoğlu, M.: MINING-VIRTUAL: a comprehensive virtual reality-based serious game for occupational health and safety training in underground mines. Saf. Sci. **166**, 106226 (2023). https://doi.org/10.1016/j.ssci.2023.106226

12. Feng, Z., González, V.A., Amor, R., Lovreglio, R., Cabrera-Guerrero, G.: Immersive virtual reality serious games for evacuation training and research: a systematic literature review. Comput. Educ. **127**, 252–266 (2018). https://doi.org/10.1016/j.compedu.2018.09.002

13. Khan, H.U., Ali, Y., Khan, F., Al-antari, M.A.: A comprehensive study on unraveling the advances of immersive technologies (VR/AR/MR/XR) in the healthcare sector during the COVID-19: challenges and solutions. Heliyon **10**(15), e35037 (2024)

14. Milgram, P., Kishino, F.: A taxonomy of mixed reality visual displays. IEICE (Inst. Electron. Inf. Commun. Eng.) Trans. Inf. Syst. **77**(12), 1321–1329 (1994)

15. Dede, C.: Immersive interfaces for engagement and learning. Science **323**, 66–69 (2009). https://doi.org/10.1126/science.1167311

16. Slater, M., Sanchez-Vives, M.V.: Enhancing our lives with immersive virtual reality. Front. Robot. AI **3**, 74 (2016). https://doi.org/10.3389/frobt.2016.00074

17. Kwegyir-Afful, E., Kantola, J.: Simulation-based safety training for plant maintenance in virtual reality. In: Cassenti, D., Scataglini, S., Rajulu, S., Wright, J. (eds.) AHFE 2020. AISC, vol. 1206, pp. 167–173. Springer, Cham (2021). https://doi.org/10.1007/978-3-030-51064-0_22

18. Liu, R., Peng, C., Zhang, Y., Husarek, H., Yu, Q.: A survey of immersive technologies and applications for industrial product development. Comput. Graph. **100**, 137–151 (2021). https://doi.org/10.1016/j.cag.2021.07.023

19. Choi, S., Jung, K., Noh, S.D.: Virtual reality applications in manufacturing industries: past research, present findings, and future directions. Concurr. Eng. **23**(1), 40–63 (2015). https://doi.org/10.1177/1063293X14568814

20. Nussipova, G., Nordin, F., Sörhammar, D.: Value formation with immersive technologies: an activity perspective. J. Bus. Ind. Mark. **35**(3), 483–494 (2020). https://doi.org/10.1108/JBIM-12-2018-0407

21. Tu, X., Autiosalo, J., Ala-Laurinaho, R., Yang, C., Salminen, P., Tammi, K.: TwinXR: method for using digital twin descriptions in industrial eXtended reality applications. Front. Virtual Real. **4**, 1019080 (2023)

22. Brauner, P., Ziefle, M.: Beyond playful learning – serious games for the human-centric digital transformation of production and a design process model. Technol. Soc. **71**, 102140 (2022). https://doi.org/10.1016/j.techsoc.2022.102140
23. Beat Games: Beat Saber game (2018). https://beatsaber.com/. Accessed 13 Feb 2025
24. Niantic: Pokémon Go (2016). https://pokemongolive.com/. Accessed 13 Feb 2025
25. Anastasiadis, T., Lampropoulos, G., Siakas, K.: Digital game-based learning and serious games in education. Int. J. Adv. Sci. Res. Eng. **4**(12), 139–144 (2018). https://doi.org/10.31695/IJASRE.2018.33016
26. Gomes, D.F., Lopes, M.P., de Carvalho, C.V.: Serious games for lean manufacturing: the 5S game. IEEE Revista Iberoamericana de Tecnologias del Aprendizaje **8**(4), 191–196 (2013)
27. Simões, J., Díaz Redondo, R., Fernández Vilas, A.: A social gamification framework for a K-6 learning platform. Comput. Hum. Behav. **29**(2), 345–353 (2013). https://doi.org/10.1016/j.chb.2012.06.007
28. Almeida, F., Simões, J.: The role of serious games, gamification and industry 4.0 tools in the education 4.0 paradigm. Contemp. Educ. Technol. **10**, 120–136 (2019). https://doi.org/10.30935/cet.554469
29. Teichmann, M., Ullrich, A., Knost, D., Gronau, N.: Serious games in learning factories: perpetuating knowledge in learning loops by game-based learning. Procedia Manuf. **45**, 259–264 (2020). https://doi.org/10.1016/j.promfg.2020.04.104
30. Freina, L., Ott, M.: A literature review on immersive virtual reality in education: state of the art and perspectives. In: Proceedings of the International Scientific Conference Elearning and Software for Education, pp. 1–8 (2015)
31. Chittaro, L., Buttussi, F.: Learning safety through public serious games: a study of "prepare for impact" on a very large, international sample of players. IEEE Trans. Vis. Comput. Graph. **28**(3), 1573–1584 (2022)
32. Feng, Z., et al.: Towards a customizable immersive virtual reality serious game for earthquake emergency training. Adv. Eng. Inform. **46**, 101134 (2020)
33. Ulmer, J., Braun, S., Cheng, C.-T., Dowey, S., Wollert, J.: Gamification of virtual reality assembly training: effects of a combined point and level system on motivation and training results. Int. J. Hum. Comput. Stud. **165**, 102854 (2022). https://doi.org/10.1016/j.ijhcs.2022.102854
34. Chen, P.-H.: The design of applying gamification in an immersive virtual reality virtual laboratory for powder-bed binder jetting 3DP training. Educ. Sci. **10**(7), 172 (2020). https://doi.org/10.3390/educsci10070172
35. Palmas, F., Labode, D., Plecher, D.A., Klinker, G.: Comparison of a gamified and non-gamified virtual reality training assembly task. In: 2019 11th International Conference on Virtual Worlds and Games for Serious Applications (VS-Games), Vienna, Austria, pp. 1–8 (2019)
36. Singhaphandu, R., Pannakkong, W.: A review on enabling technologies of industrial virtual training systems. Int. J. Knowl. Syst. Sci. (IJKSS) **15**(1), 1–33 (2024). https://doi.org/10.4018/IJKSS.352515
37. Tezel, A., Dobrucali, E., Demirkesen, S., Kiral, I.A.: Critical success factors for safety training in the construction industry. Buildings **11**(4), 139 (2021). https://doi.org/10.3390/buildings11040139
38. Jeelani, I., Han, K., Albert, A.: Development of virtual reality and stereo-panoramic environments for construction safety training. Eng. Constr. Archit. Manag. **27**(8), 1853–1876 (2020). https://doi.org/10.1108/ECAM-07-2019-0391
39. Wahidi, S.I., Pribadi, T.W., Rajasa, W.S., Arif, M.S.: Virtual reality based application for safety training at shipyards. IOP Conf. Ser. Earth Environ. Sci. **972**, 012025 (2022). https://doi.org/10.1088/1755-1315/972/1/012025

40. Hussain, R., Pedro, A., Lee, D.Y., Pham, H.C., Park, C.S.: Impact of safety training and interventions on training-transfer: targeting migrant construction workers. Int. J. Occup. Saf. Ergon. **26**(2), 272–284 (2018). https://doi.org/10.1080/10803548.2018.1465671

41. Naranjo, J.E., Sanchez, D.G., Robalino-Lopez, A., Robalino-Lopez, P., Alarcon-Ortiz, A., Garcia, M.V.: A scoping review on virtual reality-based industrial training. Appl. Sci. **10**, 8224 (2020). https://doi.org/10.3390/app10228224

42. De Groote, S.L., Raszewski, R.: Coverage of Google Scholar, Scopus, and Web of Science: a case study of the h-index in nursing. Nurs. Outlook **60**(6), 391–400 (2012). https://doi.org/10.1016/j.outlook.2012.04.007

43. Kniestedt, I.: Engagement in applied games. [Dissertation (TU Delft), Delft University of Technology] (2023). https://doi.org/10.4233/uuid:e6fedd21-5130-4311-a4bd-e1d5a87b89ec

44. Sauer, P.C., Seuring, S.: How to conduct systematic literature reviews in management research: a guide in 6 steps and 14 decisions. Rev. Manag. Sci. **17**, 1899–1933 (2023). https://doi.org/10.1007/s11846-023-00668-3

45. Tranfield, D., Denyer, D., Smart, P.: Towards a methodology for developing evidence-informed management knowledge by means of systematic review. Br. J. Manag. **14**, 207–222 (2003). https://doi.org/10.1111/1467-8551.00375

46. Strauss, A., Corbin, J.: Basics of Qualitative Research: Techniques and Procedures for Developing Grounded Theory, 2nd edn. Sage Publications Inc, Thousand Oaks (1998)

47. Borges, L.F.M.R., et al.: Inspection and training using virtual reality applied a new wheel loader model. In: Proceedings of the 26th Symposium on Virtual and Augmented Reality (SVR 2024), New York, NY, USA, pp. 113–121. Association for Computing Machinery (2024). https://doi.org/10.1145/3691573.3691575

48. Rey-Becerra, E., Barrero, L.H., Ellegast, R., Kluge, A.: Improvement of short-term outcomes with VR-based safety training for work at heights. Appl. Ergon. **112** (2023). https://doi.org/10.1016/j.apergo.2023.104077

49. Ogunseiju, O.O., Akanmu, A.A., Bairaktarova, D.: Mixed reality based environment for learning sensing technology applications in construction. J. Inf. Technol. Constr. **26**, 863–885 (2021). https://doi.org/10.36680/j.itcon.2021.046

50. Boyes, H., Hallaq, B., Cunningham, J., Watson, T.: The Industrial Internet of Things (IIoT): an analysis framework. Comput. Ind. **101**, 1–12 (2018). https://doi.org/10.1016/j.compind.2018.04.015

51. de Oliveira, T.R., et al.: Virtual reality system for inspection and training in wheel loader. In: Proceedings of the 24th Symposium on Virtual and Augmented Reality, pp. 11–20 (2022). https://doi.org/10.1145/3604479.3604503

52. Bruzzone, A.G., et al.: Promoting safety, security, awareness and productivity in Port Plants. Procedia Comput. Sci. **232**, 358–367 (2024). https://doi.org/10.1016/j.procs.2024.01.035

53. D'Agostino, P., Antuono, G., Elefante, E.: Management and dissemination for dismissed religious architecture. an approach fusing HBIM and gamification. In: Ródenas-López, M.A., Calvo-López, J., Salcedo-Galera, M. (eds.) EGA 2022. SSDI, vol. 22, pp. 399–407. Springer, Cham (2022). https://doi.org/10.1007/978-3-031-04703-9_40

54. HTC, Valve (2016). https://www.vive.com/us/. Accessed 13 Feb 2025

55. Meta Platform Technologies (2020). https://about.meta.com/. Accessed 13 Feb 2025

56. Google (2014). https://arvr.google.com/cardboard/. Accessed 13 Feb 2025

57. Wolf, M., Teizer, J., Wolf, B., Bükrü, S., Solberg, A.: Investigating hazard recognition in augmented virtuality for personalized feedback in construction safety education and training. Adv. Eng. Inform. **51**, 101469 (2022). https://doi.org/10.1016/j.aei.2021.101469

58. Chan, P., Gerven, T.V., Dubois, J.-L., Bernaerts, K.: Study of motivation and engagement for chemical laboratory safety training with VR serious game. Saf. Sci. **167** (2023). https://doi.org/10.1016/j.ssci.2023.106278

59. López-Fernández, D., Mayor, J., Pérez, J., Gordillo, A.: Learning and motivational impact of using a virtual reality serious video game to learn scrum. IEEE Trans. Games **15**(3), 430–439 (2023). https://doi.org/10.1109/TG.2022.3213127

60. Hilfert, T., König, M.: Low-cost virtual reality environment for engineering and construction. Vis. Eng. **4**(2) (2016). https://doi.org/10.1186/s40327-015-0031-5

61. Charissis, V., Khan, M.S., Harrison, D.K.: Servitization through VR serious games: from manufacturing to consumer electronics. In: Meiselwitz, G., et al. (eds.) HCII 2022. LNCS, vol. 13517, pp. 545–555. Springer, Cham (2022). https://doi.org/10.1007/978-3-031-22131-6_40

62. Checa-Cruz, D., Martinez-Garcia, K., Osornio-Rios, R., Bustillo-Iglesias, A.: Virtual reality opportunities in the reduction of occupational hazards in industry 4.0. DYNA **96**(6), 620–626 (2021)

63. Gutiérrez-Rodríguez, A., López-García, J.D., Sanabria, R.A., Acevedo-Zapata, S.: Industry 4.0 and digital transformation in higher education through the perspective of smart cites. In: Workshops at the Fourth International Conference on Applied Informatics, October 28–30, Buenos Aires, Argentina (2021)

64. Sofri, S., Reddy Prasad, D.M., Azri, H., Timbang, A.: 3D non-immersive VR game for process safety education. AIP Conf. Proc. **2643**, 060011 (2023). https://doi.org/10.1063/5.0110924

65. Hart, S.G., Staveland, L.E.: Development of NASA-TLX (task load index): results of empirical and theoretical research. In: Hancock, P.A., Meshkati, N. (eds.) Human Mental Workload, North-Holland, pp. 139–183 (1988). https://doi.org/10.1016/S0166-4115(08)62386-9

66. Bangor, A., Kortum, P.T., Miller, J.T.: An empirical evaluation of the system usability scale. Int. J. Hum. Comput. Interact. **24**(6), 574–594 (2008). https://doi.org/10.1080/10447310802205776

67. Qu, J., Kizil, M.S., Yahyaei, M., Knights, P.F.: Developing a digital twin for a laboratory ball mill operation – a step towards mining metaverse. Min. Technol. **133**(1), 3–16 (2024)

68. Sloan, H., Zhao, R., Aqlan, F., Yang, H., Zhu, R.: Adaptive virtual assistant for virtual reality-based remote learning. Paper presented at 2022 ASEE Annual Conference & Exposition, Minneapolis, MN (2022). https://doi.org/10.18260/1-2—41234

69. Al-Ansi, A.M., Jaboob, M., Garad, A., Al-Ansi, A.: Analyzing augmented reality (AR) and virtual reality (VR) recent development in education. Soc. Sci. Humanit. Open **8**(1) (2023). https://doi.org/10.1016/j.ssaho.2023.100532

70. Garcia Fracaro, S., Glassey, J., Bernaerts, K., Wilk, M.: Immersive technologies for the training of operators in the process industry: a systematic literature review. Comput. Chem. Eng. **160** (2022). https://doi.org/10.1016/j.compchemeng.2022.107691

71. de Souza Cardoso, L.F., Martins Queiroz Mariano, F.C., Zorzal, E.R.: A survey of industrial augmented reality. Comput. Ind. Eng. **139** (2020). https://doi.org/10.1016/j.cie.2019.106159

72. Har, L L., Rashid, U.K., Chuan, L.T., Sen, S.C., Xia, L.Y.: Revolution of retail industry: from perspective of retail 1.0 to 4.0. Procedia Comput. Sci. **200**, 1615–1625 (2022). https://doi.org/10.1016/j.procs.2022.01.362

73. Damiani, L., Demartini, M., Guizzi, G., Revetria, R., Tonelli, F.: Augmented and virtual reality applications in industrial systems: a qualitative review towards the industry 4.0 era. IFAC-PapersOnLine **51**(11), 624–630 (2018). https://doi.org/10.1016/j.ifacol.2018.08.388

74. Bonfield, C.A., Salter, M., Longmuir, A., Benson, M., Adachi, C.: Transformation or evolution?: education 4.0, teaching and learning in the digital age. High. Educ. Pedagog. **5**(1), 223–246 (2020). https://doi.org/10.1080/23752696.2020.1816847

75. Freese, M., Zürn, B., Lukosch, H.: Unterschiede zwischen Expert* innen und Noviz* innen beim Planspielen. In: Alf, T., Hahn, S., Zürn, B., Trautwein, F. (eds.) Planspiele: Erkenntnisse aus Praxis und Forschung, pp. 127–136. ZMS-Schriftenreihe. Books on Demand GmbH, Norderstedt (2022)

76. Song, F., Hooper, L., Loke, Y.: Publication bias: what is it? How do we measure it? How do we avoid it? Open Access J. Clin. Trials **5**, 71–81 (2013). https://doi.org/10.2147/OAJCT.S34419
77. Rendevski, N., et al.: PC VR vs standalone VR fully-immersive applications: history, technical aspects and performance. In: 57th International Scientific Conference on Information, Communication and Energy Systems and Technologies (ICEST), Ohrid, North Macedonia, pp. 1–4 (2022)

'Judging a Book by Its Cover': Simulation, Bias, and Intercultural Learning

Korryn D. Mozisek[✉] and Sebastien Dubreil

Carnegie Mellon University, Pittsburgh, PA 15213, USA
`{kmozisek,sdubreil}@andrew.cmu.edu`

Abstract. This paper examines the potential and effectiveness of *Kaleidoscope* (an immersive simulation) and accompanying pedagogical intervention to foster intercultural learning in an interdisciplinary first-year college seminar by encouraging participants to confront their cultural bias and guiding them to reflect on their cultural assumptions. Using a mixed-method approach, we assessed the effectiveness of immersive simulation and debriefing as an educational practice. Qualitative analysis of student reflections showed that the pairing encouraged students to realize how easy it is to make assumptions but that the critical reflection and debriefing also enabled them to envision a change in their behavior and recognize the links one makes between physical appearance on the one hand and cultures/values/behaviors on the other hand. These themes illustrate the potential of immersive educational experiences coupled with debriefing to bring learning alive and make it more impactful.

Keywords: Immersive simulation · intercultural learning · debriefing

1 Introduction

How many snap inferences, judgements, and perceptions do we make in a day? How many do we even consciously perceive? The signs are all around us - the type of shoes a person is wearing, their haircut, and the accent within their speech, among countless others. We process these signs nearly unconsciously; we may not even notice that we've heard an accent and placed it as French, Chinese, or Texan and shifted our perception about the person. But what results from processing these signs into perceptions framing and influencing our interactions with people?

Scholars and trainers of intercultural competence face challenges as to how to get students to recognize these very inferences occurring or acknowledge that they are imbued with cultural meaning and (symbolic) power. Immersive simulations and their debriefing techniques are potentially a powerful instructional tool in this regard and may help us shape the future of intercultural learning and the way we relate to each other. While prior intercultural competence simulation structures have focused on role-playing, immersive experiences, like *Kaleidoscope*, can leverage virtual and augmented reality technologies to advance vital educational aims and challenge us to refine known methods as we prepare students for a diverse world. While role play and simulation

F. Trautwein et al. (Eds.): ISAGA 2025, LNCS 16439, pp. 331–345, 2026.
https://doi.org/10.1007/978-3-032-20129-4_22

are sometimes used interchangeably, they have different affordances, for example with simulation allowing the user to try things out in a lower-stakes environment. With the advances in immersive technology, the question poses itself to examine the potential of immersive simulations to tackle complex problems such as intercultural learning.

Kaleidoscope is an immersive experience (powered by HTC Vive) that simulates an encounter with a stranger where the user is asked a range of questions about the person they are meeting on screen. The strangers within *Kaleidoscope* were recruited by the developers for their diverse backgrounds and willingness to be within the experience; they honestly answered all of the questions. The questions range from the inconsequential and benign, like the type of shoes the person is wearing, to more intimate, personal questions, such as whether they would marry someone of a different ethnicity. The user is only provided a few short audio recordings by the stranger on the screen and a volumetrically captured headshot of them. *Kaleidoscope* uses an interactive voting system whereby the user utilizes the controllers to select an on-screen answer from a small set of potential answers surrounding them on the walls to the user's left and right. When the user selects an answer, there is haptic feedback to its selection and the user then drags their selected answer to the stranger on the screen (Image 1); the user's choices are charted under the headshot on the main screen in front of them. After answering all questions, the user is faced with a polygon illustrating which questions they've answered correctly and incorrectly (Image 2) and prompts them explicitly to confront their assumptions. In so doing, *Kaleidoscope* challenges the user to acknowledge the presence of these snap judgements and evaluate their impact. After answering the last question, users see how their answers match with the reality of the person they just met (Image 2) and compare to the answers chosen by prior users (Image 3). With *Kaleidoscope*, the haptic experience of physically selecting and moving an answer about the stranger on the screens serves to bring the unconscious to the conscious, thus leveraging the power of simulation [13] by encouraging users to reflect on the assumptions they've made.

Image 1. A user (in shadows) answering questions inside the Kaleidoscope experience, using the controller to drag the answer from the wall to the person they meet.

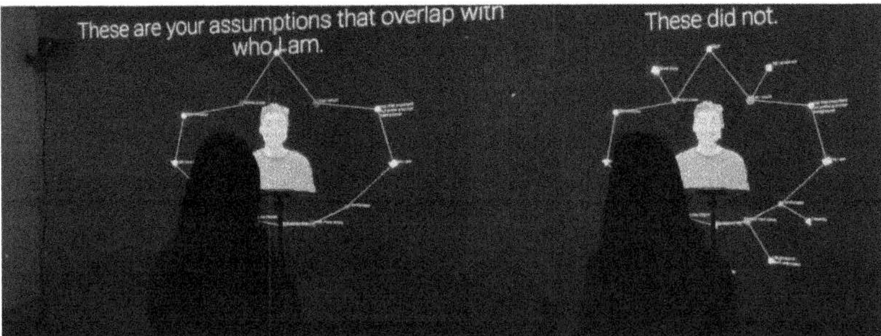

Image 2. A user (in shadows) finding out how their answers match reality inside the Kaleidoscope experience with color-coded visuals - red dots indicate incorrect responses.

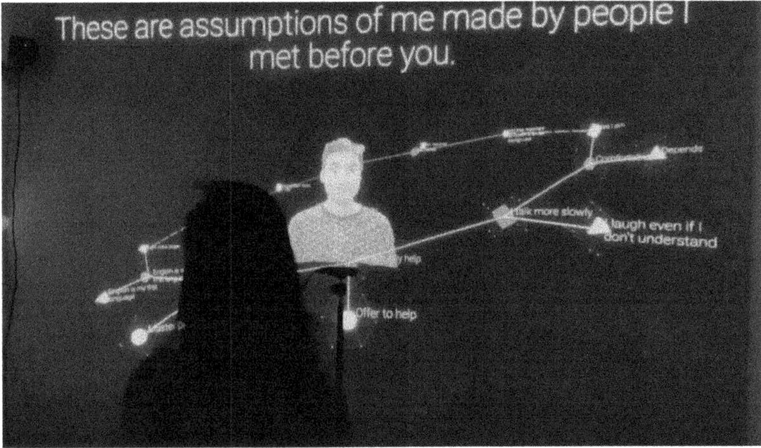

Image 3. A user (in shadows) finding out what assumptions were made about the person they just met inside the Kaleidoscope experience.

As Fowler and Pusch [7] note, "simulation games being used for intercultural training in the United States dates back to the 1970s with the publication of the first edition of *Beyond Experience.*" A central aspect of simulation games is that they "couple thinking and doing. Participants are constantly thinking, acting, and considering" [13]. In prompting users to answer questions and review their accuracy, *Kaleidoscope* provides opportunities for users to confront their unconscious biases without harm or defensiveness. While *Kaleidoscope* prompts users to reflect, a more defined debriefing process was tested to see how this would improve intercultural competence, thus leveraging prior work by Fowler and Pusch [7] who argue that intercultural simulations can cement learning. In asking participants to confront simultaneously who they are as cultural beings and their own cultural bias through the simulation and debriefing process, we aim to have them take their first steps into the intercultural learning voyage. In qualitatively analyzing student reflections, we found that the pairing of simulation and debriefing encouraged students to realize how easy it is to make assumptions, envision a change in their behavior, and recognize the links one makes between physical appearance on the one hand and cultures/values/behaviors on the other hand. These themes illustrate the potential of immersive educational experiences coupled with debriefing to bring learning alive and make it more impactful, thus further confirming the value of 21st century technological simulations for intercultural training.

2 Literature Review: The Intersections of Intercultural Competence, Immersive Learning, and Debriefing

Before defining intercultural competence, let's pause on the notion of culture. Hofstede [12] defined culture as "the collective programming of the mind which distinguishes the members of one category of people from another". As such, a culture is "an aggregate of multi-faceted reality, representing many different subcultures (generational, occupational, education, regional, age, race or gender-related)" [17]. In other words, culture is marked by symbolic and semiotic systems (including language): "Culture is membership in a discourse community that shares a common social space and history, and common imaginings" and "its members may retain, wherever they are, a common system of standards for perceiving, believing, evaluating, and acting" [16]. Following Geertz's [8] lead, we believe people are suspended in "webs of significance" that they themselves have spun and we espouse this view of culture "to be those webs, and the analysis of it to be therefore not an experimental science in search of law but an interpretive one in search of meaning." It is on the basis of this definition of culture that we envision intercultural competence. In this sense, cultural competence and intercultural competence can be used interchangeably here in that being aware of oneself as a cultural being and understanding what culture is and how it operates on shaping one's identity are *sine qua non* conditions to engage successfully with other cultures.

Intercultural competence is characterized by three dimensions: sociolinguistic ability, cultural knowledge, and cultural attitudes [17]. Claire Kramsch [17] critically notes that "the knowledge and attitudes that lead to the competence can only be taught and acquired through the interaction of the individual with fellow individuals from the same or from a different culture, in and outside the classroom." Through these encounters individuals engage in (hopefully) appropriate interactions, thus illustrating a certain level of cultural awareness [5, 17]. Scholars and administrators agree that students need to gain expertise across these dimensions rather than a single area [4]. As Deardorff [4] has offered, intercultural competence is also a positionality where "curiosity, general openness, and respect for other cultures" is exhibited. Additionally, there is agreement among scholars and administrators that "understanding of others' world views" is critical to being interculturally competent [4]. Study abroad has been a foundational experience connected with student development of intercultural competency. But as rates of students participating in study abroad decline, there is a need for curricular and co-curricular experiences to fill the gap left behind [5]. Immersive experiences like, *Kaleidoscope*, then, provide potential opportunities for its users to practice intercultural interactions. With *Kaleidoscope*'s incorporation of authentic individuals, users have an opportunity to interact and reflect in a low-risk environment; they are meeting a person who they otherwise may not meet in real life due to various factors. Our contention is that with a need for the curricular and co-curricular to fill the study abroad gap, there are opportunities to integrate immersive experiences into courses focused on teaching culture and that research to evaluate their feasibility and effectiveness becomes more necessary.

The process of intercultural competence development is divided into six stages: "denial, defense, minimization, acceptance, adaption, and integration" [1], the first three being known as ethnocentric and the last three as ethnorelative. Those demonstrating denial are unaware of culture or stereotype others while those who are defensive espouse superiority of their own culture in comparison to others. Those in the minimization phase likely offer that they are color-blind or minimize cultural differences. Those in the acceptance phase are aware of their own culture and can suspend judgement of other cultures. This stage sees difference as "intriguing rather than threatening" thus allowing training "with more complicated and risky strategies, demanding complex analysis" [1]. The next phases (adaptation and integration) focus on the ability to recognize cultural situations and adapt to them by shifting frames of reference and embracing a multicultural identity [1]. It is our contention that *Kaleidoscope* can simulate the types of intercultural encounters that Kramsch encourages [17] and aid in teaching perspective-taking when coupled with debriefing strategies. This draws upon prior studies which have shown immersive experiences addressing stigmatization and discrimination as well as ignorance about other groups, thus allowing individuals to be defter at negotiating intergroup contexts as individuals become more sensitive to discriminatory barriers [26].

While role-playing is an established pedagogical approach for intercultural competence development, it does have limitations related to authenticity, realism, and inconsistent enactments within classroom settings that immersive experiences, like *Kaleidoscope*, can potentially address [19]. Through immersive experiences, "virtual humans can induce feelings of social presence in learners, that these feelings are enhanced through personalization and simulation of social and relational behaviors, and, ultimately, that we should expect a concomitant improvement in learning" [19]. Further research, though, has been encouraged in developing and testing perspective change due to feedback within immersive environments [19].

Immersive experiences provide opportunities for intercultural role-playing and simulations that would otherwise be difficult or infeasible to enact within a classroom setting [11]. Importantly, self-reflection is an agreed upon dimension in processing immersive experiences and in relation to developing intercultural competencies. The processing of immersive experiences also should be understood as limited and shaped by the designed simulations [21], including what learning goals the learner environment is imbued with [3, 22]. This means acknowledging the values, structures, and aims for the immersive experiences, which in the case of *Kaleidoscope* means evaluating the extent to which users question their own cultural assumptions. As Leigh and Levesque [22] offer, "experiential learning activities like simulation and games inevitably move learners away from passive reception into direct engagement with activity and experience... [and] relocate power into the hands of learners during the action."

In that sense, this resonates with Kolb's [14, 15] experiential learning cycles, which are anchored in experience but, for learning to occur, necessitates a highly active involvement in the learning process [9]. Indeed, Kolb [14, 15] posits that learning occurs when a participant processes knowledge, skills, and attitudes cognitively, affectively, and behaviorally. Envisioned that way, learning requires, beyond the sensory experience, a reflective component and an abstracting phase (or conceptualization phase – i.e., what does it mean? What principles can I derive from this and test?), leading, in the best-case scenario, to an implementation phase (apply what I have learned in a real-life context). This reflective moment can be especially critical when it comes to games or game-like environments where the pressure to perform can take away from the learning component and taking the time to reflect, through either focus groups or reflective essays, becomes a critical strategy to retain the educational potential of the activity [10, 18]. In the case of a simulation, the reflection and conceptualization phases can occur through debriefing.

Debriefing is a common technique prescribed in relation to simulations as it gives a space for processing and comparisons with learning outcomes [1, 20]. As David Crookall [2, 3] notes, debriefing is a necessary aspect of experiential learning (especially simulations), and where the learning occurs. With an educational aim, the debriefing associated with simulations functions to "facilitate an understanding of what has happened, to find out what the participant learned, and to test that against the instructor's learning objective" [20]. The power of immersive experiences lies within the debriefing because it "should make the experiences of the learning activity come alive. It should connect those experiences to the content of the course and assist participants in putting theory into practice and constructing their own lessons. It should make the process feel personal and real, and increase the likelihood that the students will remember and use their new learning" [1].

Within a debriefing session, space for recollections and processing about the experience should be provided [20]. As with simulations, the focus should be on the learner, not what the facilitator expects [20]. Deason, et al. [6] contend that in centering student experience within the simulation that student learning is more likely to be retained. They added that such debriefings can occur as entire class sessions to develop a shared vocabulary and understanding; reflective writing can prepare students for such discussions [6].

Such an emphasis by simulation scholars aligns strongly with intercultural competency practice. It is a common ground because it acknowledges the on-going processes and developmental foundations of both fields. An interculturally competent reflection would be one that communicates respect, openness, and curiosity [5]. This can be exhibited through the ways that users talk about their reactions to and processing of the immersive experience, as well as its meaning.

3 Context, Methods, and Procedures

This study occurred in a required first-year seminar, entitled "Sports, Culture, Conflict, and/in Virtual Reality," focused on culture and virtual reality. As part of the course, students were asked to participate in the immersive experience, *Kaleidoscope*, complete a critical reflection of learning as a course assignment, and discuss their experiences during a class session. In leveraging the practice of reflection with debriefing, we hoped student learning outcomes related to (inter)cultural competency and awareness of implicit bias would be strengthened. The study asked the following research question:

How can immersive simulations be used in the development of students' (inter)cultural competency?

There were 33 students enrolled in the course. They were all first-semester, first-year undergraduate students in the humanities and social sciences. Fourteen students identified as women and 19 as men. Twenty were Asian (with roots in India, China, South Korea, and the Philippines and eight identified as Asian-American), three were Black, two Latino, and eight Caucasian. For the purpose of this study population, they are a more diverse group that tend not to exhibit the denial or defense stages as articulated by Bennett [1] and acknowledge the importance of culture when they step foot on our university campus and on the first day of our course, an assessment that was confirmed by results on the pretest and early class conversations as observed by the instructors. *Kaleidoscope,* and the course it was used in are, consequently, more focused on the minimization, acceptance, and adaptation categories by developing cultural self-awareness, acceptances of cultural differences without judgement, and capacity for adaptation.

All students were asked to: 1) complete a pre- and post-survey around the immersive experience participation, 2) write a critical reflection of learning (CRL), and 3) participate in a class-wide debrief. Students were given completion points for completing the pre- and post-survey. In addition to demographic information, the pretest survey aimed to better understand students' perspective on cultural bias. We did this by asking open-ended questions (e.g., what does it mean to be inclusive?) and administering an adapted version of the Miville-Guzman Universality-Diversity Scale, which aims to measure attitudes such as comfort with difference, openness to diversity, and intercultural sensitivity [24]. The critical reflection of learning was framed as a journal entry with a specific prompt leading students to reflect on their initial reaction to *Kaleidoscope*, what their process was for answering questions, which questions were easier/harder to answer, and what they took away from the experience. It was graded using a course-specific rubric. Ultimately, the study included 30 students. Three students were removed from the study as they either did not complete the pre- or post-survey or they had not completed the critical reflection of learning prior to the class discussion and opening of the post-survey.

Our university's teaching and learning center colleagues stripped all identifying data from the student written assignments and assigned them code numbers to allow for anonymous review of the qualitative data and enable matching to the quantitative measures. All names used in the results correspond to the coding number and letter of the alphabet, i.e. 1) Adele, 2) Ben, 3) Christine. Common names are used and none of the names of students enrolled in the course were used. Both authors were certified by the university's CITI Responsible Conduct of Research Training and the university's teaching and learning center has IRB approval for research related to teaching. Students in the course were notified by a teaching and learning center representative of their ability to opt-out of the study and their rights as participants during a class session prior to the pre-survey being administered. A decision to opt-out had no impact on a student's completion points related to the survey or on their course grade. The requirements and responsibilities by the authors were codified in a Teaching as Research agreement with the university's teaching and learning center.

After the pretest survey, students were asked to go in pairs or trios to engage with the *Kaleidoscope* experience. Originally thought of as an individual experience, it had become clear, during the development of *Kaleidoscope*, that letting people go through in pairs yielded fascinating dynamics and interactions. Consequently, we used this format for the class; 9 pairs and 5 trios went through the experience at least once in their designated 30-minute time slot. After completing their engagement with *Kaleidoscope*, students were asked to individually write a CRL entry (part of a series of reflection-focused assignments in the course). Depending on when the students signed up for engagement with *Kaleidoscope*, they had between a week or a few days to complete their reflection. On the day the assignment was due, a class-wide debrief occurred. Our teaching and learning colleagues compiled and analyzed the pre- and post-survey results.

The decision to use a multi-pronged assessment approach is based in strong agreement with intercultural scholars on the need for qualitative and quantitative measures when assessing intercultural competence [4]. In addition, this aligns with accepted practice of simulation scholars on the importance of debriefing when a debriefing occurs as part of the assessment process.

Following an emergent coding approach [25, 27], we identified major thematic categories within the written student reflections (CRLs). The categories include: discomfort, stereotyping, closed/open mindedness, active listening, cultural expression, and ultimate takeaways. These categories were developed as they represented the connections and points offered by the students. These categories also align with *Kaleidoscope*'s learning design which emphasizes cultural attitudes and perspective-taking as aspects of intercultural competency development. For the purpose of this paper, we focused only on analyzing the ultimate takeaway category. The ultimate takeaway category was identified as this was the last aspect of the prompt; it asked students to provide their takeaways from the experience and how their behavior would or would not change moving forward. The last paragraph or sentences of the paper were identified as where this should be occurring. Both authors reviewed all 30 eligible responses and coded quotations representative of the categories.

4 Results

If we envision culture as the lens through which one sees the world, acknowledging one's own cultural perspectives is paramount to being able (and willing) to engage with alterity. The mechanics of *Kaleidoscope* and accompanying pedagogical CRL wrapper provided a low-risk environment that allowed for this disequilibrium to take place, for the intercultural encounter to happen (albeit a simulated one), for a student's willingness to confront their own biases to emerge, and for the reflective dimension to provide the critical distance and cement the learning process. Data showed that students took this experience seriously and, even though they met a "random person" in *Kaleidoscope*, they became aware of the fact that they do have biases and sometimes make snap judgments. Indeed, the way the simulation is built can lead to discomfort but does so in a safer space than if the visitors were confronted to a real-life actor or person, or even their peers. As anticipated, the format did have an impact on students' experience.While one might expect that such a short experience would not yield significant changes on measures of intercultural competence (and our quantitative survey results verify this presumption), the quantitative results stand in contrast to the qualitative comments students provided on their experience when they realized that their intercultural competence may not be as polished as they thought but rather is, in fact, still developing (as are all of ours). Students' realization that they are, in fact, on a journey can be unsettling (and may also explain the slight quantitative dip - albeit not significant - from pretest to posttest). Such simulations demand to be done carefully and strategically to allow for the discomfort to exist, while enabling the students to transcend it and acknowledge their shortcomings. In so doing, students show their willingness to grow, improve, and move forward, even though they don't all show the same level of concreteness in their proposed behavioral and attitudinal changes.

Our analysis shows that there is no doubt that *Kaleidoscope* had an impact on students. Indeed, at the end of the course, when asked to reflect on how the course helped them develop their intercultural learning, over 43% of the students spontaneously mentioned *Kaleidoscope*. Not surprisingly, we found a statistically significant correlation ($r = .54$, $p < .01$; rho (ρ) $= .59$, $p < .001$) between growth from pretest to posttest and performance on the CRL entry related to the *Kaleidoscope* experience. In other words, students who exhibited a score increase from pretest to posttest also tended to receive high scores on the qualitative reflection post experience.

Importantly, the quantitative measures were not enough to capture the vulnerability the students showed in their CRLs or in the class debriefing. As we'll see in the qualitative analysis, the students were willing to express and confront the stereotypes that emerged during the simulation, thus creating an opportunity for their intercultural competency to improve.

We proceeded to code students' post-experience CRL using emergent coding. Six main themes and eight sub-themes (for a total of twelve distinct labels) emerged from this exercise. For each label, we calculated interrater reliability. For the ultimate takeaway category, there was 100% agreement.

The final portion of the CRL prompt asked students what their takeaway was, therefore, it comes as no surprise (or does it?) that all 30 participants offered comments in that category. Among the takeaway themes that emerged, three are particularly salient: 1) how easy it is to make assumptions, 2) envisioning a change in one's behavior, and 3) the realization of the link one makes between physical appearance on the one hand and cultures/values/behaviors on the other hand.

Eighteen of the 30 participants (60%) expressed that going through *Kaleidoscope* had made them aware of how prone they were to make assumptions about other people and how these assumptions were often influenced by societal stereotypes. Courtney, for example, wrote, "This experience helped me recognize just how easy it is to make assumptions about someone (whether they're right or wrong) simply based on appearance and a few facts about them." This is clearly something that participants almost always lamented about since they were striving to do better. Naomi offered, "I know that it is wrong and biased to create an entire image of someone's character simply based on typical generalizations made of people with similar characteristics, yet I can't help but make those assumptions upon first glance." These considerations were often accompanied by the realization that assumptions can quickly lead to bias or prejudice. For example, Iris realized that "(…) we tend to make quite a few incorrect judgments based on prior perceptions and learned stereotypes." Additionally, Yolanda wrote, "[f]rom this experience, I can reflect upon my own assumptions and see how they often come from places of cultural bias." These comments were often accompanied by a perceived need for a broader and more diverse perspective. For example, Velvet wrote, "[t]he main takeaway from this experience is that the biases that I have is [sic.] not always valid. Furthermore, I learnt that even if I know the culture well, I should not use that to make assumptions about other people because a culture is shaped by various factors and not everybody shares the same values." This double realization on the part of students (quick to judge/make assumptions and need to keep assumptions in check and a multi-perspectival approach to mind) led them to envision how they could change their behaviors.

Although 4 students reported that they would not change anything, mostly because they thought they were doing just fine (for example, Courtney wrote, "I don't think many of my behaviors will change as I tend to always assume the best in everyone and when I make assumptions, they are usually as neutral," a posture that revealed little self-awareness and critical thinking), this was a small minority of the students. Twenty-two of them (nearly 75%) made comments that pointed to an introspective posture that included both self-reflection and call for behavioral change. For example, Christine wrote:

> After this experience, I am revisiting the cardinal value that my immigrant parents instilled in me, and modifying it to be slightly more realistic. Rather than expecting to eliminate bias completely, I am amending it to include the habitual practice of introspection and self-reflection. Having difficult conversations about race and stereotypes will now become a part of my daily routine to learn about those who are different from me. Whether it be someone from a different country, familial situation, or belief system, I am now more open to learning from them than I ever have been before. My eyes have been opened to stereotyping and implicit bias, and I am eager to evolve my thinking patterns to support our diverse world.

While making conversations about race/stereotypes a daily practice may be hyperbolic or wishful thinking, the fact that Christine was willing to actually have these conversations is a clear response to *Kaleidoscope*'s takeaway message, "are you ready to start that conversation?" (image 4).

Another aspect of students' willingness to change behaviors was manifested in their understanding of differentiating the individual from the group. For example, Ben offered, "[o]ne way in which my behavior will change is that I will desist from drawing conclusions on others based on the image that I have of a particular group." Interestingly, beyond this realization or urge to do better, students also expressed how empowering *Kaleidoscope* was in that it was OK not to be perfect and that the work of intercultural learning was worth doing and maybe even fun. Naomi wrote, "I felt empowered to change these preconceived notions and to understand everybody for who they truly are before I presume anything. This experience has left me motivated to get to know people beyond their outside appearance. I want to break through any preconceived notions I have and learn about other peoples' perspectives and cultures."

Image 4. A user (in shadows) receiving the final takeaway message inside the Kaleidoscope experience.

A good place to start doing this work is by critically examining the perceived relationship between physical appearances and culture, values, and behaviors. These considerations often led to multifaceted, and complex reflections such as the one offered by Olivia:

> (...) I notice that there's a consistent reluctance to use visible identities to assume invisible identities from both myself and my peers. This is most apparent with questions that caused the group to choose an answer separate from the individual, instead based on "the average person." I believe the fact that these questions were answered in a social environment deterred me from basing my answers on more specifically applicable standards to the individual like "the average Asian man" that would theoretically lead to more accurate answers. (...) I believe the social pressure of avoiding racial/ethnic stereotypes has positive and negative effects on how things are perceived. While trying to overcome this pressure may be difficult or even counterproductive in certain areas, I believe that being cognisant [sic] of how it may affect perception and decision-making is important for me to consider when deciding how to behave.

What Olivia realizes here is the ambiguous origin of stereotypes and the tightrope one must walk between understanding why they came to being, their degree of truth, and their problematic potential for essentialization, which must be resisted.

This is the conclusion that Zoe reached when she wrote, "In totality, *Kaleidoscope* has taught me that appearance doesn't always correlate with background and lifestyle. Furthermore, it displays how important it is to actually speak to people about their experiences and culture to truly learn about them and be educated on a larger spectrum of backgrounds." Ultimately, participants demonstrated on occasion the ability to envision the other not only as a self, but as themselves, which is a key ingredient to hospitality (as understood by Levinas). Armon, for example, concluded, "[t]his experience taught me the importance of asking questions. Identity is at the core of who I am, so I must give others the ability to talk about their values instead of defining them by their appearance."

So when *Kaleidoscope* closes on the following takeaway message, "Inside this room, you have been prompted to make certain assumptions. Now you have the opportunity outside of this room to have conversations with others and get to know who they really are. Are you ready to start that conversation?", the message clearly resonated with the participants.

5 Discussion and Conclusion

We set out to examine the impact of *Kaleidoscope* in initiating and supporting intercultural learning. The quantitative measures do not offer a clear picture of the complexity of *Kaleidoscope*'s impact on students. However, moving from being unaware of what they didn't know to knowing where some of their biases or shortcomings might be, the ultimate takeaways that they offer in their CRL responses illustrate how students move between phases of intercultural competency development as a result of the immersive experience and debriefing. Within their reflections and in the class-wide debrief, students are challenging themselves to acknowledge and address their unconscious biases, thus illustrating the potential of and need for simulation-based exercises to enhance intercultural learning as well as the need for further research in this area. Students, like all of us, are prone to think, believe, or offer that they are open-minded and avoid stereotypes, but without confronting that thinking then movement between the phases of intercultural development cannot be achieved. *Kaleidoscope*'s simulated experience, though, illustrates how to see our blind spots and confront them without a real-life consequence. The debriefing aspects also provide students with an opportunity to process their cognitive, affective, and behaviors as a journey, which is central to intercultural competence development [5]. Further, the debrief illustrates more context and texture to student perspective regarding their intercultural competency development than the survey measures could provide, further illustrating the difficulty in measuring intercultural learning. Their CRL responses illustrate and support the importance of providing space to process the learning from immersive experiences or simulations; themes that emerged matched collective course themes, but there was also a significant amount of individual expression of positive intercultural learning. Their efforts affirmed and solidified our belief that a good debrief can effectuate movement between stages of intercultural learning.

We were surprised, though, by the depth with which students engaged in this pedagogical sequence as it illustrated their vulnerability and willingness to develop as interculturally competent learners. In our opinion, their honesty and transparency within the CRL and class-wide debriefs centered openness and respect within the wider class environment. Such vulnerability and transparency gave us as facilitators within the debrief session and future class sessions more opportunity to emphasize the on-going development work that each of us faces in relation to intercultural competency, a tactic that we appreciated and freed us from our own potential defensiveness over the concept's importance. Through the debrief, we learned our students' motivation and investment in their intercultural learning, thus heeding Lederman and Kato's [21] call for facilitators to reflect on how a debrief impacts them as much as the participants themselves.

With 43% of the class students coming back to *Kaleidoscope* in their final CRL, we can also see how the immersive experience and its debrief lasted with students. We were both pleased and surprised to see how students, owing in part to the *Kaleidoscope* simulation, embarked on this intercultural journey, first through an introspective gesture whereby they recognized and acknowledged their own biases. In accepting their discomfort and expressing their vulnerability, students also engaged in meaningful reflection on how visible and invisible identities shape cultural perspectives, and ultimately envisioned pathways to change their perspectives and behaviors. In returning to *Kaleidoscope* weeks after the activity, students demonstrated the complexity of intercultural learning. They are illustrating Lederman's [20] point, "An educational experience is a complex event. … It must convey to the learners that they have the capability of using this new knowledge not only in the classroom in which they learn it, but in other contexts to which they take that which has been learned." With further experiences, students crafted new connections with *Kaleidoscope* and new ways of understanding how it would impact their intercultural competency; they embody the learning as a continuous journey and enactment of their takeaways. But what if they were not given the opportunity to reflect once again?

While there is clear value in immersive experiences and debriefs to understand intercultural learning processes, we would be remiss if we did not note a few limitations of this study. First, while it provided students with an interesting first step to engage with their positionality as cultural beings and the cultural bias and prejudice they may hold, which was confirmed by how many of them acknowledged stereotypes they harbor, our methodology around *Kaleidoscope* did not engage critically with the notion of stereotypes, where they come from and how they are perpetuated. This is a notion that was broached at other times in the course but not specifically around the *Kaleidoscope* activity. As a result, the only way these stereotypes appeared in the results was through self-disclosure. Additionally, this simulation was within one course that was focused on investigating culture and its role in society. This provided further opportunities for students to make connections and investigate culture with more depth than other first-year seminars offered at the same university and semester. Use of the simulation comprised an extensive amount of course time - both for students outside of class and within a dedicated class session. This is not available to every course offering. Additionally, *Kaleidoscope* is a stand-alone experience that lacks the debriefing wrapper on a daily usage basis that was the focus of our course assignment and class-wide debrief. Considerations as to how much impact it has on a random user and not within such a structured class setting could indicate much different results than those offered within this study. And, finally, it is difficult to isolate *Kaleidoscope* as a variable in effectuating intercultural development. It is our contention that it can be a positive contribution, as evidenced by the qualitative analysis, but it cannot be seen as a singular or only intervention on students' development.

The simulation provides both distance and intimacy – distance to acknowledge the biases while also seeing the stranger as a real person that deserves respect. More importantly, this study shows the critical importance of the debriefing phase. Indeed, the debriefing process has two underlying assumptions: "first, that the experience of participation has affected the participants, and second, that a discussion of the experience will enhance the participants' ability to learn from that experience" [21]. In sum, the simulation and accompanying debriefing are effective in initiating reflection by participants, even though it is with a "person" who participants will not meet in their everyday lives. In this sense, *Kaleidoscope*, as an immersive experience, blurs the lines between simulation and a real-life intercultural encounter in two ways: while it offers a kind of sandbox for users to engage with interculturality (the simulation aspect), 1) it made users engage with themselves as culturally situated individuals (a necessary gesture intercultural learning) and 2) it invites users to reinvest the social world and seek, invite, and appreciate intercultural encounters. In this sense, as McGonigal [23] advocated, it may help users apply the attitudes and skills they learned in the simulation to make the world a better place.

References

1. Bennett, J.M.: Transformative training: designing programs for culture learning. In: Moodian, M.A. (ed.) Contemporary Leadership and Intercultural Competence: Exploring the Cross-Cultural Dynamics Within Organizations, pp. 95–100. SAGE Publications, Los Angeles (2008)
2. Crookall, D.: Serious games, debriefing, and simulation/gaming as a discipline. Simul. Gaming **41**(6), 898–920 (2010). https://doi.org/10.1177/1046878110390784
3. Crookall, D.: Debriefing: a practical guide. In: Angelini, M.L., Muñiz, R. (eds.) Simulation for Participatory Education. STE, pp. 115–214. Springer, Cham (2023). https://doi.org/10.1007/978-3-031-21011-2_6
4. Deardorff, D.K.: Identification and assessment of intercultural competence as a student outcome of internationalization. J. Stud. Int. Educ. **10**(3), 241–266 (2006). https://doi.org/10.1177/1028315306287002
5. Deardorff, D.K.: Assessing intercultural competence. New Directions Inst. Res. **149**, 65–79 (2011). https://doi.org/10.1002/ir.381
6. Deason, E.E, Efron, Y., Howell, R., Kaufman, S., Lee, J., Press, S.: Debriefing the debrief. Public Law and Legal Theory Working Paper Series, vol. 202, pp. 301–332 (2013). https://papers.ssrn.com/sol3/papers.cfm?abstract_id=2251940
7. Fowler, S.M., Pusch, M.D.: Intercultural simulation games: a review (of the United States and beyond). Simul. Gaming **41**(1), 94–115 (2010). https://doi.org/10.1177/1046878109352204
8. Geertz, C.: The Interpretation of Cultures. Basic Books, New York (1973)
9. Gentry, J.W.: What is experiential learning? Guide Bus. Gaming Exp. Learn. **9**(1), 20–32 (1990)
10. Harviainen, J.T., Lainema, T., Saarinen, E.: Player-reported impediments to game-based learning. Trans. Digit. Games Res. Assoc. **1**(2), 55–83 (2014). https://doi.org/10.26503/todigra.v1i2.14
11. Hickman, L. Akdere, M.: Developing intercultural competencies through virtual reality: Internet of Things applications in education and learning. In: 15th Learning and Technology Conference (L&T), Jeddah, Saudi Arabia, pp. 24–28. IEEE (2018). https://doi.org/10.1109/LT.2018.8368506
12. Hofstede, G.: National cultures and corporate cultures. In: Samovar, L.A., Porter, R.E. (eds.) Communication Between Cultures, Wadsworth, Belmont, CA (1984)
13. Hofstede, G.J., de Caluwe, L., Peters, V.: Why simulation games work – in search of the active substance: a synthesis. Simul. Gaming **41**(6), 824–843 (2010). https://doi.org/10.1177/1046878110375596
14. Kolb, D.A.: Experiential Learning: Experience as the Source of Learning and Development. Prentice Hall, Englewood Cliffs (1984)

15. Kolb, D.A., Boyatzis, R.E., Mainemelis, C.: Experiential learning theory: previous research and new directions. In: Sternberg, R.J., Zhang, L.-f. (eds.) Perspectives on Thinking, Learning, and Cognitive Styles, New York, pp. 227–247. Routledge (2001)
16. Kramsch, C.: Language and Culture. Oxford University Press, Oxford (1998)
17. Kramsch, C.: Teaching language along the cultural faultline. In: Lange, D.L., Klee, C.A., Paige, R.M., Yershova, Y.A. (eds.) Culture as the Core: Interdisciplinary Perspectives on Culture Learning in the Language Curriculum, Minneapolis, MN, pp. 15–31. Center for Advanced Research on Language Acquisition (2000)
18. Lainema, K., Syynimaa, K., Lainema, T., Hämäläinen, R.: Organizing for collaboration in simulation-based environments: an affordance perspective. J. Res. Technol. Educ. **55**(2), 307–323 (2023). https://doi.org/10.1080/15391523.2021.1962451
19. Lane, H.C., Hays, M.J., Core, M.G., Auerbach, D.: Learning intercultural communication skills with virtual humans: Feedback and fidelity. J. Educ. Psychol. **105**(4), 1026–1035 (2013). https://doi.org/10.1037/a0031506
20. Lederman, L.C.: Debriefing: toward a systematic assessment of theory and practice. Simul. Gaming **23**(2), 145–160 (1992)
21. Lederman, L.C., Kato, F.: Debriefing the debriefing process: a new look. In: Crookall, D., Arai, K. (eds.) Simulations and Gaming Across Disciplines and Cultures, pp. 235–242. Sage, Thousand Oaks (1995)
22. Leigh, E.E., Levesque, L.L.: Facilitating Simulations. Edward Edgar Publishing, Cheltenahm (2024)
23. McGonigal, J.: Reality is Broken: Why Games Make us Better and How They Can Change the World. Penguin Press, New York (2011)
24. Miville, M.L., et al.: Miville-Guzman Universality-Diversity Scale (M-GUDS) [Database record]. APA PsycTests (1999). https://doi.org/10.1037/t09436-000
25. Saldaña, J.: The Coding Manual for Qualitative Researchers, 4th edn. Sage Publications Ltd., Thousand Oaks (2021)
26. Todd, A.R., Bodenhausen, G.V., Galinsky, A.D.: Perspective taking combats the denial of intergroup discrimination. J. Exp. Soc. Psychol. **48**(3), 738–745 (2012) https://doi.org/10.1016/j.jesp.2011.12.011
27. Williams, M., Moser, T.: The art of coding and thematic exploration in qualitative research. Int. Manag. Rev. **15**(1), 45–55 (2019)

Anywhere Academy — Avatar-Based Collaborative Teaching and Learning in VR

Patrick Querl[(✉)] [ID], Raymond Leonardo Chandra [ID], Koen Castermans [ID], Djamel Berkaoui [ID], and Heribert Nacken [ID]

Academic and Research Department Engineering Hydrology and UNESCO Chair of Hydrological Change and Water Resources Management, RWTH Aachen University, Mies-van-der-Rohe Straße, 52074 Aachen, Germany
{querl,chandra,castermans,berkaoui,nacken}@lfi.rwth-aachen.de

Abstract. Virtual reality (VR) has emerged as a transformative technology in higher education, offering vast potential for immersive learning experiences and innovative pedagogical approaches. This paper presents *Anywhere Academy*, a new VR platform designed to leverage the benefits of virtual reality while addressing open challenges. It discusses the motivation for developing this platform despite existing alternatives. It compares current platforms against identified requirements derived from prominent concerns about using VR in higher education. This work explores technical key components and design choices informed by relevant literature and highlights the role of artificial intelligence (AI) in creating dynamic virtual environments for learners. It also presents Learning Experience Design (LXD), a novel approach to create effective educational interventions that consider the experience of learners as a whole, creating learning scenarios suited to learners' needs. The development status of Anywhere Academy is presented alongside ethical considerations and future research opportunities.

Keywords: virtual reality · immersive learning · learning experience design · higher education · unity

1 Introduction

Virtual reality (VR) has garnered increasing attention in university teaching over the past decade [25,33], offering potential across diverse pedagogical contexts and subjects. Various VR-based teaching scenarios have emerged, including communicative scenarios in the domain of SocialVR [20], role-playing applications for social skills acquisition [4], virtual excursions [27], and simulations in disciplines like chemistry [12], medicine [24], mechanical engineering [6], civil engineering [32] among others [17]. Universities can also leverage VR in marketing to enhance monetary and personal capacities [5].

Key characteristics of VR in teaching include heightened immersion and interactivity, which can psychologically impact learners by enhancing presence

F. Trautwein et al. (Eds.): ISAGA 2025, LNCS 16439, pp. 346–361, 2026.
https://doi.org/10.1007/978-3-032-20129-4_23

and agency, thus improving learning outcomes if designed effectively [25]. Studies consistently report positive attitudes towards VR and increased student engagement compared to traditional methods [15,19,32]. The strong sense of presence in VR offers significant potential for collaborative learning with complex social components, recently gaining attention [26]. VR supports autonomous student work through customizable environments and complex interactions. This potential is further amplified by AI advancements, such as intelligent avatars and conversational agents, which enable individualized forms of education [28,31,39].

The integration of VR into teaching faces challenges such as limited educational content availability [3,14,19], complexity in curriculum integration, and the need for university staff to acquire necessary skills [3]. VR still must overcome fear and familiarity barriers [14]. Additionally, inherent difficulties like increased cognitive load from wide fields of view, high immersion levels, and interactivity as well as cybersickness [14,25]. Although VR devices are becoming more powerful and cost-efficient, distributive justice issues persist due to cost barriers [3], alongside reliance on few global players like *Meta* or *PICO*, raising data security concerns.

Solutions for VR in higher education must balance positive potentials with negative aspects while understanding learner needs. Learning Experience Design (LXD) is a promising paradigm addressing these elements by emphasizing the interconnected relationship between learners as users, designed interventions, and learning contexts. LXD practice is inherently transdisciplinary, requiring extensive knowledge across multiple disciplines [35].

This work introduces *Anywhere Academy*, a new VR platform. In Sect. 2, the rationale behind creating a new platform despite existing options is discussed. Furthermore, it compares existing platforms against requirements identified earlier. Section 3 explores technical design choices referencing relevant literature. A process for scene design is proposed in Sect. 4, emphasizing key affordances of VR and plans how to harness AI capabilities to create rich experiences variably involving instructors. Section 5 provides insights into the current development status, ethical considerations and opportunities for further research and enhancements.

2   Motivation

2.1   Requirement Analysis

The following core requirements are derived from the problems described in Sect. 1:

Ease of Availability is essential to address the scarcity of educational content and ensure access for as many users as possible. VR software should minimize technical barriers, with modern applications often supporting web browsers. This is a core requirement for Anywhere Academy, ensuring quick access from various devices without extensive preparation. Additionally, the software should function on both immersive and non-immersive platforms to accommodate users unable to wear head-mounted devices and those prone to severe cybersickness.

Cross-Platform support stems from the need for easy availability, enabling seamless and inclusive integration into university curricula by connecting users across different devices.

Multi-User capabilities, enabling remote connections, are essential for developing communication and collaboration skills, which are critical competencies for future careers [30]. This feature reduces environmental impact by minimizing travel and fosters immersive connections between learners and educators. Additionally, there is evidence suggesting that meaningful and productive collaboration enhances learning outcomes [26].

Complex Interactivity is a crucial aspect of VR in learning, significantly enhancing feelings of presence and agency, thereby promoting learning success [25]. Interactivity extends beyond navigating immersive scenes and viewing media; it involves the capability to touch, move, and manipulate the virtual environment in complex and meaningful ways.

Self-Hostable platforms offer a high degree of data privacy, as universities are in control of what data is sent over their networks. Data privacy is crucial in educational environments. Being able to host a system also increases independence from third parties, which can increase robustness and longevity of the product.

AI Capability is fundamental for implementing innovative AI-supported teaching methods such as adaptive scenes or generative conversational agents. However, this requires careful consideration of data privacy due to the cloud-based nature of many AI services.

Open Source development is sustainable by being reusable and costs-efficient. It is transparent and allows universities to contribute to development while adapting solutions to their needs. Open source projects encourage innovation and viability through shared expertise and resources.

2.2   Existing VR Platforms

In this article, we present a comparison of various VR platforms based on the requirements identified in Sect. 2.1. The selection of platforms was made based on the authors' personal experiences and discussions with various colleagues within cross-university networks in Germany. While not exhaustive, it provides a suitable insight into the landscape of available VR platforms in the higher education sector to the best of our knowledge. A brief analysis of the platforms is summarized in Table 1. For more details, see below.

CoSpaces Edu is a commercial, closed-source tool for educators and students, supporting mobile devices, AR, and VR with visual scripting for object behavior modeling. It is not self-hostable but claims GDPR compliance. While featuring full-body avatars, it lacks browser support and AI capabilities [10].

ENGAGE is a renowned VR content platform offering extensive cross-platform and multiuser functionalities with high-quality 3D environments and realistic

Table 1. Comparison of existing VR platforms regarding the requirements from Sect. 2.1.

	CoSpaces Edu	ENGAGE	Figments.nrw	FrameVR	Hubs	MyScore	ShapesXR
Accessibility				✓	✓		✓
Cross-Platform	✓	✓	✓	✓	✓	✓	✓
Multi-User	✓	✓	✓	✓	✓	✓	✓
Complex Interactivity	✓		✓			✓	
Self-Hostable			✓		✓	✓	
AI Capability		✓		✓			✓
Open Source			✓		✓	✓	

avatars. It includes a content editor for customized creation but offers limited behavioral options. Integrated with OpenAI for AI-driven intelligent avatars and asset creation, ENGAGE lacks behavior modeling tools like coding or visual scripting editors, limiting object interactivity. The platform does not support web browsers, is closed source, non-self-hostable but claims GDPR compliance [11].

Figments.nrw is an open-source project providing a low-code toolkit for educators to create content with custom asset spawning and behavior modeling via a custom visual scripting language. Featuring multi-user capabilities with self-hostable servers, it claims GDPR compliance using Ready Player Me full-body avatars. Supporting HMDs, desktop PCs, and mobile devices with cross-platform functionality, Figments.nrw lacks browser support and AI capabilities [42].

FrameVR is a commercial browser-based software built in JavaScript, offering multi-user cross-platform support emphasizing AI capabilities through generative agent interactions and automated transcripts. Despite potential for AI-assisted asset creation, the absence of behavior modeling tools limits interactivity control over objects. FrameVR cannot be self-hosted; no GDPR compliance statement was found on its website [43].

Hubs, an open-source project provides a browser-based VR application with a low-code web interface to create scenes allowing self-hosting of instances where multiple users can collaborate across immersive systems. Simple behavior modeling via visual scripting is in early development stages; specific AI capabilities are absent [16].

MyScore, an open-source VR platform tailored for avatar-based teaching features multi-user configurations with server architecture facilitating game state synchronization and user communication. Self-hostable with claimed GDPR compliance, it supports cross-platform use across Meta Quest, PICO devices as well

as Windows(VR) setups among others. Content is developed directly in C#
and Unity offering flexibility if high-code development suits needs. It is lacking
browser support or integrated AI functionalities [1].

ShapesXR, primarily designed as an extended reality (VR/AR) design tool,
enables easy instantiation of assets during runtime facilitating world scene
designs collaboratively across platforms albeit without comprehensive behavior
modeling systems nor being self-hostable itself [38].

This analysis remains concise due to scope limitations. For more details,
the individual websites should be considered. None of the presented platforms
fulfills all requirements from Sect. 2.1, which is the goal of *Anywhere Academy*.
This work continues to outline important technological components and suggests
a design process for new teaching content based on recent immersive learning
theory.

3 Platform Architecture

The Unity 3D engine [41] was chosen as the foundation for Anywhere Academy
due to its widespread adoption and significant market share in 3D software
and gaming. Supported by a large community and extensive learning resources,
Unity's recent advancements focus on AI integration during development and
runtime, with tools like Unity Muse and Unity Sentis enabling AI inference
directly on devices. These innovations offer potential for pioneering educational applications. Unity supports a diverse range of devices, including desktop
PCs, smartphones, VR equipment, and modern web browsers without significant coding overhead. While this multi-device support enhances availability, it
also increases complexity regarding scalability and performance considerations.
Mobile devices like smartphones and VR headsets have fewer computational
resources than most modern computers, similar to browser versions due to less
efficient hardware resource access compared to native versions.

3.1 Multi-user and AI Capabilities

To enable multi-user capabilities, Anywhere Academy employs a self-hostable
dedicated server architecture. This approach ensures independence from individual hosts typical of peer-to-peer networks and allows universities to
autonomously manage data traffic. By using a dedicated server as the central
authority for learning sessions, centralized coordination is facilitated. Various
open-source networking libraries for Unity were evaluated based on performance
metrics such as data usage, frames per second, CPU utilization relative to concurrent user numbers, and cross-platform compatibility [8]. The study identified *FishNet* [13] as the most efficient open-source solution, supporting all platforms mentioned in Sect. 2.1, making it the chosen network library for Anywhere
Academy.

A challenge arose in implementing a voice chat system compatible with both
native applications and browser versions while maintaining development simplicity. Unity's default Microphone API is unavailable for browser-based builds

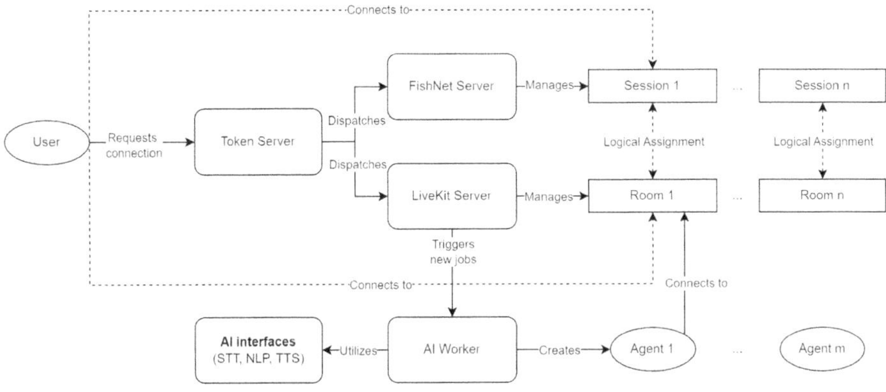

Fig. 1. Anywhere Academy server setup.

but is commonly used in voice transmission libraries. This issue was resolved using *LiveKit* [21], an open-source real-time service offering audio and video capabilities. LiveKit provides numerous SDKs for integration into various software types along with open-source server code allowing self-hosting, ensuring independence from third parties. Recent updates include integration with LLMs (Large Language Models), enabling users to interact with generative agents via oral conversation [21].

Using LiveKit increased the complexity of the server setup depicted in Fig. 1. Anywhere Academy needs three servers: a Token Server, FishNet Server, and LiveKit Server, plus an additional AI Worker if AI capability is desired. The Token Server acts as an intermediary between users and software so that only one host address needs to be known by users and verifies them to the LiveKit server. FishNet manages main game state synchronization – such as avatar movement – while LiveKit facilitates voice communication. Each FishNet session within Anywhere Academy corresponds to one LiveKit room, managed by the Token Server. To integrate AI functionality, an AI worker created using LiveKit SDK registers with the LiveKit Server to dispatch new agents when necessary; these agents connect to LiveKit rooms behaving like regular users – listening and speaking interactively. The AI worker utilizes interchangeable AI models, enhancing adaptability according to university-specific requirements while allowing simultaneous use of commercial alongside open-source AI models.

3.2   Avatar System

Avatars serve as virtual representations of users, enhancing embodiment, which can positively impact learning outcomes [25]. Embodiment involves the sensation of possessing a virtual body [25], and the theory of Embodied Cognition posits that perception is shaped by one's sensorimotor system and environmental interactions [25]. Controlling a detailed avatar differs perceptually from navigating without a body. The Proteus Effect suggests avatar appearance can significantly influence user behavior [45]. Avatars across multiple VR platforms vary in realism and customization; studies indicate VR users prefer realistic avatars in educational contexts for increased seriousness and trustworthiness [7,36]. While similarity between avatar and owner enhances body ownership, it minimally affects presence overall [18], with potential anxiety arising from identity exposure [18]. Conversely, using avatars may reduce social interaction quality, like peer criticism during reviews, due to identity disconnects [22]. However, they can alleviate the "lonely learner" experience [22].

Research indicates avatar customizability influences learning performance. Positive effects are generally associated with customization, yet excessive or insufficient options may distract and negatively affect outcomes [29]. Based on these insights, Anywhere Academy includes an Avatar Creation Toolkit offering naturalistic human representations with moderate customization flexibility. Users can tailor full-body avatars in aspects like facial structure, hairstyle, clothing, skin and hair color, physique among others within a predefined framework. An example is shown in Fig. 2. Users decide their avatar's appearance and how much of their identity to reveal. Autonomous customization aims to enhance body ownership and self-presence for improved learning outcomes [25].

The 3D models were crafted using Blender and rigged to a Mixamo skeleton ensuring compatibility with its animation library. This integration enables expressive gestures for avatars.

Fig. 2. Example avatars of Anywhere Academy. It features a naturalistic full-body representation of a human body.

In order to achieve a strong resemblance between avatars and their owners for specific applications, the incorporation of photo-based avatars is planned. These avatars will be generated using photogrammetry techniques [7], primarily targeting instructors, though their use will remain optional. The implementation of photo-based avatars aims to foster a productive social environment, which in turn is expected to enhance learning outcomes [26].

3.3   Interactivity

Interactivity is a key affordance of VR and plays a crucial role in VR-supported learning [25]. As discussed in Sect. 2.2, many platforms were deemed unsuitable due to their limited interactivity. Unity, with its *XR Interaction Toolkit* (XRI toolkit), provides a robust set of VR functionalities that enable the implementation of diverse VR-based interactions. These include 3D and UI interactions utilizing Unity's event system, which offers haptic and visual feedback. The toolkit is compatible with the OpenXR standard, granting us significant freedom in designing interactive experiences. This flexibility arises because Unity's event system can directly invoke C# methods, allowing for highly customized and sophisticated behaviors.

The base XR Rig from the XRI toolkit is adapted to function seamlessly in both immersive and non-immersive PC environments. The PC character controller interfaces directly with the XRI toolkit using Unity's new input system, facilitating easy implementation and modification. This setup allows for future integration of hand tracking capabilities. Similarly, mobile controls can be incorporated later with low effort, thereby expanding the platform's accessibility to additional groups of learners.

3.4   Optimization

Benchmarking was conducted on the Meta Quest 3 to ensure stable operation across mobile (including VR) and desktop platforms. Performance optimization involved minimizing materials and textures through atlas baking to reduce GPU bottlenecks. Real-time lighting is limited to one light source while other lighting data is baked in, preserving capacity for additional users and dynamic content such as videos or 360° images. Occlusion culling ensures only visible elements are rendered, enhancing efficiency. Current tests indicate the platform can support approximately 25 avatars in a single scenario; further testing is ongoing to confirm this limit. These measures collectively contribute to a scalable design suitable for multi-user immersive experiences focused on performance-consciousness.

4   Scene Design Process

Immersive learning models such as CAMIL and TICOL provide valuable insights into the relationships between the technological properties of VR, its unique affordances, psychological phenomena, and ultimately, learning outcomes [25, 26]. Scene design in VR encompasses considerations related to representational fidelity, control factors, and pedagogical techniques. The visual style of a virtual environment can prime perception and influence learning success. While realistic environments may enhance the sense of presence [25] and potentially improve learning outcomes, some researchers suggest a trade-off between realism and abstraction due to cognitive load [44]. Similarly, collaborative activities in VR have the potential to create engaging learning experiences; however, the presence of bystanders can increase cognitive load during task execution [34]. Understanding the relationship between scene design and cognitive load is crucial for creating environments that facilitate rather than hinder learning. Anywhere Academy focuses on simple scene environments with naturalistic-looking assets to ensure scenarios convey the necessary seriousness for a learning context without overwhelming learners with information. Some examples are illustrated in Fig. 3.

Fig. 3. Scene designs used in Anywhere Academy featuring a personal learning area, a group work scene and a virtual auditorium.

4.1   Virtual Rooms as Third Educators

In educational theory, the concept of the environment as the third educator [2] emphasizes the influential role of surroundings in shaping learning experiences. VR extends this principle by offering immersive environments that can actively engage learners. Virtual environments do not have to be static in the same way a room in reality is static by nature. Virtual classrooms can react and adapt to learners actions, creating dynamic and individual experiences without a necessary need for further instructors [32]. This potential is amplified by the uprise of powerful and easily accessible AI tools that can be incorporated into VR, like explained in Sect. 4.3. This improves scalability and independence of learners. Necessary are learning environments which are suitably tailored towards reaching learning objectives. Without instructors, self-regulation is crucial to facilitate learning success [25].

4.2   Learning Experience Design

The design process of a VR learning scene should be iterative and flexible, as requirements can vary significantly based on use cases and learning objectives. One major advantage of utilizing VR in higher education is its ability to increase enjoyment and engagement. Beyond just meeting learning objectives or achieving outcomes, affective qualities also influence learners' experiences.

This concept is embedded in *Learning Experience Design* (LXD), which lies at the intersection of classical Learning Design and User Experience Design. LXD focuses on enhancing the overall quality of learning experiences from a holistic perspective rather than solely targeting specific results [9]. It adopts a human-centered approach that necessitates an empathetic understanding of learners, aiming to provide personalized experiences that cater not only to what learners want but also what they need. A hallmark of LXD is its strong connection to established learning theories and theories from user experience design [35].

In LXD, learners should understand their goals align with overarching learning objectives [9], often featuring multiple pathways for problem-solving and knowledge acquisition. Designers must consider numerous factors and influences while possessing a deep understanding of subject matter, sometimes requiring complex models of problems and strategies integrated into the design process [9].

Unlike traditional learning design, LXD typically involves co-design with learners, integrating them as equal contributors, or participatory design where learners are included but LXD designers retain ultimate decision-making authority [35]. Gaining a comprehensive understanding may also require involving experts in the design process [9].

Another defining feature of Learning Experience Design (LXD) is its iterative process, which alternates between design phases and evaluation cycles [40]. The basic process is outlined in Fig. 4. Typically, the process begins with identifying a problem that needs to be solved. Following initial research, a design is developed and then implemented. This implementation is tested in collaboration with learners. If the problem is resolved, the product can be released. Otherwise, the process loops back to the research phase for further refinement [37]. LXD places a strong emphasis on collecting data in situ and using data-informed iterations. This approach underscores the advantages of establishing robust connections with learning analytics techniques capable of capturing real-time learner data [40].

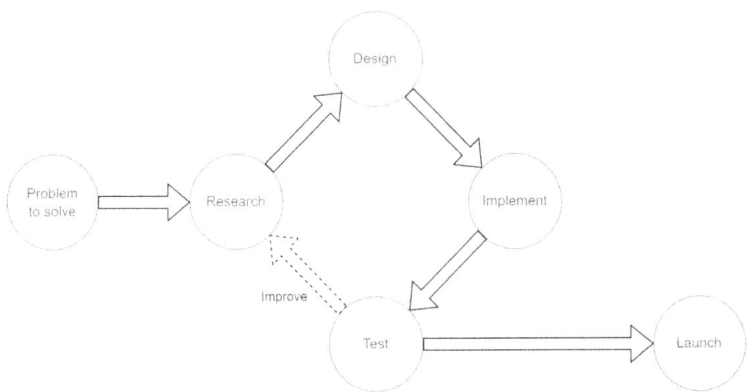

Fig. 4. Basic learning experience design process [37]

4.3   Usage of Artificial Intelligence

As discussed in Sect. 1 and Sect. 2.1, AI-based technologies hold significant promise for enhancing VR learning experiences. Many contemporary educational software platforms already leverage machine learning algorithms extensively, owing to their ability to adapt to individual users. The integration of VR hardware amplifies this potential by offering unique and additional data streams. Anywhere Academy plans to harness this data to develop adaptive digital assistance systems that provide tailored support to users [28], predicting and optimizing cognitive load and aiming to improve learning outcomes [25]. These techniques can also be applied to adapt the environment in a data-driven manner, both visually and audibly, while enabling novel interaction methods.

One such example of innovative interaction methods is the use of advanced conversational agents linked with generative AI models [31,39]. This approach allows for the simulation of unique social interactions, empowering students to train autonomously in safe environments without concerns about negative consequences or social judgment.

Given that the development of Anywhere Academy is still in its nascent stages, this list is not exhaustive. As technology evolves over time, numerous new use cases are expected to emerge. Therefore, it is crucial to establish a scalable infrastructure capable of accommodating various AI-based technologies as they develop.

5   Conclusion

This work presents *Anywhere Academy*, a virtual reality (VR) platform designed for avatar-based teaching and learning, offering browser compatibility and expandability through AI systems. The platform accommodates both immersive and non-immersive setups to improve ease of availability and accessibility, addressing challenges in VR adoption within higher education, such as content scarcity, technological barriers, and distributive fairness. The rationale behind creating Anywhere Academy despite existing VR platforms is articulated alongside technical details and design choices informed by relevant research, emphasizing learning theories in the design process. Learning Experience Design (LXD) is highlighted as a novel approach for creating educational VR content foundational to upcoming learning environments. This work aims to guide creators of educational VR content by sharing insights from the implementation of Anywhere Academy.

Anywhere Academy is a high-code solution, posing development barriers for those lacking expertise in Unity and C#. While low-code solutions often lead to functional limitations we sought to avoid, Anywhere Academy empowers researchers to develop novel VR scenes with complex interactions tailored to user needs. Although still under development, this report aims to offer valuable insights for researchers who may utilize our platform or benefit from its design considerations.

Enhancing Anywhere Academy with a low-code content creation tool could significantly improve usability for other researchers. Other research projects offer effective low-code tools that could inform this development [42]. Furthermore, leveraging AI capabilities within Anywhere Academy presents opportunities to integrate learning analytics tools or existing learning management systems, enhancing usability and supporting the LXD approach proposed here.

Ethical considerations are to be made; while aiming for inclusivity, new technologies can inadvertently exclude some individuals in higher education. We strive to minimize exclusion and address distributive fairness issues to our best extent. Data privacy is paramount; XR devices collect extensive data sets necessitating safe university environments where risks like harassment are mitigated through safety mechanisms.

Mental health concerns such as anxiety, PTSD-related issues, and dissociative experiences require attention [23]. Studies highlight reporting inadequacies regarding these adverse effects across VR studies [23], underscoring the need for better monitoring and documentation.

Challenges exist for individuals with visual or motor impairments using immersive VR technology. Involving affected individuals in the design process is essential; LXD's iterative methodology encourages inclusion of diverse perspectives throughout development cycles. Supporting multiple end devices further mitigates access limitations.

Data privacy concerns intensify with AI systems due to varying global legislation standards compared to regions like the EU. Ensuring compliance with local laws is vital while educating users about potentials and risks associated with technologies like VR and AI. Anywhere Academy will prioritize local data storage whenever feasible; cloud services will comply with GDPR regulations. Additionally, releasing it as open-source software under GPL-3-or-newer licenses and Open Educational Resources ensures transparency and reusability.

Acknowledgments. The authors want to thank the great students that assisted them in implementing Anywhere Academy so far. The authors have used GPT4o for grammatical improvement of this work.

Disclosure of Interests. The authors have no competing interests to declare that are relevant to the content of this article.

References

1. Academic and Research Department Engineering Hydrology, RWTH Aachen University: Myscore (2024). https://myscore.lfi.rwth-aachen.de/en/. Accessed 2025 Feb 12
2. Cabello, V.M., Ferk Savec, V.: Out of school opportunities for science and mathematics learning: environment as the third educator. Lumat: Int. J. Math, Sci. Technol. Educ. **6**(2) (Sep 2018). https://doi.org/10.31129/lumat.6.2.353
3. Cabrera-Duffaut, A., Pinto-Llorente, A.M., Iglesias-Rodríguez, A.: Immersive learning platforms: analyzing virtual reality contribution to competence development in higher education—a systematic literature review. Front. Educ. **9** (2024). https://doi.org/10.3389/feduc.2024.1391560, https://www.frontiersin.org/journals/education/articles/10.3389/feduc.2024.1391560

4. Cardenas, M.M., Alvarez, I.M., Romero, A., Manero, B.: A teacher training proposal for classroom conflict management through virtual reality. In: Proceedings of the ICALT. IEEE, Tartu, Estonia (Jul 2021). https://doi.org/10.1109/icalt52272.2021.00120

5. Chandra, R.L., Berkaoui, D., Castermans, K., Nacken, H.: Utilizing virtual reality in higher education marketing through open-source and open-educational software. In: Proceedings of the 2023 7th International Conference on Big Data and Internet of Things, pp. 98–102. BDIOT '23, Association for Computing Machinery, New York, NY, USA (2023). https://doi.org/10.1145/3617695.3617724

6. Chandra, R.L., Berkaoui, D., Querl, P., Castermans, K., Nacken, H.: Student perceptions of vr labs modeled after traditional physical labs in non-destructive measurement testing. Int. J. Inform. Educ. Technol. **15**(3), 419–427 (2025). https://doi.org/10.18178/ijiet.2025.15.3.2253

7. Chandra, R.L., Castermans, K., Berkaoui, D., Querl, P., Heribert, N.: Creating realistic human avatars for social virtual environments using photographic inputs. J. Inform. Syst. Inform. **6**(3), 2110–2129 (Sep 2024). https://doi.org/10.51519/journalisi.v6i3.842

8. Chandra, R.L., Querl, P., Berkaoui, D., Castermans, K., Nacken, H.: Comparison of open-source networking libraries for unity engine in higher education. J. Comput. Scie. Technol. Stud. **6**(3), 65–75 (Aug 2024). https://doi.org/10.32996/jcsts.2024.6.3.7

9. Chang, Y.K., Kuwata, J.: Learning experience design: Challenges for novice designers. Learner and user experience research: An introduction for the field of learning design & technology. EdTech Books. https://edtechbooks org/ux/LXD_challenges (2020)

10. DelighteX GmbH: Cospaces edu (2024). https://www.cospaces.io/. Accessed 13 Feb 2025

11. ENGAGE: Engage (2024). https://engagevr.io/. Accessed 12 Feb 2025

12. Ferrell, J.B., et al.: Chemical exploration with virtual reality in organic teaching laboratories. J. Chem. Educ. **96**(9), 1961–1966 (2019)

13. FirstGearGames: Fishnet: Networking evolved (2025). https://fish-networking.gitbook.io/docs. Accessed 14 Feb 2025

14. Gavin Lai, N.Y., Wei, S., Halim, D., Fow, K.L., Kang, H.S., Yu, L.J.: Why not more virtual reality in higher ed teaching and learning? In: 2021 IEEE International Conference on Engineering, Technology & Education (TALE), pp. 248–254. IEEE (Dec 2021). https://doi.org/10.1109/tale52509.2021.9678523

15. Gya, R., Bjune, A.E.: Taking practical learning in stem education home: examples from doityourself experiments in plant biology. Ecol. Evol. **11**(8), 3481–3487 (Feb 2021). https://doi.org/10.1002/ece3.7207

16. Hubs Foundation: Hubs foundation (2025). https://hubsfoundation.org/. Accessed 13 Feb 2025

17. Jongbloed, J., Chaker, R., Lavoué, E.: Immersive procedural training in virtual reality: a systematic literature review. Comput. Educ. **221**, 105124 (Nov 2024). https://doi.org/10.1016/j.compedu.2024.105124

18. Kim, H., Park, J., Lee, I.K.: "to be or not to be me?": Exploration of self-similar effects of avatars on social virtual reality experiences. IEEE Trans. Visual. Comput. Graph. **29**(11), 4794–4804 (Nov 2023). https://doi.org/10.1109/tvcg.2023.3320240

19. Kluge, M.G., Maltby, S., Keynes, A., Nalivaiko, E., Evans, D.J.R., Walker, F.R.: Current state and general perceptions of the use of extended reality (xr) technology at the university of newcastle: Interviews and surveys from staff and students. Sage Open **12**(2) (Apr 2022). https://doi.org/10.1177/21582440221093348

20. Kumari, G., Knutzen, K., Schuldt, J.: Exploring the Use of Social Virtual Reality Conferences in Higher Education. In: 2023 IEEE 2nd German Education Conference (GECon), pp. 1–6. IEEE (Aug 2023). https://doi.org/10.1109/gecon58119.2023.10295104

21. LiveKit: Livekit (2025). https://livekit.io/. Accessed 14 Feb 2025-02-14

22. Lukosch, H., Broekhans, B., Gordijn, J.: Effects of using avatars in a game-based learning environment. In: Proceedings of the 13th European Conference on Games Based Learning, ECGBL, pp. 441–449. ECGBL 2019 (Oct 2019). https://doi.org/10.34190/gbl.19.051

23. Lundin, R.M., Yeap, Y., Menkes, D.B.: Adverse effects of virtual and augmented reality interventions in psychiatry: systematic review. JMIR Mental Health **10**, e43240 (May 2023)

24. Mahling, M., Wunderlich, R., Steiner, D., Gorgati, E., Festl-Wietek, T., Herrmann-Werner, A.: Virtual reality for emergency medicine training in medical school: prospective, large-cohort implementation study. J. Med. Internet Res. **25**, e43649 (2023)

25. Makransky, G., Petersen, G.B.: The cognitive affective model of immersive learning (camil): a theoretical research-based model of learning in immersive virtual reality. Educ. Psychol. Rev. **33**(3), 937–958 (Jan 2021). https://doi.org/10.1007/s10648-020-09586-2

26. Makransky, G., Petersen, G.B.: The theory of immersive collaborative learning (ticol). Educ. Psychol. Rev. **35**(4) (Oct 2023). https://doi.org/10.1007/s10648-023-09822-5

27. Markowitz, D.M., Laha, R., Perone, B.P., Pea, R.D., Bailenson, J.N.: Immersive virtual reality field trips facilitate learning about climate change. Front. Psychol. **9** (2018). https://doi.org/10.3389/fpsyg.2018.02364, https://www.frontiersin.org/journals/psychology/articles/10.3389/fpsyg.2018.02364

28. Mukherjee, R., Lu, J.L., Ochiai, Y.: Designing AI-Support VR by Self-supervised and Initiative Selective Supports, pp. 241–250. Springer International Publishing (2022). https://doi.org/10.1007/978-3-031-05039-8_17

29. Okita, S.Y., Turkay, S., Kim, M., Murai, Y.: Learning by teaching with virtual peers and the effects of technological design choices on learning. Comput. Educ. **63**, 176–196 (Apr 2013). https://doi.org/10.1016/j.compedu.2012.12.005

30. Paolini, A.C.: Social emotional learning: Key to career readiness. Anatolian Journal of Education **5**(1), 125–134 (Apr 2020).https://doi.org/10.29333/aje.2020.5112a

31. Park, J.S., O'Brien, J., Cai, C.J., Morris, M.R., Liang, P., Bernstein, M.S.: Generative agents: Interactive simulacra of human behavior. In: Proceedings of the 36th Annual ACM Symposium on User Interface Software and Technology, pp. 1–22. UIST '23, ACM (Oct 2023). https://doi.org/10.1145/3586183.3606763

32. Querl, P., Chandra, R.L., Berkaoui, D., Castermans, K., Nacken, H.: Does self-paced learning in mobile flood protection unit construction in virtual reality have advantages over traditional measures? Front. Virtual Real. **5** (2024). https://doi.org/10.3389/frvir.2024.1447288, https://www.frontiersin.org/journals/virtual-reality/articles/10.3389/frvir.2024.1447288

33. Radianti, J., Majchrzak, T.A., Fromm, J., Wohlgenannt, I.: A systematic review of immersive virtual reality applications for higher education: Design elements, lessons learned, and research agenda. Comput. Educ. **147**, 103778 (2020). https://doi.org/10.1016/j.compedu.2019.103778, https://www.sciencedirect.com/science/article/pii/S0360131519303276

34. Rettinger, M., Schmaderer, C., Rigoll, G.: Do you notice me? how bystanders affect the cognitive load in virtual reality. In: 2022 IEEE Conference on Virtual Reality and 3D User Interfaces (VR), pp. 77–82. IEEE (Mar 2022).https://doi.org/10.1109/vr51125.2022.00025
35. Schmidt, M., Huang, R.: Defining learning experience design: Voices from the field of learning design & technology. TechTrends **66**(2), 141–158 (Aug 2021). https://doi.org/10.1007/s11528-021-00656-y
36. Seymour, M., Yuan, L.I., Dennis, A.R., Riemer, K.: Have we crossed the uncanny valley? understanding affinity, trustworthiness, and preference for realistic digital humans in immersive environments. J. Assoc. Inform. Syst. **22**(3), 591–617 (2021). https://doi.org/10.17705/1jais.00674
37. Shapers: Learning experience design process (2024). https://lxd.org/fundamentals-of-learning-experience-design/learning-experience-design-process/. Accessed 14 Feb 2025
38. Shapes Corp.: Shapesxr (2024). https://www.shapesxr.com/. Accessed 13 Feb 2025
39. Shoa, A., Oliva, R., Slater, M., Friedman, D.: Sushi with Einstein: enhancing hybrid live events with LLM-based virtual humans. In: Proceedings of the 23rd ACM International Conference on Intelligent Virtual Agents, pp. 1–6. IVA '23, ACM (Sep 2023). https://doi.org/10.1145/3570945.3607317, http://dx.doi.org/10.1145/3570945.3607317
40. Tawfik, A., Schmidt, M., Payne, L., Huang, R.: Advancing understanding of learning experience design: refining and clarifying definitions using an Edelphi study approach. Educ. Technol. Res. Develop. **72**(3), 1539–1561 (Apr 2024). https://doi.org/10.1007/s11423-024-10355-z
41. Unity Technologies: Unity (2024). https://unity.com/. Accessed 14 Feb 2025
42. University of Wuppertal: Figments.nrw (2024). https://figments.nrw/en/figments/. Accessed 13 Feb 2025
43. Virbela, LLC: Framevr (2025). https://framevr.io/. Accessed 13 Feb 2025
44. Voinov, A., Çöltekin, A., Chen, M., Beydoun, G.: Virtual geographic environments in socio-environmental modeling: a fancy distraction or a key to communication? Int. J. Digital Earth **11**(4), 408–419 (Aug 2017). https://doi.org/10.1080/17538947.2017.1365961
45. Yee, N., Bailenson, J.N., Ducheneaut, N.: The proteus effect: implications of transformed digital self-representation on online and offline behavior. Commun. Res. **36**(2), 285–312 (Jan 2009). https://doi.org/10.1177/0093650208330254

Business Simulation in the Context of Emerging Technologies the SPEE Case Study

Gércia Sequeira[1]([⊠]) , Ruben Pereira[1] , Gildo Cossa[1] , Ana Calado Pinto[2] , and Licínio Roque[3]

[1] ISTAR-Iscte, Instituto Universitário de Lisboa (ISCTE-IUL), Lisboa, Portugal
`Gercia_Sequeira@iscte-iul.pt`
[2] The School of Social and Political Sciences (ISCSP), Lisbon University, Lisboa, Portugal
[3] Department of Informatics Engineering, University of Coimbra, Coimbra, Portugal

Abstract. This study analyzed the factors to consider for updating business simulation systems within the context of digital transformation driven by emerging technologies. To achieve this, a qualitative research approach was adopted, focusing on the Business Practices and Entrepreneurship System (SPEE), the leading business simulator in Mozambique, to identify critical factors for its modernization. The investigation, conducted as a single case study, incorporated a literature review, document analysis, and interviews, which revealed five key dimensions: realism, multidisciplinary approach, communication and interaction, ease of use and support, and accessibility and scalability. The research concluded that the most significant factors include the complexity of the local market, automation and operational efficiency, the level of digital literacy and technological infrastructure, the anticipation of future scenarios, and the enhancement of user experience. These findings suggest that integrating emerging technologies such as Artificial Intelligence (AI), Blockchain, and Virtual Reality (VR) could enhance realism, adaptability, and user engagement. Additionally, hybrid solutions combining online and offline accessibility were recommended to address technological infrastructure limitations in developing countries. The study provides practical guidelines for aligning SPEE with contemporary educational and market demands, reinforcing its relevance in higher education.

Keywords: Business simulation · emerging technologies · higher education · digital transformation

1 Introduction

In the context of Education 4.0, the development of 21st-century skills, such as cooperation, creativity, leadership, effective communication, and problem-solving, is essential to preparing students for the challenges of the global market [1]. Serious games, or business simulation games, emerge as effective pedagogical tools, offering safe virtual environments for practical learning, which is often unfeasible in the real world due to cost or risk constraints [2, 3]. Simulation games, such as Business Practices and Entrepreneurship System (SPEE), not only transform students into active learners but also develop skills

F. Trautwein et al. (Eds.): ISAGA 2025, LNCS 16439, pp. 362–378, 2026.
https://doi.org/10.1007/978-3-032-20129-4_24

such as critical thinking and teamwork [4, 5]. These benefits are particularly significant in developing countries, such as Mozambique, where these tools can mitigate structural limitations in the educational system [6, 7].

The integration of emerging technologies, such as Artificial Intelligence (AI), Blockchain, and Virtual Reality (VR), expands the pedagogical possibilities of business simulators [8, 9]. These technologies can align academic curricula with contemporary market demands, reducing the gap between theory and practice [10]. However, the implementation of these technologies faces challenges, such as the perception that digital tools are optional and the need for an assertive selection of the most suitable technologies [11, 12].

This research explores the update of SPEE, a simulator widely used in Higher Education Institutions (HEIs) in Mozambique. SPEE plays a crucial role in business skills training but needs to adapt to global trends and local needs [13]. The relevance of this study is based on three main pillars: institutional recognition, with organisations such as Association for Advance Collegiate Schools of Business (AACSB) and Accreditation Council for Business Schools and Programs (ACBSP) encouraging the use of simulations as core methodologies in business education [14, 15], and with National Council for the Assessment of the Quality of Higher Education (CNAQ) and the Order of Accountants and Auditors promoting business simulators in Mozambique (OCAM) [16]; educational impact, with studies showing that simulators improve pedagogical effectiveness and prepare students for dynamic markets [17]; and the local context, where, in environments with financial and infrastructure constraints, such as Mozambique, simulators offer an accessible and effective solution for business skills training [6].

The central objective of this research is to identify the critical factors for updating SPEE in the context of emerging technologies. The guiding question is: "what factors should be considered when selecting emerging technologies to update SPEE, aiming to enhance its pedagogical effectiveness and align it with the contemporary market?".

This study is structured to address the challenges and propose solutions related to the update of SPEE. The introduction contextualises the topic and presents the research objectives and relevance. The literature review analyses key concepts and the role of emerging technologies in higher education. The methodology includes a case study, and interviews conducted with lecturers, assistants, and SPEE programmers. The case study details the functionalities and challenges of SPEE in the Mozambican context. The discussion of results identifies critical factors and relates them to market and higher education needs. Finally, the concluding remarks summarise the key findings, highlight limitations, and suggest future directions.

2 Literature Review

This analysis adopts a systematic approach consistent with the PRISMA guidelines (Preferred Reporting Items for Systematic Reviews and Meta-Analyses), ensuring methodological rigour in the identification and selection of relevant literature [18]. Within this qualitative study, PRISMA was employed as a procedural framework to structure and document the stages of literature search, screening, and inclusion, thereby enhancing the transparency and reproducibility of the review process.

Although originally designed for quantitative meta-analyses, the PRISMA framework has been meaningfully adapted for qualitative evidence synthesis [19–21]. In this study, PRISMA was therefore used as a procedural and transparency framework rather than a statistical one. Following qualitative research standards, the stage traditionally associated with *bias assessment* was reconceptualised as an appraisal of *trustworthiness* [20], focusing on credibility, dependability, and confirmability instead of statistical bias. This adaptation ensured methodological rigour while maintaining interpretative depth, aligning the review process with the qualitative orientation of the study.

Accordingly, databases such as IEEE Xplore, Scopus, ScienceDirect, and Google Scholar were consulted, prioritising publications from the last decade, in either English or Portuguese. In contrast to quantitative meta-analyses, the selection emphasised conceptual diversity over numerical exhaustiveness, seeking theoretical saturation at the intersection of *business simulation games*, *higher education*, and *emerging technologies*. This process culminated in the inclusion of 38 studies addressing pedagogical dimensions, technological innovations, and associated challenges of these simulation games (see Fig. 1).

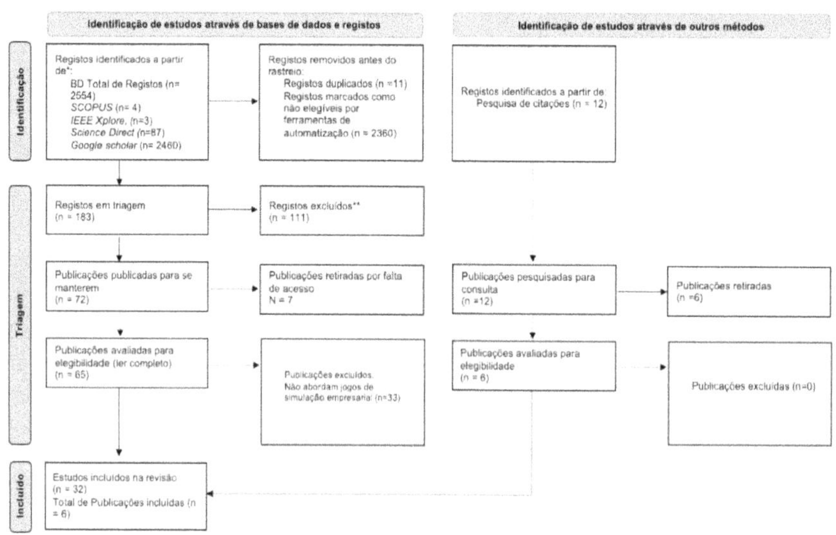

Fig. 1. PRISMA Flow Diagram, Scope Delimitation Analysis

Following the logic of the PRISMA flow diagram, 183 records were initially screened by title and abstract, with those not addressing the research question subsequently excluded. The remaining 38 papers were then thematically coded into three interpretative categories (trends, technological applications, and pedagogical evaluations), representing the qualitative adaptation of PRISMA's data extraction stage [20, 22]. During the synthesis phase, rather than calculating effect sizes, the selected studies were analysed narratively to identify conceptual dimensions such as realism, communication, usability, compatibility, multidisciplinarity, and accessibility, which informed the subsequent qualitative interpretation of the case study [19].

Business simulation games have gained prominence since the 1960s as innovative learning tools, often associated with terms such as "Business Game" and "Serious Game" [15]. These games differ from gamification, as they are designed to simulate administrative processes and economic contexts, whereas gamification uses game elements to motivate behaviours in various processes [16, 19]. Additionally, business simulation games promote realistic and controlled experiences, allowing participants to make decisions in simulated environments and acquire transferable skills applicable to the real world [10, 12].

These games are classified into categories based on their area of knowledge and learning approach. In terms of knowledge areas, they include decision-making games, functional games, and conceptual games [15]. Regarding learning approaches, they can serve as teaching tools or training methods, helping students formulate strategies and analyse business problems [5]. Among the reported benefits are the development of skills such as critical thinking, creativity, teamwork, and leadership [10, 17]. Furthermore, these games enhance student motivation, facilitate active learning, and strengthen the connection between theory and practice [5].

Despite their extensive benefits, the adoption of business simulation games faces challenges. Educational institutions must address limitations such as inadequate infrastructure, insufficient teacher training, and the need for curriculum restructuring [17, 24]. Additionally, there is a significant reliance on multifaceted lecturers capable of integrating various disciplines in a business context [9]. These challenges are further exacerbated by technological compatibility requirements and a lack of resources for developing modern laboratories.

The architecture of business simulation games requires expertise in business process modelling and content validation with specialists to ensure consistency and realism [25, 26]. Key guidelines include the representation of real-world phenomena, a balance between complexity and simplicity, and meaningful feedback for players, all of which are crucial to the success of these games [26]. Realism is one of the core dimensions, directly influencing learning outcomes and participant engagement [10, 17].

Technological advancements have expanded the impact of business simulation games, enabling the integration of emerging technologies such as Artificial Intelligence (AI), Virtual Reality (VR), and Blockchain. These technologies provide more realistic scenarios, increased interactivity, and greater transparency in simulated operations [8, 9]. Examples include the use of AI for adaptive feedback, VR to create immersive environments, and Blockchain to ensure security and asset ownership in educational games [12, 27]. These innovations also enhance the accessibility and scalability of simulation games, allowing a greater number of participants to engage in enriching learning experiences.

Recent publications highlight the potential of emerging technologies to transform the dynamics of business simulation games. A table created in this research synthesises key dimensions such as realism, communication, ease of use, multidisciplinary approach, and accessibility, linking them to the technologies implemented in specific games (see Table 1). For example, the JA TITAN simulator uses AI to personalise learning, while UNISIM applies Augmented Reality to enhance interactivity [12, 27]. These studies emphasise the significance of emerging technologies in creating more dynamic experiences aligned with market needs.

However, despite these advancements, there is a lack of research exploring the relationship between technological evolution and business simulation games in depth. Most studies focus on pedagogical benefits, game architecture, and motivations for their adoption in higher education, with few investigations dedicated to the implementation of emerging technologies. Additionally, technological integration requires a balance between simplicity and complexity, ensuring that implemented tools do not compromise user experience [5, 10].

In summary, business simulation games represent an innovative and effective methodology for higher education, with the potential to transform learning and prepare students for the challenges of the global market. The integration of emerging technologies, despite its challenges, offers significant opportunities to enhance pedagogical effectiveness and align higher education with contemporary demands.

3 Methodology

The research adopted a qualitative approach, seeking to understand the meanings that participants attribute to their experiences and the contexts in which they operate [38]. It therefore employed a qualitative methodological design that combined a systematically structured literature review, guided by the PRISMA framework, with an in-depth case study of the SPEE in Mozambique. The research question, *"What factors should be considered when selecting emerging technologies to update SPEE, with the aim of enhancing its pedagogical effectiveness and aligning it with contemporary market demands?"*, guided the investigation. While PRISMA served as a procedural and transparency tool, organising the identification, screening, and inclusion of relevant studies, the qualitative case study enabled the exploration of complex social and educational phenomena within the Mozambican context, supporting a holistic and contextually grounded analysis [39]. The systematic review provided the theoretical and conceptual foundation for the empirical work, particularly through the identification of six key dimensions (realism, communication, usability, compatibility, multidisciplinarity, and accessibility), corresponding to the qualitative reinterpretation of PRISMA's data extraction stage [20, 22]. These dimensions directly informed the design of interview protocols, document analysis, and coding categories applied to the SPEE case, ensuring coherence between the literature-based framework and field investigation.

The study involved a total of 20 participants, including lecturers, programmers, assistants, and monitors, all of whom had substantial experience in business simulation, particularly in the SPEE (Sistema de Práticas Empresariais e Empreendedorismo). The selection of interviewees followed purposive sampling criteria, based on professional experience, role, and relevance to the development and use of the simulator, as recommended by Lucas Pereira et al. [7, 40, 41]. Most participants had more than ten years of professional experience, with ages typically ranging between 30 and 40 years, corresponding to the typical user profile of the simulator, which primarily serves final-year higher education students [42]. Data saturation was reached after approximately fifteen interviews, when no new categories or insights emerged, confirming that the sample size

Table 1. Dimensions of Business Simulation Games

N⁰	Keys Dimension	Concepts	Articles
1	Realism	The level at which users perceive that the simulation reflects real-life situations, with a positive correlation between this perception and the degree of learning achieved	[7, 9, 10, 15, 16, 23–29]
2	Communication and Interaction	Represented by all systems that enhance and enable communication and interaction among participants—multiplayer teams, including email, live chats, video conferencing with webcams, etc.	[7, 8, 12, 15, 16, 23, 30–32]
3	Ease of Use and Assistance	It means the ease of playing without neglecting the necessary challenge to engage players. It includes tools that support the player throughout the entire process	[7, 15, 16, 23, 30]
4	Compatibility	It refers to the evolution of games and their continuous need for technological updates, ensuring compatibility across different machines, software, and operating systems	[15]
5	Multidisciplinary approach	It corresponds to the opportunity to simulate business operations, considering the correlation between marketing, finance, technology, human resources, and other areas	[9, 15, 33]
6	Accessibility and Scalability	Any tool that allows an unlimited number of participants and supports the player throughout the entire game process	[15]

was sufficient and the data collection process complete in accordance with qualitative research standards.

Data collection drew on multiple qualitative sources to capture complementary perspectives, following Yin's [39] methodological guidelines for triangulation and analytical depth. Semi-structured interviews involved coordinators, lecturers, assistants, and SPEE developers, allowing the collection of detailed insights into teaching practices and technological adoption. Open-ended questions encouraged participants to reflect freely on their experiences, while active observation enabled contextual interpretation of interactions and decision-making processes during simulation activities. Document analysis encompassed the review of strategic plans, meeting minutes, promotional materials, technical and financial proposals, institutional websites, and national or international programmes related to business simulation. This documentary evidence was essential in corroborating interview findings and constructing a comprehensive understanding of the phenomenon.

The authors, drawing on their professional experience in business simulation training in Mozambique, adopted an active and reflective stance throughout the research process. This insider position facilitated privileged access to relevant documents, networks, and institutional knowledge, enriching the depth of analysis. However, such proximity also raised potential concerns regarding researcher bias, which were mitigated through methodological triangulation, the use of multiple data sources, and critical self-reflection [39]. These strategies strengthened the credibility, dependability, and confirmability of the findings.

In summary, the methodological design combined the systematic discipline of the PRISMA-guided literature review with the contextual depth of the qualitative case study, ensuring both transparency and interpretative richness. The categories derived from the PRISMA-based review informed the analytical framework applied to the SPEE case, ensuring conceptual continuity between the literature review and the empirical investigation. The integration of multiple data sources (interviews, observation, and documentary evidence), strengthened the internal validity of the study through triangulation and reflexive analysis. This design was particularly suited to the complexity of the research question, allowing the identification of critical factors for integrating emerging technologies into business simulation practices while remaining grounded in the realities of Mozambican higher education. The following section presents the main findings that emerged from this process, highlighting how the methodological approach enabled a comprehensive and context-sensitive interpretation of the data.

4 SPEE Case Study

The SPEE, developed by the Institute of Technology, Innovation and Services (ITIS, SA.)[1], represents a technological solution for business simulation in Mozambique. Created in response to the lack of quality internships and the need to improve professional qualifications, SPEE stands out as one of the first serious games implemented in the country. Since its founding in 2010, ITIS envisions transforming Mozambique into a

---

[1] https://itis.ac.mz/.

technologically competent country, with a centralised team of professionals working in a hybrid system, pioneering the field of business games within the Mozambican context. This system is used by more than 17 HEIs, covering various provinces, including Maputo, Manica, Nampula, Gaza, and Tete.

The initial mission of SPEE was to address the shortage of professional internships by promoting a digital alternative that not only provided practical training but also strengthened key skills required in the job market. Through a network of national partners, such as the Mozambique Tax Authority (ATM), Mozambique Stock Exchange (BVM), Institute for the Promotion of Small and Medium Enterprises (IPEME), National Institute of Social Security (INSS), Commercial Investment Bank (BCI) and the Confederation of Economic Associations (CTA), the system has been expanded and updated over time. The integration of virtual companies, governed by legal procedures in compliance with Mozambican legislation, has enabled the creation of a safe and controlled environment where students can manage multiple areas of business operations, including accounting, human resource management, and commercial activities.

SPEE has been developed into three main modules: Student Module, Web Module, and Lecturer Module (see Fig. 2). Each module includes specific functionalities that allow users to simulate business operations, comply with tax regulations, and perform administrative tasks. For example, the Student Module includes tools such as business model canvases, entrepreneurial journals, and inventory management, while the Lecturer Module facilitates assessment and student progress tracking through automated reports and behavioural metrics. The platform also supports collaborative activities and the creation of simulated companies, fostering interaction between students and strategic partners.

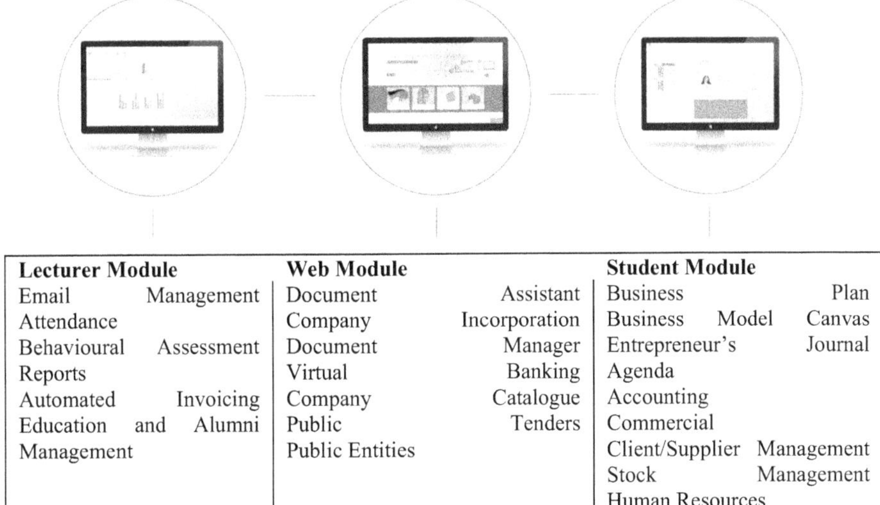

Lecturer Module	Web Module		Student Module	
Email Management	Document	Assistant	Business	Plan
Attendance	Company	Incorporation	Business Model	Canvas
Behavioural Assessment	Document	Manager	Entrepreneur's	Journal
Reports	Virtual	Banking	Agenda	
Automated Invoicing	Company	Catalogue	Accounting	
Education and Alumni	Public	Tenders	Commercial	
Management	Public Entities		Client/Supplier Management	
			Stock Management	
			Human Resources	

Fig. 2. SPEE Logical Architecture

Throughout its evolution, SPEE has undergone significant technological transformations, initially starting as an offline application before transitioning into an online system, allowing for greater accessibility and flexibility. In 2022, a distance learning management feature was introduced, further expanding its reach and pedagogical impact. This evolution was driven by the expansion of digital infrastructure in Mozambique, with the introduction of 3G and 4G networks in urban areas. As a result, the system has been used by an annual average of 800 students, with a total of 5,217 graduates between 2018 and 2023 (see Fig. 3).

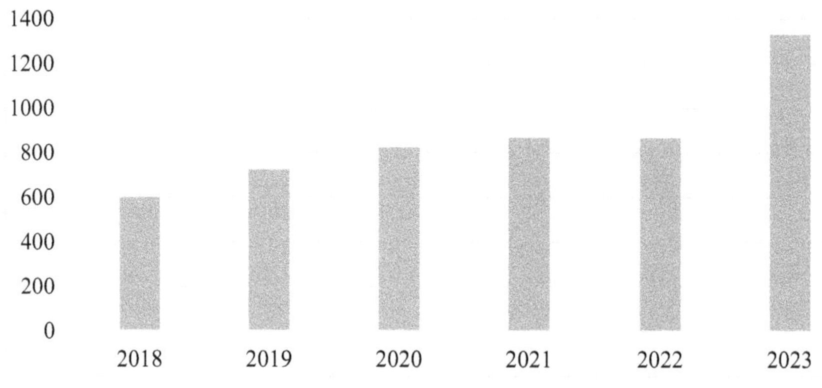

Fig. 3. SPEE users, from 2018 to 2023

The impact of SPEE extends beyond Mozambique's borders. Projects such as the Pan Africa Business Simulation and Business Simulation Bootcamp[2] have demonstrated the scalability of the system, integrating young people from different African countries[3] and promoting entrepreneurship as a tool for socio-economic development. International events, such as the International Simulation and Gaming Association (ISAGA2023)[4] conference, further highlight the relevance of SPEE in business skills training in emerging markets. Additionally, the system is often referenced as a tool for combating corruption, educating students on legal and regulatory processes required in the Mozambican market.

However, the success of SPEE depends on robust infrastructure and the engagement of facilitators and partners. The implementation of modern features, such as document assistants and automated notification systems, has been essential in enhancing the user experience. Similarly, the adoption of emerging technologies, such as artificial intelligence and blockchain, has been considered strategic for improving simulation realism and providing more dynamic business scenarios. The integration of virtual reality has also been explored to create immersive environments, increasing student engagement and enthusiasm.

---

[2] https://www.youtube.com/@businesssimulationbootcamp6539.

[3] https://www.youtube.com/watch?v=HvqKWQlBZL0&t=461s.

[4] https://shs.hal.science/halshs-04209935.

Challenges faced by the Business Practices and Entrepreneurship System (SPEE) include the ongoing need for teacher training, technological upgrades, and the expansion of access in remote regions. Despite these constraints, SPEE has proven to be an effective solution for practical business education, with numerous success stories of young people who launched their own ventures after participating in the programme. With a user-centred approach tailored to local realities, SPEE continues to serve as a benchmark in business education in Mozambique, fostering innovation and entrepreneurship in complex and demanding environments.

The growing number of higher education institutions in the country—currently around 50 universities—reflects the increasing demand for quality training and under-scores the importance of practical methodologies such as business simulation. However, Mozambique still faces significant technological barriers, including low levels of internet access—only 23.2% of the population in 2024—with approximately 71% accessing the internet via mobile phones and just 28% using computers. Moreover, internet services remain expensive and generally poor in quality. In 2022, only 33.2% of the population had access to electricity, further limiting digital inclusion and the effective use of educational technologies.

5 Results Discussion

The qualitative analysis of the interview data revealed a high level of consistency across participants, reflecting their substantial professional experience in business simulation and, in particular, in the SPEE. As illustrated in Fig. 4, thematic saturation was achieved after the fifteenth interview, when the proportion of new topics dropped below five per cent, confirming that the data collected were sufficient to capture all major perspectives. This pattern demonstrates the convergence of views among participants, supporting the robustness of the thematic coding used in subsequent analyses.

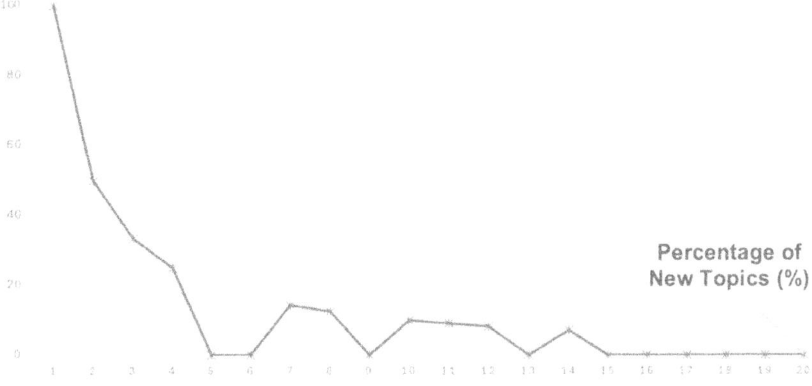

Fig. 4. Analysis of Response Saturation in Interviews on SPEE

Building upon this analytical stability, the following sections present the findings organised according to the six qualitative dimensions identified in the PRISMA-guided literature review: realism, communication, usability, compatibility, multidisciplinarity, and accessibility. Each dimension synthesises participants' perceptions, supported by evidence from interviews and document analysis, and is interpreted in relation to the theoretical insights outlined earlier.

Realism Dimension in SPEE

Realism was the first dimension explored, defined as the extent to which users perceive the simulation as reflecting real-world situations. According to Faria [15], there is a positive correlation between realism and learning effectiveness. Interviewees highlighted the need to enhance functionalities to better represent real processes in the business ecosystem, such as mobile wallet transactions, sector-specific cost differentiation, and the inclusion of a virtual stock exchange. These improvements aim to increase the representation of the local market, particularly in the Mozambican context [15, 33].

Additionally, interviewees suggested the integration of emerging technologies, such as blockchain, cryptocurrencies, and artificial intelligence (AI), to anticipate global trends and create dynamic scenarios that react in real time. Virtual and augmented reality were also identified as valuable tools for creating more immersive experiences, although their implementation in the local context presents challenges due to financial and infrastructure limitations [43, 44].

Regarding global market realism, interviewees emphasised the need to design the simulator as a trend-forecasting tool, incorporating elements such as the replacement of physical cash with cryptocurrencies and digital currencies. According to Stal [43], high technology and transaction cost-based economic theories are more important than local market knowledge in building global enterprises. Furthermore, Shami et al. [44], highlight that cooperation between businesses is becoming increasingly crucial in international business environments.

Interviewees also suggested improvements across the three SPEE modules:

- Student Module: Inclusion of digital signatures and automated feedback systems.
- Web Module: Integration of political instability scenarios, natural disasters, and corruption cases.
- Lecturer Module: Automation of routine tasks, such as audits and automatic reports.

Multidisciplinary Dimension

Multidisciplinary was another key area of analysis, focusing on interactions between different knowledge areas within the simulator. Ke [9], highlights that interdisciplinary interactions occur naturally, fostering a symbiotic experience. Interviewees stressed the importance of integrating Accounting, Stock Management, and Human Resources to create a more balanced and connected learning experience. However, the workload burden on lecturers was identified as a barrier to students fully exploring all modules [45].

To address this limitation, interviewees suggested improvements such as automating feedback and creating inter-modular dashboards, which would facilitate post-activity analysis and reflection. Artificial intelligence and augmented reality were highlighted as key technologies for developing interdisciplinary skills, enabling interdisciplinary reports and the creation of dynamic business scenarios [9, 45].

Communication and Interaction Dimension
Communication and interaction between participants were considered essential for the success of SPEE. Business simulation games promote social interactions among participants [15]. Interviewees emphasised the need to enhance communication tools within the simulator, such as automated notifications, internal chats, and progress dashboards.

Currently, students and lecturers rely on external tools such as WhatsApp and Zoom to complement interactions within the simulator, highlighting the need for modernising communication functionalities [34]. Communication fluidity was also affected by the lack of adequate technological resources, such as shared computers in laboratories. To overcome these challenges, interviewees suggested implementing more efficient support and navigation systems, enabling a more autonomous and productive use of the platform [15].

Ease of Use and Assistance Dimension
The ease of use of SPEE was widely acknowledged by interviewees, who considered the simulator intuitive and functional. However, gaps were identified in the assistance system, with reports of significant delays in responses to students.

To improve this dimension, suggested technological enhancements included:

- Interactive tutorials
- Integrated help systems
- Automated assistance tools

These improvements would reduce reliance on manual support and alleviate lecturers' workload [12, 24].

Accessibility and Scalability Dimension
Accessibility and scalability were central discussion points, with interviewees emphasising the need to make the simulator more accessible via mobile devices. Although some students access SPEE via mobile phones, the experience is not always responsive across different screen sizes, compromising usability. To address these challenges, interviewees suggested the integration of Progressive Web Applications (PWAs), which function offline and automatically sync data when the device reconnects to the internet [46]. Additionally, automation of the Lecturer Module was highlighted as an effective solution to reduce lecturers' workload and promote greater scalability of the simulator. Cultural, educational, and economic factors were also considered, with interviewees stressing the need to adapt SPEE to local limitations, such as limited access to technology and financial resources [17, 46].

6 Conclusion

The SPEE, widely used in HEIs in Mozambique, is an essential tool for business skills development, particularly in contexts where technological and socio-economic challenges demand innovative solutions. This study aimed to identify critical factors for updating SPEE in the context of emerging technologies, adopting a qualitative approach that included interviews with programmers, lecturers, monitors, and assistants, complemented by document analysis and literature review. The analysis highlighted key dimensions, such as realism, multidisciplinary approach, communication, interaction, ease of use, assistance, accessibility, and scalability, which guided the identification of crucial factors to align SPEE with contemporary educational needs.

Despite the variety of explored dimensions, they are all interconnected and consider local technological adaptability. From these dimensions, essential factors were identified for the integration of emerging technologies and the enhancement of SPEE's pedagogical benefits. Notably, these include the complexity of the local market, which requires technologies capable of creating diverse and adaptive scenarios; automation and operational efficiency, by reducing lecturers' workload; the state of digital literacy and technological infrastructure; anticipation of future scenarios; and the improvement of user experience, with technological solutions that foster interactivity, personalisation, and continuous support.

Among the proposed solutions, AI integration enables personalised learning processes and dynamic scenario modelling. Blockchain emerges as a tool to simulate secure financial transactions and smart contracts, while virtual and augmented reality provide immersive experiences. Process automation, including audits and personalised feedback, was identified as a strategy to increase student engagement and reduce lecturers' workload. Realism was reinforced, both in the local market context, through the integration of Mozambican business practices, and in the global market, with broader simulations such as foreign exchange operations and cryptocurrency usage.

Recognising the resource and infrastructure limitations in many educational contexts, interviewees prioritised high-impact, immediately implementable improvements. The integration of mobile wallets, automated notifications, and interactive dashboards were identified as initial strategies to enhance interaction and performance analysis. These accessible and easy-to-adopt solutions establish a foundation for future incorporation of more advanced technologies, such as blockchain and augmented reality, enabling a gradual and sustainable evolution of SPEE.

Multidisciplinary approach emerged as a priority, with recommendations for new subject areas, such as sustainability and digital economy, and greater integration between disciplines such as business strategy, finance, marketing, and human resources. Accessibility and scalability, through hybrid solutions and sustainable financial models, are crucial to overcoming technological limitations and ensuring adoption by institutions with budget constraints. Furthermore, the creation of an effective debriefing system, with interactive dashboards and interdisciplinary reports, was identified as central to reducing lecturers' manual workload, fostering flipped classrooms, and strengthening critical and reflective learning.

This study also underscored the importance of strengthening the link between academia and the market, fostering practical and contextually grounded learning within business simulation education. Although the research was limited to the SPEE and a sample drawn exclusively from Mozambican higher education institutions, it offers valuable guidelines for updating the simulator and enhancing its pedagogical relevance. Future research should involve strategic partners such as accreditation bodies, industry associations, and international academic networks, to broaden perspectives and reinforce the practical applicability of findings. Moreover, while PRISMA was adapted in this study as a qualitative structuring tool rather than a quantitative meta-analytic framework, subsequent investigations could employ mixed-method approaches that combine systematic evidence mapping with computational text analysis, thereby deepening the integration between literature review and empirical case design.

In conclusion, updating SPEE in the context of emerging technologies represents a strategic opportunity to strengthen the impact of higher education in Mozambique. With the proposed recommendations, it is expected that SPEE will enhance its educational relevance and establish itself as an essential tool for training managers and entrepreneurs aligned with the demands of digital transformation in Africa and globally, promoting its internationalisation and global impact.

References

1. Mukul, E., Büyüközkan, G.: Digital transformation in education: a systematic review of education 4.0. Technol. Forecast. Soc. Change **194**, 122664 (2023). https://doi.org/10.1016/J.TECHFORE.2023.122664
2. Djaouti, D., Alvarez, J., Jessel, J.-P., Rampnoux, O.: Origins of serious games. Serious Games Edutainment Appl., 25–43 (2011). https://doi.org/10.1007/978-1-4471-2161-9_3
3. Luísa, A., Baltazar, G.: Educação 4.0: Desafios e Oportunidades, September 2021. https://run.unl.pt/bitstream/10362/143941/1/Baltazar_2022.pdf. Accessed 15 Dec 2024
4. Oliveira, M.R.N.S.: Inovação Educacional e Recursos Didáticos no Trabalho Docente. Trabalho Educação **30**(1) (2021). https://doi.org/10.35699/2238-037x.2021.25671
5. Rogmans, T.: Teaching with business simulation games: identifying and overcoming hurdles to adoption. In: European Conference on Games Based Learning, vol. 17, no. 1, pp. 896–903, October 2023. https://doi.org/10.34190/ECGBL.17.1.736
6. Dos, E.P., Nunes, S., Roque, L.G.: Visual computing and the progress of developing countries measuring knowledge acquisition in 3D virtual learning environments (2016)
7. Lucas Pereira, L., Gomes Roque, L.: Breaking new ground: innovation in games, play, practice and theory (2009)
8. Bruzzone, A.G., Massei, M., Sinelshchikov, K., Fabbrini, G., Gotelli, M., Molinari, A.: Machine learning to support industrial digitalization and business transformation. In: 31st European Modeling and Simulation Symposium, EMSS 2019, Dime University of Genoa, pp. 390–393 (2019). https://doi.org/10.46354/i3m.2019.emss.055
9. Ke, M.: Research on the design of virtual simulation teaching platform in business education. In: European Alliance for Innovation, November 2023. https://doi.org/10.4108/eai.8-9-2023.2340054
10. Clarke, E.: Learning outcomes from business simulation exercises: challenges for the implementation of learning technologies. Educ. Train. **51**(5), 448–459 (2009). https://doi.org/10.1108/00400910910987246
11. BCG: Mind the Tech Gap (2022). https://media-publications.bcg.com/BCGX-mind-the-tech-gap.pdf. Accessed 05 May 2024
12. Peterková, J., Repaská, Z., Prachařová, L.: Best practice of using digital business simulation games in business education. Sustainability **14**(15) (2022). https://doi.org/10.3390/su14158987

13. Rugnath, B.D.: O papel das plataformas e-learning de estágios virtuais para geração de competências profissionais e graduados de ensino superior residentes na cidade de Maputo. Maputo (2023)
14. Dick, G.N., Akbulut, A.Y.: Innovative use of the ERPsim game in a management decision making class: an empirical study **19**, 2020 (2020). https://doi.org/10.28945/4632
15. Faria, A.J., Hutchinson, D., Wellington, W.J., Gold, S.: Developments in Business Gaming A Review of the Past 40 Years (2009). https://scholar.uwindsor.ca/odettepub/82
16. Cossa, G., Roque, L.G., Alturas, B., Pinto, A.C.: Pan Africa business simulation game. In: Iberian Conference on Information Systems and Technologies, CISTI (2023). https://doi.org/10.23919/CISTI58278.2023.10211280
17. Binsztok, A., Butryn, B., Holowinska, K., Owoc, M.L., Sobinska, M.: Business computer simulations and its role in educational processes from the students' perspective. Procedia Comput. Sci., 4006–4014 (2023). https://doi.org/10.1016/j.procs.2023.10.396
18. Haddaway, N.R., Page, M.J., Pritchard, C.C., McGuinness, L.A.: PRISMA2020: an R package and shiny app for producing PRISMA 2020-compliant flow diagrams, with interactivity for optimised digital transparency and open synthesis. Campbell Syst. Rev. **18**(2), e1230 (2022). https://doi.org/10.1002/CL2.1230
19. Flemming, K., Noyes, J.: Qualitative evidence synthesis: where are we at? Int. J. Qual. Methods **20** (2021). https://doi.org/10.1177/1609406921993276
20. Lockwood, C., Munn, Z., Porritt, K.: Qualitative research synthesis: methodological guidance for systematic reviewers utilizing meta-aggregation. Int. J. Evid. Based Healthc. **13**(3), 179–187 (2015). https://doi.org/10.1097/XEB.0000000000000062
21. Booth, A., Sommer, I., Noyes, J., Houghton, C., Campbell, F.: Rapid reviews methods series: guidance on rapid qualitative evidence synthesis. BMJ Evid. Based Med. **29**(3), 194–200 (2024). https://doi.org/10.1136/BMJEBM-2023-112620
22. Thomas, J., Harden, A.: Methods for the thematic synthesis of qualitative research in systematic reviews. BMC Med. Res. Methodol. **8** (2008). https://doi.org/10.1186/1471-2288-8-45
23. Behl, A., Jayawardena, N., Ishizaka, A., Gupta, M., Shankar, A.: Gamification and gigification: a multidimensional theoretical approach. J. Bus. Res. **139**, 1378–1393 (2022). https://doi.org/10.1016/j.jbusres.2021.09.023
24. Protil, R.M.: Utilização de Simuladores Empresariais no Ensino de Ciências Sociais Aplicadas: Um Estudo na República Federal da Alemanha. Revista de Economia **31**(2) (2005). https://doi.org/10.5380/RE.V31I2.5570
25. Classe, T.M., Araujo, R.M., Xexéo, G.B., Siqueira, S.W.M.: View of the play your process method for business process-based digital game design. Int. J. Ser. Games. https://journal.seriousgamessociety.org/index.php/IJSG/article/view/269/323. Accessed 27 Dec 2024
26. Pereira, R., Velez Lapão, L., Scalabrin Bianchi, I., Amaral, D.: Improving emergency department through business process redesign: an empirical study (2020)
27. Stamatakis, D., Kogias, D.G., Papadopoulos, P., Karkazis, P.A., Leligou, H.C.: Blockchain-powered gaming: bridging entertainment with serious game objectives. Computers **13**(1) (2024). https://doi.org/10.3390/computers13010014
28. Dai, X., Zhou, C., Li, Q.: Research on teaching mode of experiential learning environment based on VR virtual simulation technology. In: 2023 2nd International Conference on 3D Immersion, Interaction and Multi-Sensory Experiences (ICDIIME), pp. 471–476, June 2023. https://doi.org/10.1109/ICDIIME59043.2023.00097
29. Poonnawat, W., Lehmann, P., Connolly, T.: Teaching business intelligence with a business simulation game. In: Proceedings of the European Conference on Games-Based Learning, pp. 439–448 (2015)

30. Dallasega, P., Revolti, A., Sauer, P.C., Schulze, F., Rauch, E.: BIM, augmented and virtual reality empowering lean construction management: a project simulation game. Procedia Manuf., 49–54 (2020). https://doi.org/10.1016/j.promfg.2020.04.059

31. Barker, S., Davy, M.: Learning business through digital simulation: an analysis of student reflections. In: ASCILITE 2019 - Conference Proceedings - 36th International Conference of Innovation, Practice and Research in the Use of Educational Technologies in Tertiary Education: Personalised Learning. Diverse Goals. One Heart, pp. 29–38 (2019)

32. Binsztok, A., Butryn, B., Holowinska, K., Owoc, M.L., Sobinska, M.: Business computer simulation supporting competencies. Potential areas of application and barriers. Procedia Comput. Sci., 3875–3883 (2022). https://doi.org/10.1016/j.procs.2022.09.449

33. Coitinho, T.: Simulação Empresarial: qual sua importância para obter bons resultados? https://www.voitto.com.br/blog/artigo/simulacao-empresarial#google_vignette. Accessed 11 Mar 2024

34. Bach, M.P., Ćurlin, T., Stjepić, A.M., Meško, M.: Quo Vadis business simulation games in the 21st century?, 01 Mar 2023. MDPI. https://doi.org/10.3390/info14030178

35. Brandl, L.C., Schrader, A.: Serious games in higher education in the transforming process to education 4.0—systematized review. Multidisciplinary Digital Publishing Institute (MDPI) (2024). https://doi.org/10.3390/educsci14030281

36. Wu, S., Tian, Y., Li, J., Li, F., Feng, Y.: Research on virtual reality exhibition teaching platform in teaching reform of new economics. In: 2022 International Conference on Education, Network and Information Technology (ICENIT), September 2022, pp. 87–92 (2022). https://doi.org/10.1109/ICENIT57306.2022.00026

37. Hall, J.J.S.B., Marketing, H.: Existing and emerging business simulation-game design movements. In: Developments in Business Simulation and Experiential Learning: Proceedings of the Annual ABSEL conference, vol. 36 (2009). https://absel-ojs-ttu.tdl.org/absel/article/view/350. Accessed 27 Dec 2024

38. Creswell, J.W., Poth, C.N.: Qualitative Inquiry and Research Design: Choosing Among Five Approaches. https://books.google.pt/books?hl=pt-PT&lr=&id=DLbBDQAAQBAJ&oi=fnd&pg=PP1&dq=Creswell+%26+Poth,+2018&ots=-iq55aHPOt&sig=UJhlao2y9CMNmPWDIDJtcPJBr-k&redir_esc=y#v=onepage&q=Creswell%20%26%20Poth%2C%202018&f=false. Accessed 28 Dec 2024

39. Yin, R.K.: Case Study Research and Applications: Design and Methods, 6th edn. SAGE, Los Angeles, London, New Dehli, Singapore, Washington DC, Melbourne (2018)

40. Klabbers, J.H.G.: The magic circle: Principles of gaming & simulation (2006). https://www.researchgate.net/publication/273947293

41. Titton, L.A.: Parameterised business simulation game development for education in supply chain management and logistics. In: Meijer, S.A., Smeds, R. (eds.) ISAGA 2013. LNCS, vol. 8264, pp. 230–236. Springer, Cham (2014). https://doi.org/10.1007/978-3-319-04954-0_27

42. Tapscott: Grown_Up_Digital_-_How_the_Net_Generation_Is_Changing_Your_World_(Don_Tapscott) (2009)

43. Stal, E.: Multinacionais: O Papel da Tecnologia na Conquista do Mercado Externo (2005)

44. Shami, N.S., Bos, N., Fort, T., Gordon, M.: Designing a Globalization Simulation to Teach Corporate Social Responsibility (2004). http://www.bus.umich.edu/islands

45. Blažič, A.J., Novak, F., Blažič, A.J., Novak, F.: Challenges of business simulation games — a new approach of teaching business. E-Learn. Instr. Des. Organ. Strategy Manag. (2015). https://doi.org/10.5772/61242

46. Bhatt, K.: Progressive Web Application-Present and Future (2019). https://www.researchgate.net/publication/337544344. Accessed 05 Jan 2025

Author Index

GPSR Compliance
The European Union's (EU) General Product Safety Regulation (GPSR) is a set
of rules that requires consumer products to be safe and our obligations to
ensure this.

If you have any concerns about our products, you can contact us on

ProductSafety@springernature.com

In case Publisher is established outside the EU, the EU authorized
representative is:

Springer Nature Customer Service Center GmbH
Europaplatz 3
69115 Heidelberg, Germany